Kant on Laws

This book focuses on the unity, diversity, and centrality of the notion of law as it is employed in Kant's theoretical and practical philosophy. Eric Watkins argues that, by thinking through a number of issues in various historical, scientific, and philosophical contexts over several decades, Kant is able to develop a univocal concept of law that can nonetheless be applied to a wide range of particular cases, despite the diverse demands that these contexts give rise to. In addition, Watkins shows how Kant comes to view both the generic conception of law which he develops and its different particular instances as crucial components of his systematic philosophy as a whole. This volume's new and unified account of a major current running through Kant's work will be important for scholars interested in numerous aspects of his philosophy, from the theoretical and abstract to the practical and empirical.

ERIC WATKINS is Professor of Philosophy at the University of California, San Diego. He is author of the prizewinning *Kant and the Metaphysics of Causality* (Cambridge, 2005) and editor of *Kant on Persons and Agency* (Cambridge, 2017).

Kant on Laws

Eric Watkins
University of California, San Diego

CAMBRIDGE
UNIVERSITY PRESS

CAMBRIDGE
UNIVERSITY PRESS

University Printing House, Cambridge CB2 8BS, United Kingdom

One Liberty Plaza, 20th Floor, New York, NY 10006, USA

477 Williamstown Road, Port Melbourne, VIC 3207, Australia

314-321, 3rd Floor, Plot 3, Splendor Forum, Jasola District Centre, New Delhi - 110025, India

79 Anson Road, #06-04/06, Singapore 079906

Cambridge University Press is part of the University of Cambridge.

It furthers the University's mission by disseminating knowledge in the pursuit of
education, learning and research at the highest international levels of excellence.

www.cambridge.org
Information on this title: www.cambridge.org/9781107163911
DOI: 10.1017/9781316683026

© Eric Watkins 2019

This publication is in copyright. Subject to statutory exception
and to the provisions of relevant collective licensing agreements,
no reproduction of any part may take place without the written
permission of Cambridge University Press.

First published 2019

A catalogue record for this publication is available from the British Library

Library of Congress Cataloging in Publication data
Names: Watkins, Eric, 1964–
Title: Kant on laws / Eric Watkins, University of California, San Diego.
Description: Cambridge, United Kingdom ; New York, NY, USA : Cambridge
    University Press, 2019. | Includes bibliographical references and index.
Identifiers: LCCN 2018049317 (print) | LCCN 2018049941 (ebook) |
    ISBN 9781107163911 (Hardback) | ISBN 9781316615560 (Paperback)
Subjects: LCSH: Kant, Immanuel, 1724-1804. | Law–Philosophy.
Classification: LCC K230.K364 (ebook) | LCC K230.K364 W38 2019 (print) |
    DDC 340/.1–dc23
LC record available at https://lccn.loc.gov/2018049317

ISBN   978-1-107-16391-1   Hardback
ISBN   978-1-316-61556-0   Paperback

Cambridge University Press has no responsibility for the persistence or
accuracy of URLs for external or third-party internet websites referred to in
this publication, and does not guarantee that any content on such websites is,
or will remain, accurate or appropriate.

For my mother, Dona Jeanne Malan, whose love and support is itself an exceptionless law, one that has made my life, and much in it, possible.

Contents

Preface	*page* ix
Acknowledgments	xi
Note on Texts, Translations, and Abbreviations	xiv
Introduction	1

Part I Kant's Concept of Law	9
1 What Is, for Kant, a Law of Nature?	11
2 Kant on Transcendental Laws	30

Part II The Laws of Mechanics	49
3 The System of Principles	51
4 The Argumentative Structure of Kant's *Metaphysical Foundations of Natural Science*	69
5 The Laws of Motion from Newton to Kant	89
6 Kant's Justification of the Laws of Mechanics	118

Part III Teleological Laws	147
7 The Antinomy of Teleological Judgment	149
8 Nature in General as a System of Ends	174

Part IV Laws as Regulative Principles	189
9 Kant on Rational Cosmology	191
10 Kant on *Infima Species*	212

viii   Contents

Part V   The Moral Law   225

11 Autonomy and the Legislation of Laws in the *Prolegomena*   227

12 Kant on the Natural, Moral, Human, and Divine Orders   247

Conclusion   268

Bibliography   284
Index   293

Preface

Many years ago, I had wanted to write a book titled *Kant's Metaphysical Physics*. It would have argued that one could not understand Kant's abstract metaphysical principles without appreciating his physics but also that one could not understand Kant's physics without a firm grasp of his metaphysics. Though I still firmly believe both theses, it became clear that such a book was in some sense impossible to write, at least for me. The first chapter obviously could not be about Kant's metaphysics, because according to the very view I was arguing for, that presupposed an understanding of his physics. But by reason of parity, it could not be about his physics either. (Nor could it be about both at once, since that was supposed to be the subject of the entire book, not its first chapter.) In addition, executing this project according to proper scholarly standards would have resulted in a book whose length would have exceeded what a publisher would reasonably allow as well as what one could reasonably expect a reader to digest.

Instead of undertaking an impossible task, I decided to pursue something akin to the well-established strategy of "divide and conquer" (sometimes rendered somewhat less aggressively as "divide and rule"). I thus decided to write *Kant and the Metaphysics of Causality* first, which focused primarily on Kant's views on causation in the *Critique of Pure Reason*, though I drew heavily both on his pre-Critical works (especially in light of the historical context of eighteenth-century Germany) and on his views on physics so as to provide support and illustration for the abstract model of causality I saw Kant developing. I then thought that I would turn immediately to Kant's physics by writing a book whose title would be *Kant's Justification of Newtonian Science* and whose main thesis would be that Kant's justification of his distinctive version of Newtonian physics, as articulated most fully in the *Metaphysical Foundations of Natural Science*, depends in central ways on his metaphysics (especially on his model of causality). Though I continue to accept this thesis, for various reasons I ended up not writing that book either. For one, I thought that I would need to provide a sustained interpretation of the entirety of the

ix

Metaphysical Foundations, a task that presented seemingly insurmountable obstacles at every turn. For another, I did not want to write another big book right after completing the first one. So instead I focused on a number of more manageable tasks (which we academics call "papers," "articles," or "chapters") on a number of seemingly different topics that interested me, such as Kant's views on teleology, the emergence of his doctrine of autonomy, his rejection of Leibniz's doctrine of complete concepts, and his notion of a law of nature. At some point, it dawned on me that even after giving myself a break from thinking in book-length units, I still did not want to write the book I had originally envisioned, though for a different reason. For I realized that what most interested me about Kant's views in the topics I was working on was his conception of law, both in general and in the particular. Once I realized that, it was clear that the book I ought to write should be titled *Kant on Laws*.

Writing *Kant on Laws* proved, however, to be more of a challenge than I had anticipated. (Now that I stop to think about it, so did *Kant and the Metaphysics of Causality*. Perhaps I should have learned something from that first experience. At any rate, *now* I really know.) The main difficulty was not strictly scholarly or philosophical, though I encountered plenty of those kinds of difficulties along the way. Rather, it was that I had already published articles on most of the topics that I wanted to cover in the book, but I did not want to publish a "collected papers" volume, since I did not believe that the original articles on their own would make sufficiently clear the vision I had of Kant's view. What's more, I wanted the whole to be more than the sum of its parts. Thus began the process of "lightly revising" the previously published articles so that, if all went well, they would fit together seamlessly. I suspect that in the process, I have stretched the boundaries of what could reasonably count as "light revision" well beyond what is permissible. In several cases, two articles merged into a single chapter, and I also found it necessary on occasion to add (or subtract) sections. And then there were the surprising twists and turns on particular issues that one would naturally expect. Despite all of this (or because of all of this), the vision that originally inspired this book slowly took concrete form and one can see the results in the following chapters. I hope that what I have written is of some use to readers who have an interest in Kant's philosophy, in the notion of law, or, for that matter, in Kant's notion of law.

Acknowledgments

I am extremely grateful to many individuals with whom I have interacted productively over the years about the issues discussed in this book. Though I am sure to forget to mention many with whom I have had important exchanges, I thank Bob Adams, Marilyn Adams, Peter Anstey, Stefano Bacin, Angela Breitenbach, Kim Brewer, Martin Carrier, Andrew Chignell, Alix Cohen, Dina Emundts, Steve Engstrom, Mark Fisher, Eckart Förster, Dan Garber, Hannah Ginsborg, Ina Goy, Stefanie Grüne, Paul Guyer, Des Hogan, Rolf Horstmann, Tim Jankowiak, Anja Jauernig, Pauline Kleingeld, Heiner Klemme, Jim Kreines, Lorenz Krüger, Manfred Kuehn, Wolfgang Lefevre, Michela Massimi, Peter McLaughlin, Ernan McMullin, J. P. Messina, James Messina, Georg Mohr, Dalia Nassar, Konstantin Pollok, Andy Reath, Tobias Rosefeldt, Tad Schmaltz, Oliver Sensen, Lisa Shabel, Susan Shell, Sheldon Smith, Werner Stark, Thomas Sturm, Peter Thielke, Jens Timmermann, Daniel Warren, Marcus Willaschek, Falk Wunderlich, Peter Yong, and Rachel Zuckert. I am also deeply grateful to my students and colleagues at UC-San Diego, especially to regular participants in the History of Philosophy Roundtable and the German Philosophy Reading Group, since their perfect blend of criticism, charity, and constructive suggestions has been crucial to the development of my views. I would like to single out Rosalind Chaplin, who provided comments on an early draft of the entire manuscript, and Lucy Allais and Clinton Tolley, who have been particularly important to my thinking about these (and many other) issues. Special thanks go to Nancy Cartwright, whose healthy skepticism about some of Kant's most fundamental ideas has kept me honest and whose own views have been suggestive in many ways; to Michael Friedman, whose work has long been an inspiration to me and whose support, in spite of our disagreements on some crucial details, has been greatly appreciated; to Marius Stan, from whom I have learned a lot about the history of mechanics and who read and made many helpful suggestions regarding the chapters on the laws of mechanics; and especially to Karl Ameriks, who, in addition to all else (which exceeds all measurement), read and provided helpful comments on the entire manuscript. This list makes it clear that I have been blessed with a rich and wonderful philosophical community on my intellectual journey. On a more personal note, I am, as always, immensely grateful to my immediate family – Teresa, Christa Grace, Nick, and Dona – for their love and support.

I would also like to express my gratitude to a number of institutions for their support of this project. The Max Planck Institute for the History of Science in Berlin, the National Endowment for the Humanities, the National Science Foundation, the Humboldt Foundation, the Templeton Foundation, the Deutsche Akademische Austauschdienst, and the Gutenberg Forschungskolleg of the University of Mainz have all provided generous financial support for projects of which this is one important part. Virginia Tech, Yale, Notre Dame, the Humboldt University Berlin, the Gutenberg University Mainz, the Goethe University Frankfurt (including the Forschungskolleg Humanwissenschaften in Bad Homburg), and UC-San Diego (especially their philosophy departments) have all provided indispensable support for my research, for which I am thankful. Cambridge University Press, personified for me by Hilary Gaskin and her colleagues, has also been a wonderful publishing partner at every step in the process.

Last, but not least, I am thankful for permission to publish revised versions of the following papers.

1. "The Laws of Motion from Newton to Kant," *Perspectives on Science* 5 (1997): 311–48.
2. "Kant's Justification of the Laws of Mechanics," *Studies in History and Philosophy of Science* 29 (1998): 539–60.
3. "The Argumentative Structure of Kant's Metaphysical Foundations of Natural Science," *Journal of the History of Philosophy* 36 (1998): 567–93.
4. "Kant on Rational Cosmology," in *Kant and the Sciences*, ed. Eric Watkins (New York: Oxford University Press, 2000), pp. 70–89.
5. "Kant on Transcendental Laws," in *Thinking about Causes: Past and Present*, ed. James Machamer and Gereon Wolters (Pittsburgh: Pittsburg University Press, 2007), pp. 100–22.
6. "Die Antinomie der teleologischen Urteilskraft und Kants Ablehnung alternativer Teleologien §§69–71 & 72–73," in *Kooperativer Kommentar zu Kants Kritik der Urteilskraft*, ed. Otfried Höffe and Ina Goy (Berlin: Akademie Verlag, 2008), pp. 241–58.
7. "The Antinomy of Teleological Judgment," *Kantian Yearbook* 1 (2009): 197–221.

Acknowledgments xiii

8. "The System of Principles," in *The Cambridge Companion to Kant's Critique of Pure Reason*, ed. Paul Guyer (New York: Cambridge University Press, 2010), pp. 151–67.

9. "Making Sense of Mutual Interaction: Simultaneity and the Equality of Action and Reaction," in *Kant and the Concept of Community*, ed. Charlton Payne and Lucas Thorpe (Rochester: Rochester University Press, 2011), pp. 41–62.

10. "Shifts and Incompleteness in Kant's *Critique of Pure Reason*?: On Förster's *The Twenty-Five Years of Philosophy*," in *Übergänge: diskursiv oder intuitiv?*, ed. Johannes Haag and Markus Wild (Frankfurt: Klostermann Verlag, 2013), pp. 81–98.

11. "Kant on the Natural, Moral, Human, and Divine Orders," in *The Divine Order, the Human Order, and the Order of Nature: Historical Perspectives*, ed. Eric Watkins (New York: Oxford University Press, 2013), pp. 219–36.

12. "Kant on *Infima Species*," in *Kant und die Philosophie in weltbürgerlicher Absicht*, ed. Claudio La Rocca, Stefano Bacin, Alfredo Ferrarin, and Margit Ruffing (Berlin: de Gruyter, 2013), vol. V, pp. 283–94.

13. "What Is, for Kant, a Law of Nature?," *Kant-Studien* 105 (2014): 271–90.

14. "Nature in General as a System of Purposes," in *Kant's Theory of Biology*, ed. Ina Goy and Eric Watkins (Berlin: de Gruyter, 2014), pp. 117–30.

15. "Kant on the Unity and Diversity of Laws," in *Kant and the Laws of Nature*, ed. Michela Massimi and Angela Breitenbach (Cambridge: Cambridge University Press, 2017), pp. 11–29.

16. "Autonomy and the Legislation of Laws in the *Prolegomena* (1783)," in *Kant and the Emergence of Autonomy*, ed. Stefano Bacin and Oliver Sensen (Cambridge: Cambridge University Press, 2018), pp. 122–40.

Note on Texts, Translations, and Abbreviations

Bibliographic information for all works other than Kant's is supplied in the notes to each chapter, with full bibliographic information provided at the first occurrence in each chapter and a short title thereafter. Full bibliographic information is also supplied in the Bibliography. References to Kant's works are to the standard German edition: *Kants gesammelte Schriften*, ed. Deutsche [formerly Königlich Preussische] Akademie der Wissenschaften, 29 vols. (Berlin: de Gruyter, 1900–), and are cited by volume: page number, except for the *Critique of Pure Reason*, which is cited according to the pages of the first (A) and second (B) edition, as is standard practice. I consistently refer to Kant's *Metaphysical Foundations of Natural Science* simply as *Metaphysical Foundations*. Similarly, I refer to the *Critique of Pure Reason* as the first *Critique* and the *Critique of the Power of Judgment* as the third *Critique*, as is customary in the literature. All translations of passages from Kant's own works are my own, though I have consulted, and often followed, the Cambridge Edition of the Works of Immanuel Kant (by Cambridge University Press).

Otherwise, I have used the following titles, sometimes abbreviated, of Kant's writings:

> *Attempt to Introduce the Concept of Negative Magnitudes into Philosophy*
> *Concerning the Ultimate Ground of the Differentiation of Directions in Space*
> "Continued Observations on the Earthquakes That Have Been Experienced for Some Time"
> "History and Natural Description of the Most Noteworthy Occurrences of the Earthquake That Struck a Large Part of the Earth at the End of the Year 1755"
> *Inaugural Dissertation*
> *Jäsche Logik*
> *Logik Dohna*
> *Metaphysics Dohna*

Note on Texts, Translations, and Abbreviations   xv

Metaphysics Mrongovius
"On the Causes of Earthquakes"
The Only Possible Argument
Physical Monadology
Prolegomena
Refl
Thoughts on the True Estimation of Living Forces
*Universal Natural History and Theory of the Heavens, or Essay on
    the Constitution and Mechanical Origin of the Entire Universe,
    Treated in Accordance with Newtonian Principles*

Introduction

> Now the legislation of human reason (philosophy) has two objects, nature and freedom, and thus contains the law of nature as well as the moral law, initially in two separate systems, but ultimately in a single philosophical system. (A840/B868)

The focus of this book is on the unity, diversity, and centrality of the notion of law as it is employed in Kant's theoretical and practical philosophy. It argues that by thinking through a number of issues in various historical, scientific, and philosophical contexts over several decades Kant is able to develop a univocal concept of law that can nonetheless be applied to a wide range of particular cases, despite the diverse demands that these contexts give rise to. What is more, Kant comes to view both the generic conception of law he develops and its different particular instances as crucial components of his systematic philosophy as a whole. None of this, I take it, is immediately obvious, at least not on the basis of Kant's scattered pronouncements about law throughout his corpus. It is the point of the chapters that follow to make these points more readily apparent; they aim to do so by (1) introducing the generic conception of law that underlies the particular instances and that includes a notion of necessity that is interestingly different from some of the notions currently under discussion, (2) considering four different contexts in which Kant develops an account of a particular kind of law that can be seen as instantiating this generic conception, (3) showing how the diversity of the different particular cases is consistent with the univocal notion that underlies them all, and (4) explaining how laws perform crucial functions within Kant's conception of a single and complete system of cognition that would unify theoretical and practical philosophy while also satisfying reason's essential ends. Though the primary point of this book is descriptive – it describes some of the complex relations that obtain between different kinds of laws and the conception of law that unifies them – the comprehensive systematic vision that it gives rise to should also put one in a position to see its central philosophical merits.

2   Introduction

Now Kant's most generic conception of law, which applies to both laws of nature and the moral law, includes two essential elements: (1) necessity and (2) the act of a spontaneous faculty whose legislative authority prescribes that necessity to a specific domain through an appropriate act. These two elements put Kant in a unique position in contemporary discussions of laws of nature. In such discussions, it is standard to contrast empiricist and necessitarian views. Put very roughly, the empiricist view maintains that laws are general statements contained in the best (deductive) system that accounts for the totality of events that occur in the world, and they are important insofar as they organize these events in especially useful ways (with the best such system being both simple and explanatorily powerful). For example, on this view mechanical laws might be characterized as whatever mathematically precise general statements are able to collect together descriptions of a large number of changes of motion. The fewer the number of statements, the simpler the system, and the more changes of motion these statements can capture, the more powerful they are, where the best set of statements excels at both. Note that, on this account, there is nothing metaphysically necessary about the laws. If the events were significantly different, the laws would be different as well, since the laws' dependence on whatever events happen to occur in the world makes them contingent.

By contrast, the necessitarian view asserts that laws of nature express necessity relations, typically between universals or natures. For example, "all humans are mortal" is a law of nature on this view not because it is an accurate general summary of past, current, and future deaths, but because the universal 'humanity' necessitates 'mortality' or because the nature of humanity necessitates its mortality. That is, this law obtains because of the nature of humanity, not because of the mortality rates observed among humans. On this account, even if there were no humans, the law that humans are mortal would still be true, for in that case if there had been humans, they would have been mortal (given that being mortal follows from being human). On this view, strictly speaking, the laws govern the world in the sense that they determine what can and cannot happen in the world rather than having the events that occur in the world determining what the laws are. In this respect, the empiricist and the necessitarian views are diametrically opposed.

The first element of Kant's conception of law places him squarely in the necessitarian camp. However, Kant's position has two interesting twists in this context that can lead one to view it as a distinct alternative to standard versions of necessitarianism. First, he recognizes that "necessity" comes in different forms, depending on the kind of law at issue. Though "necessity" might well mean "determination" (in the sense of

Introduction 3

"natural necessity") in the case of laws of nature, in the case of the moral law it amounts to "necessitation" or "obligation" in the case of human beings. Second, Kant's account of transcendental laws is based (at least in part) on natures of a specific kind, namely what one might call our cognitive or epistemic natures (rather than on the natures of particular empirical objects, as is the case for empirical laws). More specifically, what counts as a transcendental law for him depends essentially on the nature of our cognitive faculties, such as that of the understanding (or reason), and on the fact that it makes experience possible. This feature is relevant in considering whether one should "relativize" the a priori to new scientific theories as they emerge and to the linguistic frameworks that they require for their formulation. For by basing laws on unchanging epistemic natures and the way that they make experience possible rather than on the linguistic frameworks that each new scientific theory brings with it, Kant is able to support the kind of necessity that laws must have on his account. Moreover, this second twist provides a glimpse of some of the implications of the second element of Kant's conception of law, which stems from the idea that there can be no law without a lawmaker. For the faculties that belong to our epistemic natures play a role in the legislative act that allows a necessary principle to be a law. In this way, Kant develops an account of laws that would occupy a unique place in the current debate about the nature of laws of nature.

Though this general conception of law is fundamental to Kant's overall account of law, it is useful to see how he fills it out in different contexts for different kinds of laws. One important context in which the notion of law played a dominant role both in Kant's thinking and in European thought more generally is that of normative political theory, since legitimate rulers, whether monarchs or legislatures, were taken to govern by enacting, interpreting, and enforcing laws. Kant becomes increasingly interested in this issue throughout his career, so much so that he ultimately articulates an elaborate and fundamentally new philosophy of law in the Doctrine of Right in the *Metaphysics of Morals* (1797). However, because Kant's most explicit reflections on the issue occur relatively late in his career and are largely derivative on a concept of law that he had already developed on the basis of other considerations, I will refrain from attempting to address this topic here.

Instead, I begin with the subject matter that Kant himself started with and that he devoted significant attention to for more years than any other, namely natural philosophy and the most basic laws of nature that lie at its foundation. From his very early *Thoughts on the True Estimation of Living Forces* (1746/7) and *Universal Natural History and Theory of the Heavens* (1755) up through the *Critique of Pure Reason* (1781/8) and the

4   Introduction

Metaphysical Foundations of Natural Science (1786), to his latest unpublished writings in the *Opus postumum*, Kant investigated a wide range of topics in natural philosophy. Though the scope of his interests was extremely broad (including quite specific topics pertaining to volcanoes, earthquakes, the rotation of the earth, and fireballs), one of his most sustained interests lay in working out the nature, presuppositions, and implications of the laws of motion, one that took place against the background of a specific historical, scientific, and philosophical context. For in the first half of the seventeenth century, as the so-called Scientific Revolution was radically changing the content, practice, and authority of natural science, Descartes (along with others) upended the Scholastic Aristotelian tradition by reconceiving of natural philosophy as a search for laws of nature rather than substantial forms. And the publication of Newton's *Principia* in the second half of the century (1687) marked in some ways the culmination of that movement, since the law of universal gravitation was viewed as a (single) law of nature that could unify the behavior of all bodies. Despite the near universal acclaim with which Newton's achievement was met, there was still vigorous debate throughout the rest of the seventeenth and then eighteenth century (and beyond) about the precise formulation of the laws of motion presupposed by the law of universal gravitation, the kind of argumentative support that one could provide these laws with, and their role within natural science more broadly.

It is primarily in this context that Kant develops his most detailed account of what he takes to be the most fundamental laws of nature. He articulates such laws at an extremely general level in the first *Critique*'s "System of Principles," since the "principles" that he identifies there as laws of nature are justified insofar as they are conditions of the possibility of experience; that is, they make possible our empirical cognition of a single spatio-temporal world. However, Kant also accepts somewhat more specific, though still quite general, laws of nature in the form of three Laws of Mechanics in the *Metaphysical Foundations of Natural Science*. Because Kant thinks that Newton has not provided a proper justification of his laws of motion, and because his own Laws of Mechanics cannot be derived immediately from more general laws (e.g., by means of straightforward substitution), he sees the need to provide a different justification for them. However, it turns out that Kant does not think that he can justify the laws of motion that Newton formulated. As a result, he is forced to formulate his Laws of Mechanics in ways that required significant departures from the formulations of Newton and of those in Germany who were similarly engaged in attempting to identify the proper formulation, justification, and interpretation of these laws.

Introduction 5

This line of argument represents a first major set of complex considerations relevant to Kant's thought on law, one that adds both substance and detail to his generic conception of law.

Another set of considerations in which Kant's conception of law is highly relevant is to be found in the *Critique of the Power of Judgment* (1790), where he distinguishes between the kinds of mechanical principles found in the Laws of Mechanics and the kind of teleological principles suggested by our experience of organisms, which seem to defy purely mechanistic explanation. In the Antinomy of Teleological Judgment, in particular, Kant draws a fundamental contrast between mechanical and teleological explanatory principles, one that generates an antinomy for judgments about the possibility of organisms. Though Kant's resolution of this antinomy is notoriously obscure and remains puzzling in several respects, it is important to understand the considerations that generate the antinomy, including his conception of organisms, his reasons for thinking that organisms both must be and yet cannot be explicable by purely mechanical means, and the sense in which mechanistic explanations could be subordinate to teleological ones. For these considerations shed light on several further features of mechanical laws and teleological principles, including their relationship to each other and to the supersensible ground Kant invokes in the resolution to the antinomy.

Several infrequently discussed passages in other sections of the third *Critique* reveal that Kant is interested in applying teleological considerations not only to organisms but also to other natural objects. For he thinks that reason prods us both to consider purposive relations between organic and non-organic beings (in what we might call ecosystems) and to ask whether everything in nature (and not only organisms) must be judged teleologically. On Kant's view, once reason begins its quest for explanation, which can take either mechanical or teleological form, it naturally ends up considering whether nature as a whole must be a system of purposes that itself has a purpose and, if so, what that purpose might be. By means of these considerations, one is led not only to human beings as the ultimate ends of nature (in virtue of their status as free moral beings) but also, ultimately, to what a philosophical system ought to be and what ends it should satisfy. Teleological considerations of various kinds thus shed important light on Kant's conception of mechanical and other explanatory laws.

A third set of considerations that are significant for understanding laws and their role in Kant's broader philosophy derives from a number of diverse principles that Kant describes (implicitly or explicitly) as regulative rather than constitutive (the status Kant attributes to the a priori laws

6   Introduction

of nature found in the System of Principles which make possible not only experience but also the objects of experience). First, immediately following the Refutation of Idealism, Kant discusses a series of a priori laws of rational cosmology that he refers to as the principles of no gap, no leap, no chance, and no fate (A229/B282). The principle of no fate, for example, specifies that causal laws cannot involve "blind" necessity but must rather be comprehensible. Each of these principles is, in its own way, relevant to determining what kinds of laws and explanations invoking them one is permitted to accept as genuine, which places a significant constraint on the content of laws of nature. A second set of regulative principles can be found in the Appendix to the Transcendental Dialectic, where Kant discusses at length the "logical laws" of homogeneity, specification, and the continuity of forms. These principles specify the kinds of concepts that one should look to apply to the world (namely, increasingly general concepts, increasingly specific concepts, and a continuity of those that fall in between the more general and the more specific). Though Kant is clear that these principles regulate the kinds of judgments one should make, he also thinks that this kind of regulative principle "is not merely a principle of economy for reason, but becomes an inner law of its nature" (A650/B678). Relatedly, this kind of "logical" principle presupposes, Kant repeatedly maintains, a corresponding "transcendental principle" (A650/B678), which pertains to the world and not simply to our activities. These principles thus have a significant bearing on Kant's conception of laws of nature, just as the principles of rational cosmology do.

A fourth set of considerations relevant to understanding Kant's conception of law concerns morality and God's role with respect to both it and laws of nature. Kant's decision to conceive of morality in terms of a moral law and moral obligation has a two-fold significance. First, given the availability of non-law-based conceptions of morality (such as moral sense theories), Kant was not forced either by tradition or by a lack of alternatives to invoke the notion of law in this way; that he decided to do so is significant. Second, that decision raises a philosophical challenge for his conception of law. Is he playing fast and loose with the term "law," with no concept that could apply to both the moral law and laws of nature, which derive from distinct philosophical traditions, or is there some abstract univocal concept that holds of both? Asserting the latter demands a detailed explanation of the content of that concept, an explanation that describes how morality can be understood in terms of its elements and demonstrates a close analogy between theoretical legislation of laws of nature and the practical legislation of the moral law. Fortunately, Kant's account of theoretical legislation, especially as

Introduction

presented in the *Prolegomena*, displays a structure that is remarkably similar to the account of autonomy that he first develops explicitly in the *Groundwork*. In fact, it is not easy to dismiss the suspicion that Kant's reflections on theoretical legislation while writing the *Prolegomena* were at least partially responsible for his acceptance of his doctrine of autonomy, even if moral considerations surely played a significant role as well.

These parallels between theoretical and practical legislation give rise to the question of what God's role is with respect to law. It was not uncommon in the early modern period to maintain that the laws of nature derived from God, whether it be from his immutable nature (Descartes) or from his will (Malebranche). Similarly, divine command theorists of morality maintain that the moral law just is the divine law, or God's command. Thus, for laws of nature as for morality, God plays the starring role in such accounts. Kant's doctrine of theoretical and practical legislation can seem to be a complete reversal of this kind of position. Since laws depend on the nature of human beings rather than on that of God, who is no longer needed for any act of legislation, human beings might appear to be able to replace God altogether (especially in light of Kant's probing criticisms of the traditional theistic proofs). Though it is true that with his doctrines of theoretical and practical legislation, Kant attributes great importance to "the human order," he nonetheless retains several interrelated roles for God. First, in the first *Critique*, Kant continues to see the (rational) need for the idea of an *ens realissimum* to serve as the ground of all possibility, even if the argument that leads to this conclusion does not justify the attribution of traditional divine moral properties (such as omnibenevolence) and also does not support the assertion of full-fledged theoretical cognition. Second, in the second *Critique*, Kant develops his "practical" argument for the postulate of God's existence (where the *ens realissimum* is now understood to have moral attributes), and he also allows for a modified (non-voluntarist) kind of divine command theory, since nothing stands in the way, he thinks, of viewing the moral law that reason legislates as a command of God's, given that God is rational and the moral law applies to God (albeit not in the form of an imperative), just as it does to us. Third, by the end of the third *Critique*, Kant indicates that God may play a further role not only in reconciling mechanism and teleology but also in underwriting empirical laws. What thus emerges from these considerations about the moral law and God's relation to it, as well as to laws of nature, is a picture much more complex than is typically recognized, and one in which Kant's notion of law clearly plays a central role.

With this complexity comes a further challenge, all the more so if one keeps in mind the previous sets of considerations concerning law.

8   Introduction

Given the univocal conception of law that can be identified in each of the different kinds of laws, how is all the diversity in laws possible? If all laws involve necessity and a legislative authority from whose act of legislation it becomes law, how can there be so many different kinds of laws? The resources that Kant makes available for developing an answer to this line of questioning are many, since they include different kinds of necessitation, faculties, and acts, as well as different objects of reason (freedom and nature) and its essential ends. However, the fact that reason's essential ends are implicated in this answer allows one to see how the different kinds of laws contribute in different ways to the complete systematic unity of cognition demanded by reason. Thus, one can not only account for the diverse kinds of laws that Kant accepts, but also see how they fit into his rich conception of a single philosophical system.

That, in abbreviated form, is the overarching narrative of this investigation, which is structured accordingly. Part I describes Kant's most generic account of law, focusing on the univocal concept of law that is instantiated in both laws of nature and the moral law (Chapter 1) and on the most generic kind of law of nature (Chapter 2). Part II considers the most general a priori laws of nature (Chapter 3) and Kant's justification of the laws of mechanics in their historical context (Chapters 4–6). Part III addresses the nature and status of teleological principles, how they are distinct from mechanical principles, and how the two can be reconciled (Chapter 7), as well as how they fit into Kant's conception of nature as a whole (Chapter 8). Part IV looks closely at various regulative principles that bear immediately on laws of nature and their explanatory power (Chapters 9 and 10). Part V explains the parallels between the moral law and laws of nature as well as between practical and theoretical legislation (Chapter 11) and sketches Kant's complex considerations involving the role that God plays with respect to laws (Chapter 12). The Conclusion considers how the diversity of laws is consistent with the univocity of Kant's generic concept of law, and how these laws contribute to the complete systematic unity of cognition that is, on Kant's view, reason's ultimate goal.

Part I

Kant's Concept of Law

Before investigating the different roles that the concept of law plays in Kant's theoretical and practical philosophy, it is useful to form a general idea of Kant's conception of what a law is. Chapter 1 explores Kant's conception of law by considering his frequent use of the terms "law of nature" and "moral law" and by identifying a univocal notion of law that underlies both terms. It argues that the notion of law that is fundamental to both contains two elements: an objective or necessary rule and the notion of a proper authority that prescribes that necessary rule to a particular domain through an appropriate act. This chapter then offers a description of how these two elements are involved in Kant's conception of laws of nature and the moral law, showing how, in both cases, we have a spontaneous and active faculty that legislates a necessary rule, even if the kind of necessity involved in each can be different.

Chapter 2 considers Kant's conception of transcendental laws in detail, arguing that the necessity that is inherent in them is best understood as being based on our epistemic (or cognitive) natures, making it into an attractive alternative to empiricist and standard necessitarian accounts of laws. It also considers challenges that have been raised against Kant's conception – challenges that stem from developments in science such as the discovery of non-Euclidean geometry and relativity theory – and articulates two types of response, one that is more orthodox by appealing only to resources that Kant explicitly endorses, the other less traditional insofar as it makes appeal to the notion of the relativized a priori. While both responses have their advantages, this chapter proposes that Kant's traditional conception is able to mount the stronger response. However, regardless of one's stance on this issue, the chapter offers clarification of Kant's conception of law by showing how it compares and contrasts with a range of contemporary views.

1 What Is, for Kant, a Law of Nature?

1.1 Introduction

The concept of a law of nature plays a number of highly visible roles in Kant's theoretical philosophy. For one, it allows Kant to provide an illustration of synthetic a priori cognition and the distinctive kind of transcendental argument he uses to justify it. The Second Analogy of Experience, which attempts to establish the necessity of causal laws for the possibility of experience, is perhaps Kant's most famous example of such a synthetic a priori cognition and of the kind of justification he offers in support of it. For another, Kant thinks that laws of nature are important to science in various ways. For example, he thinks that empirical science involves empirical laws of nature, which depend for their apodictic certainty on a priori laws of nature that are established in the *Critique of Pure Reason* and the *Metaphysical Foundations of Natural Science* (4:469). And insofar as he thinks that science must be systematic, that is, a whole of cognition ordered according to rational principles (4:468), he ends up devoting significant resources (constitutive principles of the understanding, regulative principles of reason, and reflective principles of the power of judgment) to explaining how laws of nature can be discovered, related, and justified so as to satisfy the strict requirements demanded by his conception of science. Laws of nature are thus crucial to the metaphysics of nature that Kant envisions.

We can appreciate the various roles that laws of nature are called on to play in Kant's philosophy only if we also have an accurate understanding of what his conception of a law of nature is. In the wake of Hume's analysis, it is often assumed that a law of nature is an exceptionless regularity concerning types of events in nature (perhaps conjoined with a subjective expectation that this regularity will hold in the future) and that Kant accepts this minimal conception such that he can then assert and argue for his distinctive claims regarding the modal status of the laws of nature. This assumption can thus make it appear as if the crucial differences between Hume and Kant primarily concern whether causality

12   Kant's Concept of Law

involves purely contingent regularities or rather some kind of necessary connection, and what non-question-begging argument Kant could offer in support of his claim to necessity. Yet it is worth stepping back from this assumption and the larger picture of which it is a part to consider whether such an interpretation of Kant's conception of laws of nature captures what is truly most central to his view.

As it turns out, Kant's explicit statements about what in general a law is consistently speak against such an interpretation.[1] What's more, investigating the broader historical and philosophical tradition out of which Kant's conception of a law emerged provides a further compelling reason to question this interpretation.[2] For this tradition contains two uses of the term "law" that, when taken together, present a challenge to the very idea of a law of nature, and one can view Kant as responding to this challenge in a novel way. One use of the term derives from the so-called natural law tradition, which asserts that moral obligation arises on the basis of natural law, where a natural law can be established only through the act of a (superior) lawgiver who governs (inferior) subjects by placing them under an obligation to perform certain actions. This conception thus assumes that natural law can apply only to beings endowed with reason and free will, since only such beings can understand the obligation that the law places them under, and can decide whether or not to obey that law.

A second use of the term "law" derives from the conception and practice of natural science in the early modern period and presupposes that natural science consists in the identification of a small number of mathematically precise laws of nature from which one can derive, e.g., the motions of bodies. Descartes, building on Galileo's results, was influential in establishing this conception of laws of nature as a desideratum of scientific inquiry, and Newton's *Principia* was often taken to represent its fulfillment for the realm of bodies.

Though each of these uses is perfectly intelligible on its own, if taken together, they reveal an important challenge to the very idea of a law of nature: How is it possible for a law to *govern* the inanimate objects found in nature? If no legislator enacts such a law or if many of the objects in nature are not rational and free beings and cannot therefore be obligated to act as the law demands, how can there be such a thing as a *law* of *nature*?

---

[1] This is not to deny that there is a disagreement between Hume and Kant on whether there are necessary connections in nature, but rather simply to claim that it is not the only or even most important distinguishing feature.

[2] For a different case against the traditional reading of the relation between Hume and Kant, see Eric Watkins, *Kant and the Metaphysics of Causality* (New York: Cambridge University Press, 2005), esp. chapters 4 and 6.

One natural response to this challenge would be simply to deny that the notion of law involved in the laws of nature is at all the same as that involved in natural law. If natural law requires that a law be established through the act of a lawgiver who governs subjects by placing them under an obligation to act in some way, then, one might think, natural law has nothing in common with the laws of nature, which cover inanimate objects that cannot be said to either obey or disobey, and one should therefore refrain from saying, as people are wont to do, that the laws of nature *govern* what happens in the world.[3] Similarly, if the laws of nature determine what *must* happen in the world in every (non-miraculous) case, then, one might think, they have nothing to do with natural law, which is concerned instead with obligation and what *ought* to happen.[4] On either version of this response, the use of the term "law" is equivocal.

A second natural response to this challenge would be to assert that a univocal concept does in fact underlie both the concept of natural law and that of laws of nature, but that one of these concepts is simply not instantiated. For example, one could deny that the world is governed by laws of nature on the grounds that all observed regularities are not truly exceptionless since they obtain only with significant ceteris paribus restrictions, and are therefore not truly laws at all.[5] Or one could argue that it is not necessary to posit a natural or moral law as such on the grounds that one can describe morality entirely in terms of obligations and permissions and thereby avoid all reference to the notion of a law that would be commanded by God, a strategy that might appear attractive, or at least fitting, in an age more secular than Kant's own. Indeed, even in Kant's own time, not all thought it necessary to invoke the notion of a moral law. Hume, to cite one notable example, never speaks of a moral law in either his *Treatise of Human Nature* or his *Enquiry Concerning the Principles of Morals*.[6] Kant's decision to interpret morality in terms of a moral law is thus important. That he places the moral law at the foundation of his practical philosophy in what he calls the metaphysics of morals is similarly significant.

---

[3] For one contemporary illustration of this general approach, see Helen Beebee, "The Nongoverning Conception of Laws of Nature," *Philosophy and Phenomenological Research* 61 (2000): 571–94.

[4] Kant displays sensitivity to this kind of difference between domains by distinguishing "what does happen" (nature) and "what ought to happen" (morality) (B830).

[5] One prominent proponent of this option is Nancy Cartwright, *How the Laws of Physics Lie* (Oxford: Oxford University Press, 1983), *Nature's Capacities and Its Measurement* (Oxford: Oxford University Press, 1989), and *The Dappled World: A Study of the Boundaries of Science* (Cambridge: Cambridge University Press, 1999).

[6] Hume does repeatedly refer to laws of justice and civil law, but does not seem to conceive of morality in terms of a moral law.

14   Kant's Concept of Law

Without denying the consistency or coherence of either of these two responses, I maintain that Kant pursues a different and, to my mind, more interesting option by articulating a concept of law that has a genuinely univocal meaning at its core, but one that can be instantiated in different ways in the theoretical and practical contexts of laws of nature and the natural or moral law. For as Kant remarks in the Introduction of the *Critique of the Power of Judgment*: "morally practical precepts, which are grounded entirely on the concept of freedom to the complete exclusion of the determining grounds of the will from nature, constitute an entirely special kind of precept: which are also, like the rules that nature obeys [*gehorcht*], simply called laws" (5:173).

But what is the content of the univocal concept of law that is involved in laws of nature and the moral law? The core meaning of law that is univocal between laws of nature and the moral law contains two elements. First, the concept of law requires an objective or necessary rule, where it is the element of necessity that constitutes its distinctive component. Second, a law can be valid only if a proper authority has prescribed it to a particular domain through an appropriate act. This core meaning of law is then instantiated in somewhat different ways in the different cases of laws of nature and the moral law. While Kant insists on every law being the result of a spontaneous legislative act (of, e.g., the understanding or reason), the notion of necessity takes on different forms in each case, since the laws of nature involve *determination*, while the moral law can give rise to *obligation*. In light of these differences, Kant is then in a position to respond to the challenge raised earlier by noting that the requirement that subjects must be rational and free to be governed by law obtains for the case of obligation, but not for determination, despite the fact that both involve a necessary rule that is the result of legislation, and, given the univocal concept of law he endorses, both allow for an appropriate sense in which the law can be said to govern subjects.

In the following, I begin (in Section 1.2) by presenting textual evidence concerning Kant's generic conception of a law, arguing that it contains the elements of necessity and legislation just mentioned. I then turn (in Section 1.3) to a brief description of two seemingly unrelated contexts in which the term "law" is used in the early modern period – that of laws of nature in science and the natural law tradition – and state the challenge that these contexts pose if taken together. With that background in mind I turn (in Section 1.4) to describing how Kant's generic concept of law is instantiated in his accounts of the laws of nature and the moral law so that I can then explain how these accounts help to provide a response to the challenge described above. What the discussion shows is that Kant's description of law in terms of notions of necessity and an act

What Is, for Kant, a Law of Nature? 15

of legislation is consistent with different kinds of necessity (determination and obligation) obtaining in different contexts such that one need not appeal to a purely metaphorical sense of law in speaking of laws of nature. It also suggests that Kant's conception of law is not an isolated and detachable element of his position, but rather is related to fundamental features of his overall philosophy.

1.2 Laws as Necessary Rules

Kant states explicitly what he understands a law in general to be in several prominent passages in his corpus. In the A-edition Transcendental Deduction, for example, he connects laws to rules as follows: "Rules, so far as they are objective, ... are called laws" (A126). Since he thinks of objectivity as being opposed to subjectivity and as including necessity, this statement is consistent with the description of law that he had offered a few pages earlier (A113), according to which a law is a necessary rule. In addition, in the *Metaphysical Foundations of Natural Science*, Kant states that laws are "principles of the necessity of what belongs to the existence of a thing" (4:469). Insofar as a principle is a rule from which something else follows, this passage likewise provides a description of law that refers to necessity and a rule. What is new in this passage is that the necessity in question can pertain to the existence of a thing.

In the so-called Kaehler transcripts on moral philosophy, Kant provides a somewhat more detailed and official-sounding definition of law as follows: "Every formula that expresses the necessity of an action is called a law."[7] Again, the elements of necessity and being a rule (in the guise of a formula) are present, but this description brings out that necessity can also pertain to an action (and not only to the existence of a thing). Now Kant thinks of an action very broadly as the determination of a power in a substance to cause an effect (28:564–5). According to this definition, then, a law expresses the necessity of the action by which a substance causes an effect (i.e., determines the existence or change of state of another thing). Since Kant's lectures on moral philosophy form the context for this definition, one might think that it is restricted to the volitional actions of human beings, but the very next sentence clarifies that the notion of law is intended to have broader application: "Thus we can have natural laws, where the actions stand under universal laws, or else practical laws. Accordingly, all laws are [either] physical

---

[7] Immanuel Kant, *Vorlesung zur Moralphilosophie*, ed. Werner Stark, (Berlin: Walter de Gruyter, 2004), p. 53.

16   Kant's Concept of Law

[i.e., natural] or practical [and] the practical ones express the necessity of free actions."[8] Kant's idea here is that a law involves a rule expressing the necessity of an action, where the substance responsible for the action and its necessity can be either an object in nature or what we might call a free agent. Though this idea would need to be filled out with various details in concrete cases, it is striking that the abstract notion of law at issue here has a univocal meaning at its core, one Kant describes in terms of a rule that expresses the necessity of an action or of what belongs to the existence of a thing.

In the B-edition Transcendental Deduction we find further evidence regarding Kant's conception of law. There he says: "Categories are concepts that prescribe laws *a priori* to appearances, thus to nature as the sum total of all appearances" (B163). Two points are of note here. First, the fact that Kant talks about the categories *prescribing* laws to appearances reveals that he is committed to the idea that law, even in a theoretical context, involves not just a necessary rule, but also the prescription, or legislation, of that necessary rule. Second, this passage reveals that Kant does not restrict his notion of law to the category of causality, as one might expect, but rather holds that it is relevant to all of the categories. Thus, even the categories of quantity and quality prescribe laws in the sense that they represent a necessary rule with respect to the objective properties of things, which fits with the passage quoted from the *Metaphysical Foundations* above; the breadth of his use of the term "law" is thus consistent with his remark about necessity pertaining to the existence of a thing (and not just action and causality).[9]

What becomes clear by considering several of those passages that read like definitions of law is that Kant is quite distant from a Humean conception that would define law in terms of purely contingent regularities of events. Instead, Kant's position is closer, at least considered at this level of generality, to the rationalist position that has been developed in recent times by David Armstrong and Michael Tooley, who describe laws in terms of relations of necessity between universals.[10] However, Kant's account also involves the notions of action and legislation, which are not emphasized in these accounts, a fact that ought to give one pause before identifying Kant's position too closely with them.[11] To gain a

---

[8] Kant, *Vorlesung zur Moralphilosophie*, p. 53.

[9] See Chapters 3 and 10 in this book for more discussion.

[10] David Armstrong, *What Is a Law of Nature?* (Cambridge: Cambridge University Press, 1983), and Michael Tooley, "The Nature of Laws," *Canadian Journal of Philosophy* 7 (1977): 667–98.

[11] See Chapter 2 in this book for a more detailed description of how Kant's account of law differs from both empiricist and necessitarian accounts.

What Is, for Kant, a Law of Nature? 17

fuller understanding of Kant's conception of a law, it is useful to consider two historical contexts in which the concept of law played an ineliminable philosophical role and to reflect on how Kant's views can be seen as responding to the challenge that arises from considering them together.

1.3 The Natural Law Tradition, Laws of Nature in Early Modern Science, and a Challenge

One major tradition in practical philosophy, broadly construed, is often referred to by the term 'natural law theory.' The basic idea is that what is good for us, what our end is, what we ought to do, or what we are obliged to do is based on natural law as opposed to positive law or common law. This idea, or variants thereof, can be found among the ancients (including Aristotle and the Stoics), but is developed in greater detail first by Thomas Aquinas and then by Francisco Suarez, before being modified further by several early modern thinkers. Although there were intellectualist (or naturalist) versions of natural law theory, according to which natural law is determined solely by the divine understanding (and thus by the natures of things), and voluntarist versions, according to which natural law is due exclusively to the (potentially arbitrary acts of) divine will, it is instructive to consider the basic features of Suarez's account. For his account is often interpreted as an attempt to forge a middle path between these two extremes, one that distinguishes nicely some central features that were regularly ascribed to natural law.[12]

Suarez agrees with the intellectualist that there is a basis in nature itself for an action being appropriate or inappropriate, independent of God's willing the appropriateness or inappropriateness of that action. That is, an action is good, and one has a reason to perform it, simply on the basis of the nature of the action itself (including relevant circumstances), and the voluntarist is wrong to think that God could command, and thereby make good, any action at all, regardless of its nature. At the same time, Suarez agrees with the voluntarist that nature itself, or the appropriateness or inappropriateness of an action, cannot suffice to create an obligation to perform an action or to refrain from acting. That is, unlike the intellectualist, he thinks that if one is obligated to perform an action, then the obligation that prescribes the performance of that action must be created by an appropriate act of will of a superior, that is, of one with the

---

[12] For a detailed discussion of Suarez's theory of natural law, see Terence Irwin's *The Development of Ethics*, vol. 2 (New York: Oxford University Press, 2008), chapters 30 and 31, pp. 1–69.

18   Kant's Concept of Law

authority to generate an obligation that binds an inferior.[13] For on his view, the lawfulness of natural law includes the notion of obligation, and obligation as such requires the command, or act of will, of a superior that places one under an obligation.[14] In short, it is one thing for an action to be good (and for me to be motivated to do it simply because it is good) and quite another for me to be obligated to perform that act (and to be motivated to perform it because I am under an obligation to do it). The extra element that is involved in obligation beyond the intrinsic goodness of the action in question must derive, Suarez thinks, from an act of will of one who has the authority to bind me.[15] Thus, according to Suarez's intermediate position, natural law contains both a precept, which aims to realize our ultimate end, and an obligation to follow the precept. For that reason, natural law requires both the divine intellect and the divine will, the former to give the human will its proper direction (to what is truly our ultimate end) and the latter to give rise to its obligatory or binding force for us.[16]

Natural law theory underwent significant changes with the onset of early modern philosophy. For example, Grotius is often interpreted as rejecting a teleological conception of natural law, while Hobbes based natural law on our interest in self-preservation (rather than on a broader conception of the good, as Aquinas and Suarez did), holding that commands generate obligations only insofar as they are associated with sanctions enforced by a superior power that motivate our compliance.[17] Leibniz, Wolff, and Crusius then react to these further developments in complex ways.[18] As a result, by Kant's time, there is a rich philosophical tradition with sophisticated views on what law is, what natural law is, how

---

[13] Francisco Suarez, *On Laws and God the Lawgiver*, 8 vols., ed. and trans. L. Perena et al. (Madrid: Consejo Superior de Investigaciones Cientificas, 1971–81): Law is "the act whereby a superior wills to bind an inferior to the performance of a particular deed" (Book I, chapter 5, §24). In Book I, chapter 6, sec. 4 of *De Jure Naturae et Gentium*, Pufendorf similarly defines law as a decree by which a superior obligates a subject to adapt his actions to the former's command.

[14] The latin "lex" derives from "ligare," which means "to bind."

[15] Thomas Aquinas holds that obligation is the result of an act of will by a superior on an inferior (see, e.g., *Summa Theologiae* II.ii.q104).

[16] Suarez, *On Laws and God the Lawgiver*, pp. 70 and 72.

[17] For discussion of Grotius's and Hobbes's positions, see Irwin, *The Development of Ethics*, vol. 2, chapters 32–6.

[18] For accounts of the development of natural law in Germany, see Knud Haakonssen, *Natural Law and Moral Philosophy: From Grotius to the Scottish Enlightenment* (Cambridge: Cambridge University Press, 1996); Haakonssen, "German Natural Law," in *Cambridge History of Eighteenth-Century Political Thought*, ed. Mark Goldie and Robert Wokler (Cambridge: Cambridge University Press, 2006), pp. 249–90; Tim Hochstrasser, *Natural Law Theories in the Early Enlightenment* (Cambridge: Cambridge University Press, 2000); Ian Hunter, *Rival Enlightenments: Civil and Metaphysical Philosophy in*

What Is, for Kant, a Law of Nature? 19

it relates to morality, and what is required for moral obligation. In light of this historical context, it is significant that Kant chooses to speak not only of morality, but specifically of a moral *law*, and that he views this law, when stated in the form of a Categorical Imperative, as giving expression to moral *obligations*; in the context of the natural law tradition, these views immediately give rise to questions about what the exact content of the law is, what its source is, and whence it derives its obligatory or binding force.[19]

The notion of law was also a central topic when natural philosophy underwent a revolutionary change in the early modern period. In addition to the various social, cultural, and intellectual transformations that took place at the time concerning how scientific authority was established, maintained, and questioned, dramatic shifts were taking place in the content of natural philosophy: Heliocentric astronomy replaced geocentric accounts of the heavens; teleological schemes gave way to purely mechanistic models of explanation; mathematical physics challenged the primacy of theology; and the metaphysics of substantial forms and prime matter was rejected in favor of a seemingly more austere ontology of bodies in motion. Amid all this doctrinal unrest, however, a crucial change took place in the ultimate goal of natural science. Instead of trying to discover the essential features of substantial forms, the causal powers that such forms possessed, and the ends they tended to pursue, many natural scientists in the early modern period, especially those working in rational mechanics (a branch of mixed mathematics), hoped to formulate a small number of mathematically precise laws that could be used to predict the future state of the world with much greater exactness and certainty than had been previously possible. Galileo was an important initiator of this project with his discovery of the law of free fall, which contradicted Aristotle's widely held account of the motion of bodies. However, Descartes played an especially crucial role insofar as he expanded the scope of scientific inquiry from finding laws of motion that would describe the states of a small subset of bodies (e.g., those in free fall) to discovering laws of motion that would hold for all bodies. As a

---

Early Modern Germany (Cambridge: Cambridge University Press, 2001); Gerald Hartung, *Die Naturrechtsdebatte: Geschichte der Obligatio vom 17. bis 20. Jarhhundert* (Freiburg: Verlag Karl Alber, 1998); and Richard Tuck, *The Rights of War and Peace: Political Thought and the International Order from Grotius to Kant* (Oxford: Oxford University Press, 1999).

[19] For an argument that Kant was working in the natural law tradition, see Jerome Schneewind, "Kant and Natural Law Ethics," *Ethics* 104 (1993): 53–74, esp. 60–4.

20   Kant's Concept of Law

result, an important part of Descartes's legacy is that discovering laws of nature came to be viewed as one of the primary goals of science.[20]

Once one understands the centrality of laws of nature to the conception and practice of science at the time, one can see how several central features of early modern natural philosophy fell into place.[21] For example, one major task of natural philosophy, conceived of in this way, lay in formulating laws of nature that would cover the widest possible range of phenomena. To accomplish this task for bodies, Descartes proposed three laws of motion along with several rules of impact meant to amplify these laws. Though the counterexamples that Leibniz and Huygens brought to light discredited Descartes's particular formulations of the laws of motion, many natural philosophers (including Kant) simply took that as a challenge to formulate laws that would not suffer the same fate.[22] Indeed, one of the major accomplishments of early modern science was Newton's formulations of three laws of motion, which were remarkably successful at describing the motions of bodies in various media and which could also be used to derive the law of

---

[20] Cf. Edward Zilsel, "The Genesis of the Concept of Physical Law," *Philosophical Review* 51 (1942): 245–79; Francis Oakley, "Christian Theology and the Newtonian Science: The Rise of the Concept of the Laws of Nature," *Church History* 30 (1961): 433–57; John R. Milton, "The Origin and Development of the Concept of the Laws of Nature," *Archives Européennes de Sociologie* 22 (1981): 173–95; Jane E. Ruby, "The Origins of Scientific 'Law,'" *Journal of the History of Ideas* 47 (1986): 341–59; Friedrich Steinle, "The Amalgamation of a Concept – Laws of Nature in the New Sciences," in *Laws of Nature: Essays on the Philosophical, Scientific and Historical Dimensions*, ed. Friedel Weinert (Berlin: de Gruyter, 1995), pp. 316–68; Peter Harrison, "Voluntarism and Early Modern Science," *History of Science* 40 (2002): 63–89; and John Henry, "Metaphysics and the Origins of Modern Science: Descartes and the Importance of Laws of Nature," *Early Science and Medicine* 9 (2004): 73–114.

[21] For a broader perspective on the shifts that occurred in the modern period and their implications, see the discussions in *The Divine Order, the Human Order, and the Order of Nature: Historical Perspectives*, ed. Eric Watkins (New York: Oxford University Press, 2013).

[22] In fact, the so-called *vis viva* dispute, which dominated much of Europe for several decades, concerned this issue directly insofar as it focused on Descartes's third law of motion and on whether mv, as Descartes thought, or mv^2, as Leibniz held, was conserved throughout the various changes in nature. For discussion of this historical episode and its complexities, see a series of articles by Carolyn M. Iltis, "D'Alembert and the Vis Viva Controversy," *Studies in the History and Philosophy of Science* 1 (1970): 135–44; "Leibniz and the Vis Viva Controversy," *Isis* 62 (1971): 21–35; "The Leibnizean-Newtonian Debates: Natural Philosophy and Social Psychology," *British Journal for the History of Science* 6 (1972): 341–77; and "The Decline of Cartesian Mechanics: The Leibnizian-Cartesian Debates," *Isis* 64 (1973): 356–73; as well as articles by Thomas Hankins, "Eighteenth Century Attempts to Resolve the Vis-viva Controversy," *Isis* 56 (1965): 281–97, and David Papineau, "The Vis Viva Controversy," *Studies in History and Philosophy of Science* 8 (1977): 111–42.

What Is, for Kant, a Law of Nature?

universal gravitation, a single law that was able to cover the motions of all bodies, both celestial and terrestrial.

In addition, many natural philosophers at the time saw the need to provide a justification of the laws of nature that was not based on their empirical adequacy.[23] For example, Descartes attempted to derive his three laws of motion from the immutability of God, while Newton referred to his three laws of motion as axioms, which at least suggests that they were to be viewed as self-evident (though Aristotelians would obviously have contested such a view).[24] As it turned out, Kant was also quite interested in this aspect of natural philosophy, since the *Critique of Pure Reason* and *Prolegomena* attempt to provide a (transcendental) justification of the very notion of a law of nature, while the *Metaphysical Foundations* offer a priori justifications of his three Laws of Mechanics.[25] As a result, the task of formulating and justifying laws of nature was central to natural philosophy at the time, and Kant was by no means alone in devoting significant attention to this task.

Given these two traditions, the central roles that they attribute to the concept of law, and the fact that Kant is clearly drawing on these traditions when he places laws of nature and the moral law at the center of his metaphysics of nature and morals (respectively), we can now see how an important challenge arises if one attempts to bring these elements together into a single coherent philosophical framework (as Kant does). On the one hand, the early modern conception of the goal of science requires the formulation and justification of laws of nature, that is, laws that would govern the behavior of all bodies in nature. On the other hand, the natural law tradition is often held to require that (1) a legislator must be endowed with authority (e.g., on the basis of some kind of superiority) for a law to govern or have binding force, and (2) whatever is subject to a law must be a rational being who is aware of the law and its obligatory force and must be free to obey or disobey it, for only under these conditions is it appropriate to speak of obligation. Taking these two traditions together, significant challenges arise in how to understand the very idea of a law of nature. One is that not all natural philosophers at the time accepted that the laws of nature must have a legislator.[26] As we saw above, Newton labeled the laws of motion axioms and, at least in the

---

[23] For discussion of the formulation and justification of laws of motion in the eighteenth century, see Chapters 5 and 6 in this book.

[24] Passages in Newton suggest that these "axioms" can be empirically confirmed indirectly by way of their explanatory power with respect to the phenomena they can account for.

[25] See Chapters 4 and 6 in this book.

[26] Although Malebranche and Leibniz both hold (in different ways) that the laws of nature instantiated in the world depend on the will of God, there is still a difference between

22 Kant's Concept of Law

context of the *Principia*, did not see the need to speculate further about their ultimate source, and Descartes thought that the laws of nature follow immediately from God's immutability, which is an essential attribute of God, rather than from any legislative act of the divine will. A second challenge lies in understanding how the laws of nature could be said to *govern* inanimate bodies if such bodies lack the rationality and freedom required to be aware of the law and its binding force and to choose whether or not to obey them. In fact, Suarez is perfectly explicit about this second point: non-rational creatures "are not properly capable of the law, just as they are not properly capable of obedience either."[27] For this reason, Suarez explicitly maintains that one can speak of laws of nature only in a metaphorical sense.[28] In short, these developments generate a very basic question: Can one speak of a law of nature and mean it literally?

1.4   Kant's Solution

Though one can, as noted above, answer this question in different ways, I maintain that Kant is in a position to develop an affirmative response that is also philosophically interesting, for he has at his disposal a concept of law that is univocal between the cases of laws of nature and the moral law even though it is instantiated differently in each case. To appreciate the main features of this response we must first understand better how the two components of the concept of law described above (in Section 1.2), namely, necessity and legislation, are instantiated in Kant's specific accounts of the laws of nature and the moral law, beginning with the former.

The concept of necessity that is contained in the generic notion of law takes on a particular form in the case of the laws of nature. Specifically, the notion of necessity involved in the laws of nature is that of *determination*, which Kant understands as the positing of a reality or property to the exclusion of its opposite (1:391). The most straightforward illustration of determination would be a case of *causal* determination. For example, when one body communicates its motion to another in impact according to the Laws of Mechanics, the one body *causally determines* an acceleration in the other body just as the second body causally determines a corresponding deceleration in the first. It does so by acting

what God wills and what God legislates, since the latter requires that further conditions be met.

[27] Suarez, *On Laws and God the Lawgiver*, 1 1.2.
[28] Suarez, *On Laws and God the Lawgiver*, 1 1.2.

What Is, for Kant, a Law of Nature? 23

according to its nature (as an extended and impenetrable object endowed with a certain mass), by means of the exercise of its distinctive causal powers (e.g., its repulsive force), and such that its action is necessarily equal and opposite to the reaction of the other body (according to the Third Law of Mechanics).[29] In this example, the body that serves as a cause determines, or makes necessary, the effect and does so according to the law of the equality of action and reaction, where it is this law that expresses the necessity of the actions that cause the precise changes that occur in the two bodies such that the acceleration and deceleration are necessarily equal. Though the notion of necessity involved in the laws of nature can be illustrated by an example of causal determination in this way, the notion is, as we saw above, more general. For insofar as the categories are defined as concepts that *determine* an object (B128–9), it will also apply to, e.g., the relation between a substance and its accidents, since in that case something is determined to be ontologically dependent just as something else is determined to be ontologically independent (yet without that determination being causal in any typical sense). Analogous points hold for the other categories. Thus, in the case of laws of nature, the notion of necessity involved is that of determination, understood broadly.

The second element that is contained in Kant's notion of law is that of legislation. There must be some authority that enacts, brings about, or serves in some way as the source of the lawfulness of the law. In the early modern period, it was not unusual to disregard this feature of the laws of nature and to treat laws of nature as in some sense primitive. The fact that Kant takes the idea of legislation seriously is a striking feature of his position, and Kant recognizes it as such. For in the *Prolegomena*, he explicitly asserts that the understanding must legislate laws to nature a priori in the following terms: "even though it sounds strange at first, it is nonetheless certain, if I say with respect to the universal laws of nature: *the understanding does not draw its* (a priori) *laws from nature, but prescribes them to it*" (4:320).[30]

Moreover, Kant's argument for this strange-sounding claim provides important details concerning his understanding of the legislation of the a priori laws of nature and of the necessity that they entail. In the passage that leads up to this quotation, Kant argues that the only way to explain how we could have a priori cognition of nature (which we do in what he refers to as the pure part of natural science) is if there is a necessary

---

[29] For a more detailed description of Kant's model of causality, see Watkins, *Kant and the Metaphysics of Causality*, esp. chapters 3, 4, and 6.
[30] Cf. the passage from B163 quoted in main text above.

24   Kant's Concept of Law

correspondence between the laws of the possibility of nature and the principles of the possibility of experience.[31] For if our cognition of these laws were to be derived from nature, our cognition would have to be a posteriori rather than a priori. But then Kant argues, in a second step, that these principles of the possibility of experience are themselves possible only on the basis of the activity of our understanding and its a priori laws. For the understanding must actively combine appearances into a single experience (i.e., into cognition of a single world) and it can do so only according to the laws that are inherent in it. Thus, our a priori cognition of the laws of nature is possible only on the basis of the a priori laws that the understanding uses to actively prescribe lawfulness to nature.

In this context it is striking that it is Kant's characterization of the understanding as an a priori faculty of rules that allows him to hold the understanding responsible not for the *empirical* content of the laws of nature, but rather for their lawfulness.[32] That is, by actively employing rules that are general, a priori, and constitutive of the possibility of experience, the understanding has the authority to determine that nature must be rule-governed; it gives rise to the lawfulness of nature, or the necessary conformity of nature to law (4:296). Thus, though the empirical content of empirical laws derives from the empirical natures of the objects that are found in nature, Kant makes it clear that the *a priori* content of the *a priori* laws, which is just the lawfulness of these laws (including their universality and necessity), derives from the understanding, since the understanding is an active faculty that is able to prescribe, or legislate, lawfulness to nature a priori.[33]

In light of this account, it is relevant to note that Kant does not make a similar claim about sensibility. For example, in the *Prolegomena*, Kant asserts that sensibility too makes possible cognition of nature (though in its material rather than its formal sense), but he does *not* for that reason assert that sensibility is responsible for prescribing or legislating laws to nature, as he does with respect to the understanding. (Kant does on occasion refer to "laws of sensibility," but these references do not state that sensibility prescribes laws.) The reason for the disanalogy lies, I suspect, in the fact that Kant characterizes sensibility in terms of

---

[31] Kant's most explicit statement of the argument is at 4:319–20. This passage is discussed in detail later in Chapter 11.

[32] In the third *Critique*, Kant emphasizes the importance of the principles of reflective judgment for the empirical content of empirical laws.

[33] That the laws of nature that are cognized a priori pertain to appearances and not things in themselves is possible, Kant holds, only because of the specific status of appearances (as things whose existence depends on human cognition).

What Is, for Kant, a Law of Nature? 25

receptivity, or passivity, whereas the understanding is spontaneous and active with respect to the functions on which its concepts and judgments rest, which makes it what Kant refers to as a "higher" faculty. In other words, it is in virtue of its spontaneous activity of combining representations into a single experience according to its own independent rules that the understanding is authorized to legislate to nature. As a result, not only does the understanding legislate laws to nature, but we can see that it does so because it *acts* according to its *own a priori rules* (by unifying the disparate appearances given through sensibility), which gives it the authority to legislate laws to the natural world.[34]

We can now turn to the moral law and to how it instantiates the two elements that Kant identifies as indispensable components of his concept of law. In this case, Kant is quite explicit about how the moral law (which he calls the law of freedom) involves necessity, providing one account of necessity that obtains for God, and another that holds for human beings:

Now the laws of freedom are either

1. *purely necessary*, or *leges objective mere necessariae*. These are found only in God. or
2. *necessitating*, *necessitantes*. These are found in man, and are objectively necessary, but subjectively contingent. Man, that is, has an urge to trespass against these laws, even when he knows them, and thus the legality and morality of his actions are merely contingent. (27:481)

Kant distinguishes here between objective and subjective aspects of the law, stating that the moral law is objectively necessary (for any purely rational being, such as God), but subjectively contingent for human beings (for whom it is possible not to act rationally). For this reason, the necessity of law for human beings is characterized as necessitation or necessitat*ing* rather than determination or determin*ing*. He explains further the special kind of necessitation that is involved in human action as follows:

The necessitation of an action by the moral law, is obligation; the necessity of an action from obligation, is duty. Necessity and necessitation are different: the former is objective necessity. Necessitation is the relation of a law to an imperfect will. In man, the objective necessity of acting in accordance with the moral laws is necessitation. Necessitation is making necessary. (29:611)

In short, the specific kind of necessity that the moral law entails for the actions of human beings is that of necessitation or *obligation*. Even

---

[34] Cf. §38 of the *Prolegomena* for a discussion of the necessity of laws that apply to mathematical objects. Kant is quite clear that the necessity of such laws derives not from the object represented in sensibility but rather from the understanding.

26   Kant's Concept of Law

though we may decide not to act in accordance with the moral law, it still places us under an obligation to do so and is necessary in that sense; it is objectively what we ought to do.

The second element of the generic concept of law, namely, legislation, is also clearly present in Kant's account of the moral law. It is a novel feature of Kant's account of morality that practical reason is said to be autonomous in its legislation of the moral law. Though Kant's doctrines of practical reason and autonomy are quite complex, we can, for present purposes, focus on two main features. First, reason is autonomous insofar as it is responsible for the content of the moral law, that is, for the kinds of actions that one is morally obligated to do or to refrain from doing. Reason's responsibility for the content of the moral law is especially clear when it is expressed in terms of the universalizability of one's maxim in the so-called Formula of Universal Law, since the universality of reason gives rise to the notions of universalizability and lawfulness in that formula.[35] Thus, just as the understanding prescribes lawfulness to nature, reason legislates the universalizability, or lawfulness, of moral actions. Second, and more importantly, reason is autonomous in the sense that we can explain how the moral law has obligatory force for us, that is, how and why it can bind us.[36] Part of Kant's explanation derives from the fact that we view reason as a highest authority, one that is independent of and higher than other faculties, and part of his explanation of reason having that status is that it *actively* and *spontaneously* gives the law *to itself*. That is, the law is not imposed on one from without, but rather lies within and finds application to itself. Indeed, these two elements, the necessity of obligation and acts of legislation, come together when Kant asserts: "The act whereby an obligation arises is called an **actus obligatorius**" (27:261).[37]

In light of these descriptions of how Kant's accounts of the laws of nature and the moral law incorporate the two elements of his notion of

---

[35] While the formula of universal law emphasizes the universality and thus rationality of the moral law, the so-called formula of the law of nature ("Act as if the maxim of your action were to become by your will a universal law of nature" (4:421)) draws even stronger parallels between the moral law and laws of nature.

[36] In other domains, reason's interests take on different forms, such as issuing regulative principles rather than legislating constitutive laws. See Part IV of this volume for discussion.

[37] In fact, he goes on to provide a fuller description of how obligation arises as follows: "Obligation is divided into **positiva** and **naturalis**. The former has arisen by a positive and voluntary choice; the latter from the nature of the action itself. All laws are either natural or arbitrary. If the obligation has arisen from the **lex naturalis**, and has this as the ground of the action, it is **obligatio naturalis**; but if it has arisen from **lex arbitraria**, and has its ground in the will of another, it is **obligatio positive**" (27:261–2).

What Is, for Kant, a Law of Nature?

law, we are now in a position to see how he can respond to the challenge to the very idea of a law of nature described above. One aspect of the challenge concerned whether laws require a legislator, one endowed with the proper authority to enact laws. It is clear that Kant not only accepts but even insists on the idea that every law requires some kind of legislator who enacts, or authorizes, the law. Whereas many medieval thinkers were inclined to think of God as the legislator of the natural law (as reflected, e.g., in the Ten Commandments), what is distinctive about Kant's position is that he ascribes the role of legislator to reason.[38] Taken in the broad sense, as we have seen, reason legislates both the formal content (i.e., lawfulness) of these laws and the kind of necessity that is appropriate to each context. For it legislates what is universal (whether it be nature's conformity to law or the universalizability of maxims) and it legislates something necessary, whether it be the necessity of (e.g. causal) determination or the necessity of obligation. Given Kant's characterization of reason as an absolutely spontaneous and active faculty, which is therefore superior to all others, it has the authority that is needed to legislate both laws of nature and the moral law.

A second aspect to the challenge described above concerns what kind of being is governed by the law, and whether such beings must be rational and free. To appreciate the resources at Kant's disposal in responding to this aspect of the challenge, it is important to recall that his notion of law can be univocal between laws of nature and the moral law precisely because the notion of necessity it involves is relatively abstract and can thus take on more specific forms in the case of the different kinds of laws – namely, determination and obligation. In light of this, we are able to see that Kant can agree that whatever is governed by a law must in fact be subject to the necessity it contains, but deny that every kind of necessity requires rationality and freedom of the subjects in question. Specifically, obligation requires the rationality and freedom of whoever is obligated, whereas determination does not. For obligation has two distinguishing features. First, obligation requires rationality since whoever is

---

[38] Kant does occasionally claim that the moral law can be viewed as resulting from a divine command such that the moral law has an explicit legislator (5:129), but he is also quite clear that he rejects the voluntarist conception of divine law, since it is only insofar as God is rational that his commands are moral. (Kant is also clear that we should not take any divine promises or threats to be our motive for acting according to the moral law, since that would prevent our actions from having moral worth. See Eric Watkins, "Kant on the Hiddenness of God," *Kantian Review* 14 (2009): 81–122. Also, though Kant ascribes the legislation of the laws of nature to the understanding rather than reason, he often views the understanding as a faculty that falls under reason in a general sense (as opposed to reason in the narrow sense, as a faculty that seeks the totality of conditions and thus the unconditioned).

28   Kant's Concept of Law

obligated must be in a position to understand and evaluate the scope and force of the obligation as well as the content of the action in question. Second, it must allow for the possibility of deviations, and that requires transcendental freedom. Determination, by contrast, does not display either of these features. Thus, the requirement of rationality and freedom derives from features specific to obligation, rather than either determination or necessity.

If one accepts this line of reasoning, one can still say (as Kant does) that the laws of nature govern whatever objects are found in nature as long as these objects are subject to the conditions of the notion of necessity contained in the laws of nature, that is, whatever conditions are presupposed by determination. And there is a genuine sense in which bodies are subject to the necessity of the laws of nature. For, as we have seen above, when a body acts (e.g., by causing an acceleration in another body), its action, its behavior, is governed by laws that determine how it can and cannot act and what effects it can and cannot bring into existence. For example, Kant's Second Law of Mechanics entails that a body *cannot* act on itself, and the Third Law of Mechanics dictates that when it acts on another, it *must* act in such a way that its action is equal and opposite to the action of the body on which it is acting. The actions of the relevant bodies are determined by, or subject to, the necessary rules expressed by the Second and Third Laws of Mechanics. Thus, what the laws of nature govern are the actions of objects in nature along with the effects that they bring about. If Kant's account can be understood in this way, it can then make perfectly good sense to talk about laws of nature and how they can govern what happens in nature, yet without having to resort to either a metaphorical or an equivocal notion of law.

1.5   Conclusion

This response reveals two larger points. First, it provides a specific answer to the question posed in the title of this chapter, namely "What is, for Kant, a law of nature?" For we have seen that a law of nature is, for Kant, a rule, legislated by a spontaneous and active faculty, that expresses the necessity by which some objective feature of the world is determined. Second, we now have a broader and more insightful perspective on the importance of laws of nature in Kant's theoretical philosophy. For we have seen that although the issue of necessary connections in nature is an important one, it represents only one aspect of a much larger set of interconnected issues involving (1) a generic concept of law that allows for different kinds of necessity (obligation and determination), (2) the specific conditions under which these different kinds

What Is, for Kant, a Law of Nature? 29

of necessity can obtain, and (3) the idea that necessity requires a legislative act of a very specific kind by a higher faculty. What this third point in particular reveals is not that the notion of law is an isolated feature of Kant's position, but rather that Kant understands the notion of a law as intimately connected to his analysis of what reason is capable of and thus an important part of his Critical project. By considering what a law of nature is, one is thus drawn into some of the most foundational issues in Kant's metaphysics of nature and freedom.[39]

---

[39] I thank the Templeton Foundation for its financial support of a larger research project (titled "God's Order, Man's Order, and the Order of Nature") that Nancy Cartwright and I co-directed from 2009 to 2013 and of which this chapter is a part. I also thank the International Leverhulme Network for funding a research project on Kant on laws of nature, which supported a conference at the University of Edinburgh at which this chapter was presented. In addition, I received helpful feedback on the chapter at the Center for the Philosophy of Science at the University of Pittsburgh. I especially benefited from comments on an earlier version of the chapter by Angela Breitenbach, Andrew Chignell, Michael Friedman, Anja Jauernig, Michela Massimi, Konstantin Pollok, and Clinton Tolley.

2 Kant on Transcendental Laws

2.1 Introduction

In this chapter, I clarify the nature of what I call transcendental laws, that is, laws for which Kant provides a transcendental or a priori justification, i.e., a justification that is not based on experience, but rather that makes experience possible in the first place. I begin (in Section 2.2) by briefly describing several standard accounts of the laws of nature, laying out what I take to be their essential differences as well as their respective advantages and disadvantages, while also allowing for the development of hybrid versions. I argue that, in this context, what is unique to Kant's account of transcendental laws is the idea that they are based (at least in part) on our epistemic natures (rather than exclusively on the natures of empirical objects that we might encounter in the world). I then (in Section 2.3) present two influential objections that have been raised against Kant's account of transcendental laws, objections that are based on foundational discoveries in the sciences of geometry and physics. Two strategies (in Section 2.4) for responding are then considered. The first strategy (in Section 2.4.1) is essentially conservative, striving to preserve an orthodox core to Kant's view by arguing that our epistemic natures are in fact necessary and unchangeable in fundamental ways, despite these new discoveries in science. The second strategy (in Section 2.4.2), developed in detail by Carnap, pursues the idea that the notion of the a priori that underlies transcendental laws should be understood not as fixed for all time, but rather as relativized to a class of objects that might change as new scientific theories are developed. Finally (in Section 2.5), I compare and contrast the accounts of transcendental laws that are based on the orthodox and the relativized notions of the a priori, concluding that while relativized notions are not inconsistent, the orthodox interpretation of Kant's position provides a genuine alternative to other accounts of the laws of nature.

2.2 Laws of Nature

Contemporary discussions of the nature of laws of nature typically present us with the following three options. First, there is the traditional empiricist position represented by David Hume and David Lewis, according to which a law of nature is based primarily on regularities among events. Since it is typically possible to describe one and the same set of events at different levels of generality, there are many alternative descriptions of regularities that could count as laws of nature. As a result, to determine which descriptions are genuine laws of nature, the view is often supplemented with further criteria, e.g., apparently pragmatic ones such as simplicity and strength. Since the events we experience in the world are, according to the empiricist, entirely contingent and the laws of nature are based on regularity relations among such events, the laws of nature must be contingent as well and cannot in any way "govern" or constrain what happens in the world; events determine the laws of nature and not vice versa. Three consequences immediately follow from this conception: (1) Since nothing constrains what events occur in the future, the problem of induction arises; (2) since the structure of the account starts with events and then constructs laws out of them, there can be no laws of nature that are not instantiated by events, which would seem, at least at first glance, to preclude Newton's law of inertia from being a law of nature; and (3) if simplicity and strength are not empirical criteria, it can seem at least awkward for empiricists to adopt them as genuine constraints on reality.[1]

Second, there is the necessitarian option developed by Michael Tooley, Fred Dretske, and David Armstrong. Its fundamental idea, as articulated, e.g., by Armstrong, is that laws of nature express necessary relations among universals. For example, it is a law of nature that all ravens are black, not because all ravens happen to be black, but rather because the universal "raven" necessitates the universal "black." Since the laws of nature are based not on what events happen to occur in the world, but rather on necessitation relations among universals, they can be said to govern (constrain or impose necessity on) what happens in the world insofar as worldly events instantiate such universals. However, two questions immediately arise: (1) What reason do we have for believing

---

[1] This is not to suggest that other serious objections have not been raised against Humean accounts. In particular, one can question whether the categorical nature of Humean events is a coherent conception.

32 Kant's Concept of Law

that such necessitation relations between universals actually exist? (2) Are relations among such universals in fact able to constrain what happens in the world and if so, how?

In short, we seem to face the following dilemma. Either we accept an empiricist conception of the laws of nature, but then the laws of nature are not necessary, can exercise no constraint on events, and the problem of induction arises. Or we adopt the necessitarian view, according to which the laws of nature have an element of necessity, but then one faces the task of identifying evidence for positing what is supposed to be the source of their necessity, and there is also no immediate explanation of how this necessity can be efficacious with respect to what happens in the world, given its origin in universals.

Given this impasse, a third, skeptical option might appear attractive. For one could avoid the problems faced by Humeans and necessitarians simply by denying that there are any such things as laws of nature. This skeptical position has been developed in different ways by Bas van Fraassen, Ronald Giere, and Nancy Cartwright. While one could rest content with the negative project of showing that laws of nature do not exist, Cartwright goes on to suggest that the absence of laws of nature has no negative implications for science, since it is, she thinks, in the business of discovering the *capacities* things have. While it is undeniable that the skeptical position has its attractions, the prominence that laws of nature have had in science at least since the seventeenth century suggests that it might be premature to give up on them before making sure that all possibilities have been duly considered.

Against this background of options, there can appear to be an intriguing fourth alternative, the *Kantian* position, which posits transcendental laws, that is, a priori laws that are supposed to make experience possible in the first place. By positing *a priori* laws that are directly tied to conditions of the possibility of our *experience* of the world, this position seems designed to avoid the perils of sheer contingency faced by empiricism, the mysteries of inaccessible and potentially irrelevant necessary relations among universals adopted by the necessitarians, and the void left by unmitigated skeptics. For as Kant himself articulates this option, at least on the traditional interpretation of his line of thinking, transcendental laws reflect necessary conditions on objects that are, at least in part, subjective, that is, conditions in us that objects must satisfy for us to be able to cognize them at all. For example, in the *Critique of Pure Reason*'s Transcendental Aesthetic, Kant famously argues that space and time are subjective forms of intuition, that all objects of experience must be given through these forms, and that such objects must therefore be spatiotemporal and subject to the laws of mathematics that are based on them.[2] Similarly, in the Transcendental Analytic, he maintains that the categories are forms of thought that place constraints on how we understand the objects that are given to us in intuition. Thus, the Second Analogy of Experience is typically read as asserting that objects must be subject to conditions represented by the category of causality and thus to causal laws if we are to understand their states as occurring in succession.

These examples illustrate, at least at a very high level of generality, how the Kantian option can seem to provide a solution to the difficulties faced by the alternative accounts. Because what happens in the world we experience is constrained by our forms of intuition and thought – and thus by the mathematical and causal laws based on them – this position is obviously distinct from any empiricist account, which allows for no (non-empirical and non-pragmatic) constraints.[3] However, because these constraints are required on subjective grounds – space, time, and the categories are *subjective* principles that serve as conditions of the possibility of experience – the modal aspects of transcendental laws are, in principle, accessible to us; after all, they stem from subjective principles in us. So they should not be either mysterious or easy to deny.

At the same time, concerns have been raised about the coherence, or, at least, the plausibility, of the Kantian position. The central question here is: What exactly does it mean to assert that something is a condition of the possibility of experience? And even a tolerably clear answer to this question is simply a preliminary step toward addressing our primary question, namely: How precisely do conditions of the possibility of experience justify laws containing some kind of necessity? Thus even if the Kantian view of transcendental laws of nature might occupy an interesting systematic position, it faces several serious questions that can make it appear vague and circumspect.

The standard options briefly sketched above are by no means as neat and tidy as I have presented them. For example, I have argued at length that Kant's own overall project, in effect, combines elements of both the Kantian and the necessitarian accounts.[4] While the subjective dimension of Kant's view has (rightly) received tremendous attention given its central position in the *Critique of Pure Reason*, it is a mistake to overlook what one might naturally call ontological aspects of his project by

---

[2] In this chapter, I abstract from the fact that Kant does not emphasize that there are mathematical laws that derive from sensibility. (For brief discussion of this issue, see Chapter 1 in this book.)

[3] For discussion of Kant's "solution" to the problem of induction, see Eric Watkins, *Kant and the Metaphysics of Causality* (New York: Cambridge University Press, 2005), pp. 230–97.

[4] Watkins, *Kant and the Metaphysics of Causality*, pp. 101–80, 230–97, and 389–422.

34   Kant's Concept of Law

assuming that its revolutionary elements *exhaust* his position.[5] Rather than presume that Kant is an arch-epistemologist whose sole concern is to refute skepticism on the basis of resources available to empiricists – a presumption that conspicuously lacks both adequate historical support and consensus with regard to its philosophical success – it is more fruitful to see Kant as motivated in deep and systematic ways by the exact sciences of his day, Newtonian physics in particular, e.g., by providing a realist phenomenal ontology for the laws of mechanics.[6] Specifically, appreciating this point can help us to see in a particularly clear way the necessitarian aspect of his account of the laws of nature in particular.

Kant's commitment to Newtonian physics – or rather to the way in which he develops Newtonian physics – leads him to accept as his starting point a different, non-Humean model of causality (which underlies his account of at least some transcendental laws). Instead of thinking that one event, the motion of one billiard ball at one moment in time, brings about another event, the motion of a second billiard ball at a later moment in time, Kant holds that the deceleration of the first billiard ball and the acceleration of the second billiard ball at impact are caused by both billiard balls jointly exercising their repulsive forces in accordance with their (respective) masses and motions.[7] When this Newtonian example is interpreted in terms of the more abstract ontology of the first *Critique*, it is to be understood as a case of two spatial substances exercising their causal powers in accordance with their natures and circumstances. This ontological redescription of the Newtonian case is important, because the mass functions as (part of) the nature of such substances, and the fact that substances exercise their causal powers in accordance with their natures explains how it is that there can be necessary connections in nature. The necessity of the causal relations is not an inexplicable free-floating modality, but rather is based on the natures of things that substances act in accordance with in exercising their causal powers.

If this richer description of Kant's model of causality is accurate, then it is clear that some laws of nature will be based on the specific natures that objects in our world have. As Kant points out in the very first sentence of the *Metaphysical Foundations of Natural Science*: "if the word

---

[5] Such a mistake has led some scholars to act as if Kant is really an "empiricist-plus," that is, just like Hume, but with the addition of necessary connections where the latter could not find them.

[6] See Chapters 3–6 in this book for detailed discussion.

[7] The same is true (perhaps even more clearly) for attraction (gravity), since only the masses of the bodies, the distance between them, and their motions are relevant to determining what changes in motion occur.

'nature' is taken simply in its *formal* meaning, where it means the first inner principle of all that belongs to the existence of a thing, then there can be as many different natural sciences as there are specifically different things, each of which must contain its own peculiar inner principle of the determinations belonging to its existence" (4:467). Yet if we are considering laws of nature that are based on the specific natures of things, then the specifically *transcendental* dimension of Kant's account appears to have been lost, since it might seem that we must discover what natures things have through standard empirical inquiry.

However, Kant explicitly distinguishes between empirical and transcendental laws.[8] In fact, in several contexts Kant goes so far as to claim that the former require the latter.[9] While this latter claim is controversial and would call for detailed clarification in its own right, what is of immediate interest to us is the status of transcendental laws. Kant certainly views both the Analogies of Experience and the *Metaphysical Foundations'* Laws of Mechanics as instances of transcendental laws, since they are both necessary for experience of a very general sort to be possible, namely experience of temporal relations and of the communication of motion, respectively. The difference between empirical and transcendental laws is that the former are based in part on the specific kinds of things that we encounter in the world, whereas the latter hold for any kind of thing that could be an object of possible experience for us (since everything we could experience is temporal and every spatial object we could encounter is capable of communicating motion to other spatial objects).[10] As a result, Kant will not be able to show that highly specific empirical laws of nature can be given a fully transcendental justification, since one must appeal to the particular empirical natures that are exemplified by things in the world. At the same time, even if the scope of the transcendental account is not completely universal, it still represents a genuine alternative to the empiricist and necessitarian accounts for certain very general laws of nature, such as the Laws of Mechanics. It is one thing to justify, say, the law of the equality of action and reaction by performing experiments on particular bodies, quite another to do so by showing that this law is a requirement on the possibility of our experiencing the communication of motion for any bodies whatsoever.

---

[8] For example, in the *Prolegomena* (4:318–20). I discuss this passage at length later in Chapter 11.

[9] The sense in which a priori laws support empirical laws is a complex issue that I do not consider in this context.

[10] I set aside here the question of whether the contrast between transcendental and empirical laws is a difference of degree or of kind.

36   Kant's Concept of Law

Accordingly, the reading of Kant I want to suggest is that both empirical and transcendental laws are based on natures and can derive their necessity from these natures, but the way in which these natures are identified is different in each case. The natures that underlie empirical laws include the natures of the relevant empirical objects. By contrast, some of the natures that give rise to transcendental laws are, in one important sense, subjective in character and are identified on the basis of the fact that they are required for us to have experience of a very basic kind. That is, the natures of things in the world stand in a certain relation to beings whose cognitive nature is such that experience of those things is possible only in certain ways, namely, according to spatiotemporal forms of sensible intuition and categories as discursive forms of thought. Transcendental laws, therefore, are a special kind of law insofar as they are based on relations among the natures of things and our nature as cognitive beings. By focusing on our subjective cognitive nature in this way Kant is entitled to posit transcendental laws that contain a blend of necessitarian and subjective elements (which also leave open the possibility that more specific laws of nature will not be transcendental per se, but rather empirical and thus partially explicable according to one of the other standard accounts).

2.3   Challenges to Kant's Alternative

To begin to assess the merits of Kant's distinctive account of transcendental laws, it is important to consider two influential challenges that were raised against it on the basis of scientific developments in the nineteenth and twentieth centuries.[11] The first objection (or set of objections) arises from the discovery of non-Euclidean geometries. If non-Euclidean geometries are possible, then Euclidean geometry is obviously not necessary and the question of what geometry holds for objects we experience turns out to be empirical. It also follows that Euclidean geometry cannot consist of synthetic a priori cognition, since it is, if cognition at all, either a posteriori or analytic, depending on whether it is supposed to refer to empirical objects or rather be considered a set of definitions that determine the meanings of terms for an abstract formal framework. As a result, Euclidean geometry cannot contain transcendental laws, since its laws either are gained through empirical discovery

---

[11] This is not to suggest that other significant challenges have not been raised against it. Quantum mechanics, in particular, has been the source of serious questions (concerning concepts of substance), questions that are problematic for Kant's position as well, though Kant may be in no worse shape than anyone else in this respect.

or are analytic statements that place no constraint on objects of experience. Finally, it also seems to follow that space and time cannot be *forms* of intuition in any weighty sense, since space and time appear to be empirical features that must be given to us just as other features of objects are.

The second objection stems from the overthrow of Newtonian physics with the discovery and establishment of Einstein's relativity theory. The consequences of this discovery for Kant's position seem to be analogous to what was the case for geometry, except that here it is the forms of thought rather than the forms of intuition that come under attack. That is, if Kant's broadly Newtonian Laws of Mechanics are not even true, much less necessary, then they are obviously not synthetic a priori cognition, and do not express transcendental laws. Similarly, it would seem that the categories on which the Laws of Mechanics are based are not truly forms of thought by means of which we must understand any object of experience, since they must, it seems, be revisable so as to accommodate whatever demands relativity theory places on them.

Taken together, these objections are thought to entail two consequences that are allegedly fatal to the distinctive core of Kant's position: (1) What Kant took to be the primary instances of synthetic a priori cognition – Euclidean geometry and the "pure" principles of Newtonian science – are not in fact synthetic a priori. Either they are analytic (in the case of formal geometries that may or may not apply to any objects), or they are a posteriori (if one takes the questions of which geometry and which mechanical laws apply to physical objects to be settled by empirical inquiry into these objects). (2) Since there is no synthetic a priori cognition, there is no reason to accept either forms of intuition or forms of thought to which all objects of experience must be subject. They are as changing as the sciences they are alleged to make possible, and the question of what cognitive capacities we have is thus a purely empirical matter just as everything else is. From these two consequences, there follows a third: If there are no a priori forms of intuition or thought, then there are, it might seem, no subjective principles that can serve to constrain what objects we can experience and thus no distinctively transcendental laws of nature. As a result, these objections appear to jeopardize the distinctively Kantian alternative account of transcendental laws described above.

2.4   Two Strategies for Response

At this point, two general strategies for responding seem most tempting. First, one can attempt to mount a detailed defense of Kant against these

38 Kant's Concept of Law

charges by identifying elements of his position that undercut the two lines of objection described above. Second, one can concede the objections and attempt to develop a different account of transcendental laws of nature, an account whose differences from Kant's are still not so great as to force it into either the straight empiricist or necessitarian options. Let us first consider what might be said in defense of the orthodox Kantian position.

2.4.1 Strategy 1: In Defense of Orthodoxy

Whether Kant was in fact committed to Euclidean geometry in an essential way has been widely discussed in the literature, and I do not propose to add to that discussion here. Distinguishing between perceptual and physical space and considering whether our perceptual space might be Euclidean even if physical space is not is an issue that I set aside. For what is of immediate interest in the current context is whether the objection based on non-Euclidean geometries truly threatens the necessitarian aspect of transcendental laws.

The crucial question to raise at this point is what the source of the necessity of transcendental laws is on Kant's account. For the contingency of the forms of intuition calls into question the necessity of transcendental laws only if the necessity of those transcendental laws actually depends on the forms of intuition (or on their special status, as a priori or necessary). On this question Kant clearly asserts that the necessity of transcendental laws depends not on sensibility's forms of intuition, but rather on the understanding's categories (insofar as they are applied to objects given to us in experience). In the *Prolegomena*, for example, Kant explicitly addresses this point as follows:

Now I ask: Do the laws of nature lie in space and does the understanding learn them merely by trying to find out the enormous wealth of meaning that lies in space or do they inhere in the understanding and in the way in which it determines space according to the conditions of the synthetic unity that governs all of its concepts? Space is something so uniform and, with respect to all special properties, so indeterminate that we should certainly not seek a treasure of natural laws in it. By contrast, what determines space to assume the form of a circle or the figures of a cone and a sphere is the understanding insofar as it contains the ground of the unity of their constructions. The mere universal form of intuition, called space, must therefore be the substratum of all intuitions that could be determined as particular objects and of course the condition of the possibility and of the variety of these intuitions lies in it, but the unity of the objects is determined *entirely by the understanding* and according to conditions that lie *in its own nature*. Thus the understanding is the origin of the universal order of nature in that it comprehends all appearances under its own laws and thereby first constructs *a priori* experience (as to its form), by means of

Kant on Transcendental Laws

which whatever is to be cognized only through experience is necessarily subjected to its laws. (4:321–2, emphasis added)

What this passage illustrates is that mathematical objects have necessary features and the necessity inherent in them is due, in the case of mathematics, not to space – since space is too indeterminate – but rather to the understanding and, specifically, to the rule for constructing spatial objects that is contained in its concepts. As a result, Kant's view is that the necessity contained in transcendental laws is due, even in the case of laws concerning *mathematical* objects, to the understanding. It follows that any contingency in our sensibility's forms of intuition does not necessarily affect the necessity of transcendental laws, for it is the understanding that forms the basis for the necessity and thus the distinctive status of transcendental laws.[12] Thus, even if there is a contingent manifold, the laws that order that manifold are no less necessary for ordering the contingent manifold. As Kant sometimes puts it, the "lawfulness of the laws of nature" involves a necessity that is distinct from their content.

But if the first objection can be handled in this way, the second objection might seem all the more urgent, since it calls into question the necessity of the understanding's categories. Once again, the issues raised by this objection are complex and cannot be treated with all the attention they deserve. However, three remarks can perhaps help to put this objection into perspective. First, it is important to keep in mind how complex the philosophical presuppositions are of both Newtonian mechanics and relativity theory. On Kant's account, empirical claims asserted in actual Newtonian physics that might be tested through experiment emerge only *after* considerable philosophical analysis and argument. As a result, if aspects of Newtonian physics must be rejected, it does not immediately follow that *every* assumption that led to Newtonian physics must likewise be rejected. For the premise that leads Newtonians astray and that must therefore be rejected could be peripheral rather than fundamental to Newton's account. Of course, what relativity theory calls into question about Newton's physics are not incidental details, but rather his understanding of the fundamental concepts of space, time, and mass. However, Kant, too, rejected Newton's conceptions of space and time, and, as we just saw, space and time end up not being crucial

---

[12] This interpretation fits well with, though it does not in all respects go as far as, Sellars's reading of Kant's distinction between intuition and concept, according to which even intuitions are both conceptually determined and derive their content from concepts.

40 Kant's Concept of Law

to the necessity of transcendental laws, so it is not obviously the case that even fundamental problems in Newton's physics have immediate consequences for the status of transcendental laws, even if it is problematic for other elements of his natural philosophy.

Second, Kant's table of categories has, I think, received less than the most charitable interpretation in the literature. Whatever one thinks of his derivation of the table of categories from the table of judgments, one could simply consider whether at least some of the categories he lists are minimally necessary ways in which we must understand objects of experience. Now formal logicians are quick to point out that one needs very little conceptual machinery to represent objects – perhaps only existential quantification and negation – but this objection to Kant's richer set of categories misses the point of his project. His table of categories is part of a project of explaining how *empirical cognition of a single world* is possible (and not simply what is required for representation per se). And while no extensive argument for it can be developed in this context, the basic ontology argued for in Kant's Analogies of Experience can appear in many ways commonsensical and fairly attractive. There are objects with properties (i.e., substances and accidents), and the temporal relations of succession and coexistence that are necessary components of the single temporal world we inhabit require asymmetrical and symmetrical causal relations as their ground. As a result, if one keeps in mind the purpose to which the categories are supposed to contribute, it seems disputable that there are not fundamental concepts, such as causality, that we must use to understand our world.

These two points suggest the third regarding how an orthodox Kantian might respond to objections based on recent scientific developments. What motivates the various responses is the idea that our subjective cognitive nature may not be linked as closely to cognition in Euclidean geometry and Newtonian physics as the objections assume. Specifically, the central point lies in seeing that transcendental laws are based on unchanging or a priori forms of thought that constitute the very nature of our understanding, such as that of causality, rather than on other aspects of Kant's position.[13] Given the immutability of our understanding's most basic forms of thought, one can acknowledge revolutionary changes in science without thereby immediately sacrificing the subjective cognitive natures that form the basis for transcendental laws.

---

[13] Though I emphasize the role of the understanding here, I grant that the understanding is also relevant when applied to objects given to us through sensibility (and thus according to the latter's forms).

2.4.2 Strategy 2: The Relativized A Priori

With this understanding of how an orthodox interpretation of Kant might respond to these two objections, we can now turn to a second kind of response, one that still claims to be Kantian in spirit, even if it rejects one central element of Kant's account. This position, initiated by Poincaré and developed further in different ways by Hans Reichenbach, Rudolf Carnap, and Michael Friedman, maintains that what the discovery of non-Euclidean geometry and relativistic physics shows is that one must distinguish two different senses of the a priori. Whereas Kant held that a priori principles (1) make experience possible and (2) are necessary and unrevisable, these thinkers argue that only the former aspect of the a priori can be retained. For given that the objects of science change (whether in geometry or in physics), so too must the principles that make them possible. The notion that remains has come to be known as the "relativized" a priori, because what principles are a priori is relative to the body of scientific knowledge that they are to explain. Despite this departure from Kant's official view, the position is still thought to be distinctively Kantian, since it continues to advance as part of its core doctrine the view that certain principles make experience possible, e.g., by accepting as principles that are, according to Reichenbach, constitutive of the concept of the object of scientific knowledge.

To appreciate the structure of this position better, consider the way it was articulated by Carnap in "Empiricism, Semantics, and Ontology." Central to Carnap's view in this article is the distinction between "internal" and "external" questions. Internal questions are those questions that can be posed once a linguistic framework that defines the elements of one's basic ontology is in place, and answers to them are based either on empirical evidence or on logical methods, depending on whether the framework is empirical or logical. (In fact, if the answers are based exclusively on logical methods, they will be analytic propositions; otherwise, synthetic.) External questions, by contrast, are those that concern the adoption of the very linguistic framework within which internal questions about (scientific) objects can be posed. Importantly, Carnap denies that external questions can be answered by empirical or logical means. Instead, he asserts that it is a "practical question, a matter of a practical decision concerning the structure of our language," where the decision will be based on pragmatic criteria, such as "efficiency, fruitfulness, and simplicity."[14]

---

[14] Rudolph Carnap, "Empiricism, Semantics, and Ontology," *Revue Internationale de Philosophie* 11 (1950): 20–43, p. 40.

42   Kant's Concept of Law

Given Carnap's basic terminology, we can see how it provides a clear illustration of the distinctive features of the "relativized a priori." Internal questions are the kind of questions that are answered by standard scientific means, but they presuppose for their very meaningfulness a linguistic framework within which they can be framed. As a result, the linguistic framework functions as a source of constitutive principles; the linguistic framework makes possible meaningful reference to objects of experience, which is necessary to answer internal questions that arise in, e.g., scientific inquiry. In that sense, the linguistic frameworks at the heart of his view are akin to the transcendental aspect of the a priori. However, unlike Kant's forms of intuition (space and time) and thought (categories), linguistic frameworks are not simply given as part of our nature, but rather must be constructed. Moreover, we have a choice about which one to construct for any given purpose in such a way that the linguistic framework is relative to the kinds of objects that we want to be able to refer to meaningfully. In other words, there is not a single linguistic framework for all purposes, and what linguistic framework we adopt will be determined by what kinds of objects can satisfy different goals we might have. Thus, linguistic frameworks provide constitutive or a priori principles that are relative to different classes of objects, principles that could, it seems, still be called transcendental laws given that they make possible meaningful reference to objects of experience.

2.5   Kant and Carnap on the Nature of Transcendental Laws

On the basis of this brief description of Carnap's version of the "relativized a priori," we can now see more clearly how it compares and contrasts with Kant's position. On the one hand, the similarities are undeniable. For one, Kant and Carnap both accept a version of the analytic-synthetic distinction and are thus committed to the possibility of analytic truths, even if Carnap's notion of analyticity must be relativized just as his notion of the a priori is. That is, since analytic truths are possible only after a linguistic framework has been accepted, the fact that linguistic frameworks can be replaced entails that analytic truths are in principle revisable. This feature of Carnap's position entails that he is able to account for even fundamental changes in our beliefs, and therefore that the flexibility typically associated with Quine's position is equally available to Carnap.

For another, and of greater relevance to our current line of inquiry, Kant and Carnap are, as we have seen, both committed to some version of transcendental laws, that is, subjective principles that are in some way conditions of the possibility of objects of experience. This commitment forms a fundamental shared point of contrast with empiricists such as Hume and Quine. For both Hume and Quine hold that every event is both contingent in itself and does not stand in necessary connection with anything else in such a way that rejecting the one would require giving up the other. Kant and Carnap, by contrast, maintain that without certain subjective constitutive, a priori principles, we would be unable to stand in specific kinds of cognitive relationships with objects.

On the other hand, there are at least two fundamental differences between Kant's and Carnap's accounts of transcendental laws. First, on Kant's account, transcendental laws are based, at least in part, on our cognitive natures. Specifically, transcendental laws rest on our sensibility's forms of intuition, space and time, and our understanding's forms of thought, or categories. For Carnap, by contrast, transcendental laws depend entirely on linguistic frameworks, or on the relationship between linguistic frameworks and the objects and properties defined by means of them. That is, Kant appeals to subjective faculties and types of representations, while Carnap draws on linguistic frameworks.[15]

Second, the most significant difference between Kant's and Carnap's accounts is that Kant is committed to *necessary* and *immutable* transcendental laws, whereas Carnap allows for revisions or, rather, replacements of such laws, though he acknowledges that such revisions may entail the adoption of entirely new linguistic frameworks. As a result, the notion of necessity that can be attributed to transcendental laws on Carnap's account is ultimately hypothetical; *given* the adoption of a certain linguistic framework, then certain laws (and analytic truths) will be necessary, but there is nothing necessary about the adoption of any particular linguistic framework. While the notion of necessity that Kant employs might seem to be conditional in a similar sense – transcendental laws are necessary *given* the forms of intuition and thought – there is a real difference here, since these natures are, he thinks, both immutable and definitive of human cognitive capabilities, not one set of options among others for humans.[16]

Taken together, these differences reveal that transcendental laws end up exercising different *kinds* of constraint for Kant and Carnap. For one, there is an important difference in scope. Because Kant's project is based on our cognitive capacities, it turns out that transcendental laws, on his

---

[15] One might naturally expect (complex) connections between linguistic frameworks and the types of representations of which our subjective faculties are capable.

[16] Kant does allow for the possibility of fundamentally different kinds of cognitive capacities. He simply rejects the idea that (finite) human beings could have them.

44   Kant's Concept of Law

account, do not constrain what objects can *exist*. For transcendental laws preclude neither the existence of things in themselves nor representations thereof. Instead, they can constrain only what objects we can *cognize*, with things in themselves – or ultimate reality – being famously excluded from this class, though not from the class of objects we can think. For Carnap, by contrast, the scope of constitutive principles is broader insofar as it includes any and all objects that we can contemplate or meaningfully refer to at all, and not just those that fall under the purview of our specifically epistemic faculties (i.e., faculties that provide theoretical justification for cognitive claims).

For another, and more importantly, while Kant's transcendental laws and Carnap's constitutive principles can *appear* to provide the same *kind* of constraint on objects – both assert what empiricists regularly reject, namely, that there are conditions of the possibility of objects of experience – in this case appearances are somewhat misleading regarding the precise nature of this constraint. For Kant, transcendental laws, such as the Second Analogy of Experience, are instances of synthetic a priori cognition, whereas for Carnap, constitutive principles are not synthetic a priori, but rather principles that define (by means of pure stipulation) what constitutes an object. In fact, Carnap rejects the idea that there could be synthetic a priori cognition, asserting that his constitutive principles are, in effect, analytic (given that they are ultimately merely definitions). As a result, Kant's transcendental laws provide a substantive (or synthetic) constraint on the possibility of experience, whereas Carnap's constitutive principles are merely analytic and thus generate only analytic constraints. (While one might question whether the idea of analytic constraints is coherent, it represents an important part of Carnap's position, since it is what allows his view to be distinct from Quine's, who, in effect, denies that there are any non-empirical constraints.)

Moreover, even if one were to set aside the difference between synthetic and analytic constraints, there is a crucial sense in which Carnap's constitutive principles do not constrain in precisely the same way that Kant's transcendental laws do. For transcendental laws are based on necessary and thus unrevisable, cognitive natures, whereas constitutive principles are contingent and thus, in principle, revisable.[17] The crucial point here is that if constitutive principles are contingent, then they provide no empirically *unconditioned* constraints at all, since any restriction

---

[17] While Kant is committed to necessity, especially if our natures are to give rise to *necessary* connections in the world, he could still account for a (weaker) notion of constraint by asserting that our natures are immutable, i.e., do not in fact change (even if they could in some sense).

that a given set of constitutive principles might seem to provide can be overcome through the adoption of a new set of constitutive principles. To illustrate this point, consider how the problem of induction can still arise for Carnap's position. If a given linguistic framework entails that Fs are always followed by Gs, it is not necessary that Fs are always followed by Gs. In fact, if we encounter an F that is not followed by a G, all we have to do is reject our initial framework and replace it with a new one. The revisability of linguistic frameworks and of the constitutive principles that follow from them entails that these principles cannot generate unconditioned constraints.

To be sure, constitutive principles could represent unconditioned constraints if there were limits on what linguistic frameworks one can adopt. However, as we saw above, Carnap emphasizes that decisions about linguistic frameworks (and thus of the constitutive principles embodied in them) are not cognitive, but rather are to be made on purely pragmatic grounds. Pragmatic grounds, however, would seem to be thoroughly contingent and thus, at least in principle, if not in practice, highly variable. Moreover – and this is a crucial point that should not be overlooked – even pragmatic grounds are not independent of the objects constituted by linguistic frameworks. As a result, there are no independent constraints on constitutive principles and the linguistic framework that they are associated with, beyond the objects made possible by these principles. Therefore, on Carnap's view objects end up constraining constitutive principles (via the pragmatic interests they serve) rather than vice versa (except for logical constraints).

At this point, our description of Carnap's account of constitutive principles should sound more than vaguely familiar. These principles are contingent, do not constrain what occurs in the world (except purely logically), still face the problem of induction, and are selected on purely pragmatic grounds. In short, Carnap's constitutive principles seem to be similar to the empiricist account of the laws of nature attributed to Hume and Lewis. Given that Carnap is a logical empiricist, this result ought to come as no surprise (even if it is also true that Carnap is heavily influenced by Kantian considerations about judgment, concepts, and the role of logic in our empirical cognition, as Friedman rightly emphasizes).

Does it follow from these considerations, then, that describing Carnap's constitutive principles as conditions of the possibility of objects of experience is nothing more than a deceptive rhetorical move, designed to mislead and confuse? Not at all. Instead, it can be stressed that Carnap was looking for a way in which to distinguish himself, perhaps ever so slightly, from Quine's extreme form of empiricism, and was pursuing an ingenious strategy: Take Kant's anti-empiricist idea that there are

46 Kant's Concept of Law

conditions of the possibility of experience, but instead of resting them on controversial (and, one might think, scientifically discredited) subjective cognitive natures (spatiotemporal forms of intuition and non-empirical categories), make them depend only on logical principles that can be revised as needed. In this way, one can fashion a much more modest innovation on an otherwise controversial, albeit orthodox, Kantian idea. The only cost is that in the process of remaking Kant's distinctive position for a new audience and a different set of concerns, one has given up on the specifically *transcendental* idea that our subjective cognitive natures can provide substantive and unconditioned constraints on the world of experience that differ from those that an empiricist can adopt.

2.6   Conclusion

At this point, I have clarified – through straightforward description and via comparison and contrast with both closely related and rather remote positions – what is at the heart of Kant's conception of transcendental laws, that is, laws that make experience of the world possible at all. The crucial idea is that transcendental laws are based on our primitive forms of intuition and thought, which constitute our immutable cognitive natures. Because these natures are necessary and unchanging, they can provide unconditional constraints on whatever the laws cover, unlike various empiricist accounts of the laws of nature – even those accounts, like Carnap's, that can sound much like Kant's on the surface. However, because these natures are subjective principles (in that they are part of our nature), we have reason to think that we can, at least in principle, become acquainted with them, especially if they are so basic that we must use them to have any experience at all, a point that makes them very different from the kinds of relations between universals stressed by necessitarians. In this way, Kant's account can appear to be not only a coherent and intelligible option regarding at least some laws of nature, but also one that represents an attempt to occupy a systematically attractive middle position between necessitarian and empiricist extremes.

This is not to say, however, that I have described the nature of Kant's account in nearly enough detail. For a number of substantive questions have not even been posed, much less answered. To cite one obvious example, it is one thing to claim that space and time are forms of intuition (and thus elements of our cognitive natures), quite another to claim that space and time are *merely* forms of intuition and not also objects or relations between objects distinct from us. As a result, the clarification I have provided so far does not take a stand on one particularly controversial feature of Kant's broader metaphysical position, namely, Transcendental Idealism. For given what I have said above, transcendental laws could make experience of the world possible by giving us access to features that the world exemplifies completely independently of our cognitive faculties, but they might also do so in a much stronger sense, namely, by *constituting* the objects of our experience in the first place. It is, I take it, a virtue of the account described above that it can accommodate either of these positions.[18]

---

[18] For helpful comments on earlier versions of this chapter or discussions of the topics treated in it, I thank Karl Ameriks, Craig Callender, Nancy Cartwright, Susan Castro, Robert Hanna, Michael Hardimon, Wayne Martin, James Messina, Sam Rickless, Donald Rutherford, and Bernard Thöle, as well as audience members at the Pittsburgh-Konstanz conference held in Konstanz in May 2005, at a colloquium sponsored by the Department of the History and Philosophy of Science at Indiana University, in October 2005, and at a conference held at UCLA in November 2005.

Part II

The Laws of Mechanics

From his time as a student, when he wrote *Thoughts on the True Estimation of Living Forces*, until his final productive days, when he composed the pages that would be collected together into the *Opus postumum*, Kant was especially interested in scientific issues. These interests were extraordinarily broad in scope, ranging from foundational questions in physics concerning cosmogony, matter theory, the ether, and the conservation of force (e.g., the vis viva controversy) to highly specific issues, such as the causes of earthquakes (occasioned by events in Lisbon in 1755), the rotation of the Earth, volcanoes on the moon, and the fireball that was visible in the night sky over nearly a quarter of Germany in July of 1762. Kant's interest in these issues is best understood insofar as they are placed in the broader context of the Scientific Revolution, which viewed science as attempting (in the ideal case) to provide explanations of all natural events in terms of a small set of highly general, mathematically precise laws of motion. To make a foundational contribution to natural science, one that would be both rich in scope and capable of rigorous philosophical justification, Kant attempted to formulate and justify laws of mechanics that would be foundational for the rest of natural science.

Chapter 3 describes part of the broader philosophical framework within which Kant's thinking about the laws of mechanics is situated. It provides his account of the most general principles that govern our experience of a single world, which includes inanimate bodies causing changes of motion in each other on impact, and it does so by presenting those a priori principles that result from applying the categories to objects of possible experience according to the System of Principles in the first *Critique*. Chapter 4 then considers how the more specific principles stated and defended in the *Metaphysical Foundations* are related to the more general principles described in the System of Principles. Specifically, while it would be natural to expect the more specific principles to follow deductively from the more general principles (e.g., by simply substituting the term "matter" or "body" for the term "object" or "substance" wherever it occurs in the more general principles), this chapter shows

49

50   The Laws of Mechanics

that such an interpretive suggestion cannot be defended. It shows how Kant instead developed an extended transcendental argument specifically for the fundamental principles put forward in the *Metaphysical Foundations*. The basic idea behind his argument is that just as the first *Critique*'s Principles of Pure Understanding are necessary for experience of objects that belong to the same *temporal* world, so too the more specific principles of the *Metaphysical Foundations* are necessary for experience of matter understood as *spatio*temporal objects of outer sense.[1] In this way, Kant provides a transcendental justification of some of the laws of natural science.

Kant's formulation and justification of his three Laws of Mechanics do not, however, take place in a vacuum. While the laws of motion that Newton identified as axioms and made crucial use of in the overall argument of his *Principia* were accepted in certain circles as a canonical statement of the laws of nature, such a view came to be in the minority as the eighteenth century progressed, since different natural philosophers pursued different interests with different commitments, arriving at significantly different formulations of the laws of motion. Chapter 5 provides a broad overview of the reception of Newton's laws of motion throughout eighteenth-century Germany so that one can see what is distinctive about Kant's formulation of his three Laws of Mechanics. Chapter 6 then draws the previous chapters together by offering a detailed interpretation and justification of Kant's three Laws of Mechanics. Insofar as Kant takes his Laws of Mechanics as his paradigm case of what a law of nature is, having a detailed account of these laws provides an indispensable illustration of some of the distinctive elements of his conception of law.

---

[1] Kant revises his position in the second edition of the first *Critique* in ways that reflect conditions of our experience of spatiality.

3   The System of Principles

3.1   Introduction

In the *Critique of Pure Reason*, the "System of all principles of pure understanding" is the second of three chapters in the Analytic of Principles. It is preceded by the Schematism chapter, in which Kant provides schemata, or time-determinations (in effect, temporal meanings), for the pure concepts of the understanding in such a way that they can then be applied to objects given in sensible intuition. It is followed by the Phenomena/Noumena chapter, which summarizes the restrictions on cognition that Kant has established so far and draws out some consequences thereof, especially insofar as they make clear the mistakes of earlier philosophers such as Leibniz and Locke. Despite the clear significance of these chapters, however, it is the System that forms the core of Kant's Analytic of Principles. For it contains his most detailed and specific positive account of how the categories – whose existence and legitimacy were established collectively in the Metaphysical and Transcendental Deductions – are to be applied to appearances, that is, to objects given to us in sensible intuition. It does so not only by arguing for particular conditions under which each category must be applied, but also by providing insight into what Kant thinks any spatiotemporally unified world of experience must be for us, namely a plurality of substances that stand in causal relations of mutual interaction, a view radically different from Hume's empiricism, though it has important parallels with the views of several of his immediate predecessors, such as Wolff, Knutzen, Crusius, and Tetens.[1]

The System contains three sections. The first two sections succinctly state the supreme principles of all analytic and synthetic judgments, a topic directly relevant to the central Critical question about how

---

[1] For translations of selected texts of Kant's most important immediate predecessors, see Eric Watkins, *Kant's Critique of Pure Reason: Background Source Materials* (New York: Cambridge University Press, 2009).

51

52   The Laws of Mechanics

synthetic a priori cognition is possible. The long third section, the "Systematic representation of all synthetic principles of pure understanding," contains four subsections that argue for particular synthetic a priori principles stating "rules of the objective use of the categories" (A161/B200). Accordingly, the Axioms of Intuition explain how the quantitative categories are to be applied to intuition; the Anticipations of Perception establish the use of the categories of quality; the Analogies of Experience prove the employment of each of the relational categories; and the Postulates of Empirical Thought explicate the meaning of the modal categories. In the second edition, Kant adds the Refutation of Idealism.

After briefly presenting the supreme principles of analytic and synthetic judgments (in Section 3.2), I explain the principles of the Axioms of Intuitions and Anticipations of Perception and state the main arguments Kant develops for them (in Section 3.3). I then describe the general principle of the Analogies of Experience (in Section 3.4), focusing on the problem of time-determination, which forms a basic framework for all three Analogies. The rest of the chapter is devoted to explaining the main positions, arguments, and consequences of the First, Second, and Third Analogies (in Sections 3.5–3.7). Reference to Kant's broadly Newtonian account of physics provides guidance on several difficult issues of interpretation along the way.[2]

3.2   The Supreme Principles of Analytic and Synthetic Judgments

Kant states that the principle of contradiction can be used as a *negative* criterion (or necessary condition) of *all* truth insofar as any judgment that contradicts itself cannot be true, given that such a judgment annihilates itself (A151/B191) and is thus "nothing" (A150/B189). It can also be put to *positive* use insofar as it is sufficient to establish the truth of all *analytic* judgments. It is not, however, a *sufficient* criterion (or condition) of truth simpliciter, since it is not a determining ground of *synthetic* judgments.

Synthetic cognition requires, in addition to subject and predicate concepts, some "third thing" to allow for their combination. Kant claims that the third thing is the possibility of experience, which consists of three elements: inner sense (along with its a priori form, time), the imagination's synthesis of representations (in inner sense), and the unity of

---

[2] How the laws of nature that are established in the Principles of Pure Understanding apply to the laws of nature expressed in the *Metaphysical Foundations* is the topic of Chapters 4–6 in this book.

The System of Principles 53

apperception's synthetic unity (in concepts and judgment). Synthetic a priori judgment is possible, therefore, insofar as it can be supported by a priori intuition, a priori synthesis of the imagination, and the transcendental unity of apperception with its use of a priori concepts. Kant summarizes his discussion with a rhetorically catchy, but (potentially misleading) conclusion: "the conditions of the **possibility of experience** in general are at the same time conditions of the **possibility of the objects of experience**" (A158/B197). While some think that this statement sets aside ontological in favor of purely epistemological or semantic conditions (by focusing exclusively on conditions of experience instead of on conditions of objects), it can be understood simply as asserting that epistemological or semantic conditions can be, or at least involve, ontological conditions for a certain class of objects.

3.3   Axioms of Intuition and Anticipations of Perception

The principle of the Axioms of Intuition, which is supposed to state a synthetic a priori principle for the applicability of the categories of quantity – unity, plurality, and totality – asserts: "**All intuitions are extensive magnitudes**" (B201). The import of this principle is that when we represent any "formal" feature of an appearance as having a determinate magnitude, we must represent it as having an extensive magnitude. An extensive magnitude is one where "the representation of the parts makes possible the representation of the whole" (A162/B203), which occurs when the parts of a homogeneous manifold are successively synthesized, or added, to form an aggregate. For example, if I represent nine one-foot-long squares placed next to each other so as to form a large square, the area of the large square is an extensive magnitude, since it depends on the successive addition of the areas of its parts.

The Axioms involve the quantitative categories because a *plurality* of homogeneous parts is represented in terms of a particular unit of magnitude, or *unity*, and the successive synthesis of these parts is responsible for the formation of a whole, or a *totality*. It is a *synthetic* principle because one can imagine magnitudes that do not aggregate in this way, such as colors, sounds, and tastes. Insofar as the definition of an intuition – a representation that "relates" immediately to a singular object – does not immediately entail that the magnitude of its object must be extensive, this feature must derive from some specific aspect of our particular forms of intuition, such as their passivity or spatiotemporality.

Kant's argument for the principle of the Axioms, added in the second edition, is not stated particularly clearly, but seems to consist of two

54   The Laws of Mechanics

parts. The first part begins by recalling from the Transcendental Aesthetic that all empirical intuitions of appearances presuppose a priori intuitions of space and time. It then notes, as the Transcendental Deduction showed, that a priori intuitions of space and time are possible only through a synthesis of a (homogeneous) manifold, the consciousness of which involves the concept of a magnitude. Given these two points, Kant can argue that the formal features of empirical intuitions of appearances that presuppose a priori intuitions of space and time are similarly possible only through such a synthesis and the concept of a magnitude. The second part argues that because the magnitude of the a priori intuitions of space and time in general that make empirical intuitions of appearances possible is extensive, the magnitude of the formal features of empirical intuitions of appearances must be extensive as well.[3] The rest of the text of the Axioms of Intuition explains the significance of this principle for mathematics and its applicability to objects of experience.

The principle of the Anticipations of Perception, which is a synthetic a priori principle for the objective use of the categories of quality – reality, negation, and limitation – is: "**In all appearances the real, which is an object of the sensation, has intensive magnitude**, i.e., a degree" (B207). This principle claims that any "material" feature of appearances, i.e., any feature that concerns not the mere form of intuition, but rather its "matter," or the object of sensation, must have an intensive magnitude. An intensive magnitude is one that "can be apprehended only as a unity and in which multiplicity can be represented only through approximation to negation $= 0$" (A 168/B 210), thus, one that is not formed through the successive addition of equal homogeneous parts, as extensive magnitudes are. The magnitude of the motion of a body, for example, is not represented as the summation of several smaller motions. (An object does not travel at sixty miles per hour by traveling twenty miles an hour three times in succession.) Instead, the magnitude of the motion of a body, whatever it is, must be grasped immediately. Another example of an intensive magnitude might be a raw feel, such as the qualia of a color experience. Accordingly, the general idea underlying this principle is that whatever in appearance is due not to the forms of space and time, but

---

[3] For further discussion of this argument, see Paul Guyer, *Kant and the Claims of Knowledge* (New York: Cambridge University Press, 1987), chapter 7; Béatrice Longuenesse, *Kant and the Capacity to Judge* (Princeton: Princeton University Press, 1998), chapter 9; and Daniel Sutherland, "The Point of Kant's Axioms of Intuition," *Pacific Philosophical Quarterly* 86 (2005): 135–59.

The System of Principles 55

rather to sensation, is to be represented as having a certain degree of reality that can, in principle, be greater or lesser (if one had different sensations).

Kant's most explicit proof of the principle of the Anticipations of Perception, added in the second edition, runs as follows. First, Kant notes that perception is an empirical consciousness and thus involves not only pure intuitions of space and time, but also sensation, which is a subjective representation by which the subject can be conscious of being affected. He then analyzes sensation, noting that it is present to different degrees in the empirical consciousness of perception. (In the first edition, he argues this point by noting that sensation fills only an instant and is therefore not apprehended through a successive synthesis of parts.) On the basis of this analysis, he contends that sensation cannot have an extensive magnitude, because it is distinct from the extensive magnitudes of space and time, which are present independent of sensation.[4] However, because sensation does still have a magnitude – it can vary from the limiting case of zero in formal consciousness to any arbitrary magnitude in perception – its magnitude must be intensive (a conclusion that follows either immediately, if an intensive magnitude is defined negatively as a magnitude that is not extensive, or less directly, if Kant is relying on sensations being raw feels that can be grasped only as a unity). Now Kant is clear that a sensation is not an objective representation, so establishing that sensation has an intensive magnitude does not immediately entail that every *object* of perception must have an intensive magnitude. However, he asserts that since sensation is supposed to *correspond* to what is (empirically) real in such an object, it follows that if sensation has an intensive magnitude, then so too must whatever (empirically) real element is ascribed to the object on the basis of that sensation.

Though Kant does not offer explicit statements as to how the principle of the Anticipations involves the categories of quality, he seems to think of a determinate intensive magnitude of an object as a limited degree of reality, with the *limitation* arising through a *negation* of a *reality*. In the Dynamics chapter of the *Metaphysical Foundations* (1786), Kant is somewhat more explicit about how the three qualitative categories apply to matter (4:523). He says that what is real in space, namely, solid matter, fills space due to its repulsive force, while its attractive force is what is negative insofar as, if taken by itself, it would penetrate all space and destroy solidity. If taken together, however, the second force limits the first in such a way that matter fills a determinate region of space. As a

---

[4] This step is particularly difficult, both exegetically and philosophically.

56   The Laws of Mechanics

result, the degree to which matter fills a determinate region of space depends on the limitation of reality, where the limitation is a kind of negation.

The rest of the text of the Anticipations covers a range of topics that are more or less closely related to intensive magnitudes. For example, it clarifies that although one cannot anticipate the content or quality of sensations, since they are given only a posteriori, it is still possible to cognize their continuity a priori. Kant also discusses the law of continuity of change at length, explaining that the dependence of change on empirical causes precludes any a priori proof. Further, he warns that one should not mistakenly assume (on metaphysical grounds) that the real in space *must be* the same everywhere so that one must accept a void to explain differences in the quantity of matter at equal volumes. For as the Anticipations has shown, it is at least possible that what is real in space has different intensive magnitudes. He also suggests that no perception, whether direct or indirect, could prove the entire absence of everything real in experience (a void).

3.4   The Analogies of Experience

The Analogies of Experience are those principles that state conditions under which the relational categories – substance–accident inherence, cause–effect relation, and community or mutual interaction – must be applied. Unlike in the Axioms and Anticipations, in the Analogies of Experience Kant devotes a separate principle to each category.[5] However, he prefaces these three Analogies of Experience with a single principle, which, in the first edition, reads: "As regards their existence, all appearances stand *a priori* under rules of the determination of their relation to each other in **one** time" (A176). In the second, it states: "**Experience is possible only through the representation of a necessary connection of perceptions**" (B218). Though these statements provide only a glimpse of what is crucial to all three Analogies, the general idea is that each of the three relational categories represents a necessary connection that is required for experience of a single time and of objects existing and being temporally related to each other within a single time to be possible.

Time itself has, Kant argues, three modes: persistence, succession, and simultaneity. By this Kant seems to mean that time persists (or at least

---

[5] Kant also distinguishes between the "mathematical" and the "dynamical" principles (A160–2/B199–201) such that the Axioms and Anticipations belong to the former and the Analogies and Postulates to the latter class.

The System of Principles 57

does not change) and all of its moments are either successive or simultaneous (though Kant also denies simultaneity this status at A183/B226). Moreover, if appearances are supposed to be in one time and temporally related to each other in that time, then every state of every appearance must be before, after, or at the same time as every other. As a result, if our experience is to be of objects and their states existing in this one time, we must be able to represent objects as expressing these three modes of time and their states as related to each other in these ways. In light of this, Kant structures his argument as follows. Each of the three Analogies states that one of the relational categories is necessary for experience of one of the modes of time. Thus, the First Analogy states that the category of substance is required for experience of persistence (which is in turn required for experience of succession); the Second Analogy asserts that the category of causality is required for experience of succession; while the Third Analogy maintains that the category of mutual interaction is required for experience of simultaneity.

Before turning to these more specific, though still highly abstract claims, it is important to consider at a very general level why there should be any substantive requirements at all on experiencing objects in a single time. Why is it not trivial to determine, say, the simultaneity of the book in front of me and the table on which it rests (e.g., by simply looking at both)? One main task of Kant's general discussion of the Analogies is to address this issue. Two points are particularly central. First, we do not, he says, perceive "time itself" (B219) or objective time. That is, we do not immediately cognize any timeline that would allow us to cognize when objects exist nor do we directly cognize any spatial x-y-z coordinates that would make it possible for us to cognize where objects exist. Second, there is a distinction between what one might call objective time and subjective time, which is nicely illustrated by one of Kant's most famous examples, that of the ship and the house in the Second Analogy (A192/B237). Although our apprehension of an object is always successive, the various states of the apprehended object may not be, since, e.g., the parts of a house, although apprehended successively, nonetheless coexist. Once one has distinguished between the temporal relations of the states of objects and the temporal relations of the representations by means of which these states are apprehended, it is clear that substantive questions can be raised about how our judgments about objective temporal relations are possible.

These points can be illustrated by Newton's project in the *Principia*. What we are given in observation are the "apparent" motions of the heavenly bodies and the non-trivial task is to determine what their "true and objective" motions are. Newton argues that we must make

58   The Laws of Mechanics

substantive determinations about the masses of objects and the gravitational relations that they have with each other to be able to determine these motions. While Kant's argument here has important parallels with Newton's, it is both more general (by focusing on generic causal relations between substances instead of specifically gravitational attraction between bodies endowed with mass) and more explicitly cognitive (by focusing on the particular kind of representations necessary for cognition of objective temporal relations). This latter difference illustrates the point of Kant's analysis of the conditions of the possibility of experience and of the contrast he draws between what is subjective and contingent and what is objective and necessary in our representations. For at this level, Kant wants to argue that the cognition of objective temporal relations cannot be based on purely contingent, subjective empirical representations alone, but rather requires necessary, objective, a priori representations in the form of the relational categories.

Another important question that arises regarding the problem of time-determination is whether it assumes Transcendental Idealism. That is, does the problem of time-determination concern merely how we *perceive* the temporal relations that already exist between objects or does it also involve the question of how such temporal relations could *exist* in the first place? Given that Kant's arguments in each of the Analogies (as we shall see shortly) involve both cognitive and broadly ontological commitments (e.g., to real and not merely ideal causal relations) and that the Transcendental Aesthetic has already established that temporal relations do not exist independently of us, Kant thinks that he is warranted in interpreting the problem of time-determination based on the prior acceptance of Transcendental Idealism. A full evaluation of Kant's arguments would need to keep this dimension of his thought firmly in mind.[6]

3.5   The First Analogy of Experience

Kant's statement of the principle of the First Analogy in the first edition is: "All appearances contain that which persists (**substance**) as the object itself, and that which can change as its mere determination, i.e., the way in which the object exists" (A182). That is, Kant is committed to a permanent substance as an object in which any changing determinations inhere as accidents. In the second edition, Kant adds the further thought that the quantity of this permanent substance is neither increased nor diminished, despite whatever changes occur in nature.

---

[6] See, for example, Guyer, *Kant and the Claims of Knowledge*, pp. 371–83.

The System of Principles   59

Kant's primary argument for the principle of the First Analogy, added in the second edition, proceeds in the following steps. First, he notes that time is a permanently persisting substratum in which the other modes of time, succession and simultaneity, as well as all appearances must be represented. Second, we do not perceive time itself. Therefore, to have cognition of (or even represent) appearances as temporal (e.g., as successive), one must identify a permanent substratum that can represent time in appearances (in the objects of perception). The appearances that we immediately apprehend are always changing, whereas substance alone, as "the substratum of everything real" (B225), is permanent and thus the only object of perception that can represent time. Therefore, if we are to have cognition of appearances as successive, these appearances must be represented as the successive states of a permanent substance.

It is crucial to note here the difference between a permanent perception and a perception of something permanent (as Kant does in a footnote at B xli). His argument attempts to establish not that we have a permanent perception – a perception that remains the same while all of our other perceptions change – but rather that what we perceive is permanent, whether or not we are constantly perceiving it. In fact, Kant draws a further distinction between the states of a substance, which may change with some frequency, and the substance whose states are changing, and claims that only the former can be given to us immediately in intuition, but that we can still perceive the latter insofar as we apply concepts to what is given to us in such a way that sensible qualities are perceived as states *of* permanent substances. This allows Kant to avoid one objection that empiricists sometimes raise against substance, namely, that we can perceive only sensory qualities and not, as Locke says, "a supposed I know not what, to support those *ideas* we call accidents."[7] For Kant can concede that substance is not given to us immediately in intuition, while still maintaining that a permanent substance can be perceived by way of its changing states.

Even with these points duly noted, however, Kant's argument faces several serious questions. First, even if one grants that there must be something permanent in perception to represent time, why must it be substance as it is traditionally understood, namely as the bearer of properties?[8] Two lines of response can be briefly noted. First, Kant can be plausibly interpreted as starting with the traditional notion of substance in the Metaphysical Deduction, and then as simply adding

---

[7] John Locke, *An Essay Concerning Human Understanding* (Oxford: Oxford University Press, 1689), book 2, chapter 23, section 15.
[8] Guyer, *Kant and the Claims of Knowledge*, pp. 220–1.

60   The Laws of Mechanics

permanence in the Schematism chapter. Therefore, it would not be right to object to the First Analogy that it does not present an argument for understanding substance as the bearer of properties. This is not to say that no objection can be raised, but only that it would need to be aimed at a different target (such as the Schematism chapter). Second, and now facing the objection head on, substance must not only express time by being permanent, but also stand in a relation to the changing states we apprehend in direct perception that time itself does not stand in to them, and it is for that reason that substance must be the bearer of properties. For only the inherence relation that obtains between a single permanent substance and its various accidents or states can guarantee that its states are really temporally related (i.e., related in empirically determinable ways). Otherwise, we would have no reason to think that the states exist within one and the same time rather than as temporally unrelated to each other.[9]

Second, commentators have questioned whether Kant's argument establishes the *absolute* rather than the *merely relative* permanence of substance.[10] That is, even if one grants that there must be a substance underlying two changing states at t_1 and t_2, it does not follow that the same substance that underlies these states must also underlie two other changing states at t_3 and t_4 and so on, and therefore be absolutely permanent. What is ruled out, it might be argued, is only that there be *no* substance underlying any two changing states. However, several points are relevant here. For one thing, if one granted only relatively permanent substances, no single thing would represent time itself, but that time itself must be represented is a basic presupposition of Kant's argument. (For textual support, see A188–9/B231–2.) For another, insofar as substances are perceived only through the states that are their determinations, it is unclear on what grounds one could assert a plurality of relatively permanent substances rather than one absolutely permanent substance. For there is no way of determining when one substance perishes and another arises, as opposed to a single substance persisting permanently throughout all change. With no possible evidence supporting the proliferation of merely relatively permanent substances, it would be more economical to posit absolutely permanent substances.

---

[9] A further possibility here is that what is permanent must be a substratum, or bearer, of properties, because time itself is a kind of substratum for the moments of time. Accordingly, if what is permanent were not the bearer of properties, it would not express this feature of time, even if it would express time's permanence.

[10] See, e.g., Henry Allison's discussion of this objection in *Kant's Transcendental Idealism: An Interpretation and Defense* (New Haven: Yale University Press, 2004), pp. 207–9.

The System of Principles 61

If substances are absolutely permanent, however, one must be curious as to what kinds of things they are supposed to be according to Kant. Garden-variety objects (houses, ships, books, etc.) will obviously not qualify as substances, since they are not absolutely permanent. Nor, for that matter, will the sun and the planets, as is clear from Kant's own account of their origin in the *Universal Natural History and Theory of the Heavens*. However, recalling Kant's commitment to Newtonian science is helpful, because Newtonian mass would seem to fit the bill insofar as even when the sun passes out of existence, its mass does not.[11] Moreover, thinking of substance along these lines helps one to understand Kant's claim that the quantity of substance remains unchanged in nature, because the quantity of mass remains the same according to Newtonian principles.[12] This is not to say that Kant can appeal to the identification of the quantity of substance with mass in his argument for the conservation of the quantity of substance, since the concept of mass is more specific and more empirical than can be used in the first *Critique* (as opposed to the *Metaphysical Foundations*). At the same time, it can be helpful to have an appropriate concrete example of what Kant is describing abstractly in the First Analogy.[13]

3.6 The Second Analogy of Experience

Kant's statement of the Second Analogy in the second edition is: "All alterations occur in accordance with the law of the connection of cause and effect" (B232). An alteration is a *change* of state of a substance (e.g., a change of motion that a body undergoes), which Kant calls an "event" in a technical sense that is unlike contemporary Humean notions, and he often refers to the law of the connection of cause and effect simply as a causal rule, so the content of the principle of the Second Analogy is that every event occurs according to a causal rule. This much is clear and uncontroversial. There is, however, an important ambiguity in what the causal rule amounts to. Some read Kant as asserting simply that every event has a cause, while others read him as being committed to causal

---

[11] In post-Newtonian physics, mass is treated as equivalent to energy (according to $E = mc^2$), such that this kind of identification can be retained even with the rejection of Newtonian physics. (See Chapter 2 in this book for discussion of related points.)

[12] For more discussion, see Chapter 6 in this book.

[13] Unfortunately, this model does not clarify whether substance is for Kant a count noun or a mass noun. This question turns on issues discussed in the Third Analogy of Experience, the Second Antinomy, and Proposition 4 of the Dynamics chapter of the *Metaphysical Foundations*.

62   The Laws of Mechanics

laws such that the same type of event must always have the same type of cause.[14] Some textual evidence supports the latter, stronger reading: For every event, or occurrence, there must be a causal rule "in accordance with which this occurrence *always* and necessarily follows" (A193/B238–9, emphasis added; cf. A198/B243 and A200/B245). And one might suppose, on strictly philosophical grounds, that the very notion of a rule entails some kind of law-like regularity. Whether this or some other kind of argument can be identified in Kant's texts that is also philosophically plausible has been a matter of considerable debate.[15]

Kant's text in the Second Analogy is not clearly structured. As a result, there has been significant disagreement about how many arguments he is offering for its principle.[16] I find it most helpful to understand the text in terms of two kinds of arguments.[17] The first kind, which is expressed most clearly in text added in the second edition (B232–4), relies on Kant's analysis of the kinds of representations and faculties that we have. Its main thrust is that the succession of two states of an object cannot be represented either in sensibility's intuition or in the imagination's synthesis, because neither can represent the kind of objective connection that is contained in the change of its states. For if an object changes from state A to state B, in order to have cognition of this event, we must represent A first and B second and not the reverse. However, our intuitions of A and B are distinct from each other and thus do not represent their temporal relations, and our imagination is free to represent either A before B or B before A. Instead, only the understanding's category of causality is able to represent the proper kind of connection. Therefore, to have cognition of objective succession, we must apply the category of causality. This argument obviously depends heavily on Kant's account of our cognitive psychology, specifically on his taxonomy of the kinds of representations we have being not only correct, but exhaustive. That is, this argument requires that Kant's characterizations of our faculties of sensibility, imagination, and understanding and of the

---

[14] See Michael Friedman, "Causal Laws and the Foundations of Natural Science," in *The Cambridge Companion to Kant*, ed. Paul Guyer (New York: Cambridge University Press, 1992), pp. 161–99, for a discussion of both interpretations and an argument in favor of the latter.

[15] See, e.g., Lewis White Beck, *Selected Essays on Kant*, ed. Hoke Robinson (Rochester: University of Rochester Press, 2006) (esp. "Once More unto the Breach: Kant's Answer to Hume, Again").

[16] See, e.g., Norman Kemp Smith, *A Commentary to Kant's Critique of Pure Reason* (New York: Humanities Press, 1962), p. 363.

[17] For more detailed discussion of the Second Analogy, see Eric Watkins, *Kant and the Metaphysics of Causality* (New York: Cambridge University Press, 2005), chapter 3.

The System of Principles 63

representations that each such faculty can have be fully supported. In the absence of such support, this first argument is vulnerable.

The second kind of argument, which is scattered throughout this section of the text in various guises, does not rely as directly on the contrasts between sensibility, imagination, and the understanding, and can be reconstructed as follows:

> P1 Apprehension of objects (the subjective order of perceptions) is always successive.
>
> P2 There is a distinction between the subjective order of perceptions and the successive states of an object such that no immediate inference from the former to the latter is possible.
>
> C1 One cannot immediately infer objective succession from the successive order of perceptions.
>
> P3 To have cognition of objective succession, the object's states must be subject to a rule that determines them as successive.
>
> P4 Any rule that determines objective succession must include a relation of condition to conditioned, i.e., that of the causal dependence of successive states on a cause.
>
> C2 To have cognition of the successive states of an object, the object's successive states must be dependent on a cause, i.e., must stand under a causal rule.[18]

P1, P2, and C1 express the problem of time-determination discussed above and are supported by ample textual evidence (e.g., at A189/B234). They also show that one reading of the Second Analogy that, prima facie, is tempting, cannot be correct. One might think that the way to cognize whether a cause is present is to note that the order of our representations of the different states of the object in apprehension is irreversible. That is, the irreversibility of the order of our representations in apprehension might be taken as a criterion that indicates the presence of a cause. However, in addition to the fact that such an argument commits, as Strawson famously put it, "a non-sequitur of numbing grossness" by confusing conceptual with causal necessity, P1, P2, and C1 show that Kant does not (and cannot) accept irreversibility as an *assumption* of his argument.[19] Instead, as Guyer has noted, Kant brings up irreversibility as a *consequence* of our cognition of objective succession, a point Kant makes clearly when he notes: "I must therefore derive the **subjective sequence** of apprehension from the **objective sequence** of appearances" (A193/B238).[20]

---

[18] See Watkins, *Kant and the Metaphysics of Causality*, pp. 209–10.

[19] Peter Strawson, *The Bounds of Sense* (London: Methuen, 1966), p. 137.

[20] Guyer, *Kant and the Claims of Knowledge*, p. 247.

64   The Laws of Mechanics

P1, P2, and C1 also clarify Kant's strategy in the Second Analogy. Not only is he not trying to derive causality from the irreversibility of the order of our subjective representations, but his project is also not one of trying to find a sufficient condition for causality in what is given to us immediately in intuition. Accordingly, he is not trying to uncover an "impression" of causality that would allow us to distinguish accidental regularities from genuine causal bonds, as Hume is, and, more generally, he is not trying to refute a skeptic about the external world (by appealing only to what is immediately evident in our impressions). The only kind of skeptic he is addressing here is one who denies that we have cognition of causal relations or causal laws. However, even in that case, his argument presupposes a substantive premise that a hard-core skeptic would reject, namely, cognition of objective succession, whose requirements are discussed further in P3 and P4.

P3 introduces the idea that a *rule* is supposed to make cognition (or "experience") of objective succession possible. Kant seems to be expressing this point when he argues that only by assuming that a change of state proceeds according to a rule "can I be justified [*berechtigt*] in saying of the appearance itself, and not merely of my apprehension, that a sequence is to be encountered in it" (A193/B238). That is, the difference between representations that are merely apprehensions and those that are cognitions of objective succession presupposes the notion of a rule according to which the second state must follow the first. P4 then characterizes this rule as a *causal* rule:

In accordance with such a rule there must therefore lie in that which in general precedes an occurrence the condition for a rule, in accordance with which this occurrence always and necessarily follows ... I must necessarily relate it [i.e., the succession] to something else in general that precedes, and on which it follows in accordance with a rule, i.e., necessarily, so that the occurrence, as the conditioned, yields a secure indication of some condition. (A193–4/B 238–9)

Kant seems to be arguing here that the rule that is required for cognition of objective succession must (1) be such that given a preceding condition, necessarily the later state follows the earlier state, and (2) entail that the condition has been satisfied when one cognizes that the change of state occurs. As a result, the rule that Kant is arguing for is both causal – it necessitates the change of state – and semantic/epistemic – it allows one to cognize that the cause necessitates the succession. This two-fold claim is evident in Kant's summary statement: "the occurrence, as the conditioned, yields a secure *indication* of some condition, but it is the latter that *determines* the occurrence" (A194/B239, emphases added).

The System of Principles 65

In the rest of the text of the Second Analogy, Kant repeats this basic argument in different formulations, but he also discusses a number of closely related issues along the way. For example, he describes how the category of causality contains an element of necessity that Hume's empirically derived concept cannot (A195/B240ff.), and he provides illustrations of why objectivity requires rule-governedness (A196/B243). He also explains that the rule in question must be causal because only a causal relation with respect to appearances is consistent with time itself, which sensibility represents in a priori fashion in such a way that one moment in time determines the next (A199/B244). In addition, Kant considers a reservation that arises regarding simultaneity, and invokes for its clarification traditional metaphysical notions such as action, force, activity, and substance (A202/B247). He concludes with an intriguing and lengthy discussion of the law of the continuity of change (A206/B252), which stands in a complicated relation to the discussion of this law in the Anticipations.[21]

3.7 The Third Analogy of Experience

The principle of the Third Analogy of Experience in the first edition is: "All substances, insofar as they are **simultaneous**, stand in thorough-going community (i.e., interaction with one another)" (A211). The similarities with the Second Analogy are, at a certain level of generality, obvious and pervasive. For just as the Second Analogy asserts the necessity of causality for cognition of objective succession, so the Third Analogy maintains the necessity of mutual interaction for cognition of simultaneity. Kant's arguments for this principle can also be viewed as roughly analogous to those of the Second Analogy. The first of his arguments, added in the second edition (B256–8), proceeds by eliminating sensibility and the imagination as faculties that could represent simultaneity as an objective temporal relation, thereby leaving only the understanding and its category of community, while the second (A211–13/B 258–60) pushes the idea that only a certain kind of causal relation can license cognition of simultaneity. Specifically, the first step of this second argument proceeds from the problem of time determination, asserting that one cannot immediately perceive the objective simultaneity of two states nor can one immediately infer the objective simultaneity of two states from the order of apprehension (A212/B 258–9). The second step then asserts that only a rule could warrant

[21] For detailed discussion of this issue, see Chapters 9 and 10 in this book.

66   The Laws of Mechanics

an inference to objective simultaneity and, in fact, only a special kind of causal rule, called community or mutual interaction (A212–13/B259–60). (The last two paragraphs of the text of the Third Analogy attempt to clarify the notion of community, distinguishing causal from spatial community and noting that it can be direct or, if it involves more than two substances, indirect.)

Despite these extensive similarities, there are fundamental differences between the Second and Third Analogies, differences that derive from genuine philosophical features.[22] One important difference concerns the symmetrical nature of the temporal relation of simultaneity and the reciprocal kind of causality that it requires in the form of mutual interaction (rather than a "simple" asymmetrical cause–effect relation).[23] For the Third Analogy requires not only that the place in time of the states of (at least) *two* substances be determined (as opposed to the change of states of only one), but also that the states of these two substances be determined as simultaneous. If one grants that a substance cannot determine its own place in time (A212/B258–9), then it follows that, in the simplest case involving only two substances, S_1 must determine, or cause, the state of S_2 and S_2 must determine, or cause, the state of S_1. However, S_1 causing the state of S_2 cannot be completely independent of S_2 causing the state of S_1. For if they were independent, simultaneity would not be established given that the state of S_1 that S_2 caused could be later than the state of S_2 caused by S_1. So what is in fact required to account for simultaneity is that these two causal bonds must be understood *jointly*. (It would not help to say that the two causal bonds must obtain *at the same time*, since that would be viciously circular.) While such a causal notion might sound strange to contemporary ears, it is instantiated in Newtonian physics in the mutual attraction of two bodies in virtue of their gravitational forces or, in fact, in any case of the communication of motion, which is governed, Kant maintains, by the law of the equality of action and reaction. Viewed in its fuller context, mutual interaction turns out to be ubiquitous.

Another important difference between the Second and Third Analogies is that the Third Analogy makes clear how Kant's general model of

---

[22] For detailed discussion of the complexities that derive from the Third Analogy's notion of mutual interaction, see Watkins, *Kant and the Metaphysics of Causality*, chapter 4.

[23] For discussion of the implications of the difference between asymmetrical and symmetrical temporal relations, see Eric Watkins, "Making Sense of Mutual Interaction: Simultaneity and the Equality of Action and Reaction," in *Kant and the Concept of Community*, ed. Charlton Payne and Lucas Thorpe (Rochester: Rochester University Press, 2011), pp. 41–62. It turns out that Kant's Third Law of Mechanics displays in an especially clear way the differences between succession and coexistence.

The System of Principles 67

causality must be understood. It is quite common, starting with the Second Analogy, to understand Kant's model of causality as similar to Hume's, with one state causing another – with the difference, of course, that Hume rejects, whereas Kant accepts an element of necessity in the causal relation. In that case, the question is simply what Kant's argument is for the element of necessity and whether Hume is really forced to accept it. However, the Third Analogy's notion of mutual interaction is inconsistent with such a model. In mutual interaction, one state cannot cause a second state if the second state causes the first.[24] While some have held on to their Humean interpretation of Kant's model of causality and rejected the Third Analogy as a philosophical lost cause, this is a high exegetical price to pay, all the more so if rejecting the Humean assumption makes possible an interpretation that renders mutual interaction and the principle of the Third Analogy intelligible. Fortunately, it is possible to read Kant as committed not only to events as determinate changes of state but also to substances endowed with causal powers that are exercised according to their circumstances and natures in such a way that these determinate changes of state necessarily occur. Thus, as one can see by appealing to a Newtonian example, when two bodies accelerate toward each other due to their mutual gravitational attraction, the change in motion in the one body is caused by the exercise of the attractive force of the other in accordance with the distance between the two bodies and the mass of the latter (just as the change in motion of the second body is caused by the exercise of the attractive force of the first in accordance with their distance and the mass of the second body, such that this is indeed a case of mutual interaction).

On this interpretation, Kant's model is different from the Humean one along a number of dimensions. In terms of basic ontological frameworks, Kant's model involves substances and their natures, whereas Humean models do not. Further, when it comes to causation specifically, the exercise of causal powers is clearly fundamentally different from a Humean event. To keep with the example of gravitation, there are important differences, both cognitively and metaphysically, between the accelerations of bodies toward each other and the exercise of their attractive forces. Cognitively, the exercises of the attractive forces are not observable, as the accelerations of the bodies are (which Newton illustrated with his bucket experiment). Metaphysically, Kant (now perhaps unlike Newton) insists on fundamental asymmetries between the cause and the effect. For (1) the cause is active insofar as it determines the

---

[24] For extended argument, see Watkins, *Kant and the Metaphysics of Causality*, chapter 4.

68 The Laws of Mechanics

(change of) state of the effect (29:807–8), while the effect is passively determined by it, and (2) the cause is temporally indeterminate insofar as its activity is continuous (A208/B254), whereas the effect is temporally determinate insofar as it has temporally determinate initial and terminal states (29:863).[25]

Given these fundamental points of contrast, the question of how Kant is replying to Hume is not as straightforward as is often assumed. While it would be natural to expect Kant's arguments in the Analogies to make use only of those assumptions that a Humean ought to grant, Kant in fact appeals to a series of views that are, as we have seen above, rather foreign to Hume's (radical) empiricist picture: Transcendental Idealism, a distinction between our apprehension of objects and the objects themselves (though still as appearances), and a different model of causality (invoking substances, natures, causal powers, and changes of state rather than Humean events). It is also the case that Kant's overall project, including his ambitions in practical philosophy and the unity that he hopes to establish between his theoretical and practical philosophy, brings with it yet further contrasts between his and Hume's positions. In light of these radical differences, a proper evaluation of Kant's response cannot be carried out by focusing simply on one or two narrowly specified issues, but rather involves basic issues that depend on one's entire philosophical outlook.[26]

---

[25] See Watkins, *Kant and the Metaphysics of Causality* (pp. 252–97, esp. 255–82) for clarification and detailed argumentation.

[26] I thank Paul Guyer and Clinton Tolley for comments on an earlier version of this chapter.

4   The Argumentative Structure of Kant's
Metaphysical Foundations of Natural Science

4.1   Introduction

One of Kant's most fundamental aims in his theoretical philosophy is to justify Newtonian science. However, providing a detailed explanation of even the main structure of his argument (not to mention the specific arguments that fill out this structure) is not a trivial enterprise. While it is clear that Kant's *Critique of Pure Reason* (1781), his *Metaphysical Foundations of Natural Science* (1786), and his unpublished (and incomplete) *Opus postumum* should in some way constitute the core elements of this justification, it is less clear how each of these works actually does so. In this chapter I first argue that the standard view of the relationship between the first *Critique* and the *Metaphysical Foundations* is mistaken. Kant does not derive substantive new principles in the *Metaphysical Foundations* simply by substituting "matter" for "substance" in the Principles of Pure Understanding established in the first *Critique*. I then present my own interpretation of how the *Metaphysical Foundations* contributes to the justification of Newtonian science. The main line of this interpretation maintains that Kant engages in an extended transcendental argument that shows how the substantive principles of the *Metaphysical Foundations* are required for experience of matter as an object of outer sense. However, it is first necessary to present briefly Kant's conception of science (in particular what conditions a body of cognitions must satisfy for Kant to be considered science proper) as well as Kant's understanding of the relevant differences between his projects in the first *Critique*, the *Metaphysical Foundations*, and the *Opus postumum*.

Kant's conception of science is rather strict if measured by contemporary standards. For in the preface to the *Metaphysical Foundations* Kant establishes three substantive conditions that a body of cognition must satisfy in order to be considered science proper (4:468).[1] (1) It must not

---

[1] Kant does suggest further criteria. For example, he famously maintains that mathematics is a crucial requirement of natural science proper (4:470).

70   The Laws of Mechanics

consist in empirical principles, but rather must be obtained solely from pure, a priori principles. (2) It must be apodictically certain (which means that one must be conscious of its necessity). (3) It must be a systematically ordered whole (which means that its various propositions must be related as, for example, antecedents and consequents).[2] After stating these conditions, Kant argues that all natural science proper requires a pure part on which its apodictic certainty is based (4:469). Accordingly, these three conditions (and the first one in particular) imply that natural science proper presupposes a justification by something distinct from it that Kant calls a metaphysics of nature.[3] But what exactly does a metaphysics of nature encompass? Kant distinguishes two different parts of the metaphysics of nature: a transcendental part and a special part. A metaphysics of nature is transcendental insofar as it concerns "the laws that make the concept of nature in general possible, even without relation to any determinate object of experience, and [insofar as it is] thus indeterminate with respect to the nature of this or that thing in the sensible world," whereas a metaphysics of nature is special to the extent that "it is concerned with a special nature of this or that kind of thing of which an empirical concept is given, but so that except for what lies in this concept no other empirical principle is used for cognition thereof" (4:469–70). In short, transcendental metaphysics, revealing how experience in general is possible, presupposes no empirical concept, whereas a special metaphysics does make such an assumption insofar as it is concerned with the special natures of things.

How do the three works cited above relate to Kant's distinction between a transcendental and a special metaphysics of nature? In the preface to the *Metaphysical Foundations* Kant indicates that he intends the *Metaphysical Foundations* to constitute the special metaphysics of nature. Although he does not explicitly refer to the first *Critique* in the preface, he clearly sees it (or at least the 'System of Pure Reason')[4] as constituting the transcendental part of a metaphysics of nature.[5] As we have seen in

---

[2] In the following I do not explicitly discuss this third requirement.

[3] While Kant's explicit argument at 4:469 might seem to differ from the account given above, the construction of concepts is directly relevant to the a priori status of principles involving that concept.

[4] Cf. A13–14/B27–8, Bxxii, and Bxxxvi.

[5] Not all scholars agree with this identification. Peter Plaass, *Kants Theorie der Naturwissenschaft. Eine Untersuchung zur Vorrede von Kants "Metaphysischen Anfangsgründen der Naturwissenschaft"* (Göttingen: Vandenhoek & Ruprecht, 1965), argues that transcendental or general metaphysics is identical with 'Ontology' as Kant defines it at A845/B873, namely, as that which "considers only the understanding and reason itself in a system of all concepts and principles that refer to objects in general without assuming objects that would be given (*Ontology*)." Hansgeorg Hoppe, *Kants Theorie der Physik. Eine*

Chapter 3, the 'Principles of Pure Understanding' in the Transcendental Analytic argue for what could naturally be described as "laws that make the concept of nature in general possible." For instance, the Analogies of Experience establish laws that make possible experience of objective temporal relations (e.g., of duration, succession, and coexistence). Finally, since the *Metaphysical Foundations* is still a metaphysics of nature and not natural science proper (that is, the special metaphysics of nature is still pure, whereas natural science is not insofar as it contains empirical data), it is necessary to explain how to make the transition from the special metaphysics of nature to empirical natural science.[6] Kant attempts this final transition in the *Opus postumum*.[7]

Given that the first *Critique* represents the transcendental part of the metaphysics of nature and the *Metaphysical Foundations* its special part, how do these works combine to justify Newtonian science (or at least its pure part); that is, how do they jointly satisfy the three conditions stated above? In the preface to the *Metaphysical Foundations* Kant claims (4:470) that the special metaphysics of nature is an "application" of transcendental principles to the two kinds of objects of our senses (whereby it is understood that the empirical concepts of mind and matter represent the

---

Untersuchung über das Opus postumum von Kant (Frankfurt: Klostermann, 1969), argues against this identification because the first *Critique*'s architectonic chapter (e.g., at A845/B873) concerns the system of *all* philosophical cognition of pure reason next to which merely apparent cognition is to be displayed as well: "[W]ithout a doubt what is called transcendental philosophy or ontology in the introduction to the *Critique of Pure Reason*, in contrast to the transcendental part of the *Metaphysical Foundations*, belongs to mere apparent rational cognition" (Hoppe, p. 32). Ontology considers objects independently of whether they can be given or not. The *Metaphysical Foundations*, by contrast, considers the concept of nature as the sum of all things insofar as they are understood as objects of our senses. Hoppe supports this position with *Refl.* 40 (14:118–20). While Hoppe is right to criticize Plaass's claim that a general metaphysics considers objects in general without assuming objects that would be given, he goes too far in claiming that merely apparent cognition belongs to ontology as well. If this were true, then merely apparent cognition ought to have been discussed in special metaphysics as well (which does not happen in the *Metaphysical Foundations*). Daniel Dahlstrom comes to a similar conclusion in his "Kant's Metaphysics of Nature," in *Nature and Scientific Method*, ed. Daniel O. Dahlstrom (Washington: Catholic University Press of America, 1991), pp. 271–90, esp. 276–82.

[6] To put the point more clearly: The special metaphysics of nature contained in the *Metaphysical Foundations* is the pure part of natural science and thus does not contain the empirical part.

[7] Kant's *Opus postumum* will not be discussed further here. For helpful discussions of this work, see Michael Friedman, *Kant and the Exact Sciences* (Cambridge, MA: Harvard University Press 1992), pp. 213–341, and Eckart Förster, "Is There 'a Gap' in Kant's Critical System?," *Journal for the History of Philosophy* 25 (1987): 533–55.

72   The Laws of Mechanics

two kinds of objects of our outer and inner senses).[8] But which transcendental principles is Kant relying on in his special metaphysics of nature, and what is the nature of their application to matter (or to objects of outer sense)?[9]

4.2   The Standard View

The standard view presents this application as consisting merely in the substitution of the concept of matter into the first *Critique*'s Principles of Pure Understanding. More specifically, the standard view consists in two main claims.[10] First, the transcendental principles ("*Principien*") that are applied to matter to obtain a special metaphysics of nature are the first *Critique*'s Principles of Pure Understanding.[11] Accordingly, the first

---

[8] In other words, what distinguishes the transcendental from the special metaphysics of nature is that the latter contains an empirical concept. In the case of physics, the empirical concept is that of matter qua an object of outer sense.

[9] Kant argues that a science of the mind is not possible. Cf. Michael Washburn, "Did Kant Have a Theory of Self-Knowledge?," *Archiv für Geschichte der Philosophie* 58 (1976): 40–56; Karl Ameriks, *Kant's Theory of Mind* (Oxford: Oxford University Press, 1982), p. 291; and Andrew Brook, *Kant and the Mind* (Cambridge: Cambridge University Press, 1994), pp. 9–10, for discussions of this issue.

[10] Robert Butts, "The Methodological Structure of Kant's Metaphysics of Science," in *Kant's Philosophy of Physical Science*, ed. Robert Butts (Reidel: Dordrecht, 1986), pp. 163–99, esp. pp. 169–70, seems to maintain this interpretation when he calls the principles from the *Metaphysical Foundations*'s chapter on Mechanics 'instantiations' and 'instances' of 'universal metaphysics.' Philip Kitcher, "Kant's Philosophy of Science," in *Midwest Studies in Philosophy*, Contemporary Perspectives on the History of Philosophy, ed. Peter A. French, Theodore E. Uehling, Jr., and Howard K. Wettstein, vol. 8 (Minneapolis: University of Minnesota Press, 1983), pp. 387–408, seems at times at least to be committed to this interpretation as well. For example, he states: "this does not explain the fact that, in the proof of Proposition 5, and in many other parts of the *Metaphysical Foundations*, the principles and procedures of the Analytic are conspicuously absent. (The link between the *Metaphysical Foundations* and the *Analytic* is most evident in chapter 3. There Kant does try to apply the principles of the *Analogies* to derive substantive laws.) So, for example, the principle of the First Analogy serves as a premise for a law of mass conservation." Accordingly, although Kitcher notes that the standard view has some difficulties, he seems to take this as a criticism of Kant's position rather than as a reason to question it as an interpretation.

[11] The empirical nature of the concept of matter consists in the claim that to have the concept of matter, one must have perceived matter previously, i.e., one must have perceived some object or other (in motion) through outer sense (A41/B58). This sense of presupposition will not infect any inferences from matter. It may be somewhat unusual for Kant to use the term 'empirical' to describe this state of affairs, since it indicates neither the objective reality of the concept of matter nor its logical content but rather the conditions for its *acquisition*. But (1) the standard view cannot suggest that matter is an empirical concept in its typical sense, since that would render impossible the a priori and apodictic status of the *Metaphysical Foundations*'s principles, and (2) being empirical in this less standard sense does not exclude the possibility of being involved in the a priori claims required by special metaphysics in the *Metaphysical Foundations*.

Critique's Axioms of Intuitions, Anticipations of Perception, Analogies of Experience, and Postulates of Empirical Thought are to be considered assumptions in the *Metaphysical Foundations*' chapters on Phoronomy, Dynamics, Mechanics, and Phenomenology, albeit assumptions justified by the arguments Kant has provided in the first *Critique*.[12] Second, when Kant says that transcendental principles are *applied* to matter, the standard view interprets this to mean that the term 'matter' is to be *substituted* for the relevant term in the corresponding Principle. For example, the standard view reads the *Metaphysical Foundations*'s First Law of Mechanics as substituting 'matter' for 'substance' in the first *Critique*'s First Analogy ('In all change of appearances substance is permanent; its quantity in nature is neither increased nor diminished'; B224) with the resulting principle that matter is the permanent in appearances and the quantity of matter in nature is neither increased nor diminished, which corresponds to Kant's First Law of Mechanics.

The standard view claims to have two advantages (that is, beyond certain textual evidence, where the Mechanics chapter is usually cited). First, it shows how the *Metaphysical Foundations* establishes principles that satisfy the conditions of natural science proper. For if its principles are deductively derived via simple substitution from the Principles established in the first *Critique*, then this deductive relationship between the first *Critique* and the *Metaphysical Foundations* establishes that the principles of the *Metaphysical Foundations* will have the same degree of certainty and an a priori status similar to that had by the principles established in the first *Critique*. Second, it seems natural to expect that the substantive results Kant spends so much effort establishing in the first *Critique*'s Principles would be crucial to justifying natural science.

However, both of the standard view's claims are incorrect. For substitution does not correctly describe how Kant conceives of the nature of the application of transcendental principles to matter. Further, and more importantly, Kant does not necessarily assume or even use the first *Critique*'s Principles in a systematic way in his argument in the *Metaphysical Foundations*.

The standard view's second claim (regarding substitution) encounters a number of difficulties. First, the term 'matter' does not correspond in a natural and direct way to any term in all of the first *Critique*'s Principles. Consider, for instance, the Principle of the Axioms of Intuition: "All intuitions have extensive magnitude" (B202). Even granting that Kant equates matter with spatial substance, it is hardly obvious for what term

---

[12] See Chapter 3 in this book for discussion of the arguments Kant offers for these Principles.

74   The Laws of Mechanics

'matter' is supposed to be substituted. Since matter is not only spatial substance, but also an object of *outer intuition*, one could argue that 'matter' (qua object of *outer intuition*) is to be substituted for 'all intuitions.' However, a second problem immediately arises: What *justifies* one substitution over another? Although it may seem natural to take matter in the First Law of Mechanics to be substance in the First Analogy of Experience and matter in the Dynamics chapter to be an object of outer intuition in the Axioms of Intuition, such a substitution is more problematic for some of the other Principles. For example, the Second Analogy of Experience, which states that every change has a cause, might result in the following substitution: 'every change of matter has a cause.'[13] While such a substitution would be justified, it is not the principle that Kant actually states in his Second Law of Mechanics. Rather, the Second Law of Mechanics states that every change of matter has an *external* cause. However, this substitution is not at all trivial, since it must exclude the possibility that an event exemplified by a spatial substance could be brought about by the substance acting on its own. Accordingly, while some substitutions might be legitimate without further argument, others are not and would require further argument.

Finally, in the Phoronomy chapter, not only does Kant not provide an argument substituting 'matter' for 'intuitions,' he cannot do so. If we accept that matter is an object of (outer) intuition, according to the standard view its substitution in the Axioms of Intuition would result in the principle that the magnitude of matter's velocity is an extensive magnitude. However, in the Phoronomy chapter of the *Metaphysical Foundations* Kant argues for exactly the opposite position:

But if one explains a doubled velocity by saying that it is a motion by which a space doubled in size is traversed in the same time, something is assumed here that is not obvious, namely: that two equal velocities can be combined in the same manner as two equal spaces are, and it is not self-evident that a given velocity consists in smaller ones and quickness consists in slownesses as a space does in smaller ones. For the parts of velocity are not external to each other as are the parts of space, and if the former is to be considered as a magnitude, then the concept of its magnitude, since it is *intensive*, must be constructed in a different manner from that of the *extensive* magnitude of space. (4:493)

That is, Kant argues that the magnitude of matter's velocity is not extensive but, rather, intensive, which is precisely the opposite of what the standard view would have to maintain. Therefore, the second claim of the standard view cannot be maintained. Even if isolated cases are unproblematic, Kant cannot argue by substitution in a systematic way.

---

[13] Again, the first difficulty arises here as well. It might seem equally natural to substitute matter for the following principle: "every change has a material cause."

Kant's *Metaphysical Foundations of Natural Science*   75

However, one might still attempt to retain at least the first claim of the standard view as a fallback position. That is, even if 'application' is not to be understood as 'substitution,' one might still hold that the *Metaphysical Foundations*'s special metaphysics relies on the first *Critique*'s Principles (which the empirical concept of matter is supposed to instantiate in some other way). The Mechanics chapter of the *Metaphysical Foundations* might be taken to be providing strong evidence in favor of this claim. In the beginning of the proof for each of his three Laws of Mechanics, Kant states principles very similar to the three Analogies of Experience, claiming that they are taken from transcendental philosophy.[14]

However, even the standard view's first claim cannot adequately represent the argumentative structure of the *Metaphysical Foundations*, and for three reasons. First, even a superficial reading of the argument in the Dynamics chapter shows that Kant does not refer either implicitly or explicitly to the Principle of the Anticipations of Perception.[15] Instead, Kant provides explanations of how *the categories* are to be used in establishing the *Metaphysical Foundations*'s results:

> If we look back after all of the affairs of the Dynamics, we will notice: that, *first*, the **real** in space (otherwise called the solid), in the filling of space by *repulsive force*, *second*, that which is **negative** with respect to the first [force] as the object of our outer perception, namely the attractive force by which all space is penetrated to the extent this force is present, and thus the solid is completely replaced, *third*, the **limitation** of the first force by the second and thus the determination of the *degree of filling space* that stems from it, thus the *quality* of matter is completely treated under the titles of *reality*, *negation*, and *limitation* as much as it is appropriate to a metaphysical dynamics. (4:523)

That is, it is the qualitative *categories*, rather than the qualitative *Principle* (the Anticipations of Perception), that Kant draws on from the first *Critique* to explain matter under the heading of quality. In a passage added in the second edition of the first *Critique*, Kant is quite explicit about the importance of the table of categories (rather than the Principles) as being the organizing principle of the *Metaphysical Foundations*.[16]

---

[14] A close reading reveals, however, that there are variations in both their formulations and their meanings. For example, the third principle (which is supposed to be identical to the Third Analogy's principle) states that all external efficacy in the world is *mutual interaction* ("alle äußere Wirkung in der Welt *Wechselwirkung* sei" 4:544). But this principle is clearly distinct from the Third Analogy's principle, which states that mutual interaction is required for us to cognize the coexistence of substances.

[15] The same problem arises in the Phoronomy for the Axioms of Intuition.

[16] Cf. B109–10: "For that this table is extremely useful in the theoretical part of philosophy, and indeed is indispensable as supplying the complete plan of a whole science, so far as that science rests on *a priori* concepts, and as dividing it systematically according to determinate principles, is already evident from the fact that the table contains all the elementary concepts of the understanding in their completeness, nay, even the form of a

76   The Laws of Mechanics

Second, even for the Mechanics chapter, the standard view encounters serious difficulties. While Kant does acknowledge each of the Analogies of Experience, it is far from clear that they must be presupposed for systematic reasons. For while the first two Laws of Mechanics seem to state the First and Second Analogies as assumptions, the Third Law intimates a slightly weaker relationship. For Kant does not claim that the Third Analogy is presupposed, but rather suggests that it must be "*entlehnt*" (borrowed). He weakens the tie even more explicitly, however, when he apologizes for the intrusion of a metaphysical principle by noting: "only I cannot completely omit this metaphysical law of community here without impairing the completeness of insight" (4:545). Such a formulation hardly suggests that the Third Analogy is a crucial assumption; instead, the Third Analogy could provide a basic model of causality that it is useful to have in mind so as to properly understand what the Third Law of Mechanics is claiming. And even if all three Analogies were used as premises in the Mechanics chapter, this does not establish that they are essential to the argumentative structure of the *Metaphysical Foundations* as a whole; they could be simply accidental features of these particular arguments.[17]

Further, the mode of proof in the Analogies of Experience is not compatible in any straightforward way with the structure of Kant's arguments for the Laws of Mechanics. For the Analogies of Experience have a conditional form, according to which if one is to have cognition of objective temporal relations (e.g., succession and coexistence), then a certain metaphysical entity or relation must be posited (e.g., a causal bond or mutual interaction). But the Laws of Mechanics do not have this conditional form and thus cannot employ the consequent, unless they were also to assume the antecedent. More importantly, they do not concern time-determination the way that the Analogies do. For example, the Third Law of Mechanics does not state: to cognize that bodies coexist, they must act and react equally. Given the argumentative structure and aim of the Analogies of Experience, it is difficult to see how they could be used systematically as premises in arguments for the Laws of Mechanics.

Third, the standard view encounters the following difficulty with the empirical concept of matter. Given that the standard view begins by assuming the first *Critique*'s Principles and then derives more specific

---

system of them in the human understanding, and accordingly indicates all the momenta of a projected speculative science, and even their order, as I have elsewhere shown."

[17] I later show that the Analogies of Experience are not presupposed in Kant's discussion of his Third Law of Mechanics.

Kant's *Metaphysical Foundations of Natural Science*   77

principles by applying the empirical concept of matter to them, the validity of these more specific principles will depend on whether the empirical concept of matter is instantiated by the objects that we experience. If one experiences objects to which the concept of matter applies, then the principles that are derived from this concept will hold as well. However, if one does not experience objects to which the concept of matter applies, then the relevant principles will not hold. In other words, one could argue that Kant's Laws of Mechanics are false simply by rejecting the concept of matter that is presupposed. Accordingly, on the standard view the principles advanced in the *Metaphysical Foundations* would be contingent insofar as for any given object that we encounter we can say only that if it conforms to the *Metaphysical Foundations*'s principles, then it is matter, and if it does not, then it is not matter.[18] In short, according to the standard view, whether the specific principles derived in the *Metaphysical Foundations* hold for an object is a contingent matter, but Kant is clear that these principles are not supposed to be contingent in that sense, since they are supposed to constitute the pure part of natural science.[19] Thus, the standard view is unable to explain how the *Metaphysical Foundations*'s principles could have the status they do. Finally, even if the above objections were not sufficient to defeat the standard view, the issue is decided by the arguments Kant actually gives. For they clearly do not assume the first *Critique*'s Principles in a systematic way.[20]

4.3   The Transcendental Argument Interpretation

If the standard view does not describe the argumentative structure of the *Metaphysical Foundations*, what does? I suggest that the *Metaphysical Foundations* can be understood as an extended (two-step) transcendental argument.[21] More specifically, the task of the *Metaphysical Foundations* is

---

[18] Plaass's interpretation encounters this difficulty.

[19] Admittedly, the fact that we have experience at all is a contingent matter. However, given that we have experience, certain things are not contingent. Thus, the Analogies of Experience show that if we have unified temporal experience, substances, causal rules, and mutual interaction are not contingent. Similarly, if we have unified spatial experience, the principles that constitute the special metaphysics of nature are not contingent. I return to this issue below.

[20] I provide some support for this claim later in my discussion of the Third Law of Mechanics.

[21] Another proponent of what I call the "Transcendental Argument Interpretation" is Konrad Cramer, *Nicht-reine synthetische Urteile a priori. Ein Problem der Transzendentalphilosophie Immanuel Kants* (Heidelberg: Carl Winter Verlag, 1985), though he develops the interpretation differently. Friedman, too, maintains a version of the Transcendental Argument Interpretation. Though Gordan Brittan does not explicitly endorse this

78   The Laws of Mechanics

to develop the conditions necessary for an object of outer sense to be possible as an object of experience. Just as the first *Critique* asks how experience (empirical cognition) of objects in general is possible, the *Metaphysical Foundations* similarly asks how experience of objects of outer sense is possible. The first step of Kant's argument uses a transcendental argument to establish the most basic feature of matter, namely, that any object of outer sense (i.e., any matter) is essentially something movable in space. The second step uses yet another set of transcendental arguments to establish specific substantive principles. More specifically, since the first *Critique* establishes that any object of possible experience must be determinable under each categorial heading, each chapter in the *Metaphysical Foundations* first derives a 'new' determination of matter by showing how matter as something movable in space is to be determined by each categorial heading.[22] Each 'new' determination of matter then requires, by yet another transcendental argument, substantive principles that show how each new determination is possible.[23] For example, since objects of experience in general have a magnitude (which is established in the Axioms of Intuition), one must show how it is possible for objects of outer sense in particular to have a magnitude. Specifically, since movability is a necessary property of objects of outer sense, one must show how it is possible for motions to have magnitudes. Let us now consider each of these steps in more detail.

4.3.1   Matter as the Movable in Space

With respect to the first step of the argumentative structure of the *Metaphysical Foundations*, in the Preface Kant claims that matter as an

---

reading, it is compatible with his main thesis that Kant intends to give a realist interpretation of Newtonian physics; cf. *Kant's Theory of Science* (Princeton: Princeton University Press, 1978), p. 122. Though there has been considerable debate about the very possibility of transcendental arguments, I understand a transcendental argument to be an argument satisfying two conditions: (1) it is an argument that reveals the necessary conditions for (2) a general type of experience. It is not obvious that a transcendental argument, if described in this way, is subject to any of the difficulties standardly associated with transcendental arguments. For a fuller defense of transcendental arguments, see Eckart Förster, "How Are Transcendental Arguments Possible?," in *Reading Kant*, ed. Eva Schaper and Wilhelm Vossenkuhl (Cambridge: Blackwell, 1989), pp. 3–20.

[22] On this reading, the "transcendental principles" are the categories (or the categorial headings under which they fall), not the Principles of Pure Understanding.

[23] The first step of the argument is similar to Kant's claim in the first *Critique* that all objects of intuition must be temporal to be cognized (a claim Kant supports in both the Transcendental Deduction and the Schematism), whereas the second step is closer to the first *Critique*'s Principles of Pure Understanding.

Kant's *Metaphysical Foundations of Natural Science* 79

object of outer sense is essentially the movable in space.[24] Yet his explicit justification claims (rather dogmatically): "The fundamental determination of a something that is to be an object of outer senses must be motion, for only thereby can these senses be affected" (4:476). This remark hardly amounts to a satisfactory justification. It may (or may not) be true that, given the kind of physiology we happen to have, objects must be in motion for us to perceive them. However, the same is not necessarily true for beings characterized only as having a discursive understanding and space and time as forms of intuition (i.e., for the kinds of epistemic beings with which Kant is concerned), since it is entirely conceivable that beings characterized in this manner should be able to be affected by spatiotemporal objects that are not in motion. As Ralph Walker points out, it seems possible to conceive of a world in which spatial objects do not move but rather change colors instead.[25] Moreover, it seems possible to conceive of beings in such a world with similar cognitive faculties, yet with perceptual organs different from those that we have in such a way that they could cognize this color-changing world as an objective spatiotemporal world, just as the first *Critique* prescribes, but without satisfying the condition that such beings must be affected by objects in motion. Thus, Kant's remark is best taken not as a justification of the claim that matter is essentially movable, but rather as an expression of his belief that objects of outer sense must move in order to affect human beings' sense organs. Consequently, we must look elsewhere (and beyond the immediately surrounding text) for a justification of Kant's claim that matter is the movable in space.[26]

Kant makes two remarks that point in the direction of a more adequate justification for his claim. First, his claim is not that matter is necessarily in motion, but rather that matter is essentially movable. This claim excludes only the possibility that there be in principle immovable matter. It thus allows for the existence of matter that *in fact* is never moved as long as it *could have* been moved, e.g., had external forces been exercised differently. This claim does not concern whether it is metaphysically possible that some matter that is independent of the conditions under which we can experience objects is in principle immovable. Kant's claim

[24] At times, Kant claims that motion is an essential property of matter, but this must be an imprecise way of speaking, since it seems to be too strong to claim that all matter is always and necessarily in motion. Rather, as will become clearer shortly, matter is essentially the *movable* in space.

[25] Ralph C. Walker, "The Status of Kant's Theory of Matter," in *Kant's Theory of Knowledge*, ed. Lewis White Beck (Dordrecht: Reidel, 1974), pp. 151–6.

[26] Otherwise, one would have to claim that the special metaphysics of nature is limited to human beings in particular.

80   The Laws of Mechanics

implies that if there were such matter, it would not be matter *for us* in the sense that we could not cognize it as such through outer sense.

Second, just as time itself or objective time cannot be perceived, so too 'absolute'[27] or objective space cannot be directly perceived.[28] Although it may be true that we can directly perceive some spatial properties (e.g., incongruent counterparts), we cannot directly perceive position in objective space (position in space being the basic notion in terms of which motion must be understood). Rather, objective space must be constructed according to a procedure outlined in the *Metaphysical Foundations*'s chapter on Phenomenology.

But these two points have the consequence that one cannot *directly* perceive whether something is in objective motion or not (since objective motion depends on objective space). What one directly perceives is *apparent* motion. Thus, it is possible that any immediate object of outer sense that appears to be moving might really be moving in space, depending on how the construction of objective space situates that object. Consider the following four types of construction of objective space: (1) Space reveals all matter to be in motion at present. (2) Although some matter is not at present in motion, all matter will be in motion at some time or other. (3) Although some matter will be in motion at some time or other, some matter will never in fact be in motion. (4) All matter is not in motion at any time. But none of these possibilities actually contradicts Kant's claim that matter is the movable in space, since cases 1 and 2 entail this claim and it follows from cases 3 and 4 that had the construction of space been different, matter that never in fact moves could have been in motion.

Kant's claim is strengthened even further when one takes into consideration the fact that he views objective space as an idea of reason, for this fact implies that its 'construction' is never completed.[29] Accordingly, one can never exclude the possibility that although it may now appear that a given matter is not moving (or movable) according to a particular construction of objective space, a future construction of objective space might reveal it to be in fact moving (and thus movable), and this is either because the actions and thus the motions of bodies might be different in the future or because the incompleteness of the input to the prior

---

[27] Although Kant uses the term 'absolute' here, he does not mean by it the same thing as Newton (namely, an independently existing thing). I refer to it as objective space in this chapter to avoid confusion.

[28] See the Phenomenology chapter (4:556 and 4:559) for textual support. Kant claims that time is not an object of immediate perception in the General Principle of the Analogies of Experience as well as in the Second and Third Analogies.

[29] See the Phenomenology chapter for Kant's explanation, esp. 4:559.

construction makes it possible that a later construction delivers a different result. Thus, Kant has several reasons to maintain that matter is essentially movable.[30]

Now consider whether this interpretation of Kant's position is able to solve the problem expressed by Walker's color-changing world. First, it should be noted that the color-changing world example is not necessarily an instance of immov*able* objects and thus does not directly contradict Kant's claim.[31] It is at least in principle possible that these colors, which change periodically, *could* move; and if this is possible, then it is simply a *contingent* matter of fact that they do not move but rather change. Second, it is possible, depending on how the construction of objective space proceeds, that what initially appears to be a static color-changing world is actually dynamic.[32] As a result, Kant's claim turns out to be consistent with Walker's example of the color-changing world.

These considerations show how Kant could have argued for the basic determination of matter as the movable in space, namely, through a transcendental argument that maintains that an object of outer sense is possible for us only if it is movable in space. Since this claim characterizes only the general subject matter of the *Metaphysical Foundations*, it still remains to be shown how substantive principles are required to show how it is possible to experience matter as the movable in space according to each categorial heading.

4.3.2   *Matter's New Determinations and Substantive Principles*

Kant's single most helpful methodological remark in the *Metaphysical Foundations* about its argumentative structure is as follows: "Therefore, the concept of matter had to be carried out through all four functions of the concepts of the understanding (in four chapters) in each of which a new determination of matter was added. The fundamental determination of a something that is to be an object of outer senses must be motion . . . The understanding leads all other predicates which pertain to the nature of matter back to motion" (4:476–7). This remark does not, however, indicate in any detail either how each 'new determination' is established

---

[30] In fact, one might think that this final consideration is sufficient on its own to justify Kant's claim and that the earlier considerations are not in fact needed (even if Kant can seem to offer them as support).

[31] The similarity of Walker's color-changing world to Strawson's sound-world (in *Individuals*) is apparent.

[32] Walker's example cannot simply presuppose that the objects in the world are not moving, since that presupposes a construction of absolute space, a construction which Kant claims is precisely at issue here.

82   The Laws of Mechanics

or how each new determination is involved in establishing further principles. To see how these steps proceed, let us consider the Mechanics chapter, arguably the clearest case, in some detail.

The 'new determination' of matter added in the Mechanics chapter is that of the communication of motion.[33] What is the justification for this new determination? The relevant categorial heading is that of relation. Thus, for us to be able to experience matter as the movable in space, we must represent the parts of matter as somehow relating to each other as the movable in space. It seems plausible to hold that for Kant only the communication of motion could express matter's relation to other matter insofar as motion is concerned.[34] For without the type of relation involved in the communication of motion there could, it seems, be no real relation between the parts of matter insofar as motion is concerned. To see the plausibility of this claim, one can contemplate other possible relations between matter concerning motion.[35] Consider the statement "one part of matter is distinct from another." This sentence does express a relation between two parts of matter that is not an instance of the communication of motion. But such a relation does not pertain to matter *as the movable*.[36] One might also consider that one part of matter might simply impart motion to another part, but for Kant that *is* an instance of the communication of motion. For any meaningful verb, x, that one places in the locution 'One part of matter x-es another part of matter in motion,' it will be an instance of the communication of motion.[37] Though it is not feasible to consider all of the possibilities, this line of

[33] Kant seems to indicate that the new determination of matter in the Mechanics chapter is that of having a motive force (cf. 4:536). However, motive forces were already introduced in the Dynamics chapter. Kant is aware of this difficulty and proceeds to explain how the dynamic concept of force could view matter as at rest, but the mechanical concept of matter requires motion. Accordingly, it is not implausible to interpret the communication of motion to be the real new determination in this chapter.

[34] A different way of putting this point would be to emphasize the importance of moving force to the real relations that would have to obtain between bodies that are movable in space. (I discuss moving force in more detail later in Chapter 6.) Marius Stan, in "Kant's Third Law of Mechanics: The Long Shadow of Leibniz," *Studies in History and Philosophy of Science* 44 (2013): 493–504, similarly notes that moving force is understood as a property a body retains whether it is active or not, and that it is important to the communication of motion.

[35] If correct, this would imply that the determination of each chapter's 'new' determination of matter proceeds much more loosely than one might expect.

[36] The same difficulty would apply to two parts of matter being at a distance from each other.

[37] Admittedly, it would be difficult to determine what a 'meaningful verb' could be for Kant in this context. However, Kant would, I think, want to restrict these verbs to 'real' rather than 'ideal' connections. In transcripts from various metaphysics lectures, Kant, following Baumgarten and Crusius, explains that an ideal connection is one that consists in thought alone.

Kant's *Metaphysical Foundations of Natural Science* 83

thought has at least some intuitive appeal.[38] And it is not particularly contentious to assert that matter can in fact communicate motion, so not much might be needed in the way of argument.

The truly controversial move concerns how Kant intends to argue to substantive principles from this new determination of matter. In the Mechanics chapter, three Laws of Mechanics are required to explain how we can experience matter insofar as it communicates motion. Let us briefly consider the Second and Third Laws of Mechanics, which claim (respectively) that all change of matter has an external cause and that in all communication of motion action and reaction are equal to each other.[39]

In his Proof of the Second Law of Mechanics, Kant argues that all change of matter must have an external cause because all change of matter must have a cause (given the Second Analogy) and we do not experience matter *as such* as having any *internal* grounds of determination that could cause a change in its own state. As a result, the cause must lie external to the matter undergoing the change. If this argument is successful in establishing the Second Law of Mechanics, how does it make possible our experience of the communication of motion? The Second Law of Mechanics states, in stark contrast to a certain understanding of Leibniz's pre-established harmony (as applied to bodies), that we cannot experience matter acting on itself so as to determine its own motion (at least not if natural science is to be possible).[40] Consequently, if there are any changes in motion, real causal interaction must hold between two parts of matter, and since we are concerned with motion, this real causal interaction results in the *communication* of motion from one part of matter to another. We shall see in more detail in our discussion of the Third Law of Mechanics *how* two substances can communicate motion. But the Second Law of Mechanics establishes that there must be a real causal connection between two substances in the communication of motion, since as far as our experience is concerned, only an external cause can bring about a change in the motion of matter. In short, the

---

[38] This argument is not Kant's strongest and would be valid only with a considerable amount of supplementation. For example, one would have to assume that motion, rather than, say, color, is the only property in question. But there is good textual evidence (e.g., at 4:524) to think that Kant would have accepted this particular assumption.

[39] The Laws of Mechanics, especially the First Law, will be discussed in detail later in Chapter 6.

[40] Kant does not refer to the first *Critique*'s Third Analogy of Experience in this context, which would have been natural insofar as only the Third Analogy excludes pre-established harmony. This omission provides us with a further reason to think that the first *Critique*'s Principles are not required in any systematic way as assumptions in the *Metaphysical Foundations*.

84   The Laws of Mechanics

Second Law of Mechanics shows that some kind of causal bond is necessary for us to experience the communication of motion.[41]

Kant's Proof of the Third Law of Mechanics has a structure that parallels that of the Second and Third Analogies of Experience, which are similarly transcendental arguments, albeit for a different (more general) kind of experience. This kind of transcendental argument assumes that we have cognition of a certain determinate feature. In this case, the relevant feature is the communication of motion and the acceleration and deceleration of the bodies that constitute the communication of motion. It then argues that this determinate feature requires a certain kind of causal relation, exploiting the idea that there are aspects of the determinate feature that is assumed that require precisely the feature of the causal relation that is being posited as a condition on the possibility of cognition of the determinate feature. In the case of the Third Law of Mechanics, the causal relation that is required is the equality of action and reaction, and it is the equality of the acceleration and deceleration that must occur in our cognition of the communication of motion that requires the equality of the action and reaction.

In the text of his Proof of the Third Law of Mechanics, Kant devotes the bulk of his attention to showing how we must cognize the motions that are involved in the communication of motion. Take the case of two billiard balls in impact as an example.[42] Rather than thinking that the cue ball starts off in motion while the eight ball is at rest, and then after the collision, the eight ball is in motion while the cue ball is at rest, Kant argues that, given the reciprocity and symmetry of the relative motions of two bodies toward each other, the motion of the cue ball toward the eight ball must be understood as equal and opposite to the motion of the eight ball toward the cue ball. For given that the eight ball is in relative motion toward the cue ball before the collision, it cannot be at rest before the

---

[41] For Kant's rejection of pre-established harmony, see Eric Watkins, "Kant's Theory of Physical Influx," *Archiv für Geschichte der Philosophie* 77 (1995): 285–324. For fuller discussion of Kant's views on causality, which are presupposed by this analysis, see Eric Watkins, *Kant and the Metaphysics of Causality* (New York: Cambridge University Press, 2005).

[42] Kant implicitly restricts his discussion to the case of two bodies. For the sake of completeness, one would need to consider cases involving three or more bodies, but there is no reason to think that these more complex cases are problematic. Also, I am abstracting from the masses of the bodies involved, an issue that will be discussed later in Chapter 6. (This is permissible in the billiard ball case on the assumption that the billiard balls can be treated as having the same mass.) What's more, as Marius Stan rightly notes (in "Kant's Third Law of Mechanics"), Kant takes impact to be his paradigm case of the communication of motion. At the same time, Kant can extend his argument to the case of pressure and also argue along similar lines that the law obtains for cases of attraction (understood in terms of action at a distance).

collision, and given that the cue ball is in relative motion away from the eight ball after the collision, it cannot be at rest after the collision. One assumption that these claims rest on is the fact that we cannot perceive absolute space. If we could perceive absolute space, it would allow us to cognize those cases where one of the bodies was at rest in absolute space before or after the collision.[43] Instead, Kant understands motion as a relational property in such a way that the motion of one body is simply a change in its spatial relation to a second body. Since we can perceive only relative space, we can perceive only the relative motions of bodies with respect to each other.

A second assumption that Kant makes in arguing for representing the motions of the bodies that are communicating their motion in the way that he does is that the *changes* of motion that take place in the communication of motion must be equal, just as the relative motions of two bodies are. That is, if at time t_0 the cue ball is moving with velocity a toward the eight ball while the eight ball is moving toward the cue ball with a velocity $-a$, and if at time t_1 the cue ball is moving with velocity a away from the eight ball while the eight ball is moving away from the cue ball with a velocity $-a$, then the change of motion in the cue ball, its deceleration, must be equal and opposite to the change of motion in the eight ball, its acceleration. This allows Kant to characterize the communication of motion, which is the determinate feature the possibility of whose cognition he is attempting to explain, as consisting in equal and opposite changes of motion, that is, in the equality of acceleration and deceleration of the two bodies in question.[44]

In the second main step of the argument, Kant then shows that the equality of the changes of motion that the two bodies undergo requires both the action and reaction of both bodies, and that the action and reaction be equal and opposite. Kant can draw on three relatively unproblematic assumptions to show that the changes of motion involved

---

[43] Kant argues against absolute space in the Transcendental Aesthetic in the first *Critique*.

[44] In Note 2 to the Third Law of Mechanics, Kant distinguishes between the mechanical and the dynamical laws of the equality of action and reaction. The former "rests on the fact that no *communication* of motion takes place, except insofar as we presuppose a *community* of motions, and thus that no body impacts another that is at rest *relative to it*" (4:548). This is the version of the law that Kant has established at this point in the argument. Kant describes the dynamical law of the equality of action and reaction as "not insofar as one matter *communicates* its motion to another, but rather as it *imparts* this motion originally to it, and, at the same time, produces the same in itself through the latter's resistance" (ibid.). I take it that the mechanical version is purely kinematic and that the dynamical version requires dynamical actions of forces (e.g., of repulsion). And I read Kant as establishing the mechanical law first, and then showing that it requires the dynamical law.

86 The Laws of Mechanics

in the communication of motion require both action and reaction. First, the communication of motion involves changes of motion (rather than change of place), which Kant takes to be genuine changes of state of the bodies.[45] Second, in line with the thought that drives the Second Analogy of Experience, Kant holds that genuine changes of state require causes. Third, the Second Law of Mechanics states that changes in the states of bodies cannot be self-caused, but rather require external causes. Given these three assumptions, it is clear that the acceleration of the eight ball can have only the action of the cue ball as its cause, just as the deceleration of the cue ball can have only the (re-) action of the eight ball as its cause. As a result, the communication of motion is possible only with both action and reaction.[46]

However, Kant can also show that the action and reaction must be equal. For if the acceleration and the deceleration of the two billiard balls must be equal, then the action and the reaction that causes them must be equal as well. For there is no reason to attribute more of the cause to the one than to the other. Action and reaction must therefore be equal and opposite, just as the Third Law of Mechanics states.[47]

How is this argument for the Third Law of Mechanics a transcendental argument? That is, how is the equality of action and reaction a necessary condition for the experience of matter as the movable in space? The Third Law of Mechanics provides a rule for constructing the communication of motion in intuition, where construction in intuition demonstrates the possibility of what is to be constructed. In other words, the Third Law of Mechanics is a necessary condition for experience of the communication of motion, since the Third Law is necessary for construction of (changes of) motion in intuition and construction of (changes of) motion in intuition is in turn necessary for the communication of motion to be possible. In short, the Third Law of Mechanics explains the possibility of experiencing the communication of motion by showing how the communication of motion must be constructed on the basis of what is given in intuition by means of the relational categories. Although I have offered only a brief description of the main arguments of the Second and Third Laws of Mechanics, if the other chapters of the

---

[45] See Chapter 6 in this book for more detailed discussion of this point.

[46] It is worth noting explicitly that the Principle of the Third Analogy of Experience, despite being quoted just prior to the statement of the argument, is not presupposed in this argument.

[47] Marius Stan offers a reconstruction of Kant's proof that is, I believe, similar, in "Kant's Third Law of Mechanics" (pp. 501–2). For a different reconstruction of Kant's argument here, see Robert Palter, "Kant's Formulation of the Laws of Motion," *Synthese* 24 (1972): 96–116.

Metaphysical Foundations can be interpreted in a similar way, then the other specific principles that Kant argues for in the *Metaphysical Foundations* can likewise be understood as the second step of an extended transcendental argument.

4.4   Conclusion

I have suggested that the substantive principles of the *Metaphysical Foundations* are the result of an extended transcendental argument explaining both how matter in general as an object of outer sense must be the movable in space and how this concept of matter can be determined according to each of the categorial headings in the first *Critique*. This suggestion allows us to understand not only how the specific arguments in the *Metaphysical Foundations* proceed but also how Kant can claim that the *Metaphysical Foundations* as a special metaphysics of nature has a priori and apodictic status. Because Kant's account of matter as the movable in space and as subject to the Laws of Mechanics (as well as to the other principles in the *Metaphysical Foundations*) is derived via an extended transcendental argument, it is a priori and apodictic.[48]

If this is correct, then we can also understand the precise relationship between the transcendental and special parts of the metaphysics of nature. The transcendental part (in the first *Critique*) explains how experience in general (or temporal experience) is possible by establishing certain necessary conditions for experience considered under each categorial heading. The special part argues analogously, but attempts to explain the possibility of experience that is more specific and richer than that of the first *Critique* (i.e., experience in general). For it presupposes a concept of matter as an object of outer sense (i.e., outer or spatial experience) that clearly has more content than "experience in general." Since the notion of experience it attempts to explain is richer in content, the principles it presupposes will naturally have more content as well. At the same time, such an argumentative structure can preserve the a priori and apodictic status necessary for these principles to be considered part of science proper (namely, the pure part). Further, this interpretation has the two-fold advantage that the *Metaphysical Foundations*'s principles

---

[48]   It is in light of this point that this interpretation has an advantage over the standard view. Recall from the previous section that on the standard view the Laws of Mechanics (as well as the other principles stated in the *Metaphysical Foundations*) turn out to be contingent rather than a priori and necessary.

88   The Laws of Mechanics

do not rely on the first *Critique*'s Principles. First, these principles do not necessarily assume the first *Critique*'s Principles. Second, since no deductive relationship holds between these principles and the first *Critique*'s Principles, the falsity of the former (as established by relativity theory) carries no direct implications for the latter.[49]

---

[49] I thank Karl Ameriks and Michael Friedman, for providing extensive comments on earlier versions of this chapter, and Manfred Kuehn, for his helpful commentary on a shorter version of this chapter as it was presented at the 1993 Central Division APA in Chicago. I am indebted to audiences at Virginia Tech, Stony Brook University, Rutgers University, and Ohio State University. I also thank the Max Planck Institut für Wissenschaftsgeschichte Berlin as well as the National Endowment for the Humanities for a fellowship during which part of this chapter was written.

5   The Laws of Motion from Newton to Kant

5.1   Introduction

Standard accounts in the history of philosophy of science claim that one of Kant's fundamental aims is to justify Newtonian science in general and Newtonian mechanics in particular as stated in the three laws of motion of Newton's *Philosophiae Naturalis Principia Mathematica* (hereafter *Principia*). Such accounts implicitly presuppose that Newton and Kant are fundamentally concerned with both the same content and the same goal.[1] Michael Friedman's recent interpretation of Kant is an excellent example of how one might emphasize Newtonian aspects of Kant's view by reconstructing a detailed argument for the Laws of Mechanics that draws on and parallels Newton's justification of the laws of motion in fundamental ways.[2] However, these accounts require clarification, supplementation, and, ultimately, some significant revision. For Kant is not actually concerned with Newton's laws of motion as such and his fundamental aim is quite different from Newton's. To substantiate these claims, I argue that Kant's Laws of Mechanics differ in important ways from Newton's laws of motion and that they do so at least in part because his specific goals are different from Newton's. These differences can be discerned more clearly if one realizes that almost a century passes between the publication of Newton's *Principia* and Kant's *Metaphysical Foundations*, and that the reception of Newton's laws of motion during this period reveals incredible variety in the way that the laws of motion are formulated by other figures in Germany during the

---

[1] For different versions of this view, see Ernst Cassirer, *Das Erkenntnisproblem in der Philosophie und Wissenschaft der neueren Zeit* (Berlin: B. Cassirer, 1922), and Gerd Buchdahl, *Metaphysics and the Philosophy of Science* (Oxford: Blackwell, 1969), pp. 672ff., esp. p. 675.

[2] See Michael Friedman, *Kant and the Exact Sciences* (Cambridge, MA: Harvard University Press, 1992).

90   The Laws of Mechanics

eighteenth century.[3] In fact, in very few cases are Newton's laws of motion accepted without change. Rather, the variety in these formulations stems in significant ways from contexts or traditions within Germany that are all distinct, in one way or another, from Newton's own situation.

To begin to see that Kant's Laws of Mechanics are not identical to Newton's laws of motion, first recall Newton's formulations of the laws of motion as stated in the *Principia*:

> Law I Every body continues in its state of rest, or of uniform motion in a right line, unless it is compelled to change that state by forces impressed upon it.
>
> Law II The change of motion is proportional to the motive force impressed; and is made in the direction of the right line in which that force is impressed.
>
> Law III To every action there is always opposed an equal reaction: or, the mutual actions of two bodies upon each other are always equal, and directed to contrary parts.[4]

Now consider Kant's formulations of the Laws of Mechanics in the Mechanics chapter of the *Metaphysical Foundations*:

> First Law of Mechanics: With regard to all changes of corporeal nature, the quantity of matter taken as a whole remains the same, and is neither increased nor decreased.
>
> Second Law of Mechanics: Every change of matter has an external cause. (Every body remains in its state of rest or motion in the same direction and with the same velocity unless it is compelled by an external cause to forsake this state.)
>
> Third Law of Mechanics: In all communication of motion, action and reaction are always equal to one another. (4:541–4)

Three points of contrast are immediately apparent. First, Kant states a conservation law explicitly, whereas Newton is silent about whether any particular quantity of matter must be conserved throughout the communication of motion. Second, Kant does not even mention Newton's

---

[3] Despite my disagreements with particular points of Friedman's interpretation, I am in fundamental agreement with his overall approach to Kant, according to which Kant can best be read as reacting philosophically to the exact sciences of his day.

[4] Isaac Newton, *Mathematical Principles of Natural Philosophy and His System of the World*, trans. Andrew Mott, revised by Florian Cajori (Berkeley: University of California Press, [1729] 1934), p. 13.

second law.[5] Third, Kant provides a different formulation of Newton's law of inertia, citing change of matter and external causality rather than change of motion and forces. Kant does restate a principle very similar to Newton's law of inertia in parentheses following his own formulation (so that one might think that the difference between the two is merely apparent, due perhaps to a looseness in translation from the Latin), but such a principle could be simply an instance of his more general law rather than an equivalent formulation.[6] Only Kant's Third Law, that of the equality of action and reaction, *seems* to be (nearly) the same as Newton's.[7] Accordingly, at least prima facie there would appear to be several significant differences (in addition to some overlap) between Newton's laws of motion and Kant's Laws of Mechanics.

To show that these varieties in formulation are not merely apparent but, rather, reflect fundamental differences, I present a brief characterization of Newton's primary aim in the *Principia* so that it can then be compared and contrasted with the projects and formulations of the laws of motion undertaken by a number of important figures in eighteenth-century Germany prior to Kant. Insofar as Kant was influenced by the earlier German context, it is clear that his project would naturally fit in with the projects and formulations of these figures. There are three different types of figures whose discussions of the laws of motion Kant

---

[5] Friedman argues that Kant thinks that Newton's second law can be derived from the law of the equality of action and reaction. "However, since Kant formulates the equality of action and reaction in terms of equal and opposite *momenta*, and states that a 'dynamical law' of moving *forces* corresponds to his 'mechanical law' of the community of *motions* (Note 2 to Proposition 4 of the Mechanics: 548.13–29), Newton's second law appears to be contained in Kant's third law: in modern terms, Kant's third law states that any two interacting masses m_A, m_B have accelerations a_A, a_B such that $m_A a_A = -m_B a_B$; Kant's dynamical law then states that $F_{AB} = -F_{BA}$, where F_{AB}, F_{BA} are the forces exerted by A on B and by B on A, respectively. It appears, then, that Kant is presupposing $F_{BA} = m_A a_A$ and $F_{AB} = m_B a_B$" (*Kant and the Exact Sciences*, p. 168 n. 6). However, Friedman's interpretation encounters two difficulties. First, it does not fit Kant's text. For if Kant were presupposing $F = ma$, then, given his third law ($m_A a_A = -m_B a_B$), he would be in a position to infer immediately, and thus not have to provide an independent argument for, $F_{AB} = -F_{BA}$. However, Kant does provide an independent argument for the equality of $F_{AB} = -F_{BA}$ (and not through trivial substitution). Second, there is no independent reason to think that Kant must assume $F_{BA} = m_A a_A$ and $F_{AB} = m_B a_B$ in this derivation, since the derivation would work with a wide variety of laws relating force to the momenta. For example, the derivation would work if $F^3_{BA} = m_A a_A$ and $F^3_{AB} = m_B a_B$, since substituting this principle into $m_A a_A = -m_B a_B$ would give $F^3_{BA} = -F^3_{AB}$, which of course entails $F_{BA} = -F_{AB}$.

[6] Newton's law of inertia specifies in a way that Kant's formulation does not that the changes to be explained by external causes must be changes in motion.

[7] However, even this identification has been persuasively challenged by Martin Carrier, "Kant's Relational Theory of Absolute Space," *Kant-Studien* 83 (1992): 399–416, esp. 405.

92   The Laws of Mechanics

would have been familiar with: (1) Wolff and his followers (and opponents) who publish metaphysics textbooks, (2) "Newtonian" members of the Berlin Academy of Sciences, and (3) authors of influential physics textbooks that Kant used (either in his own studies or in his physics lectures). What will emerge from a consideration of the figures working in these different contexts is that the differences between Newton's formulation of the laws of motion and Kant's formulation of his Laws of Mechanics do not constitute an isolated incident, since there are significant differences between Newton's and these figures' formulations of the laws of motion, and that the projects undertaken by most of these figures are fundamentally different from Newton's insofar as they reflect a concern with (1) providing primarily non-empirical justifications of the laws of motion and (2) developing an intelligible ontological account of motion in terms of substances, accidents, and forces. Thus, we can see that Kant's differences with Newton are not an anomaly, but rather reflect a fundamental difference in interest and context in eighteenth-century Germany, a difference that one must take into account to be in a position to understand how Kant's Laws of Mechanics differ from Newton's laws of motion.

As its full title indicates, in the *Principia* Newton's fundamental aim is to develop the fundamental mathematical principles of natural philosophy. Accordingly, Book One postulates laws of motion, which are applied to bodies or point masses, in particular those orbiting attracting centers. Book Two discusses the motion of bodies through resisting fluids, culminating in an attack on Descartes's theory of the vortices (the leading account of celestial motions at the time). Book Three then presents a positive theory of astronomy, in which the demonstration of the derivation of Kepler's three astronomical laws from Newton's own laws of motion represented the fundamental challenge. It turns out that such a derivation is possible only given the law of universal attraction, a law that Newton applies to both celestial and terrestrial bodies, thereby significantly strengthening the explanatory power of his account. It is important to point out, however, that Newton's account consists of *mathematical* principles. That means not only that both the laws of motion and the derivations undertaken from them must be in mathematical form, but also that Newton does not purport to be explaining the actual mechanisms through which bodies are moved. This restriction applies especially to the force of attraction, since Newton does not explicitly accept that bodies could act on each other immediately at a distance. What this brief account of Newton's fundamental project in the *Principia* shows is that the laws of motion stated in Book One are absolutely fundamental to his entire argument. Even the slightest of variations in their formulations could invalidate the derivations of the later Books. Accordingly, significant changes in the laws of motion imply that one might not be able to carry out Newton's project. Thus, if eighteenth-century German thinkers posited significantly different laws, it would be natural to expect that their fundamental concerns were different as well.

Given the fact that Newton presents a host of other views in the *Principia*, one might object that the above characterization of Newton's project is overly narrow and, further, that this narrowness renders trivially true the claim that Kant's project is different from Newton's.[8] However, the law of universal gravitation along with its derivation (which centrally involves the laws of motion) forms the principal content that can be reasonably attributed to Newton (as opposed to, say, Bacon or Locke) and this law came to be generally acknowledged in the eighteenth century as representing the main element of Newton's famous achievement.[9]

5.2 Metaphysics: Wolff, Thümmig, Bilfinger, Reusch, and Crusius

The person who had the most lasting and direct influence in metaphysics in the first half of the eighteenth century in Germany was Christian

---

[8] In fact, Kant rejects a wide range of these other views (e.g., atomism, absolute space and time, mechanism) so that even a broader construal of Newton's project would not imply the truth of this claim. I am not claiming that Newton had no influence on Kant. Rather, the claim is that his influence is not as direct as is often thought and is more complicated due to the historical context in which he was working. In a series of important articles, Marius Stan has argued that, for reasons both intellectual and political, Christian Wolff and several of his followers attempted to substitute broadly Leibnizian principles for Newton's metaphysical and epistemological presuppositions, and they did so on a number of issues that were fundamental to matter theory and mechanics: absolute space, dynamical laws of motion, his general theory of gravitation, and different notions of force, such as inertia. See, for example, Marius Stan, "Newton's Concepts of Force among the Leibnizians," in *Reading Newton in Early Modern Europe*, ed. Mordechai Feingold and Elizabethanne Boran (Leiden: Brill, 2017), pp. 244–89; "Rationalist Foundations and the Science of Force," in *The Oxford Handbook of 18th Century German Philosophy*, ed. Brandon Look and Frederick Beiser (New York: Oxford University Press, forthcoming); "Newton and Wolff: The Leibnizian Reaction to the Principia, 1716–1763," *The Southern Journal of Philosophy* 50 (2012): 459–81; "Euler, Newton, and Foundations for Mechanics," in *The Oxford Handbook of Newton*, ed. Chris Smeenk and Eric Schliesser (New York: Oxford University Press, 2017) pp. 1–22; and "Emilie du Chatelet's Metaphysics of Substance," *The Journal of the History of Philosophy* 56 (2018): 477–96.

[9] This account of Newton's principal aim in the *Principia* is in the same spirit as Friedman's interpretation according to which Newton's ultimate goal is to distinguish true from apparent motions. For true motions can be distinguished from apparent ones when Newton "applies his laws of motion to empirically given 'phenomena' so as to derive first the inverse-square law and then the law of universal gravitation. The argument then culminates in Proposition XI: 'That the common center of gravity of the earth, the sun, and all the planets, is immovable'"; Friedman, *Kant and the Exact Sciences*, pp. 141–2.

94   The Laws of Mechanics

Wolff. However, Wolff relies on Leibniz for significant aspects of his own view, despite displaying some degree of independence, especially regarding systematic issues. The laws of motion are a case in point. Leibniz's best-known discussion of the laws of motion occurs in the context of dynamics in his *Specimen Dynamicum*,[10] and the discussion there is too brief to clarify sufficiently the issues surrounding the laws of motion. In the course of presenting a detailed argument (against Cartesians) in favor of dynamical forces (as being the necessary complement to purely geometrical properties such as extension), Leibniz offers what he calls systematic laws of motion: "that all change comes about by stages,[11] that all action has a reaction, that a new force is not produced unless an earlier one is diminished, and therefore that a body that carries another off with it is always slowed by the one it carries off, and that there is neither more nor less power in an effect than there is in its cause."[12] Leibniz's only other remark in this context that sheds light on these laws is that they arise "by adding the metaphysical laws of this something [i.e., dynamical force] to the laws of extension."[13] In other words, Leibniz holds that because geometrical considerations by themselves are insufficient to explain bodies fully and must therefore be supplemented by metaphysical ones, the laws of motion, too, must somehow involve metaphysics. However, in the *Specimen Dynamicum* Leibniz fails to explain in any clear way either how metaphysics must be involved or what place the laws of motion occupy in his overall philosophical position. Since Wolff provides an accessible, comprehensive, and systematic treatment of metaphysics that clarifies such issues (though not in uncontroversial ways), Wolff's metaphysics provides a crucial perspective on this topic.

Wolff's most general and popular presentation of his metaphysics occurs in his *Vernünfftige Gedancken von Gott, der Welt und der Seele des Menschen, auch allen Dingen überhaupt* (published in Halle in 1719–20). In this work Wolff divides metaphysics into four main parts: ontology,

---

[10] Both Leibniz's correspondence with Clarke and his articles in the *Acta Eruditorum* did receive widespread attention, but neither contains an explicit account of the laws of motion.

[11] This law is often known as the law of continuity. This particular passage obscures this connection insofar as one might think that "by stages" means discrete changes. However, other passages make it clear that Leibniz thinks that all change proceeds gradually and is continuous.

[12] Gottfried Wilhelm Leibniz, *Philosophical Essays*, ed. and trans. Roger Ariew and Daniel Garber (Indianapolis: Hackett, 1989), pp. 124–5.

[13] Leibniz, *Philosophical Essays*, p. 124.

The Laws of Motion from Newton to Kant 95

rational cosmology, rational psychology, and rational theology.[14] Since rational cosmology concerns the world and the laws that govern the changes that take place in it, Wolff discusses the laws of motion in the chapter entitled "On the World." In this chapter Wolff develops the ontology of the world further in ways that set the context for his discussion of the laws of motion. Accordingly, it is first necessary to set out Wolff's ontology insofar as it relates to rational cosmology.

Wolff begins by defining the world as "a series of mutable things that are next to each other, and follow upon each other, but in general are connected to each other."[15] Further, because the world is a composite or a whole, it must be composed of parts that are simple, which Wolff calls elements (§582). Wolff draws on his general ontology to ascribe to elements both the capacity for self-subsistence and forces through which they can change their internal states.[16] Every simple must be individuated through its internal state, which Wolff characterizes as the mode of its limitation.[17] Wolff then explains that bodies are composed of these elements.[18] Bodies fill a space, have a shape, are divisible, and can be moved. Further, every body has a force for resisting motion in such a way that it cannot be moved until its force is overcome. Wolff defines matter as what gives a body extension through its resisting force and then claims that extension along with enduring in a place stems from the elements.

Having established the fundamental components of his ontology of both simples and bodies, he turns to the laws of motion. He first argues that no body can move itself. His justification for this claim is: "Since matter has a force of resisting motion, no body can move itself."[19] From this principle, coupled with the principle of sufficient reason, he then derives a law of inertia similar to Newton's. "Because nothing can occur which does not have its sufficient reason why it is rather than is not (§30), the motion of a body also cannot cease once it has been placed in motion

---

[14] I should note that the superficial structure of the book does not correspond exactly to the structure of its content, in part since Wolff wants to start off his discussion from an epistemological standpoint. However, its title (along with his series of metaphysics textbooks in Latin) does indicate the four systematic topics to be considered.

[15] Christian Wolff, *Vernünfftige Gedancken von Gott, der Welt und der Seele des Menschen, auch allen Dingen überhaupt,* [Halle], reprint of the 11th edition in Abt. 1, Bd. 2 of Christian Wolff's *Gesammelte Werke* (Hildesheim: G. Olms Verlag, [1719] 1983), p. 332 (§544).

[16] Wolff, *Vernüfftige Gedancken,* p. 360.   [17] Wolff, *Vernüfftige Gedancken,* p. 361.

[18] Wolff's elements are perhaps best understood as being similar in nature to Leibniz's monads. See Eric Watkins, "On the Necessity and Nature of Simples: Leibniz, Wolff, Baumgarten, and the pre-Critical Kant," *Oxford Studies in Early Modern Philosophy* 3 (2006): 261–314.

[19] Wolff, *Vernüfftige Gedancken,* p. 377 (§608).

96   The Laws of Mechanics

unless one meets with a cause from without for why it happens."[20] Wolff understands this "rule of motion" as stemming from Newton (rather than, say, Descartes) because he explicitly calls it "an immutable law of nature," citing (§610) the second edition of Newton's *Principia*.

Three features of Wolff's discussion are particularly striking. First, it is clear that Wolff intends to be providing an adequate (i.e., intelligible) ontology for the laws of motion. He explicitly shows how bodies are to be understood as composites of simple elements, which are clear and distinct to reason. Second, Wolff intends to provide arguments for the laws of motion that are not empirical in nature. Newton calls his laws of motion axioms, but these axioms seem to be justified only by their success in accounting for Kepler's "laws," which are simply descriptions of empirical astronomical regularities. In this sense they depart from Euclid's axioms in geometry, which lay claim to the status of immediately self-evident principles. Wolff's laws, by contrast, are supposed to be evident on the basis of more primitive, non-empirical principles (such as the principle of contradiction and the principle of sufficient reason). Third, Wolff does not explicitly designate any other "rules of motion" as laws of nature or of motion, though he does proceed to discuss the equality of action and reaction as well as the measure of motive force. He does not, however, mention Newton's second law of motion.

To determine more precisely the nature of Wolff's account of the laws of motion, it is helpful to consider his discussion of this issue in his *Cosmologia Generalis* (first published in Frankfurt in 1731). For in this text Wolff devotes considerably more attention to the laws of motion. Though many of the points Wolff makes in this work either are very similar in nature to those made in the *Vernünfftige Gedancken* or go beyond them in predictable ways, three points are worth special note. First, once again, Newton's second law of motion is never mentioned. Second, Wolff provides a lengthy and explicit justification of the law of the equality of action and reaction. After laying out in considerable detail a series of necessary conditions that must be satisfied for bodies to act on each other, he argues for the law as follows:

The action of one body is equal to the reaction of another. For a body reacts on another through inertia (§316); consequently, it strives against the effort of the agent (§319). Hence, equal actions are produced when both efforts are equal (§343)

---

[20] Wolff, *Vernüfftige Gedancken*, p. 377 (§609). Note the slight differences in formulation between Newton's and Wolff's laws of inertia. Newton explicitly talks of direction and of impressed force being the cause of the change of motion, whereas in this passage Wolff does not mention direction and does not identify the cause of the change of motion as a force. Wolff's law of inertia is thus less specific than Newton's.

The Laws of Motion from Newton to Kant 97

and action and reaction occur at the same time (§316 & §319), [produced] at the same time by the same forces (§733 Ontol.) which are equal (§349, §737 Ontol.); accordingly action and reaction must be equal.[21]

Wolff thus provides a non-empirical justification for this law, much as he does for the law of inertia in the *Vernünfftige Gedancken*.

Third, tracking down Wolff's numerous cross-references, one finds that his argument for the equality of action and reaction relies on a claim made earlier in the chapter (§315), namely: "There is no action in bodies without reaction."[22] What is interesting about this claim is not the fact that it is presupposed but rather the ontology Wolff invokes to substantiate it. His proof proceeds as follows:

For because the actions and passions of bodies are accidental changes in them (§713 §714 Ontol.), but no change can occur in them except through motion (§128); one body does not act on another except insofar as it being constituted in motion solicits the other to motion; one does not arise from the other except insofar as it is urged by the other to motion (§133). But as long as it is solicited to motion, it resists motion (§129), and it reacts to the agent through this resistance (§314). Therefore, no action is without reaction.[23]

It is one thing for Wolff to develop an account of the simple elements and their essential properties, quite another for him to present a detailed ontological account of bodies and the forces by which motions are produced (an account absent in any explicit way in Newton's *Principia*).[24] In Wolff's proof for the necessity of action and reaction, we find him developing precisely such an account (though his complete explanation is advanced only in an even wider-ranging series of cross-referenced passages). Thus, at a variety of levels we find Wolff developing a metaphysics for principles that are similar in certain ways to those advanced by Newton, though ultimately these principles have more in common with Leibniz's laws of motion.

Wolff is by no means the only eighteenth-century German metaphysician interested in discovering the proper formulation and justification of the laws of motion. Many of his followers, such as Ludwig Thümmig, Georg Bilfinger, and Johann Peter Reusch, devote extensive attention to

---

[21] Christian Wolff, *Cosmologia Generalis*, [Frankfurt], reprint of the 2nd edition in Abt. 2, Bd. 4 of Christian Wolff's *Gesammelte Werke* (Hildesheim: G. Olms Verlag 1964), p. 252 (§346).

[22] Wolff, *Cosmologia Generalis*, p. 236.   [23] Wolff, *Cosmologia Generalis*, p. 236.

[24] This account is distinct in important ways from that given for bodies and their motions, especially since Wolff, in following Leibniz, resists any attempts at making specific claims about what binds bodies and the simple elements, namely, matter and the forces inherent in matter.

98 The Laws of Mechanics

this issue.[25] Thümmig's *Institutiones Philosophiae Wolfianae* (published in Frankfurt in 1725–6) generally follows very closely, albeit in rather abbreviated form, the content of Wolff's *Vernünfftige Gedancken*.[26] However, his chapter titled "*Institutiones Cosmologiæ Generalis*" is more explicit than Wolff on two important points. First, shortly after discussing the law of inertia (which he calls "*prima lex motus naturalis*") he explicitly calls the law of the equality of action and reaction "*lex motus naturalis altera*," making it clear that Newton's second law is intentionally being omitted.[27] Second, Thümmig reveals a more direct connection between fundamental metaphysical principles and his two laws of motion. As in Wolff's account, the law of inertia is taken from the principle of sufficient reason (as well as from the claim that a body cannot move itself). More interestingly, the law of the equality of action and reaction, which might appear to be derived directly from Newton's *Principia*, is explicitly linked to Leibniz's principle that the whole effect is equal to the full cause, or, in other words, that "there is neither more nor less power in an effect than there is in its cause."[28]

Bilfinger and Reusch, while both clearly Wolffians, are more independent of Wolff than is Thümmig, an independence that reveals itself in their treatments of the laws of motion. For both provide formulations and justifications of the laws of motion that are significantly different from Wolff's. Bilfinger (in his *Dilucidationes Philosophicae de Deo, anima humana, mundo, et generalibus rerum affectionibus*, published in Tübingen in 1725) states no fewer than six laws of motion: (1) Action is equal and contrary to reaction; (2) The full effect is always equal to the forces of the whole cause; (3) A certain quantity of forces persists in the world; (4) Any body perseveres in its motion uniformly with respect to its velocity and direction, unless it is impeded or accelerated by another

---

[25] This issue is discussed in §§43–72 of Ludwig Philipp Thümmig, *Institutiones philosophiae Wolfianae*, [Frankfurt], reprinted in Abt. 3, Bd. 19 of Christian Wolff, *Gesammelte Werke* (Hildesheim: G. Olms Verlag, [1725–6] 1982), pp. 88–97; in §§167–84 of Georg Bernhard Bilfinger, *Dilucidationes philosophicae de Deo, anima humana, mundo, et generalibus rerum affectionibus*, [Tübingen], reprinted in Abt. 3, Bd. 18 of Christian Wolff, *Gesammelte Werke* (Hildesheim: G. Olms Verlag, [1725] 1982), pp. 165–79; and in §§444–50 of Johann Peter Reusch, *Systema metaphysicum antiquiorum atque recentiorum item propria dogmata et hypotheses exhibens*, [Jena], reprinted in Abt. 3, Bd. 27 of Christian Wolff, *Gesammelte Werke* (Hildesheim: G. Olms Verlag, [1735] 1990), pp. 295–301.
[26] Thümmig's textbook summarizes Wolff's entire series of textbooks, covering ethics, politics, and economics in addition to the various branches of theoretical philosophy.
[27] Thümmig, *Institutiones philosophiae Wolfianae*, §61, p. 94.
[28] Leibniz, *Philosophical Essays*, pp. 124–5.

and in its state of rest, unless moved by another;[29] (5) A body describes for a given time the diagonal of a parallelogram of forces; (6) The law of continuity.[30] Obviously, Bilfinger's laws of motion (along with the justifications he develops) differ in significant ways from Newton's and are similar in equally significant ways to Leibniz's in terms of both form and content.

Reusch's discussion in his metaphysics textbook, *Systema Metaphysicum* (published in Jena in 1735), reveals striking similarities to (though also significant differences from) Bilfinger's discussion. He starts his discussion of the laws of motion (§545) by recalling the account of action and reaction that he had given in the ontology section of his metaphysics (§191) and then, like Wolff, asserts (§549) that action cannot occur without reaction.[31] It is only after defining the different ways in which action and reaction can occur in bodies (namely, through "naked contact," impact, and pressure) that he derives a simplified law of inertia according to which "there can be no motion of the elements without an external cause."[32] Accordingly, Reusch proposes deriving the law of inertia from the fact that action cannot occur without reaction (rather than vice versa). Also, like Wolff, Thümmig, and Bilfinger, nowhere does Reusch explicitly consider Newton's second law.

Accordingly, Bilfinger's and Reusch's discussions make it apparent that, like Wolff, they are concerned to show how the laws of motion can be derived from intelligible metaphysical principles. Further, given that both Bilfinger and Reusch attempt to derive the law of inertia from a law pertaining to action and reaction, whereas Wolff attempts to derive the law of inertia from the principle that a body cannot act on itself, it is clear that a number of different options for providing derivations of the laws of motion were available to those committed to a Leibnizian or Wolffian metaphysics.[33]

Now one might think that from a metaphysical standpoint only Wolffians would deviate from Newton's laws of motion in such unusual ways. However, even Wolff's staunchest Pietist opponents follow Wolff (more or less closely) when it comes to the laws of motion. For example,

---

[29] Bilfinger's formulation of the law of inertia is closer to Newton's than is Wolff's, but it too is still more general than Newton's.

[30] Bilfinger, *Dilucidationes philosophicae*, pp. 168–74.

[31] Oddly enough, Reusch does not seem to consider in any explicit way the *equality* of action and reaction.

[32] Reusch, *Systema metaphysicum*, p. 374 (§562).

[33] A different justification of the laws of motion is attempted by another Wolffian, Friedrich Baumeister, in his *Institutiones Metaphysicae*, [Wittenberg], reprinted in Abt. 3, Bd. 25 of Christian Wolff's *Gesammelte Werke* (Hildesheim: G. Olms Verlag, [1738] 1988).

100   The Laws of Mechanics

Christian August Crusius, who is the leading philosophical Pietist in Germany in the 1740s (as well as the leading critic of Wolff), similarly singles out the law of inertia and the law of the equality of action and reaction in his metaphysics textbook, *Entwurf der nothwendigen Vernunft-Wahrheiten* (published in Leipzig in 1745).[34] Nor can one say that Crusius follows Wolff out of ignorance of physics or its relation to metaphysics. For Crusius actually provides a more detailed discussion of the ontology required in order to explain motion, distinguishing, for example, between metaphysical and physical inertia (the one depending on dead and the other on living forces).[35] Precisely because Crusius wants to distance himself from (if not attack) Wolff on every possible point, his discussion requires detail and sophistication. It is thus striking that even Wolff's opponents in metaphysics adopt his treatment of the laws of motion.

In sum, what we find among authors of German metaphysics textbooks throughout the first half of the eighteenth century is an intellectual context or tradition reflecting Leibnizian rather than Newtonian concerns and goals (much less Newton's project in the *Principia*). For these figures attempt to provide both an intelligible ontology for the bodies of physics and a non-empirical justification of the laws that govern the motions of bodies. Newton's *Principia* does not attempt either of these tasks, since it works out mathematical rather than metaphysical principles and the laws of motion are justified empirically rather than a priori. Further, in their statements of the laws of motion all of these authors deviate more from Newton than from Leibniz. However, it is also striking that they differ from each other, indicating that German metaphysicians during this period both are interested in developing the proper formulation of the laws of motion and have sufficiently rich conceptual resources

---

[34] Crusius does discuss some of the issues raised by Bilfinger. For example, somewhat surprisingly, Crusius accepts the law of continuity (or at least a physical version of it) at §410; Christian August Crusius, *Entwurf der nothwendigen Vernunft-Wahrheiten* (Leipzig: Gleditsch, 1745), pp. 786–7. Oddly, Crusius discusses a claim similar to part of Newton's second law (not explicitly noting that the topic is even discussed by Newton), namely, the claim that a change of motion is made in the direction of the right line in which that force is impressed (§411, pp. 787–8), but he does not express the more important part (which expresses a mathematical relationship between the force and the change of motion, a relationship that is crucial to the derivation of Kepler's laws). In fact, Crusius may reject Newton's second law insofar as he wants to assert that souls have the capacity to produce motion. Elsewhere, Crusius rejects conservation laws for precisely this reason. See Eric Watkins's "The Development of Physical Influx in Early Eighteenth-Century Century Germany: Gottsched, Knutzen, and Crusius," *Review of Metaphysics* 49 (1995): 295–339, for a discussion of Crusius's rejection of conservation laws.

[35] See Crusius's *Entwurf*, §397, p. 767.

at their disposal to attempt a variety of formulations and non-empirical justifications of the laws of motion. Finally, while it would be difficult to establish the point definitively, it is tempting to think that these distinct Leibnizian or metaphysical interests led to the omission of Newton's second law. For either such a law cannot be proved by means of more fundamental ontological principles alone or such a law contains empirical elements that would be out of place in discussions of rational cosmology.

5.3   Berlin Academy of Sciences

Although the Berlin Academy of Sciences has not received the scholarly attention other modern European Academies have, it clearly played an important role in the Prussian intellectual community after the early 1740s, when it was reorganized and given more funding.[36] While the Prize Essay questions it posed every year had considerable influence, the intellectual talent of its members was perhaps most impressive.[37] Its resident membership included Voltaire, Pierre-Louis Maupertuis, Leonhard Euler, Pierre Samuel Formey, and Johann Sulzer, whereas its non-resident membership included Buffon, Helvetius, Fontenelle, Holbach, the Bernoullis, Wolff, Baumgarten, Gottsched, Bilfinger, Ploucquet, Meier, and Lambert.[38] The explicit aim of the Academy was research, whereas the university system was oriented primarily toward education. Accordingly, anyone doing research on the foundations of physics in Germany during the second half of the eighteenth century (including Kant) would have been familiar with views expressed by the Academy's members.

Debate within the Berlin Academy of Sciences is typically characterized as being between Newtonians and Wolffians. Formey and, at least early in his career, Sulzer are generally faithful in a broad sense to Wolff, whereas Maupertuis and Voltaire are famous for popularizing Newton in France. However, such a characterization is somewhat misleading and is certainly unhelpful for a discussion of the laws of motion. For it is far from clear what it means to be a Newtonian in eighteenth-century Germany. Is mere acceptance of the law of universal gravitation enough?

---

[36] For reasons of space, I have removed many of the scholarly references to the secondary literature that were contained in this section of the original article.

[37] Kant submitted two essays in response to Prize Essay questions and seriously contemplated submitting an essay for at least one other.

[38] See Adolf Harnack, *Geschichte der Königlich-Preussischen Akademie der Wissenschaften zu Berlin* (Berlin: Reichsdruckerei, 1900), for the canonical account of the history of the Berlin Academy.

102   The Laws of Mechanics

Or must one accept Newton's laws of motion and the derivation of the law of universal attraction that proceeds from them? Would it be sufficient if one's own principles were consistent with Newton's account or could there be non-trivial additions, omissions, or revisions? If revisions were allowed, how significant could they be?

Despite the difficulty of establishing precisely what it means to be a Newtonian, one might think that Maupertuis and Euler are clearly Newtonians.[39] Maupertuis established his considerable reputation in France by popularizing Newton's work (along with Voltaire and Châtelet) against the Cartesian position, which by that time had become firmly entrenched.[40] Euler's prolific mathematical work included the development of Leibnizian calculus to incorporate Newtonian topics. It was precisely such work that occasioned Frederick the Great to invite Maupertuis and Euler (along with Voltaire) to the Academy of Sciences.[41] However, both Maupertuis and Euler depart from Newton in significant ways, most importantly with respect to the laws of motion.

Maupertuis is now best known for his "discovery" of the principle of least action. The principle of least action states: "Whenever any change occurs in nature, the quantity of action employed for this is always the smallest possible."[42] Maupertuis discovers this principle after becoming dissatisfied with the standard options within the vis viva debate, that is, with both Descartes's law of the conservation of the quantity of motion and Leibniz's law of the conservation of living forces, since neither one can be applied in every relevant circumstance.[43] Descartes's law does not apply to all cases (e.g., free fall) and Leibniz's law does not apply to all bodies (namely, perfectly hard, inelastic bodies). Since Maupertuis adopts a skeptical stance toward the nature of bodies, he cannot know

---

[39] That Kant is aware of the work of Maupertuis and Euler is clear from references in his pre-Critical writings. He endorses Maupertuis's principle of least action in *The Only Possible Argument* (2:99) and speaks approvingly of his other work in other passages (cf. 2:181). He refers to Euler's "Reflexion sur l'espace et le temps" in his *Concerning the Ultimate Ground of the Differentiation of Directions in Space* (2:378) and to Euler's *Letters to a German Princess* very positively at the end of his *Inaugural Dissertation* (2:419).

[40] For a helpful biography of Maupertuis, see David Beeson, *Maupertuis: An Intellectual Biography* (Oxford: Oxford University Press, 1992).

[41] Frederick II's intention to balance the Academy by inviting Wolff to be co-director with Maupertuis failed due to Wolff's decision to remain in Halle, a decision that clearly contributed to a lasting anti-Wolffian slant within the Academy.

[42] Maupertuis, "Recherche des loix du mouvement" (Berlin, 1746). Maupertuis repeats the principle of least action several times in other works.

[43] Initially, when Madame du Châtelet forces him to take a position, he tries to skirt it by claiming (as does D'Alembert) that it is merely a dispute about words. After Châtelet presses the point more forcefully, he sides with Leibniz against Descartes and the Newtonians. However, by the time he comes to the Berlin Academy, he becomes dissatisfied with Leibniz's position as well.

that bodies are not perfectly hard and thus cannot grant universality to Leibniz's law. What emerges from his arguments against both positions is the desire to find a law that would cover all cases. The principle of least action is supposed to accomplish precisely that insofar as it can be used to derive the laws not only of mechanics but also of statics, optics, the motions of celestial bodies, and, ultimately, even organic bodies.[44]

The principle of least action is important for our discussion of the laws of motion for a variety of reasons. First, it reveals that, like Wolff and his followers, Maupertuis is interested in discovering a more fundamental principle from which the laws of motion can be derived.[45] Second, despite the fact that the principle of least action is used to derive the laws of motion, it is justified only by the phenomena described by the laws of motion that can be derived from it. In other words, its justification is empirical in nature and indirect in form. If some other principle could be discovered from which one could derive laws that extended further than those that can be derived from the principle of least action, one would have to favor it over the principle of least action. Similarly, if a statement could be derived from the principle of least action that was falsified by experience, then, via modus tollens, the principle of least action would have to be rejected. Third, the principle of least action is not tied to the same kind of metaphysics that Wolff proposes. Maupertuis's skepticism about the nature of bodies means that he cannot develop an ontology in the way that Wolffians can. Fourth, Maupertuis nonetheless does think that the principle of least action has metaphysical import. For he argues (most forcefully, in the *Essai de cosmologie*, translated into German as *Versuch einer Cosmologie* and published in Berlin in 1751) that the principle of least action provides the grounds for the strongest argument for God's existence. The argument's main idea is that in creating the world according to laws, God will do no more than is needed and the principle of least action expresses this idea for the communication of motion insofar as the changes that occur in bodies are, according to that principle, as small as possible.

For our purposes, however, what is most significant is the fact that Maupertuis's adherence to the principle of least action puts him directly at odds with Newton's understanding of the second law of motion. The source of the conflict lies in Maupertuis's rejection of Newton's motive

---

[44] See Mary Terrall, "Maupertuis and Eighteenth-Century Scientific Culture," PhD thesis, UCLA, 1987, for a discussion of these extensions.

[45] Beeson makes a similar point: "What is particularly striking about Maupertuis's approach ... is that it is fundamentally rationalist, concerned with the ideas we have about the nature of things" (*Maupertuis*, p. 219).

104   The Laws of Mechanics

forces. In other words, Maupertuis thinks that since we have no knowledge of the nature of bodies, we also do not know what motive force is beyond its observable effects. Earlier in his career Maupertuis had used this skeptical point to support Newton by refuting objections to Newton's universal attraction at a distance. Since we do not understand the nature of bodies, we understand bodies' attractive forces that are alleged to underlie gravity no more poorly than we understand the repulsive forces that are alleged to underlie the essential impenetrability of bodies.[46] However, after 1746 Maupertuis draws the more radical (and now anti-Newtonian) inference that forces must be dispensed with altogether. Accordingly, Maupertuis explicitly denies that the concept of motive force has any explanatory power. Thus, Newton's second law stating that the change of motion is proportional to the motive force impressed is reduced to an empty tautology insofar as it claims that the change of motion is proportional to something we observe only as a change of motion.[47]

Euler is often considered to be a Newtonian, and there is certainly some truth to that. However, it is fair to say that, like Maupertuis, Euler draws on a variety of traditions (Newtonian, Leibnizian, and Cartesian) in developing his own position. One of the main reasons for thinking of Euler as a Newtonian is especially relevant to the laws of motion since one way of characterizing much of Euler's work is as a systematic mathematical application of Newton's second law to a vast array of possible cases (the motion of free mass points, the motion of mass points through fluids, and the motion of rigid bodies).[48] However, this characterization of Euler's accomplishments oversimplifies matters in important ways. For Newton's formulation of the second law in the *Principia* is actually ambiguous between the following two principles: (1) The change of motion (or momentum) is proportional to the motive force impressed, and (2) the rate of change of motion (or momentum) is proportional to the motive force impressed. Principle (1) can be seen as a limiting case of principle (2) insofar as the impressed force would be the same according

---

[46] See Pierre Louis Moreau de Maupertuis, *Discours sur les différentes Figures des Astres*, Paris, [1732], reprinted in Pierre Louis Moreau de Maupertuis, *Oeuvres* (Lyon, 1768), p. 95.

[47] Maupertuis is quite explicit about his rejection of Newton's second law in his *Examen philosophique de la preuve de l'Existence de Dieu employée dans l'Essai de Cosmologie* (published in Berlin in 1758, p. 411, though originally presented to the Academy in 1756).

[48] Since Newton does not employ the calculus in the *Principia*, it is a substantial undertaking to show how the mathematical structure involved in its argument can be translated into Leibniz's analytical calculus, an undertaking for which Euler is rightly praised.

The Laws of Motion from Newton to Kant 105

to both principles for cases of instantaneous impact. Current historical scholarship suggests that Newton's primary intention corresponds to principle (1). What is striking is that principle (1) is a principle that concerns the change of motion (or momentum) rather than acceleration. In other words, Newton's second law thus understood is not $F = ma$, as is often thought. Rather, Euler is the first person to introduce such a formulation *as the foundation of mechanics*. Accordingly, it is quite natural (though somewhat misleading) to think of Euler as being Newtonian. However, it is interesting to note that Euler, who is otherwise very careful about acknowledging his debts to other scholars, makes no mention of Newton on this point. In fact, Maupertuis, when commenting on Euler's formulation of "Newton's" second law in 1756, attributes the principle to Galileo. Accordingly, a number of scholars working in rational mechanics seem to have been aware of such a principle, but Euler is the first to recognize its fundamental status, and these scholars do not think of it as particularly Newtonian.[49] So even the main initial reason for thinking of Euler as a Newtonian ultimately turns out to be a reason for thinking that his position is at least in some fundamental respects different from Newton's.

However, there are other reasons for thinking of Euler as not following Newton in any strict sense.[50] First, unlike Newton, Euler holds that forces are not primitive entities; they stand in need of further explanation. More specifically, Euler suggests that they must be derived from the essential nature of bodies. Unlike Maupertuis, Euler does not attempt to solve the problem by taking a skeptical position with respect to bodies. Rather, he struggles throughout his career to provide a satisfactory explanation of forces, in particular, the force of attraction, which caused so much difficulty for Newton.[51] His account as presented in

---

[49] See Thomas Hankins, "The Reception of Newton's Second Law of Motion in the 18th Century," *Archives internationales d'histoire des sciences* 20 (1967): 43–65, for an account of the physical, logical, and mathematical problems surrounding Newton's second law that were responsible for its omission in the eighteenth century. In the first part of this chapter I have suggested yet further "problems" surrounding Newton's second law, metaphysical problems. For an analysis of the difficulties that arise for Newton's second law from the perspective of Newton himself, see Stuart Pierson, "Two Mathematics, Two Gods: Newton and the Second Law," *Perspectives on Science* 2 (1994): 231–53.

[50] Euler's optical theory is Newton's main rival at the time, but there are no clear implications between optics and mechanics so that this difference is for all practical purposes irrelevant to their relationship in mechanics.

[51] See Helmut Pulte, *Das Prinzip der kleinsten Wirkung und die Kraftkonzeption der rationalen Mechanik* (Stuttgart: Franz Steiner Verlag, 1989), for an insightful interpretation of the development of Euler's account of the force of inertia as a fundamental property of bodies.

106   The Laws of Mechanics

Gedancken von den Elementen der Cörper (published in Berlin in 1746) posits the force of inertia in addition to extension and impenetrability as a fundamental property of bodies from which the motions of bodies can be derived according to the laws he develops (given that the force of inertia is proportional to mass). He explicitly criticizes Newton's plurality of forces (e.g., centripetal, impressed, etc.), asserting that his force of inertia unifies them into a single force.[52] Later, in the "Recherches sur l'origine des forces" (published in Berlin in 1750), Euler modifies his account, replacing the force of inertia (which he now finds self-contradictory) with impenetrability, which provides the basis for his conception of forces. While this modification forces him to revise significant portions of the rest of his ontology, he remains committed to the (rather Wolffian) idea that the essential nature of bodies can contain only one force. Constant throughout all these revisions, however, is the (non-Newtonian) desire to provide an adequate ontology for the laws of motion.

Second, Euler attempts to derive one of Newton's laws of motion, namely, his law of inertia, from a more primitive principle. For both in his *Mechanica sive motus scientia analytice* (published in St. Petersburg in 1736) and in his *Reflexions sur l'espace et les temps* (published in Berlin in 1748), Euler, like Wolff, argues for the law of inertia on the basis of the principle of sufficient reason. However, despite his reliance on a Leibnizian principle of sufficient reason, Euler's derivation of the law of inertia is different from those of the Leibnizian-Wolffians, such as Reusch's, insofar as Euler's argument relies on Newtonian conceptions of absolute space and time, entities that Leibniz, Wolff, and their followers consistently reject.

Third, Euler's own ontology departs in significant ways from Newton's. For example, he accepts Leibniz's law of continuity, which precludes the possibility of absolutely hard atoms, as "an indisputably certain law of nature." However, Euler uses a Newtonian conception of force rather than Leibniz's living forces. So Euler's ontology is significantly different from both Newton's and Leibniz's, though Euler does not devote the same amount of attention to developing his ontology as do Leibniz or Wolff.

In sum, two of the most influential "Newtonians" at the Berlin Academy of Sciences are far less Newtonian than one might naturally think, at least when it comes to the laws of motion. Maupertuis's "discovery" of the principle of least action forces him to reject Newton's second law as a substantive principle as well as the forces underlying it. Maupertuis's

---

[52] This is not to say that Euler's account at this point is without difficulty. In fact, he seems to recognize some of the difficulties of such an account, e.g., when he has to introduce further qualities (such as elasticity) in his explanation of the laws of impact.

The Laws of Motion from Newton to Kant 107

skepticism about the ultimate nature of bodies prohibits him from offering any ontological account of bodies as well as any non-empirical justification of the laws of motion (thereby distancing him from the Wolffians), but the theological implications of his principle of least action reveal his interest in the metaphysical implications of his account of physics. Despite the fact that Euler might appear very Newtonian on the surface (or even in much of his work), it becomes clear on closer inspection that his attitude is at best broadly Newtonian given his differences from Newton in some of his other work. In particular, Euler sees the need to provide an ontological account of forces in terms of the nature of bodies, an account that is more similar to Wolff's interests than it is to Newton's, though Euler vehemently opposes the specific account Wolff provides in terms of simple elements. Accordingly, both Maupertuis and Euler as two of the primary specialists in rational mechanics at the Berlin Academy of Sciences pursue interests that either are at odds with or extend well beyond Newton's main project in the *Principia*.

5.4 Physics Textbooks

A third context in which Newton's laws of motion are discussed is that of the physics textbooks that were used in university curricula at the time. Since the laws of motion form a fundamental part of mechanics, which in turn is a central component of physics, it would be natural to expect Newton's laws of motion (or alternate formulations) to be presented and then perhaps be used to derive the law of universal gravitation. While it is impossible to consider all or even a majority of the textbooks used in eighteenth-century Germany in this context, it is possible to consider several of the most popular ones that Kant either explicitly refers to in his writings or uses in his own physics lectures. Accordingly, I briefly consider physics textbooks written by Wolff, s'Gravesande, Musschenbroek, Erxleben, and Karsten. As is the case with the metaphysics textbooks discussed earlier as well as with the work of Maupertuis and Euler, the fundamental aims of these physics textbooks are significantly different from Newton's in the *Principia*.

Before turning to the specific authors mentioned above, it is important to understand the nature of physics in general and the relation between physics and applied mathematics in particular in Germany in the eighteenth century.[53] For both the nature of physics and the distinction between physics and applied mathematics underwent significant and

---

[53] For a helpful account of the various shifts that physics (and physics textbooks) underwent throughout this period, see Gunter Lind, *Physik im Lehrbuch 1700–1850* (Springer: Berlin, 1992).

108   The Laws of Mechanics

non-uniform change during this period. Consider first Christian Wolff's treatment of "physics" in the 1730s.[54] We have already seen that he discusses the nature of the world in his metaphysics textbook and in his rational cosmology. However, he also retains a scholastic distinction between physics proper and applied mathematics, according to which the former deals with the causes of real objects while the latter considers abstract features of objects (i.e., features that do not pertain to bodies per se). Accordingly, he discusses the efficient and final causes of bodies in what is often referred to as the *German Physics*, his *Vernünfftige Gedancken von den Würckungen der Natur* (first published in Halle in 1723), and in his so-called *German Teleology*, *Vernünfftige Gedancken von den Absichten der natürlichen Dinge* (first published in Halle in 1724). He treats of the abstract, mathematical features of bodies in his *Anfangsgründe aller mathematischen Wissenschaften* (first published in Halle in 1710), which forms the main content for a Latin edition entitled *Elementa Matheseos* (first published in Halle in 1715).[55] In these works on applied mathematics Wolff discusses arithmetic, geometry, architecture, artillery, fortification, hydrostatics, aerometry, hydraulics, along with mechanics.[56] Thus, what we understand physics to be is divided into three separate areas: metaphysics (insofar as it includes rational cosmology), physics proper (or in the narrow sense), and applied mathematics. While Wolff may be clear about the relations between metaphysics and physics proper, he is less forthcoming about the relations between these two topics and applied mathematics, so that his treatment of what we might call physics lacks a clear principle of unity.[57]

By the time of Wenceslaw Johann Gustav Karsten's *Anleitung zur gemeinnützlichen Kenntniß der Natur* (published in Halle in 1783), physics textbooks tend to reject Wolff's formal principle of division between physics and applied mathematics as well as Newton's emphasis on the latter.[58] For they are primarily concerned with specific physical

---

[54] Lind's discussion of Wolff is particularly helpful (*Physik im Lehrbuch* pp. 91ff., 99ff., 102–7).

[55] Wolff discusses "experimental physics" in Christian Wolff, *Allerhand nützliche Versuche dadurch zu genauer Erkantnis der Natur und Kunst der Weg gebahnet wird* (Halle, 1721), collecting numerous experiments into three volumes.

[56] In the mechanics section Wolff does not discuss the most general laws of motion (as stated in his *Cosmologia Generalis*) insofar as his concern is merely with giving mathematically correct kinematic descriptions of the behavior of bodies in a wide variety of situations.

[57] Lind (*Physik im Lehrbuch*, p. 101) argues that Wolff is best seen as an eclectic in physics.

[58] Lind (*Physik im Lehrbuch*, p. 127ff.) notes that as the century progresses authors of physics textbooks become critical of both Wolff and Newton. In particular, Newton's mathematical explanations (qua applied mathematics) are criticized for not being real or physical explanations.

The Laws of Motion from Newton to Kant 109

phenomena such as air, water, light, warmth and coldness, electricity, and several other basic elements.[59] In fact, Karsten explicitly asserts that the relations between physics and applied mathematics are problematic. What Karsten dislikes about the way that applied mathematics is treated in physics is that the extensive mathematics involved in applied mathematics pushes chemistry out of physics textbooks, despite the fact that chemistry, unlike applied mathematics, is a genuine part of physics.[60] He also complains that applied mathematics considers only the measure of the effects, rather than the essential properties, of bodies.[61] Karsten's general conception of physics holds that it consists equally in physics (in the narrow sense of explaining only the most general features of bodies on the basis of their inner, essential properties), chemistry, and natural history. He explicitly rejects giving priority to physics in the narrow sense over natural history and chemistry, because he claims that we do not have sufficient knowledge of the inner nature of bodies to allow a derivation of their more specific features as treated in natural history and chemistry. Rather, experience and experiments are the primary source of our knowledge of bodies.[62] Later, in the first section of his *Anleitung*, Karsten raises further criticisms, the most serious of which is that applied mathematics gives the erroneous impression that the kind of evidence available in mathematics holds for physics as well.[63] Accordingly, insofar as Karsten's attitude is standard for the time, it is clear that physics textbooks aim at a more comprehensive empirical explanation of the more specific properties of bodies rather than a precise (Newtonian) mathematical formulation of the behavior of point forces in a variety of media. The laws of motion also do not seem to deserve a privileged place in such textbooks and thus Newton's detailed derivation of the law of universal gravitation could not be a central topic.

Newton's reception in Germany is heavily influenced by the physics textbooks of two Dutch Newtonians, Willem Jacob van s'Gravesande

---

[59] The fourth edition of Erxleben's *Anfangsgründe der Naturlehre* (published in 1787) is similar in nature. For the bulk of his discussion is devoted to air, light, warmth and coldness, electricity, and magnetism (though he does provide a brief introduction to physics ('*Naturlehre*') and a general explanation of "several" general properties of bodes as well as motion).

[60] Karsten's *Anleitung* is reprinted in the Akademie Ausgabe of Kant's works. This point is made at 29:173.

[61] 29:174.

[62] Lind (*Physik im Lehrbuch*, pp. 132ff.) also notes a stronger emphasis on experience and experiment later in the eighteenth century.

[63] 29:193.

110   The Laws of Mechanics

and Pieter van Musschenbroek.[64] s'Gravesande published several text-books introducing Newtonian philosophy, *Mathematical Elements of Natural Philosophy Confirmed by Experiments or an Introduction to Sir Isaac Newton's Philosophy* (translated into English by J. T. Desaguliers, second edition published in London in 1721)[65] and *Philosophiae Newtonianae Institutiones: in usus academicos Philosophiae Newtonianae institutiones* (published in Leiden in 1723). Despite his clear intentions as indicated by its title, s'Gravesande's *Mathematical Elements* departs from Newton's account regarding the laws of motion in two interesting ways. First, s'Gravesande is concerned with the intelligibility of the laws of motion in a way that Newton is not. Second, the position that the laws of motion occupy within his overall account is different from their position in Newton's account.

s'Gravesande is especially concerned with the intelligibility of the law of inertia. After stating Newton's law of inertia, he continues:

A Body also being once in motion, continues in Motion according to the same Direction, in the same Right Line, and with the same Velocity, as we see by daily Experience; for we never see any Change made in Motion, but from some Cause. But (since Motion is a continual Change of Place) how motion in the second Moment of Time should flow from the Motion in the first, and what should be the Cause of the Continuation of Motion, appears wholly unknown to me; but as it is a certain Phaenomenon, we must look upon it as a Law of Nature.[66]

What is of interest here is the fact that s'Gravesande is concerned with how a body can continue to be in motion over time. More specifically, he thinks that there should be some fuller explanation or cause for the continued motion of a body not acted on externally. s'Gravesande admits his ignorance of the cause of the continuation of a body's motion. Accordingly, he seems to recognize that the law of inertia is derived solely from experience, that we lack any rational account (e.g., in terms of the fundamental properties of bodies) of *why* the law is true, and that the lack of such an account is a real deficiency. While the kind of justification

[64] Andreas Kleinert, "Mathematik und anorganische Naturwissenschaften," in *Wissenschaften im Zeitalter der Aufklärung*, ed. Rudolf Vierhaus (Göttingen: Vandenhoek and Ruprecht, 1985), pp. 218–48, p. 220, reports that both Voltaire and Frederick the Great became familiar with Newton through s'Gravesande's *Mathematical Elements*.

[65] In support of the previous point, s'Gravesande notes in the preface to the *Mathematical Elements* that radically different doctrines go under the name of physics. So even early in the eighteenth century "physics" lacks any agreed-on unity.

[66] Willem Jacob van s'Gravesande, *Mathematical Elements of Natural Philosophy Confirmed by Experiments or an Introduction to Sir Isaac Newton's Philosophy*, second edition, trans. John Theophilus Desaguliers (London, 1721), pp. 49–50.

The Laws of Motion from Newton to Kant 111

s'Gravesande desires may not be exactly the same as Wolff's, it is also significantly stronger than what Newton seems to be satisfied with.

Despite the fact that the laws of motion must be derived empirically for s'Gravesande as for Newton,[67] they are not situated at the beginning of the book. Rather, they are stated only after s'Gravesande has already discussed a number of other issues. For example, Part One (Of Body in General) discusses (chapter 1) the scope of natural philosophy, (chapter 2) the nature of body, (chapter 3) extension, solidity, and the vacuum, (chapter 4) the infinite divisibility of body, and (chapter 5) cohesion, which includes hardness, softness, fluidity, and elasticity. Part Two then discusses a wide array of other issues (e.g., the comparison of the actions of powers, gravity, levers, pulleys, wedges and screws, wheels with teeth, and compound engines) before finally stating briefly Newton's laws of motion. Nor does what follows the statement of the laws of motion coincide to any great extent with Newton's project. In the dedication to Newton, the translator explains what he thinks this work should accomplish:

And as there are more Admirers of your wonderful discoveries, than there are Mathematicians able to understand the two first Books of your *Principia*: So I hope you will not be displeased, that both my author and myself have, by Experiments, endeavored to explain some of those Propositions, which were implicitely believed by many of your Readers ... And through [*sic*] some of ours [experiments] may not always prove, but sometimes only illustrate a Proposition; yet such Mathematicians as are of a communicative Temper will be glad to use them, as a new Set of Words, to give Beginners so clear a Notion of the System of the World, as to encourage them to the Study of higher Geometry; whereby they may know how to value your Solutions of the most difficult Phaenomena, and learn from You, that a whole Science may be contain'd in a single Proposition.[68]

This statement of purpose reveals that this textbook does not intend to provide Newton's derivation of the law of universal gravitation. Rather, it hopes to give the reader a "clear Notion" of Newton's worldview by illustrating (rather than proving) some of his principles by experiments. Accordingly, even in an ardent follower of Newton, as an author of a physics textbook s'Gravesande pursues a project that is significantly different from (though not at odds with) Newton's in the *Principia*.

Musschenbroek's textbook, *Elementa Physicae* (initially published in Leiden in 1734), is translated into German by Johann Christoph

---

[67] "And here we must reason from Phaenomena, (as one must do in all Natural Philosophy) and from them deduce the Laws of Nature" (*Mathematical Elements*, p. 49).

[68] *Mathematical Elements*, pp. ii–iii.

112   The Laws of Mechanics

Gottsched as *Grundlehren der Naturwissenschaft, nach der zweiten latei-nischen Ausgabe* (published in 1747 in Leipzig) and thereby gains a significant readership in Germany.[69] Gottsched notes in the translator's preface that despite the fact that Musschenbroek is heavily indebted to "the example of the great Newton ... [he] retains for himself a noble philosophical freedom," siding, for example, with Leibniz against the Newtonians in the vis viva controversy.[70] More importantly, Musschen-broek is even further from Newton regarding the laws of motion than is s'Gravesande, since Musschenbroek does not even state Newton's laws of motion. At a general level Musschenbroek's "Newtonianism" would seem to amount to an agreement with Newton's rules of philosophizing, an empiricist approach coupled with skepticism about the ultimate nature of bodies and an acceptance of a broadly Newtonian ontology of absolute space and time with atoms exhibiting impenetrability, exten-sion, inertia, and gravity.[71] His primary goal in the *Grundlehren der Naturwissenschaft* is simply a clear exposition of a variety of different physical phenomena, not an extended argument for the law of universal gravitation on the basis of laws of motion and Kepler's empirical regularities.

Erxleben's *Anfangsgründe der Naturlehre* (originally published in Göt-tingen in 1772) is one of the most popular physics textbooks in the second half of the eighteenth century in Germany, republished in numer-ous editions with substantial revisions and even many additions by Lichtenberg after Erxleben's death.[72] His approach is broadly empiricist in nature, leaving several questions about the fundamental properties of bodies to be decided by future investigation (e.g., the extent of the divisibility of bodies), though his own account is generally close to Newton's (despite a rejection of absolutely hard atoms). His treatment of the laws of motion is brief and relatively undistinguished. He does not highlight the laws of motion (e.g., by devoting a chapter to the topic). Rather, after explaining some of the fundamental concepts underlying motion he states the law of inertia. He then suggests that experience must not contradict the law and that it is ultimately nothing other than the

---

[69] Kant's library contained a copy of this German translation and he refers to Musschenbroek in *The True Estimation of Living Forces* (1747) as well as in the *Attempt to Introduce the Concept of Negative Magnitudes into Philosophy* (1763).

[70] Pieter van Musschenbroek, *Grundlehren der Naturwissenschaft, nach der zweiten latei-nischen Ausgabe*, trans. Johann Christoph Gottsched (Leipzig, 1747), unpaginated.

[71] I characterize Musschenbroek's position as "broadly Newtonian" because he seems to accept views Newton is reluctant to commit himself to in any unambiguous way.

[72] For a discussion of physics textbooks in general and Erxleben's textbook in particular, see William Clark, "German Physics Textbooks in the Goethezeit, Parts 1 and 2," *History of Science* 35 (1997): 219–39 and 295–363.

The Laws of Motion from Newton to Kant

principle of sufficient reason applied to the change of state of a body. He does, however, note a series of critical questions about inertia: "Does a body need a force in order to remain what it is? Can one think of a force that never acts of its own accord, but rather only resists? That has no intrinsic magnitude, but rather one that is large or small according to what it resists?"[73] Instead of providing answers to these questions, he turns to consider the explanations others have provided, rejecting both Euler's position, according to which inertia could be derived from impenetrability, and Gordon's view, that inertia is identical to gravity.

In the middle of his discussion of inertia, Erxleben does briefly posit the law of the equality of action and reaction. However, he provides no justification for this law and nowhere in the surrounding text does he state Newton's second law. Rather, he describes how bodies behave in the simplest kinds of impact. Although the following chapter considers statics and mechanics, at no point does he attempt anything like Newton's derivation in the *Principia*. Nor should this absence be surprising, given his stated aim in the Preface:

Since of the majority of those who listen to a lecture course on physics at the university some do not have the intention of becoming more familiar with the finer points of physics and others begin to study this science without the requisite mathematical knowledge, I have always used only the simplest mathematics in explaining physical doctrines and preferred not even to mention those that presuppose more mathematics ... Those who are not prepared with the mathematical knowledge necessary to learn physics in the appropriate manner can still be taught a lot of useful and pleasing knowledge from physics, though not the entire science or the proof of various propositions, which they must simply take on faith without being truly convinced of their correctness.[74]

Accordingly, Erxleben's goal is simply to present a sampling of knowledge about physics insofar as that is possible without presupposing much mathematical background in his audience. The views he presents may (or may not) be compatible with Newton's proofs, but he clearly recognizes that what he is doing is not the same as Newton's project.

In sum, while any generalization about physics textbooks in eighteenth-century Germany will surely have notable exceptions, it is clear that as the century progresses the task of physics textbooks becomes more and more a non-mathematical explanation of the physical properties of various kinds of bodies. It is also striking that even staunch Newtonians (such as Musschenbroek and s'Gravesande) do not emphasize Newton's

---

[73] Johann Christian Polykarp Erxleben, *Anfangsgründe der Naturlehre* (Göttingen, 1772 [first edition], 1787 [fourth edition]), pp. 45–6.

[74] Erxleben, *Anfangsgründe der Naturlehre*, p. xiv.

114   The Laws of Mechanics

laws of motion. Accordingly, while such textbooks may be compatible with the fundamental results of Newton's *Principia*, it is clear that their principal aims are fundamentally distinct insofar as they pursue a variety of projects for a variety of ends.

5.5   The Context for Kant's Laws of Mechanics

We can summarize the various views presented above that illustrate how Newton's laws of motion were received in eighteenth-century Germany, in the following main points. First, Newton's formulations of the laws of motion are rarely accepted in precisely his words. Rather, the formulations, and their content too, differ to varying degrees. In fact, Newton's second law is most often omitted or even rejected outright.

Second, many of these figures are interested in providing an ontology for natural science. Insofar as Newton's *Principia* is a treatise in mathematics, it does not emphasize the ontological presuppositions or implications of its mathematical principles. Since mathematics is still often thought of at the time as pertaining only to abstract imaginary entities of the mind, providing an ontology for natural science remedies a serious omission in Newton's account.

Third, the majority of the figures discussed above attempt to give some kind of justification of the laws of motion, though they diverge considerably with respect to the kind of justification they thought necessary (or possible). The Wolffians tend to provide non-empirical or logical derivations. Their most common strategy was to show how the laws of motion can be derived from more fundamental ontological principles, which should, ultimately, be derivable from the principles of contradiction and sufficient reason. Maupertuis and Euler both seem to prefer a more empirical justification of the law(s) of motion, though Euler does attempt to justify the law of inertia through (a seemingly Wolffian) recourse to the principle of sufficient reason. The authors of physics textbooks (especially later in the century) adopt a more empirical approach, and are not especially interested in justifying the laws of motion either systematically or mathematically, since they seem satisfied with illustrating such laws by means of experiments that could be performed in a classroom laboratory.

Taken together, these differences suggest that these figures undertake projects that differ significantly from Newton's. Insofar as Newton states laws of motion that are used to derive the law of universal gravitation by means of their empirical application to Kepler's "laws," these particular laws of motion are central to his project and it would be quite difficult to put others in their place. This difficulty reveals the importance of the differences we identified in the formulations of the laws of motion,

The Laws of Motion from Newton to Kant 115

differences that might otherwise appear insignificant. Insofar as the treatises in which the laws of motion are discussed are works of metaphysics or physics rather than mathematics, it is clear that either a fundamental ontology or a clear account of the principal properties of bodies must be developed rather than an abstract, formalized set of mathematical equations. Accordingly, the projects these figures undertake, despite their diversity, differ from Newton's project.[75]

So what new light do these main points shed on Kant's Laws of Mechanics (and on his project in the *Metaphysical Foundations* as a whole)? First, earlier we noticed a number of differences between Newton's laws of motion and Kant's Laws of Mechanics. While one might initially have thought that these differences were merely apparent, it is now clear that given the diversity of projects pursued by his predecessors Kant would not have felt constrained to adopt uncritically either Newton's laws of motion or, for that matter, his fundamental project. Specifically, the fact that Kant does not mention Newton's second law is not surprising, but rather to be expected, given that this law is absent from almost all discussions of the laws of motion in Germany prior to Kant. Kant's explicit concern with a conservation law (about which Newton is silent) ties in naturally with issues involved in the vis viva debate rather than with any Newtonian concern.[76] Even what might have seemed at first glance to be obviously taken from Newton, namely, the law of the equality of action and reaction, could easily stem from Leibniz (as it did for Thümmig) rather than Newton. In short, we cannot simply assume that Kant's Laws of Mechanics are identical to Newton's laws of motion and that any differences are merely terminological. Instead, we must take Kant's formulations of his Laws of Mechanics seriously on their own terms.

Second, given the historical views presented above along with the fact that Kant's project is formulated as providing "metaphysical foundations of natural science," it should not be surprising if it turns out that he is interested in providing an ontology for natural science (or at least for physics). His conservation law clearly reflects his concern to provide a

---

[75] One line of inquiry that would need to be investigated for a more complete picture would consider the pre-Critical Kant's reception of Newton. For example, for a discussion of how the pre-Critical Kant is both a Newtonian and an anti-Newtonian with respect to the laws of mechanics, see Eric Watkins, "The Early Kant's (Anti-) Newtonianism," *Studies in History and Philosophy of Science* 44 (2012): 429–37. See also Martin Schönfeld, *The Philosophy of the Young Kant: The Pre-Critical Project* (New York: Oxford University Press, 2000).

[76] Kant still seems to adhere to his previous solution to the problem (as developed in his *Thoughts on the True Estimation of Living Forces* from 1747), though he now thinks the issue is far less important than his principle of the conservation of the quantity of matter.

116   The Laws of Mechanics

more adequate ontology for the communication of motion, by indicating that the quantity of matter does not change in the communication of motion even if forces were (somehow) to be transferred from one body to another in the communication of motion.[77] Kant's statement of the law of inertia, which deviates in certain respects from Newton's, is characteristic of at least Wolff and his followers and is similarly indicative of his concern with providing an adequate ontology for natural science. Thus, the views discussed above suggest that we must be open to a range of ontological commitments in interpreting Kant's Laws of Mechanics.

Third, Kant is clearly concerned to provide a justification of his Laws of Mechanics. The question that emerges from taking the historical context into account is whether Kant's justification is empirical, like Newton's (or even Maupertuis's), or non-empirical, like the Wolffians'. Most of the figures discussed earlier who were interested in providing a justification of the laws of motion, and especially the metaphysically inclined Wolffians, attempt some kind of non-empirical justification. If it is plausible to view Kant as influenced by the rationalist tradition in which he was educated, his justification of the Laws of Mechanics is not likely to be empirical in any Newtonian sense. Yet Kant's justification cannot be exactly like that of the Wolffians insofar as he comes to reject (as dogmatic) Wolff's basic principles in favor of considerations that make experience (and synthetic a priori cognition) possible. As we have seen in Chapter 4 in this book, Kant develops broadly transcendental arguments in support of the basic principles of natural science, including the Laws of Mechanics.[78] But note that even transcendental arguments can be ontological in an important sense. While Kant's method of argumentation employs as a criterion for intelligibility "construction in intuition a priori" (where "a priori intuition" is a technical term denoting the formal means by which we have cognitive access to objects), many of the constraints that he places on such constructions could still be ontological in nature. Kant's "critical turn" thus need not eliminate ontological considerations, even as it adds broadly epistemological or cognitive factors. Accordingly, the views of Kant's predecessors suggest that we should be open to a range of different kinds of considerations in determining Kant's justification of his Laws of Mechanics.

But note that all these points, which derive from considering the reception of Newton's laws of motion in Germany in the eighteenth century, form nothing more than an essentially historical and contextual

---

[77] Kant argues against the transfer of either motion or (motive) forces in the communication of motion – a further interest in ontology.

[78] See Chapter 4 in this book for a detailed reconstruction of Kant's arguments.

argument, whose conclusion is at best tentative. Only a detailed interpretation of Kant's three Laws of Mechanics, a reconstruction of the justification he provides for them, and an explanation of the project within which they are situated can establish that they are in fact different from those of Newton's and how. It is to this task that I now turn.[79]

[79] I thank Roger Ariew, Lisa Downing, Mordechai Feingold, Marjorie Grene, Don Howard, and Eric Palmer as well as the audience members of the first annual History of Philosophy of Science conference for their helpful comments on an earlier version of this chapter. I have also benefited from numerous discussions of these topics with Martin Carrier, Michael Friedman, and Ernan McMullin. I also thank the Max Planck Institut für Wissenschaftsgeschichte as well as the National Endowment for the Humanities for their support of this research.

6 Kant's Justification of the Laws of Mechanics

6.1 Introduction

We are now in a position to consider the meaning and justification of Kant's Laws of Mechanics in the Mechanics chapter of the *Metaphysical Foundations*. In the last chapter, we saw that we must take seriously the historical context in which Kant's discussion occurs, since it suggested that his Laws of Mechanics cannot simply be taken to be identical to Newton's laws of motion. One main goal of this chapter is to articulate a detailed interpretation of Kant's Laws of Mechanics that both develops and supports this suggestion further.[1] The second larger aim is to show that such an interpretation is consistent with the account of law presented above in Part I.

Before we turn to these tasks, recall Newton's laws of motion:

> Law I Every body continues in its state of rest, or of uniform motion in a right line, unless it is compelled to change that state by forces impressed upon it.
>
> Law II The change of motion is proportional to the motive force impressed; and is made in the direction of the right line in which that force is impressed.
>
> Law III To every action there is always opposed an equal reaction: or, the mutual actions of two bodies upon each other are always equal, and directed to contrary parts.[2]

---

[1] For further (historical and philosophical) argument for the kind of relation between Newton and Kant that this chapter develops, see Marius Stan, "Kant's Early Theory of Motion," *The Leibniz Review* 19 (2009): 29–60, and "Rebellious Wolffian: Kant's Philosophy of Mechanics in 1758," in *Rethinking Kant*, ed. Oliver Thorndike, vol. 3 (Cambridge: Cambridge Scholars Press, 2011), pp. 158–79. In particular, in these articles Stan argues that the pre-Critical Kant is working out a more Leibnizian and Wolffian dynamics.

[2] Isaac Newton, *Mathematical Principles of Natural Philosophy and His System of the World*, trans. Andrew Mott, revised by Florian Cajori (Berkeley: University of California Press, [1729] 1934), p. 13.

Kant's Justification of the Laws of Mechanics

And also keep in mind Kant's specific formulations of the Laws of Mechanics:

> First Law of Mechanics: In all changes of corporeal nature the total quantity of matter remains the same, neither increased nor diminished.
>
> Second Law of Mechanics: Every change in matter has an external cause. (Every body persists in its state of rest or motion, in the same direction, and with the same speed, if it is not compelled by an external cause to leave this state.)
>
> Third mechanical law: In all communication of motion, action and reaction are always equal to one another. (4:541–4)

We can now consider Kant's treatment of these three Laws of Mechanics in some detail.

6.2   The First Law of Mechanics

It was common among early modern natural philosophers to be interested in establishing a conservation law, and Kant's First Law of Mechanics shows that he is no exception in that regard. However, his interest in the conservation of the quantity of *matter* rather than some kind of *motion* does represent something of a departure from that tradition. Descartes had proposed a conservation law according to which the quantity of motion, measured by speed multiplied by volume, is conserved due to God's immutability.[3] Leibniz, in turn, argued for the inadequacy of Descartes's law by showing that this quantity of motion is not conserved in the case of the free fall of bodies, countering that what he calls living forces, measured by mv^2, are conserved.[4] Considerable debate ensued in the first half of the eighteenth century over whether Descartes's "dead forces" or Leibniz's "living forces" are conserved.[5] In

---

[3] See Descartes's *Principles of Philosophy* II art. 36.

[4] See, for instance, §17 of Leibniz's *Discourse on Metaphysics*.

[5] For extended discussion of the debate, see Ronald S. Calinger, "Frederick the Great and the Berlin Academy of Sciences (1740–1766)," *Annals of Science* 24 (1968): 239–49; Ronald S. Calinger, "The Newtonian-Wolffian Controversy (1741–1759)," *Journal of the History of Ideas* 30 (1969): 319–30; Ronald S. Calinger, "The Newtonian-Wolffian Confrontation in the St. Petersburg Academy of Sciences," *Cahiers d'histoire mondiale* 11 (1968): 417–35; Thomas Hankins, "Eighteenth Century Attempts to Resolve the Vis-Viva Controversy," *Isis* 56 (1965): 281–97; Thomas Hankins, "The Concept of Hard Bodies in the History of Physics," *History of Science* 9 (1970): 119–28; Thomas Hankins, "The Influence of Malebranche on the Science of Mechanics during the 18th Century," *Journal of the History of Ideas* 28 (1967): 193–210; Thomas Hankins, "The Reception of Newton's Second Law of Motion in the 18th Century," *Archives internationales d'histoire des sciences* 20 (1967): 43–65; Thomas Hankins, *Jean d'Alembert: Science and*

120   The Laws of Mechanics

fact, Kant entered the fray in his first publication, *Thoughts on the True Estimation of Living Forces* (1747), arguing for an ambitious, complicated, and ultimately unsuccessful reconciliation of the two positions. Newton, for his part, took Descartes's side, while also acknowledging that, on his account, the universe could slowly be depleted of all motion. Since the universe did not seem to be losing motion in the way his theory allows, he suggested that God could suffuse motion into the world so as to prevent it from coming to a standstill. Kant's First Law of Mechanics thus concerns a slightly different issue. For it is asserting that whatever might change in the communication of motion, the quantity of *matter* must remain the same.[6]

Now, as we saw earlier (in Chapter 4), Kant seeks to justify all three Laws of Mechanics on the grounds that they are conditions of the possibility of our experience of the communication of motion. The First Law of Mechanics can thus be understood as asserting that to experience the communication of motion, one must presuppose that the quantity of matter remains unchanged. That is, if the quantity of matter were not conserved, then we would experience not the *communication* of motion, but rather some other kind of change (e.g., a chemical reaction). Since Kant defines the quantity of motion that is involved in the communication of motion in terms of the speed, direction, and quantity of matter, understanding the First Law of Mechanics requires a basic grasp of these notions. Kant had already discussed both speed and direction in the

---

the Enlightenment (New York: Oxford University Press, 1970); Carolyn Iltis, "D'Alembert and the Vis Viva Controversy," *Studies in the History and Philosophy of Science* 1 (1970): 135–44; Carolyn Iltis, "Leibniz and the Vis Viva Controversy," *Isis* 62 (1971): 21–35; Carolyn Iltis, "Madame du Chatelet's Metaphysics and Mechanics," *Studies in the History and Philosophy of Science* 8 (1977): 29–48; Carolyn Iltis, "The Decline of Cartesian Mechanics: The Leibnizian-Cartesian Debates," *Isis* 64 (1973): 356–73; Carolyn Iltis, "The Leibnizean-Newtonian Debates: Natural Philosophy and Social Psychology," *British Journal for the History of Science* 6 (1972): 341–77; Larry Laudan, "The Vis Viva Controversy: A Post-Mortem," *Isis* 59 (1968): 131–43; and David Papineau, "The Vis Viva Controversy," *Studies in History and Philosophy of Science* 8 (1977): 111–42.

[6] Kant is interested in establishing a conservation law (though one that is distinct from one concerning living or dead forces) as early as his *Negative Magnitudes* essay. He identifies as a first proposition: "In all the natural changes which occur in the world, the sum of what is positive is neither increased nor diminished" (2:194). Shortly thereafter, he goes on to clarify this principle by noting: "the following mechanical rule is firmly established and has long since been proved to be true … *Quantitas motus, summando viers corporum in easdem partes et subtrahendo eas quae vergunt in contrarias, per mutuam illorum actionem (conflictum, pressionem, attractionem) non mutatur.* Although, in pure mechanics, this rule is not derived immediately from the metaphysical ground, from which we have derived the general proposition, its validity does indeed, as a matter of fact, depend on this foundation. For the law of inertia, which is the foundation of the usual proof, derives its truth simply from the argument adduced, as I could easily show, if I could go into the matter in detail" (2:195).

Phoronomy chapter in the context of explaining how one should construct the concept of the composition of two motions. Given the restricted scope of that discussion, he was able to abstract from the quantity of matter and simply consider the motion of points (4:480). Since the Mechanics chapter concerns the communication of motion of bodies with different magnitudes, however, he can no longer consider matter as a point, but must clarify how to understand the quantity of matter.

Because Kant understands the quantity of matter as the quantity of spatial substance, it will be useful to start by briefly clarifying some essential features of his conception of substance. In the First Analogy and in the Schematism chapters in the first *Critique* Kant had already established that substance is not only the ultimate subject of predicates (and bearer of properties) but also "the persistence of the real in time" (A144/B183), where the real involves the "continuous action" (A208/B254) of a force. This fits in with Kant's understanding of substance in general as a permanent thing that is endowed with essential properties (which constitute its nature) and causal powers, the exercise of which can bring about change in the world.[7] Now, in the *Metaphysical Foundations* Kant takes matter to be spatial substance, more specifically, the movable in space, and in Explication 1 of the Mechanics chapter, he then describes matter even more specifically as "the movable insofar as it, as such a thing, has moving force" (4:536). How Kant understands a moving force can be nicely illustrated by billiard balls in impact, a paradigm case of the communication of motion. For in such a case a billiard ball in motion can cause an acceleration in another, whereas a billiard ball at rest cannot, and this difference in effect is due to the fact that in the one case it has a moving force, whereas in the other it does not.[8] Thus, matter insofar as it is a spatial substance that communicates motion must be a permanent and real thing endowed with essential properties and continuously active causal powers, and, in this case, those powers must include a moving force, the force a thing possesses in virtue of its motion.

If matter is conceived of as spatial substance in this way, how is its quantity to be understood? Kant takes up this issue explicitly in Explication 2:

The *quantity of matter* is the aggregate [*Menge*] of the movable in a determinate space. Insofar as all its parts are considered as acting (moving) together in their

---

[7] For more detailed discussion, see Eric Watkins, *Kant and the Metaphysics of Causality* (New York: Cambridge University Press, 2005), especially chapter 4.
[8] For the purposes of this example, I am abstracting from attractive force, just as Kant does.

122   The Laws of Mechanics

motion, it is called *mass*, and one says that a matter *acts in mass*, when all its parts, moved in the same direction, *together* exert their moving force externally. (4:538)

Kant is giving expression to two main thoughts in this Explication. One is the idea that the quantity of matter is determined by those substances in a determinate region in space that are acting (in a way that will be specified further shortly). The more substance acting in a given region, the greater the quantity of matter. At the same time, it is essential to note that because Kant accepts the infinite divisibility of matter, he cannot simply equate the quantity of matter with the number of substances in a given region, as there would be a potentially infinite number of substances in any given body and the quantity of matter would be the same, regardless of the how much spatial substance is present. The first sentence in the quotation thus cannot be his last word on the matter.

The second main thought Kant is giving expression to in this quotation is the idea, familiar in this period, that the quantity of matter depends on its mass. In the context of the communication of motion, Kant's conception of mass is necessarily connected to those parts of matter that are *acting with their moving force*, not to those that are not acting at all nor to those that are acting in some other way. For example, if a billiard ball were made out of magnetic material, its *magnetic* forces would not make any difference in the acceleration its moving force would cause in a second billiard ball in impact (provided that the second ball is not made of metal), since the acceleration of the second ball is determined by all the acting parts of the aggregate insofar as they "*together* exert their moving force externally." This is not to say that matter cannot *have* forces other than moving forces, but rather only that they are irrelevant to determining the quantity of matter in the communication of motion.

Though Kant conceives of the first two Explications in the Mechanics chapter as building up to Proposition 1, which concerns how to devise a universal measure of the quantity of matter, we can turn directly to Kant's official proof of the First Law of Mechanics, which *appears* to be relatively straightforward:

(From general metaphysics we presuppose the proposition [*wird der Satz zum Grund gelegt*] that in all changes of nature no substance either arises or perishes, and here it is shown only what substance is in matter.) In every matter the movable in space is the ultimate subject of all accidents inherent in matter, and the aggregate [*Menge*] of the movable, external to one another, is the quantity of substance. Hence the magnitude of matter, with respect to its substance, is nothing else but the aggregate of substances of which it consists. Therefore, the quantity of matter cannot be increased or diminished except in such a way that new substance thereof arises or perishes. Now substance never arises or perishes in any change of matter; so the quantity of matter is also neither increased nor diminished thereby, but remains always the same. (4:542)

Kant's Justification of the Laws of Mechanics 123

Kant's argument has the following structure. He starts by assuming, from the First Analogy, that substance does not arise or perish. He then specifies what is substance in matter, namely, the movable in space (since the movable in space is the ultimate subject of the relevant accidents, namely, motion and rest). But if the quantity of spatial substance is to be conceived of as the aggregate, sum, or number of the substances of which it consists, then it follows immediately that the quantity of matter must be the aggregate, sum, or number of the movables in space that he had just identified as the substance in matter. But then it might seem to follow as well that the only way for the quantity of matter to change would be if the number of spatial substances in matter were to change. Given the initial assumption that no substance arises or perishes, however, the number of spatial substances and thus the quantity of matter cannot change either, which is precisely what the First Law of Mechanics asserts.[9]

Though this statement of Kant's proof is faithful to the way he expresses it, it obscures the genuinely controversial point that is at issue. For this presentation makes it appear as if its central assumption is that substance cannot arise or perish; given that assumption, it can seem to follow immediately that spatial substance cannot arise or perish (since no substance can), and that the quantity of matter must therefore be conserved (since the quantity of matter just is the quantity of spatial substances, which cannot arise or perish). But if the First Analogy justifies the sole weight-bearing assumption in this argument, then nothing fundamentally new is being asserted in the First Law of Mechanics, and precisely this view of things is suggested by the remark: "Here it is shown only what substance is in matter." However, we have already seen that the quantity of matter cannot be judged simply by counting the number of substances that are present. So determining the quantity of matter is more complicated than Kant's official proof seems to suggest. What's more, we have seen that Kant views moving forces as important to the quantity of matter. But how?

In his Remark to the proof, Kant is a bit more explicit about the crucial issue. There he notes:

What is essential in this proof to the characterization of the *substance* that is possible only in space and in accordance with its condition, thus only as object of the *outer* senses, is that [1] its magnitude cannot be increased or diminished without substance arising or perishing, because [2] every magnitude of an object possible merely in space must consist of *parts external to one another*, which [3], consequently, if they are real (something movable), must necessarily be

---

[9] In the B-edition First Analogy (B224), Kant adds the claim that the quantum of substance in nature can be neither increased nor diminished.

124   The Laws of Mechanics

substances. By contrast, that which is considered as object of inner sense can, as substance, have a magnitude, which [~2] *does not consist of parts external to one another*, and whose parts [~3], therefore, are not substances, [~1] whose arising or perishing need also not be the arising or perishing of a substance whose augmentation or diminution, for that reason, is possible without compromising the principle of the persistence of substance. (4:542)

Here we see Kant both clarifying the issue that he sees the argument as turning on (in addition to the permanence of substance), and what his reasoning for it is. In [1], he is stating one assumption that we have already seen to be crucial to his argument, namely, that the quantity of matter cannot be increased or diminished unless substance arises or perishes. But here he sees the need to argue for this assumption and he does so by asserting two new claims: [2] that the magnitude of a spatial substance (i.e. of a substance that is possible only in space) must consist of parts external to one another, and [3] that the parts of a spatial substance that are external to one another must themselves be substances.[10]

In the second half of the quotation, Kant clarifies his argument by way of a contrast with objects of inner sense, which are obviously not spatial substances. For given that such objects are not spatially extended, [~2] they cannot consist of parts external to one another, and because whatever parts they might have are not external to one another, [~3] these parts are also not substances.[11] As a result, [~1] these parts could arise or perish without entailing the arising or perishing of the substance whose parts they are, for which reason the quantity of such a substance could increase or diminish.

Though this contrast case is certainly illuminating, one might still wonder: Why should it make any difference to the quantity of matter whether a substance's parts are substances external to one another? Here it is useful to recall Kant's position in the *Physical Monadology*.[12] There he maintains that what he calls physical monads fill a space only through the exercise of their attractive and repulsive forces. In other words,

---

[10] Kant adds the qualification "if they are real," which suggests that the parts of objects of inner sense might not be "real." However, the parts of matter must be real because the parts of matter are divisible into substances that are spatial, that is, are movable in space.

[11] It may not be obvious why the parts of an object of inner sense could not be substances. If spatial composition were the only relation that a plurality of substances could have, this claim would follow, but there could, it seems, be other relations between such substances.

[12] Michael Friedman provides clarification of some of the issues at stake by contrasting the "mechanical" concept of the quantity of matter with two "dynamical" concepts in *Kant's Construction of Nature: A Reading of the* Metaphysical Foundations of Natural Science (Cambridge: Cambridge University Press, 2013), pp. 180–94.

Kant's Justification of the Laws of Mechanics 125

physical monads are not themselves extended, but fill space only through their sphere of activity. The advantage Kant derives from conceiving of physical monads as non-extended, but their sphere of activity as extended, is that it allows him to reconcile the infinite divisibility of space with the absolute indivisibility of metaphysically simple substances or monads. For while the effect of a monad's activity might be infinitely divisible, the monad itself is a point and thus must be indivisible. Further, what determines the amount of space that a given monad fills is the strength or degree of the forces that the monad possesses.

Later, in the first *Critique*, Kant will explicitly distinguish between extensive and intensive magnitudes such that for an extensive magnitude the properties of the whole are determined by the properties of the parts, whereas for an intensive magnitude the properties of the whole are not determined by the properties of the parts but are "apprehended only as unity" (A168/B210).[13] For example, volume is an extensive magnitude, whereas a property like color is an intensive magnitude. Since a physical monad is not itself spatially extended, it has no spatially distinct parts in terms of which its magnitude could be explained. As a result, its magnitude must be intensive and is determined by the strength or degree of its forces.

Now the fact that a physical monad has an intensive rather than an extensive magnitude entails that it cannot perish through *division* since it has no spatially distinct parts that could be divided. However, it could seem to do so through *diminution*. As Kant points out against Mendelssohn in the first *Critique*, the soul might cease to exist, not by perishing through division – the soul likewise has no spatially extended parts that could be divided – but rather because it could vanish through the gradual remission of its degree of consciousness, a process he refers to as "elanguescence" (B414). Something analogous would seem to be true of physical monads; they could, it would seem, disappear entirely as the strength of their forces recedes into oblivion.

This background allows us to see more clearly the central question in Kant's discussion of the conservation of the quantity of matter. If Kant's own physical monads from the *Physical Monadology* or Mendelssohn's souls could perish by vanishing slowly over time, why could matter not perish in the same way? As we saw above, Kant sees important differences between matter and either physical monads or objects of inner sense (such as Mendelssohn's souls). Matter has parts that are themselves spatial substances, whereas physical monads and objects of inner

---

[13] Baumgarten and Meier also distinguish between extensive and intensive magnitudes. Accordingly, even in his pre-Critical period Kant has such a distinction at his disposal.

126   The Laws of Mechanics

sense do not. As a result, the quantity of matter can be an extensive magnitude, since its magnitude can be explained on the basis of its spatially extended parts, whereas the magnitude of a physical monad or an object of inner sense must be an intensive magnitude.

In this context, it is instructive to consider how Kant understands the infinite divisibility of matter (since it directly contrasts with the physical monadologist's account). In the passage following Proposition 4 in the Dynamics chapter, where he presents his formal proof of the infinite divisibility of matter, Kant notes:

Matter is impenetrable, through its original force of extension (Prop. 3). But this is only a consequence of the repulsive forces of each point in a space filled with matter. Now, the space filled by matter is mathematically divisible to infinity, that is, its parts can be distinguished to infinity, although they cannot be moved and thus cannot be divided (according to geometrical proofs). But in a space filled with matter, every part of it contains repulsive force, so as to counteract all the rest on all sides, and thus to repel them and to be repelled by them, that is, to be moved a distance from them. Hence, every part of a space filled with matter is in itself movable, and thus separable from the rest as material substance by physical division. Therefore, the possible physical division of the substance that fills space reaches as far as the mathematical divisibility of the space filled by matter. But this mathematical divisibility extends to infinity, and thus so does the physical [divisibility] as well. That is, all matter is divisible to infinity and, in fact, into parts such that each is itself material substance in turn. (4:503–4)

In the first observation following this proof, Kant remarks that "the proof of the infinite divisibility of space has not yet come close to proving the infinite divisibility of matter" (4:504), and then raises the possibility of the physical monadologist who admits infinite *mathematical* divisibility, but not infinite *physical* divisibility.[14]

Kant then explains how the above proof is supposed to work against a physical monadologist:

For it is thereby clear that in a filled space there can be no point that does not exert repulsion in all directions, and is itself repelled, and thus would be movable in itself, as a reacting subject external to every other repelling point. Hence the hypothesis of a point that would fill a space through mere driving force, and not by means of other equally repelling forces, is completely impossible. (4:504)

The intent of Kant's argument is clearly to show not only that matter is infinitely divisible but also that matter's divisibility cannot be explained as the physical monadologist would, but rather such that, at each step, matter must be divided into parts that are themselves spatial substances.

---

[14] Although Kant makes no explicit mention of it in this passage, Descartes appears to be one of his targets when he distinguishes between mathematical and physical divisibility.

Kant's Justification of the Laws of Mechanics 127

But how exactly does Kant's argument proceed? The background provided by Kant's immediate predecessors provides some helpful context. In the 1730s and 1740s one of the most important issues for Leibnizians and Wolffians was to determine the precise relationship between monads (or simple elements) and bodies.[15] Leibniz's position on the issue is that bodies and their motions are well-founded phenomena, implying that monads are responsible for bodies and their motions, but he rejects the idea that one could provide a detailed (e.g., scientific) explanation of the specific ways in which the motions of bodies could be derived from monads.[16] Wolff, by contrast, hopes to provide specific explanations of the ways in which the simple elements relate to bodies, but struggles to articulate a clear and consistent position. Certain Wolffians, such as Kant's teacher, Martin Knutzen, pose critical questions about this relationship, at times coming to conclusions radically different from Leibniz's and Wolff's. For example, Knutzen argues that monads must be able to act on other monads (*pace* pre-established harmony) because they have the power both to move their own bodies and to resist the penetration of other bodies.[17] That is, Knutzen's view turns on considerations that pertain directly to the relationship between monads and bodies. Given that this relationship underwent such careful scrutiny during his formative years, it is natural that Kant would focus on it as well.

In light of this context, we can see that in his argument for the infinite divisibility of matter, Kant is concerned with understanding how one body could be repulsed by another in virtue of their forces. More specifically, he is at pains to show that a physical monadologist cannot give an explanation of how a physical monad can fill a space through repulsion that is consistent with the infinite divisibility of space. The reason for the inconsistency lies in the fact that the physical monadologist is committed to the following four claims about how a physical monad fills a space. First, for any space that a physical monad fills, it fills this space through the *exercise* of its repulsive force. Second, a physical monad fills a space by

---

[15] For a more detailed account of this issue, see Eric Watkins, "On the Necessity and Nature of Simples: Leibniz, Wolff, Baumgarten, and the Pre-Critical Kant," *Oxford Studies in Early Modern Philosophy* 3 (2006): 261–314.

[16] Leibniz presents his views on this matter in, e.g., *Specimen dynamicum* (1695).

[17] Such an argument is controversial insofar as Leibniz and Wolff both reject the claim that monads (or simple elements) can act on each other. Nor could Leibniz and Wolff resolve the issue simply by denying that monads have the power of impenetrability, for that would make it difficult to see how monads are responsible for the phenomena. For a more detailed discussion of the ways in which Knutzen and others discuss the relationship between monads and bodies, see Watkins, *Kant and the Metaphysics of Causality*, chapter 1.

128   The Laws of Mechanics

acting on all the physical monads that fill the spaces that *immediately surround* the space it fills (namely, by exercising its repulsive force on them). Third, it is impossible that a physical monad fill a determinate space unless it also fills the *smaller spaces* into which that determinate space can be divided. (Since space is infinitely divisible, there must be infinitely many spaces that any given physical monad fills in virtue of filling any space at all.) Finally, no physical monad can repulse itself, since it is impossible for an unextended monad to push itself away from itself.

The inconsistency involved in these four claims can be brought to light by considering how it is that a physical monad is supposed to fill a subregion of space that does *not* border on any space filled by a different monad.[18] The third claim establishes that the physical monad itself must be responsible for repulsion in this subregion. The first claim establishes that it does so through the exercise of its repulsive force. The problem arises when one tries to incorporate the second claim's requirement that the physical monad must fill this subregion by exercising its repulsive force on the monads that fill the space that *immediately surrounds* the subregion in question. For in the case of the particular subregion chosen, the space that *immediately* surrounds it is filled by the very same monad that fills the subregion.[19] This requirement causes an inconsistency because in this case the first and third claims would demand that a physical monad exercise its repulsive force on itself, i.e., that it repulse itself, which contradicts the fourth claim.[20] As a result, the physical monadologist cannot give a consistent account of how a physical monad can fill a space through the exercise of its repulsive force.

But notice that the Critical Kant avoids such a problem by making substance as divisible as space is and by maintaining that every space must have a substance that is active, through its repulsive force, so as to

---

[18] That Kant makes precisely such a move is indicated in the text when, after reminding the reader of the infinite divisibility of space, he notes: "But in a space filled with matter *every part of the space* contains repulsive force to counteract on all sides all remaining parts" (4:503, emphasis added).

[19] One might attempt to avoid this problem by reformulating the second claim as follows: a monad fills a space by exercising its repulsive force on any *other* monad that may attempt to penetrate into this space (cf. Proposition VII of Kant's *Physical Monadology*). However, Kant's worry seems to be that such a claim cannot actually explain how a monad fills its internal spaces. One might think that a monad can fill "external" spaces only after first filling "internal" spaces, but it is unclear that Kant's model has the resources to explain how internal spaces can be filled in this way.

[20] It also violates Kant's claim that a substance cannot act on itself.

Kant's Justification of the Laws of Mechanics 129

be able to account for how that space is filled.[21] That is, like the physical monadologist, he can continue to hold that substances fill space through the exercise of their repulsive forces. However, he can avoid the problem created by the divisibility of space for the physical monadologist, because, unlike physical monads, substance can be divided whenever necessary, and when it is divided, it is divided into *substances*, that is, into what can serve as a seat of a particular kind of activity, namely repulsion.[22] As a result, regardless of the space in question, a substance will never be required to repulse itself, because, as long as substance is divided just as space is, for any two spaces that are filled two distinct substances can act so as to fill them. In short, Kant's argument is that since each filled space requires a distinct seat of repulsive forces and space is infinitely divisible, each space must be filled with infinitely divisible seats of repulsive forces, that is, substances. What Kant's proof thus shows is not only that matter is infinitely divisible – its explicit goal – but also that it is infinitely divisible *into spatially extended parts that are themselves substances*.

But note that this last result is precisely the premise that Kant identifies as crucial to his proof of the conservation of the quantity of matter. In fact, there are striking parallels between Kant's positions on the infinite divisibility of matter and the quantity of matter. In both cases, he starts with a certain determinate effect, whether it be the filling of a determinate region in space or the communication of a determinate quantity of motion. In both cases, he claims that the activity of a spatially extended substance is (at least in part) responsible for the effect, whether it be a repulsive force or a moving force of matter. What's more, in both cases, not only must the spatially extended substance that is responsible for the effect be divisible into spatially extended substances, but the activity of the original substance must also be dispersed among the spatially extended substances into which it is divided in such a way that the activities of all the individual substances jointly bring about the effect in question.

Seen in this light, we can now better understand why Kant thinks that in the communication of motion, the quantity of matter should be viewed as an extensive magnitude that must be accounted for by those spatially extended substances that are acting with their moving forces. For just as

---

[21] To distinguish Kant's position from that of the physical monadologist's, I shall use the term "substance" instead of "monad." Monads are necessarily simple, substances are not.

[22] This difference allows Kant to avoid the inconsistency of the physical monadologist's four claims by rejecting the attributability of any filled space to any *single* monad, which is implicitly asserted in the first claim.

130   The Laws of Mechanics

the divisibility of the region of space that a body occupies requires that each subregion of that space be filled by a spatially distinct substance that acts with its repulsive force, so too the (divisibility of the) quantity of motion that is being communicated from one body to another requires that each part of the body that is communicating its motion be a spatially distinct substance that acts with its moving force. In short, the quantity of the motion communicated is determined by all the moving forces of the substances that compose the body in question. And since, according to the First Analogy, none of these spatially distinct substances can arise or perish, it seems to follow the quantity of these substances and thus the matter they compose must be conserved, just as the First Law of Mechanics asserts.

At the same time, these considerations also allow one to see a serious weakness in Kant's argument. For even if one grants that the quantity of a given matter must depend on the parts that are substances external to each other and that are acting together with their moving forces, this is not incompatible with the possibility that the activities of these substances diminish over time, just as the degree of consciousness of an object of inner sense lessens as it suffers elanguescence. Whether matter consists of substances that are *spatially distinct* from each other simply does not speak to whether its *activities* can *increase or diminish* over time. And this is true regardless of whether the activities are activities of a physical monad, an object of inner sense, or, in the case of matter, an object of outer sense, and it is also true regardless of whether the effect that the activity brings about is the filling of a determinate region of space, a degree of consciousness, or the communication of motion.

Now one might try to eliminate this weakness by appealing to other features of Kant's conception of substance. For example, as we saw above, Kant conceives of substances as having essential and thus unchanging properties and as consisting of continuous activities. If the quantity of matter is an essential feature of substances and if the moving forces that give rise to the communication of motion are their continuous activities, then one might have reason to reject the supposition that the quantity of matter could change over time, given that this quantity is determined by features that cannot change. Indeed, one might draw intuitive support for this response from the fact that it is part of our Newtonian worldview to think of mass as the quantity of matter and to think of it as an essential and thus unchanging feature of matter.

But however intuitively plausible such a position might be, it is difficult to see that Kant has provided an *argument* for those features that are crucial to the response just noted. For even if one grants Kant's basic conception of substances as having unchanging essential properties and

Kant's Justification of the Laws of Mechanics 131

continuous activities, it is not obvious why the quantity of matter in particular has to be an essential property, and even if one were justified in identifying the moving forces as the continuous activities that substances engage in, a *continuous* activity is not the same as an *unchanging* one. As long as there is no break in the activity, it is continuous, but that is consistent with there being highs, lows, and everything in between. As we have seen above, Kant's own example of an object of inner sense illustrates the possibility of the activity of a substance changing over time, that is, the possibility that a continuously active representative force changes its strength and thus its effects over time. Insofar as Kant cannot rule out an analogous possibility in the case of matter, it is difficult to see that his proof of the First Law of Mechanics is fully compelling.

At the same time, it must be noted that this kind of consideration does not call into question the consistency and coherence of Kant's conception of the quantity of matter and its conservation in the communication of motion. Things could be exactly as Kant describes them. And Kant could also be right that the quantity of matter *must* remain the same throughout the communication of motion. But in the absence of an independent argument that establishes conservation of the quantity of matter for the communication of motion, the worry remains that it can sound dogmatic, or at least stipulative, to say: If the quantity of matter remains the same, then what you have experienced in, say, the collision of two billiard balls, is in fact the communication of motion, whereas if it does not, then your experience of the same billiard balls in what could seem to be the same collision is actually of something else.

6.3 The Second Law of Mechanics

As we saw above, Kant's Second Law of Mechanics states that every change in matter must have an external cause. This formulation is more general than Newton's law of inertia insofar as it does not specify exactly what would constitute a change in matter. That is, it does not explicitly assert, much less argue, that change of motion (i.e., acceleration) is a change that requires an external cause and that change of place (i.e., motion) does not.[23] Relatedly, it also makes no mention of impressed forces (a topic typically treated in mathematical physics), referring instead to external causes (something most naturally discussed in metaphysics). Immediately after stating the Second Law, Kant does add a

---

[23] In the Second Analogy Kant similarly remarks that only change of motion and not change of place counts as a change of state, but he does not argue for this (substantive) assumption there.

132   The Laws of Mechanics

parenthetical statement that comes much closer to Newton's first law insofar as it states that every body must persist in its state of rest or motion unless compelled to change its state by an external cause. However, he does not argue for this parenthetical statement, nor does he show how one could derive it from his Second Law.[24] Its status is thus unclear in the sense that he presumably accepts it as true, but not on the basis of any reasons that he presents in the text that ensues. As a result, it is tempting to think that he simply wants to give the reader to understand that his own Second Law is a more fundamental principle that one might need to assume if one wanted to argue for Newton's law of inertia. But that does not change the fact that Kant's Second Law is distinct from Newton's law of inertia. However, as noted earlier in Chapter 4, at least one of Kant's targets in Second Law is Leibniz's (or at least Leibnizian) pre-established harmony, which denies inter-substantial causation. For Kant's Second Law is explicitly rejecting that kind of conception of how the communication of motion could occur. It is, therefore, a substantive claim that not all his readers would have accepted.

But perhaps the most important difference between Kant's Second Law and Newton's law of inertia concerns the fact that Newton does not provide an explicit justification for his law, whereas Kant devotes significant attention to this task for his Second Law. Kant starts by assuming "from general metaphysics" that "every change has a cause." Since the Second Analogy of Experience shows that every event must have a cause and an event is a change of state, Kant clearly thinks that he has already justified this assumption in the first *Critique*.[25] As a result, what he thinks still has to be proved here is simply that any change in matter must have an *external* cause. Kant's basic line of argument on this point is that any change in matter must have an external cause because insofar as matter is an object of outer sense, it does not have any *internal* determinations or grounds of determination that could cause a change in its own state. All that I perceive about, say, a billiard ball is its state of motion or rest, not that it has any internal principle of change within itself. Specifically, we are, he thinks, familiar with two different kinds of internal principles of change – desiring and thinking – but we do not perceive matter (through outer sense) as having desires or thoughts. Accordingly, matter as such cannot cause changes in itself, and, since he defines life as "the faculty

---

[24] Michael Friedman similarly notes that Kant does not seem to be interested in proving "the positive part of the law of inertia – that a body acted upon by no external causes will move uniformly ... and rectilinearly" (Michael Friedman, *Kant's Construction of Nature*, p. 338).

[25] Kant's intent in the Second Analogy thus seems to be that it is noncommittal about whether the cause of an event can be internal or must be external.

Kant's Justification of the Laws of Mechanics 133

of a *substance* to determine itself to act from an *internal principle*" (5:544), matter must be lifeless.

Note, however, that Kant's Second Law does not rule out the existence of living beings, or preclude the kind of internal principles that would be characteristic of them. Instead, he claims that if something is alive, then it must exist in "another substance, different from matter, yet combined with it" (4:544).[26] After making this (relatively obscure) metaphysical remark, he goes on to make a methodological point by saying that "in natural knowledge [*Naturkenntniß*] we first have to be acquainted with the laws of matter, as such, and to purge them from the admixture of all other active causes, before we connect them with these latter, in order properly to distinguish what acts and how each of them does so in itself alone" (4:544). In other words, Kant is attempting to clarify the laws that hold for moving forces in the communication of motion, and to that end, he abstracts from other forces. Thus, in the Mechanics chapter, he is simply trying to state the laws that govern the communication of motion in matter, leaving for another occasion the existence of living beings and how such beings would interact with matter. Kant returns to this issue in the third *Critique*.[27]

As we saw in Chapter 5, (some version of) the law of inertia was widely accepted by Kant's immediate predecessors, but there was considerable disagreement about how it was to be justified, even if many of the justifications relied on metaphysical considerations (e.g., the principle of sufficient reason). The fact that Kant, unlike Newton, provides an argument for his Second Law fits well with this context. The fact that his argument invokes metaphysical and broadly epistemological considerations (the distinction between intrinsic and relational determinations and the Second Analogy as a Critical version of the principle of sufficient reason) adds further support to seeing Kant's thought here as continuous with this tradition in substantive respects, even though he also innovates in several ways.

6.4 The Third Law of Mechanics

One might concede that Kant's First and Second Laws of Mechanics are at home in the context of his Leibnizian-Wolffian predecessors, but argue that his Third Law of Mechanics is intelligible (solely) on the basis of its relation to Newton and his own Critical epistemology. However, Kant's

---

[26] It may not be clear whether Kant is claiming that matter cannot in fact have internal relations or that it can, but that we could not cognize it *as matter*.

[27] See especially Chapter 7 in this book.

134   The Laws of Mechanics

discussion of the Third Law of Mechanics reveals that he is again concerned with positions represented by Leibnizian-Wolffian figures from his rationalist background. Kant's *formulation* of the law of the equality of action and reaction is close to Newton's. One minor apparent difference is that Kant limits his claim to the communication of motion, whereas Newton's is unrestricted in scope and would thus apply to, say, statics. However, Kant's understanding of the law and its significance extends well beyond Newton's insofar as he is explicitly concerned with providing (1) an a priori proof of the truth of this law and (2) a satisfactory ontological account of how action and reaction occur.[28]

We need not concern ourselves with Kant's proof of the law of the equality of action and reaction in detail, since it has been considered earlier (in Chapter 4). In this context it is sufficient to note that in keeping with the Leibnizian-Wolffian tradition Kant thinks that since this law is a fundamental and non-trivial principle in his natural philosophy, it stands in need of some kind of derivation or proof. In fact, Kant places further requirements on *scientific* laws by requiring that they must be cognized a priori (hence with necessity) and with apodictic certainty (which includes consciousness of their necessity). Since Newton does not provide such a proof, much less one that could deliver a result with such demanding features, Kant sees the need to remedy Newton's omission and does so by providing a proof.

Kant's rationalist metaphysical background is even more important for understanding the ontology that he provides for the communication of motion and its central notions of action and reaction. As is well known, Leibniz argues that finite substances do not stand in causal interaction with each other.[29] Rather, each finite substance can act only on itself. Leibniz adopts this view for various reasons. In part, he is reacting against Descartes's position that the mind and the body can act on each other. For he thinks that the mind and the body are too different in nature to be

---

[28] Marius Stan, in "Kant's Third Law of Mechanics: The Long Shadow of Leibniz," *Studies in History and Philosophy of Science* 44 (2013): 493–504, argues that the differences between Kant's and Newton's laws of the equality of action and reaction are even more extensive. Most importantly, Kant's Third Law makes no mention of impressed force. Instead, as we have seen earlier, he speaks of moving force, but the relation between action and moving force is not specified. For example, is action to be identified with moving force, or with the effect of a moving force, or with the force that a body exerts on another in collision? Stan goes further in arguing, persuasively to my mind, that Kant formulates the Third Law as he does because he is attacking the position(s) developed by Wolff and Hermann (rather than simply adopting Newton's formulation).

[29] For fuller discussion of these issues as they bear on Kant, see Watkins, *Kant and the Metaphysics of Causality*, chapter 1.

Kant's Justification of the Laws of Mechanics 135

able to act on each other. How can something material, namely, matter in motion, cause something immaterial, namely, a thought in the mind (and vice versa)? In part he holds that inter-substantial causation is simply unintelligible. For he rejects as absurd the claim that an accident could literally migrate or be transferred from one substance to another in inter-substantial causation. But if inter-substantial causation does not occur through the migration of accidents, then it seems inconceivable how one substance could cause an accident to appear ex nihilo in a distinct substance. Due to these (and yet other) difficulties, Leibniz claims that a substance can act only on itself, and, due to God's omnipotence, benevolence, and wisdom, all substances proceed in complete harmony with one another, so as to appear as if they acted on each other. Further, since God can foresee perfectly before the substances of the world begin acting on themselves how they will do so, there is a perfect "pre-established harmony" among all of creation.

Wolff adopts Leibniz's pre-established harmony for the mind–body relation and is, as a result, expelled from Prussia since it allegedly leads to determinism, atheism, and Spinozism. To make the long story that ensues short, a number of Leibnizian-Wolffians (including Gottsched, Knutzen, Crusius, and the pre-Critical Kant) attempt to develop different versions of inter-substantial causation that could respond to some of Leibniz's main objections against inter-substantial causation, which was commonly known as physical influx (*influxus physicus*).[30] In this way the intelligibility of inter-substantial causation could be maintained. While much of this discussion takes place in metaphysical contexts, Kant clearly sees its application at the foundations of physics as well. For in his discussion of the equality of action and reaction, he explicitly argues against understanding the communication of motion as certain proponents of physical influx suggest. For example, Gottsched can be read as suggesting that only one substance must exercise its force in order for inter-substantial causation to occur. The physical analog for such a model might be that one billiard ball in motion literally transfers all of its motion to a second billiard ball initially at rest. Kant calls proponents of such a model transfusionists (4:549).

Kant has both metaphysical and physical reasons for rejecting the transfusionist's model. The metaphysical reason he cites (4:550) is that the transfusionist does not provide a genuine explanation of the communication of motion. Simply stating that motion is transferred does not

---

[30] For a fuller explanation, see Eric Watkins, "The Development of Physical Influx in Early Eighteenth-Century Germany: Gottsched, Knutzen, and Crusius," *Review of Metaphysics* 49 (1995): 295–339.

136   The Laws of Mechanics

explain *how* it is transferred or communicated. And all parties to the debate agree that *accidentia non migrant e substantiis in substantias*. Accordingly, the transfusionist position has no explanatory resources with which it can explain the communication of motion.

Kant presents three physics-based objections to understanding the communication of motion as the transfusionist suggests. First, he has provided an a priori proof that both action and reaction are required in the communication of motion, since one must appeal to both in explaining their equality. Second, Kant raises the following objection:

> It is quite inconceivable to me how the *transfusionists* of motion would explain, in their fashion, the motion of *elastic* bodies through impact. For here it is clear that the resting body does not, merely as resting, acquire motion lost by the hitting body, but that, in the collision, it exerts actual force on the latter in the opposite direction, so as to compress, as it were, a *spring* between the two, which requires just as much actual motion on its part (but in the opposite direction) as the moving body itself has need of for this purpose. (4:549)

In short, Kant's main objection here is that the transfusionist cannot explain how bodies actually behave in impact, because the transfusionist cannot account for the change of motion in the body that transfers its motion to another body. Why should that body not continue to move as it did before? Presumably, the transfusionist will say that the first body should stop because it has passed all of its own motion on to the other body. However, according to the law of inertia (which Kant assumes that the transfusionist accepts), a body will remain in its state of motion or rest unless *acted* on *by* another body. But if a body simply transfers its motion to another body, it has not been acted on by the other body and its motion should therefore not be changed (despite the fact that it has given up all of its own motion). For the first body to stop, the second body must act on it. However, this kind of reciprocal action (i.e., reaction) is inconsistent with the transfusionist's position.[31]

Third, Kant argues that the transfusionist position would render the law of the equality of action and reaction contingent. Kant puts the point as follows: "No other remedy was known but to deny the existence of absolutely hard bodies, which amounted to admitting the contingency of this law, in that it was supposed to rest on a particular quality of matters that move one another" (4:549). Here Kant is arguing that the transfusionist position implies the contingency of the law of the equality of action and reaction insofar as the equality of action and reaction would

---

[31] Even if the transfusionist does not assume the law of inertia per se, the reaction of the second body is required to explain the (lack of) motion of the first body by its own account.

Kant's Justification of the Laws of Mechanics 137

hold only for bodies that are not absolutely hard. For only with bodies that are not absolutely hard could one body transfer all of its motion to another body. If, however, bodies are absolutely hard, then the transfusionist must admit that action is not equal to reaction. Accordingly, if action is to be equal to reaction, then no body can be absolutely hard. However, whether bodies are absolutely hard is presumably a contingent matter.[32] Accordingly, if this law were true, it would be only contingently true. But since Kant clearly holds that the fundamental principles of the *Metaphysical Foundations* are a priori and apodictically certain, he rejects the transfusionist's position.

In this same context Kant rejects a second ontological account of the communication of motion, an account he attributes to Kepler (but one which could apply to Newton as well). To explain the communication of motion, one might maintain not only an active force in the agent body (i.e., the body that causes the body acted upon to change its state) but also a passive force of inertia in the patient body that resists any change in its state. Action, according to this view, is the exercise of the active force, whereas reaction is the exercise of a corresponding passive force in the patient. Since this passive force is active only when another body attempts to change the first body's state via its active force, the resistance of the passive force 'uses up' some of the agent's active force. Kant objects to this account as follows:

Regardless of the famous name of its creator, the terminology of inertial force (*vis inertiae*) must therefore be entirely banished from natural science, not only because it carries with it a contradiction in terms, nor even because the law of inertia (lifelessness) might thereby easily be confused with the law of reaction in every communicated motion, but primarily because the mistaken idea of those who are not properly acquainted with the mechanical laws is thereby maintained and even strengthened – according to which the reaction of bodies discussed under the name of inertial force would amount to a draining of, diminution, or eradication of the motion in the world; but the mere communication of motion would not be effected thereby, because the moving body would have to apply a part of its motion solely in overcoming the inertia of the one at rest (which would then be a pure loss), and could set the latter in motion only with the remaining part; but if none were left over, it would completely fail to bring the latter into motion by its impact because of its great mass. But nothing can resist a motion except the opposite motion of another body, and certainly not its state of rest. Thus here the inertia of matter, that is, the mere incapacity for self-movement, is not the cause of a resistance. A special, entirely peculiar force merely to resist,

---

[32] In Query 31 of the *Opticks* Newton asserts that the ultimate particles are hard, but it is not clear that this claim represents a necessary truth. Further, even if atoms are necessarily hard, one could still argue that the bodies that are composed of atoms are not perfectly elastic in collisions.

138   The Laws of Mechanics

without being able to move a body, under the name of an inertial force, would be a word without meaning. (4:550–1)

In this passage Kant runs through a number of objections to the force of inertia (i.e., the passive force that is supposed to "use up" some of the active force in resisting it). For example, he thinks that it is a contradiction, and hence meaningless, to assert a force that is inert, that is, that does not do anything. Further, if this account were correct, motion would continually be lost in the communication of motion. For if a body in motion had to expend any of its moving force to overcome the force of inertia, it is possible that it would have expended all of the moving force it had, in which case, a body in motion might come to rest in impact without imparting any motion at all to another. Kant rejects Newton's idea that one could invoke God (as a potential source of "new" motion) in a properly scientific explanation.[33] Finally, Kant makes the conceptual point that the mere incapacity of a body to move itself (inertia properly understood) is distinct from its capacity to resist the actions of other bodies. In fact, Kant is clear that only the motion of one body can resist the motion of another (by means of their moving forces). To lump both of these functions together under the same name is to conflate distinct capacities.[34]

Given that Kant rejects the force of inertia understood in this way, he must develop his own account of how bodies act in the communication of motion. According to Kant, in this context action is to be understood as the exercise of a force that changes the state of a body distinct from the body exercising its active force. Reaction, however, is not a passive force in an inert body, but rather simply the exercise of an active force of the second body. In other words, in the communication of motion, the first body acts on the second body, thereby changing its state, just as the second body acts on the first body, thereby changing its state. Action and reaction are not only equal, but they are of exactly the same kind as well. Only such an ontology, Kant argues, can adequately account for our experience of the communication of motion.[35]

---

[33] For Kant's scientific explanation of earthquakes, which contrasts with the theological accounts on offer at the time, see his "On the Causes of Earthquakes" (1756), "History and Natural Description of the Most Noteworthy Occurrences of the Earthquake That Struck a Large Part of the Earth at the End of the Year 1755" (1756), and "Continued Observations on the Earthquakes That Have Been Experienced for Some Time" (1756).

[34] For further discussion of Kant's objection to the force of inertia, see Marius Stan, "Rebellious Wolffian: Kant's Philosophy of Mechanics in 1758."

[35] For a fuller account of Kant's theory of causation, see Watkins, *Kant and the Metaphysics of Causality*.

6.5 Action at a Distance

Naturally, claiming that action and reaction are of the same kind does not settle all questions, not even all strictly ontological questions concerning the equality of action and reaction in the communication of motion. For both Newton and Kant consider the possibility of action at a distance as one particular instance of the communication of motion. Newton's own reservations about the physical *causes* of action at a distance are well documented, and it is perhaps fair to say that he never arrives at a stable account (or at least at any position that he is comfortable asserting in a consistent and unambiguous way).[36] The nature of the difficulty that action at a distance raises is that it might seem occult or mysterious as to how one body can cause changes in a body that is not immediately contiguous to it. How can a body act where it is not? If the ontology Kant develops to account for the communication of motion is to be adequate, it must also address the possibility of action at a distance, since on Newton's account, our solar system involves (at least apparent) action at a distance throughout.

Kant discusses the possibility of action at a distance not in the Mechanics chapter, but rather earlier in the Dynamics chapter of the *Metaphysical Foundations*, where he establishes the necessity of attractive and repulsive forces for our experience of matter as filling a determinate region of space. In his explanations of the force of attraction in particular, Kant addresses the main objection generally raised against the idea of action at a distance and argues that action at a distance actually underlies and makes possible contact action. Kant explains his position as follows:

It [i.e., matter] therefore acts immediately at a place where it is not, which is apparently contradictory. In truth, however, it is so far from being contradictory that one may rather say that every thing in space acts on another only at a place where the acting thing is not. For if it should act in the same place where it is itself, then the thing upon which it acts would not be *outside* it at all; for this *outsideness* means presence at a place where the other is not. (4:513)

Kant's line of reasoning can be reconstructed as follows. If a body is acting on a body that is distinct from it, then it is acting on a body that fills a place that is distinct from it. But if a body is acting on a body that is distinct from it, it must be acting on a body that is at a distance from it, since distinct bodies must occupy distinct locations and thus be at a distance from each other. Therefore, contact action must be understood

---

[36] See Ernan McMullin, *Newton on Matter and Activity* (Notre Dame: University of Notre Dame Press, 1978), especially pp. 106–9.

140   The Laws of Mechanics

as the action of one body on another body that is at a distance from it. Accordingly, even contact action requires bodies acting on each other at a distance, that is, action at a distance.[37]

What allows Kant to offer this analysis of action at a distance and contact action is his rationalist background. As we saw above, Kant rejects pre-established harmony in favor of physical influx, that is, inter-substantial causation. Seen from this broader ontological perspective, there is no important difference between action at a distance and contact action, because both are simply cases of inter-substantial causation. To put this point differently, if there is a difficulty with action at a distance, then there will also be a difficulty with contact action. The main difficulty associated with action at a distance is that it is difficult to see how a body can cause changes so far away, as it were, in a distinct body. However, from this ontological perspective this difficulty is simply a more specific version of the general or ontological difficulty Leibniz had already raised for inter-substantial causation, namely, how it is possible for one substance to cause a change in another (since accidents cannot migrate, whether between substances at a distance or those standing in contact). Since Kant has addressed Leibniz's more general difficulty by developing a concept of force that makes inter-substantial causation possible (by appropriating a concept of force from physics for use in a metaphysical context), he can use the same concept of force to explain both contact action and action at a distance.

Given this description of Kant's background and this explanation of how it makes possible his analysis of action at a distance, his Critical turn does not seem to be the crucial factor in explaining action at a distance. Gerd Buchdahl claims that it is only in the *Metaphysical Foundations* that Kant develops "a more articulated methodological structure of scientific hypotheses" that then allows for a more sophisticated attempt at rendering action at a distance intelligible.[38] More specifically, Buchdahl argues that Kant's intent is to show that action at a distance is an essential part of "any 'possible construction' of the concept of matter,"[39] which, if successful, would (1) show how action at a distance is possible, (2) render it intelligible in such a way that it is not occult, and (3) show the actuality of action at a distance without any recourse to hypotheses. Though Kant does not, according to Buchdahl, meet with complete

---

[37] In response to the objection that bodies in contact with each other are not at a distance, Kant argues that they are separated by a point that is not a part of either body (4:513).

[38] Gerd Buchdahl, "Gravity and Intelligibility: From Newton to Kant," in *The Methodological Heritage of Newton*, ed. Robert Butts and John Davis (Toronto: University of Toronto Press, 1970), pp. 74–102, p. 74.

[39] Gerd Buchdahl, "Gravity and Intelligibility," p. 95.

success in this project, given that attractive and repulsive forces have an empirical or material element that cannot be constructed in intuition a priori, his endeavors are still "not a total loss" due to the greater methodological articulation he achieves (as compared with the work of other figures in the eighteenth century as well as with his own pre-Critical position).[40]

However, we have just seen that it is the development of a specific ontology rather than Kant's Critical turn that contains the key to explaining his acceptance of action at a distance, even if the latter does affect many other features of his philosophy of science in the *Metaphysical Foundations*. In particular, as we have seen, Kant does not rely on any special or Critical notion of possibility, namely, construction in intuition a priori, to show that action at a distance can be conceived in such a way that the standard Newtonian and Leibnizian objections can be met. Instead, the crucial notion is the concept of force he develops, according to which one substance or body can change the state of another substance or body through the exercise of, e.g., its attractive or repulsive force.

In fact, if the Critical turn *were* truly essential to his explanation of action at a distance, then Kant would have had to have rejected action at a distance in his pre-Critical period. However, Kant not only *accepts* action at a distance in his pre-Critical period but also develops an explanation of action at a distance that is strikingly similar to the one presented in the *Metaphysical Foundations*. In his *Physical Monadology* Kant first argues for the necessity of a force of impenetrability. He then suggests that "in addition to the force of impenetrability, every element needs another force, that of attraction. If the force of attraction did not exist, then the bodies of nature would have no determinate magnitude" (1:484). Kant also makes clear that these two forces are inherent in matter and are not to be accepted on the basis of hypotheses. Even more clearly, in his (pre-Critical) *Inquiry Concerning the Distinctness of the Principles of Natural Theology and Morality*, Kant addresses action at a distance explicitly as follows:

Thus, if I say that one body acts upon another immediately at a distance then this means that it acts on it immediately, but not by means of impenetrability. But it is by no means clear here why this should be impossible, unless, that is, someone shows either that impenetrability is the only force possessed by a body, or at least that a body cannot act on any other body immediately, without at the same time doing so by means of impenetrability. But this has never been proved, nor does it

---

[40] Gerd Buchdahl, "Gravity and Intelligibility," p. 101.

142   The Laws of Mechanics

seem very likely that it ever will be. Accordingly, metaphysics, at least, has no sound reason to object to the idea of immediate attraction at a distance. (2:288)

Given that Kant has argued for a distinct force of attraction, he is convinced that impenetrability is not in fact the only force possessed by a body. Accordingly, Kant accepts action at a distance in his pre-Critical period on the basis of a certain conception of force, just as he does in the *Metaphysical Foundations*.[41]

6.6   Newton's Second Law of Motion

We noted earlier (in Chapter 5) that many of Kant's immediate predecessors did not include Newton's second law ($F = ma$) in their lists of the laws of motion. Nor does Kant. However, one might think that he must be committed to Newton's second law, given how fundamental it is to Newton's argument in the *Principia*, and given his fundamental Newtonian orientation, which finds expression in so many of his works (e.g., in the *Universal Natural History*, but also in the first *Critique* and the *Prolegomena*).

It is perhaps best to approach Kant's attitude toward Newton's second law by considering both textual and philosophical considerations. On the textual side, we face the question: What evidence do we have for thinking that Kant in fact accepts Newton's second law as a law of mechanics? On the philosophical side, we must ask: Does Kant have any argument that would establish Newton's second law as a law of mechanics? As it turns out, neither question admits of an entirely simple or straightforward answer.

On the first question, Kant does seem to accept the truth of the idea that forces are the cause of accelerations. As we saw above in our discussion of Kant's Second Law of Mechanics, he thinks that only changes in motion (i.e., accelerations) require (external) causes, and he also thinks that forces are the (external) causes of these accelerations. And there is some direct textual evidence for thinking that Kant accepts the connection between acceleration and force. Near the beginning of the Dynamics chapter, where Kant argues that there can be only two kinds of moving forces (attractive and repulsive), he notes: "all motion that one

---

[41] Of course, this notion of force must be compatible with being constructed in a priori intuition (and thus Kant is attempting to reconcile Critical concerns with other considerations), but adopting construction in a priori intuition as a criterion of possibility occurs after his endorsement of action at a distance and the attractive force necessary for its explanation. Accordingly, the crucial move (i.e., the development of a certain conception of force) lies in his pre-Critical period, although it must be consistent with any changes that occur in his Critical period.

Kant's Justification of the Laws of Mechanics 143

matter can impress on another ... must always be viewed as imparted in the straight line between the two points" (4:498). Though this falls short of an explicit endorsement of Newton's second law, it can seem to capture at least much of what that law asserts. For it does state that matter imparts motion in a straight line (and "imparting motion" could be interpreted to mean acceleration). At the same time, the fact remains that Kant does not explicitly endorse Newton's second law *as a law* of mechanics. Nor does his most fundamental project in the *Metaphysical Foundations* explicitly require it.[42]

One natural reason for thinking that Kant does not accept Newton's second law as a law of mechanics (even if he accepts its truth) would be that, like his immediate predecessors, he does not think that it is capable of the kind of proof that would be required for it to be a Law of Mechanics (in the context of the *Metaphysical Foundations*). If this is correct, then the historical question depends, at least in part, on the philosophical question: Does Kant have the resources to prove Newton's second law (e.g., a priori and with apodictic certainty)?[43]

Marius Stan has recently suggested that Kant can either prove Newton's second law or at least come very close to doing so.[44] According to Stan, Kant's argument turns on three premises. The first is what can be referred to as the parallelogram of velocities, which Kant articulates in the Phoronomy chapter of the Metaphysical Foundations (at 4:487–95). It states that if a point has two distinct velocities, one can represent them as vectors that are additive.[45] The second premise states that "all forces induce accelerations (i.e. velocity increments) in the direction of their action."[46] The third premise is that "single forces induce accelerations proportional to them."[47] In short, the idea is that since accelerations add like vectors (given that accelerations are changes in velocities, which add like vectors) and forces are collinear with and proportional to their

---

[42] For an ingenious defense of the idea that the argument of the *Metaphysical Foundations* does require Newton's laws of motion, see Michael Friedman's *Kant and the Exact Sciences* (Cambridge, MA: Harvard University Press, 1992) and *Kant's Construction of Nature*.

[43] If Kant believed himself to be in possession of a proof of Newton's Second Law, why would he not have made that law one of his Laws of Mechanics?

[44] Marius Stan, "Kant and the Object of Determinate Experience," *Philosopher's Imprint* 15 (2015): 1–19. Stan does not claim that Kant actually gives this argument. Instead, he presents it in a reconstructive mode.

[45] A point that moves west at 1 meter per second and that moves north at 1 meter per second can be represented as moving northwest at the square root of 2 meters per second.

[46] Stan, "Kant and the Object of Determinate Experience," p. 14.

[47] Stan, "Kant and the Object of Determinate Experience," p. 14.

144   The Laws of Mechanics

accelerations, the forces must add like vectors as well in accordance with the parallelogram rule.

This is certainly a tempting argument, since it seems to put Kant's commitments together in a way that delivers Newton's second law as a result. However, it is unclear that this interpretation is compelling. One concern is that the second premise can appear to be lacking in support. For even if one knows the conditional that if a force induces an acceleration, then it would do so in the direction of its action, one must know the antecedent, namely that the force actually induces an acceleration. As we saw above, Kant provides no *argument* for accepting that an acceleration (change of velocity rather than, say, change of place) is a change of state.

A second, more serious concern focuses on the third premise and on the support one might offer for it. Why think that the forces and the accelerations must be proportional? One might think that Kant's Third Law of Mechanics, along with the conservation of linear momentum, would entail proportionality. After all, if action is necessarily equal (and opposite) to reaction, then the accelerations that the action and reaction induce must be equal (and opposite) as well, and if they are equal (and opposite), then they must also be proportional. But note that what is equal and opposite (and thus proportional) are the relevant acceleration and deceleration, on the one hand, and the action and reaction, on the other hand. This does not establish that the action (or reaction) and the acceleration (or deceleration) must be proportional.

But note that a more general worry underlies these specific concerns. Newton's second law is, in effect, asserting one specific empirical meaning for the concept of an impressed force. But how could one prove a priori with apodictic certainty that the concept of an impressed force (which is a predicable, to put it in Kant's terms) must have one particular empirical meaning rather than another? This is, I think, a principled difficulty for proving Newton's second law on the basis of the resources that Kant has at his disposal. Newton could perhaps appeal to empirical data to confirm that $F = ma$ is the proper description of what happens in the world. But since Kant is attempting to provide metaphysical foundations for natural science and is thus restricted to a priori resources (except for the empirical concept of matter), it is simply not clear that he can establish such a seemingly empirical result entirely on a priori grounds.[48]

---

[48] In fact, there may well be other difficulties. For example, it is not clear that forces must be additive just because the accelerations they cause are additive.

Kant's Justification of the Laws of Mechanics 145

Perhaps there is a way to overcome this principled difficulty, and perhaps one can reconstruct an argument that delivers Newton's second law as a result. However, given the restrictions Kant places on what must be the case for the law in question to count as a Law of Mechanics (and qualifying as part of science proper), these are tall orders, and even if one could somehow make good on this, it is striking that Kant does not devote explicit attention to such an argument and that he does not need this result to establish the metaphysical foundations of his physics. As a result, it is difficult to see how to bridge the gap between Kant and Newton on this point.

6.7   The Laws of Mechanics

With this account of Kant's three Laws of Mechanics in hand, we can now see that it fits with the account of law presented above, in Part I. Consider the first main element of Kant's generic account of law, namely, the necessity expressed in the content of the law. Each of the three Laws of Mechanics gives expression to an objective (rule-based) necessity, whether it be the necessary conservation of the quantity of matter throughout the changes that occur in the communication of motion, the necessity of an external cause for bringing about a change of state in a substance, or the necessary equality of action and reaction in the communication of motion. In fact, Kant's arguments for the Laws of Mechanics are designed to reveal these necessities in our experience of the communication of motion. The Laws of Mechanics thus fit nicely with this part of Kant's account of law.

Kant's Laws of Mechanics also exemplify the second main component of his generic account of law, namely, the requirement that any law be legislated by a spontaneous and active faculty. For it is evident that the understanding, a clear case of a spontaneous and active faculty, is prescribing these laws to nature insofar as it is using the relational categories of substance, causality, and mutual interaction to construct the communication of motion (on the basis of whatever relative motions are given in intuition). That the understanding is involved in the Laws of Mechanics in this way is made explicit by the fact that Kant makes use of an extended transcendental argument, showing that the relevant categories are necessary for our experience of the communication of motion.

All three of Kant's Laws of Mechanics thus straightforwardly satisfy both of his requirements for laws. This result should not be viewed as surprising since Kant takes the Laws of Mechanics as paradigm instances of laws of nature and models his generic account of law on these laws.

Part III

Teleological Laws

Though Kant was, as we have seen, especially interested in the Laws of Mechanics (especially insofar as they came to play a particularly fundamental role in his overall philosophy by making one fundamental kind of experience possible), he was also interested in phenomena that could not be fully explained by mechanical laws. For example, in the *Critique of the Power of Judgment* he claimed that "it would be absurd for humans even ... to hope that there may yet arise a Newton who could make comprehensible even the generation of a blade of grass according to natural laws that no intention has ordered" (5:400). And mechanical laws are precisely the kind of laws that he thinks are obviously insufficient for such an explanatory task. Indeed, the *Critique of the Power of Judgment* as a whole investigates subjective and objective purposiveness, in the hopes of coming to understand the laws according to which we view purposive beings as operating and what (ontological and epistemic) status such beings can have, given that such laws are not constitutive of experience as mechanical laws are.

In attempting to shed light on the nature of objective purposiveness and the kind of teleological law that would give expression to it, Chapter 7 investigates in some detail the Antinomy of Teleological Judgment. Specifically, it reconstructs the antinomy that is at the heart of the Antinomy of Teleological Judgment – its Thesis and Antithesis as well as the arguments that could be given in favor of each – and considers a range of different interpretations of what its resolution might be. Even if the text has (so far) proven resistant to a fully satisfying interpretation, it is striking that any adequate interpretation must make good sense of Kant's appeal to a supersensible ground in attempting to reconcile what seem to be irreconcilable standpoints. Chapter 8 takes a different tack at clarifying teleological laws by looking at how Kant understands objective purposiveness in the case of organisms and how they and their interactions fit together into nature in general. For Kant seems to think that rational reflection on organisms leads

148   Teleological Laws

us to make further claims about nature, namely, that every specific thing in nature (not just organisms) must be judged teleologically as well as that nature as a whole is a system of purposes that itself has a purpose. Thus, purposiveness and the laws that govern it extend well beyond the organisms that first lead us to think in teleological terms. This gives a clearer picture of the importance of teleological laws in Kant's philosophy.

7 The Antinomy of Teleological Judgment

7.1 Introduction

In this chapter I address two deceptively simple questions: (1) What is the antinomy of teleological judgment? (2) What is its resolution? While both questions have received sustained scholarly attention over the years, it turns out that satisfactory answers have proved elusive, and in some cases very basic questions that naturally arise in answering these questions have not even been clearly posed. With respect to the first question (addressed in Section 7.2), I argue (in Section 7.2.1) that the most plausible line of interpretation of the antinomy of teleological judgment has it consisting in a contradiction between two regulative principles. At the same time, this interpretation faces two challenges. The first challenge (raised in Section 7.2.2) concerns whether there is really any contradiction between the regulative principles, a question that is motivated, at least initially, by several sentences in §70 whose intent is not patently obvious. I maintain that a careful reading of these passages allows one to see the point Kant wants to make and why he would want to make it. I also argue that straightforwardly philosophical grounds support the idea that there is a genuine contradiction in the antinomy so understood. The second challenge concerns what the proofs of the regulative principles might be. In the case of the mechanical regulative principle (addressed in Section 7.2.3), I articulate three possible lines of argument, argue that two are manifestly inadequate, and settle on the third as the most attractive option on offer, even though it too is not entirely unproblematic. In the non-mechanical case, I tentatively suggest (in Section 7.2.4) that Kant's argument is based on the limitations of our cognitive powers along with the related idea that the possibility of organisms lies in the supersensible.

With respect to the second main question (addressed in Section 7.3), I argue that a satisfactory resolution of the antinomy remains elusive, despite our very best attempts. For Kant's discussion (in §§72–3) of the four different possible alternative systems that aim to account for

149

150   Teleological Laws

teleology reveals them to be unsatisfactory and, what's more, does not shed substantive light on the nature of Kant's own resolution (Section 7.3.1). Further, taking into account the best interpretations of Kant's resolution offered up in the scholarly literature reveals the inadequacy of the appeals that have been made to the notion of an intuitive understanding (Section 7.3.1), of the claim that not everything is objectively explicable (Section 7.3.2), and of the idea that mechanism is to be subordinated to teleology (Section 7.3.3), which leaves us with a major unsatisfied desideratum. In addressing these two questions in this way, my primary intent is neither to articulate and defend definitive answers nor to find fault with the best currently available answers, but rather to advance the current state of the debate by suggesting what questions must be pursued further so that we might eventually obtain an adequate interpretation of Kant's Antinomy of Teleological Judgment.

7.2   The Antinomy of Teleological Judgment

In the Dialectic of the Teleological Power of Judgment, after first explaining (in §69) that the antinomy of teleological judgment pertains to reflecting judgment rather than reason, Kant turns (in §70) to specifying particular principles or maxims of the power of reflecting judgment and to explaining how they could come into conflict. He begins by noting that while the necessary laws that the understanding prescribes to nature a priori (e.g., the Analogies of Experience) do not involve reflecting judgment, the contingent unity of diverse empirical laws capable of giving us unified cognition of the world does, and he mentions two kinds of maxims in particular that reflecting judgment would adopt to promote this end. One kind arises because the understanding places constraints not just on a priori laws but also on empirical laws. A second kind arises because there are "particular experiences" of objects (specifically, of organisms) that we cannot explain mechanically and that require a "special principle" (5:386). If these two maxims conflict, reflecting judgment will be at odds with itself, and we will have an antinomy.

Kant then formulates and discusses two specific statements of pairs of contradictory principles. The first pair states a contradiction at the level of reflecting judgment in such a way that the one maxim requires judgments in terms of mechanical laws, while the other asserts the inadequacy of judgments in terms of mechanical laws in such a way that judgments invoking final or teleological causes are required instead. The second pair, by contrast, states a contradiction between constitutive principles possessing content that is otherwise analogous to that of the first pair. In short, in the first pair, the thesis and antithesis make a claim about

The Antinomy of Teleological Judgment   151

how bodies must *be judged* and thus take these principles to be regulative, whereas the second pair concerns how objects must *be*, thereby "transforming" the first pair's maxims into constitutive principles pertaining to the possibility of objects themselves. Specifically, they read:

> Thesis$_r$: All generation of material things and their forms must be judged as possible in accordance with merely mechanical laws.
>
> Antithesis$_r$: Some products of material nature cannot be judged as possible according to merely mechanical laws (judging them requires an entirely different law of causality, namely, that of final causality).
>
> Thesis$_c$: All generation of material things is possible in accordance with merely mechanical laws.
>
> Antithesis$_c$: Some generation of such things is not possible in accordance with merely mechanical laws. (cf. 5:387)

7.2.1   What Is the Antinomy?

In light of these two separate formulations of contradictory theses and antitheses, one fundamental question arises immediately: Which pair of thesis and antithesis statements is supposed to represent the genuine antinomy of teleological judgment? One prima facie attractive option, which gained adherents especially in the first half of the twentieth century, is that of Thesis$_c$ and Antithesis$_c$, given that they are clearly contradictory – all generation of material things either is or is not possible in accordance with merely mechanical laws – and Kant notes this feature immediately after presenting them (5:388).[1] One might think further that both Thesis$_c$ and Antithesis$_c$ could be proved straightforwardly: Thesis$_c$ by the argument of the Second Analogy of Experience and Antithesis$_c$ by the distinctive nature of organisms. Finally, the resolution of the antinomy would follow from well-established Critical principles insofar it would consist simply in distinguishing clearly between constitutive and regulative principles and in rejecting the constitutive pair in favor of the regulative version, a move that could naturally seem to be supported by several crucial sentences in §70 and §71 (esp. 5:387–8 and 5:389).

However, despite its initial appeal, this first option is not ultimately tenable. For one, it contradicts §69, whose main point is to show that the antinomy pertains specifically to reflecting judgment, and Kant reiterates

---

[1] See Ernst Cassirer, *Kants Leben und Lehre* (Berlin: B. Cassirer, 1921), and Alfred C. Ewing, *Kant's Treatment of Causality* (London: Kegan Paul, 1923).

152   Teleological Laws

this point immediately after stating the two pairs of contradictions when he notes that if Thesis$_c$ and Antithesis$_c$ represented the antinomy, then it would be an antinomy of reason, not judgment. For another, Kant explicitly states that reason cannot prove either Thesis$_c$ or Antithesis$_c$, which would be required for an antinomy to arise. Further, this option is contradicted by the very title of §71 – "*Preparation* for the Resolution of the Antinomy" – insofar as the distinction between constitutive and regulative principles would already solve the antinomy, rather than simply prepare the way for its resolution. Finally, this option would render otiose the remaining sections of the Dialectic, where the antinomy is supposed to be resolved by means of distinctions other than that between constitutive and regulative principles.[2]

The weaknesses of the first option speak strongly in favor of a second option, which holds that the antinomy consists of Thesis$_r$ and Antithesis$_r$. For this second option does concern reflecting judgment, given that Thesis$_r$ and Antithesis$_r$ pertain specifically to how we judge things, and not to how they are. It is also not in danger of trying to resolve the antinomy too quickly in one fell swoop simply by distinguishing between regulative and constitutive principles given that this distinction must be taken into account for the antinomy to be formulated in the first place. As a result, this option leaves plenty of work to be accomplished in the following sections, just as it should, and by means of whatever moves are made there, though determining what these moves are and how they resolve the contradiction are questions that still need to be addressed (later in Section 7.3).

7.2.2   The First Challenge

This second option, which has come to represent the standard view in more recent literature, faces two significant challenges that have not been squarely addressed so far.[3] The first challenge initially derives from a textual issue and is then backed up by straightforwardly philosophical considerations. In §70, after the statements of the two pairs of contradictions and the explanation referred to earlier (about why the constitutive

---

[2] For a more sophisticated interpretation of this kind of view, one that responds to these criticisms, see Marcel Quarfood, *Transcendental Idealism and the Organism* (Stockholm: Almquiest and Wiksell, 2004), pp. 166–71. Unfortunately, I do not have space to discuss Quarfood's interpretation of the nature of the antinomy here.

[3] This view is developed by Henry Allison, "Kant's Antinomy of Teleological Judgment," *Southern Journal of Philosophy* 30 (Supplement) (1991): 25–42, and especially by Peter McLaughlin, *Kant's Critique of Teleology in Biological Explanation: Antinomy and Teleology* (Lewiston: Edwin Mellen Press, 1990).

The Antinomy of Teleological Judgment

principles do not constitute the antinomy), one English translation has Kant asserting: "By contrast, the maxims of a reflecting power of judgment that were initially expounded do not in fact contain any contradiction" (5:387).[4] This sentence obviously represents a major problem for the second option, since it would be at the very least extremely bizarre if Kant were to assert an antinomy and then immediately deny that any contradiction holds between its thesis and antithesis. This difficulty, in conjunction with Kant's reference to the "mere appearance" of an antinomy in §71, could easily tempt one into rejecting this option as well and holding that the entire antinomy is a highly artificial construct motivated solely by architectonic considerations.

This purely textual issue might then be bolstered by philosophical grounds that question whether there is in fact any contradiction between these regulative principles. Why should it be a contradiction for one to look for a mechanical explanation of some phenomenon at the same time that one looks for a teleological explanation? If one takes the possibility of multitasking into account, the contradiction can seem to disappear almost immediately, and the second option can appear to be just as untenable as the first.

However, I maintain that the second option can be successfully defended against this two-fold challenge. As for the textual issue, it is essential to note that the German text reads as follows: "Was dagegen die zuerst vorgetragene Maxime einer reflectirenden Urtheilskraft betrifft, so enthält sie in der That gar keinen Widerspruch" (5:387). Literally (and inelegantly) translated, it reads: "By contrast, what concerns the initially expounded maxim of a reflecting power of judgment, it in fact contains no contradiction at all." Since it can sound strange to assert that a single maxim contains no contradiction – we expect contradictions between pairs of propositions – one can certainly understand why one might be tempted to transform the singular "maxim" into the plural "maxims." However, the text does unambiguously use the singular, and one must be open to the possibility that Kant means to refer here only to the first of the principles of reflecting judgment, namely Thesis$_r$. In light of this, I suggest that though the passage is indeed neither completely clear nor

---

[4] This is the Cambridge translation by Guyer and Matthews. The other main English translation, by Pluhar, renders it as follows: "But if we consider instead the two maxims of a power of judgment that reflects [i.e., the first thesis and antithesis above], the first of those two maxims does in fact not contradict [the second] at all"; Immanuel Kant, *Critique of Pure Reason*, trans. W. Pluhar (Indianapolis: Hackett, 1987), p. 267. While this translation is different in some respects, it is still misleading insofar as it maintains that the first maxim does not contradict the second maxim, which thus faces the exact same problem that the translation by Guyer and Matthews does.

154   Teleological Laws

fully straightforward in its intent, one can read it as asserting not that Thesis$_r$ does not contradict itself (which would be true, but not particularly significant in the context), but rather (more interestingly) that it does not contradict either the truth or the falsity of either Thesis$_c$ or Antithesis$_c$, which he had just discussed in the previous paragraph and thus could easily be referring back to without any explicit mention.

Reading the text in this way is not only more faithful to what Kant actually writes, but also allows him to be making a point that is directly relevant to the matter at hand. Insofar as it has not been shown that reason can prove either one of the constitutive principles, it is not clear whether Thesis$_c$ or Antithesis$_c$ is true. Even so, it would be a problem if the one that turned out to be true was inconsistent with Thesis$_r$. As a result, the sentence in question, as I read it, avoids this potential problem by asserting that Thesis$_r$ does not contradict the truth of either Thesis$_c$ or Antithesis$_c$, precisely because it is a principle of reflecting judgment and not a constitutive principle. This reading also makes sense of how the passage continues:

For if I say that I must **judge** the possibility of all events in material nature and hence all forms, as their products, in accordance with merely mechanical laws, I do not thereby say that they **are possible only in accordance with such laws successfully** (to the exclusion of any other kind of causality); rather, that only indicates that I **should** always **reflect** on nature, and hence research the latter, so far as I can, because if it is not made the basis for research then there can be no proper cognition of nature. (5:387)

That is, Kant explains that Thesis$_r$ is not committed to any ontological claim about what makes objects in nature possible and thus would not be threatened by whatever laws (whether mechanical or non-mechanical) in fact make them possible. In the rest of this paragraph Kant then argues that Antithesis$_r$ is similarly not threatened by the truth of Thesis$_c$ (as one might otherwise have thought). For even if we must explain some forms of nature according to a principle of final causality, as Antithesis$_r$ suggests, events in nature might still be possible by mechanical laws alone (as Thesis$_c$ asserts). Because it is the case that neither constitutive principle directly contradicts either of the regulative principles, one can see that the point of this paragraph is not to remove the force of the antinomy, but rather to show that it retains its full strength in the face of a potential difficulty.

If the text can be read in this way, the strictly philosophical part of the objection must still be faced. Is there in fact a contradiction between Thesis$_r$ and Antithesis$_r$? It is clearly possible in general to seek two different explanations at once, just as it is in principle possible to undertake two distinct actions simultaneously (e.g., to pat your head and rub your stomach). However, it must be noted that Thesis$_r$ and Antithesis$_r$ are not simply recommending that one pursue two distinct activities at once. Rather, they are concerned with judgments about what makes the generation of material things possible, and on that point, they assert both that merely mechanical laws make such judgments possible and that merely mechanical laws do not make such judgments possible. Two points are thus crucial to understanding why a genuine contradiction does in fact arise here. First, Thesis$_r$ and Antithesis$_r$ are not simply *recommendations* to seek explanations of what makes the generation of natural things possible, but rather express commitments to *judgments* about such phenomena. Second, these judgments are genuinely contradictory insofar as the one says that mechanical laws all by themselves can be used to judge the possibility of the generation of natural things, while the other says that mechanical laws alone cannot be used to make such judgments. Whatever our judgment about what makes the generation of natural things possible, it must involve either mechanical laws (alone) or laws other than mechanical ones. Accordingly, if one sought explanations that involved both mechanical and teleological laws at the same time, one would be performing activities that contradicted Thesis$_r$ insofar as one would be looking for explanations that were not restricted to mechanical laws (alone). So Thesis$_r$ and Antithesis$_r$ are in fact contradictory on strictly philosophical grounds.

7.2.3   The Second Challenge: The Proof of Thesis$_r$

If one can respond to the first challenge in this way, this line of interpretation still faces a second important challenge. Insofar as the antinomy is to be constituted by Thesis$_r$ and Antithesis$_r$, they both require proof. Given that Kant does not have separate sections of the text explicitly dedicated to this task, as he did in the first *Critique*'s Antinomy of Pure Reason, the challenge here lies in identifying their proofs. Take Thesis$_r$ first. The simplest idea here is to suppose that it is justified by the Second Analogy of Experience. However, accepting this suggestion would conflict with the first *Critique*'s contention that the Second Analogy is a constitutive principle, given that Thesis$_r$ is clearly a regulative principle. While one might think that Kant's view is genuinely problematic in this regard, the standard view – advanced first by Peter McLaughlin and then by Henry Allison – is that there is a significant difference between the Second Analogy and the notion of mechanism involved in mechanical

156   Teleological Laws

laws.[5] For however one interprets the notoriously difficult Second Analogy, it specifies that every event must be caused according to a rule (or law), but it neither asserts nor argues that the rule has to be a *mechanical* law.[6] As a result, even if the Second Analogy plays some role in the justification of the maxim expressed in Thesis$_r$, it does not suffice on its own and would require significant supplementation.

What, then, could Kant's justification of Thesis$_r$ be? Why should we think that all generation must be able to be explained mechanically? Kant's explicit statements are quite minimal. As we saw above, he notes that without mechanical explanation, "there can be no proper cognition of nature" (5:387). However, he provides no explanation in this context of why that should be the case, and (understandably) the secondary literature is silent on this very basic question.[7]

Three answers could be developed in response to this question. First, one might turn to the *Metaphysical Foundations* in the hopes that it establishes the necessity of mechanical explanation. After all, as we have seen, Kant argues for three Laws of Mechanics that might fill out and justify the content of Thesis$_r$. The fact that he has already argued for these laws would account for the absence of an explicit justification of Thesis$_r$ in the *Critique of the Power of Judgment*.[8] This line of argument, however, faces two serious problems. First, if its argument were successful, the *Metaphysical Foundations* would establish mechanical principles for explanation in science proper (in particular, physics), but it would not establish the necessity of mechanical explanation for all of nature (either for sciences other than physics or for non-scientific cognition). Given that organisms fall outside the purview of physics, one would have no reason to think that Thesis$_r$ does or even should hold for them. As a result, the scope of this argument would be too narrow to achieve the desired result. Second, even if the *Metaphysical Foundations* could establish the necessity of mechanical principles for all natural bodies, these principles would still be constitutive rather than regulative, as is required

---

[5] See McLaughlin, *Kant's Critique of Teleology in Biological Explanation*, and Allison, "Kant's Antinomy of Teleological Judgment."

[6] In fact, it does not clearly assert that the cause must be prior to the effect in time, only that the effect must "follow" from the cause (which may not be asserted in a temporal sense).

[7] For example, Allison, who is generally charitable to Kant, notes the absence of explicit proofs of Thesis$_r$ and Antithesis$_c$ – "[w]ithout any further argument, Kant affirms that there are, indeed, two such maxims presupposed by judgment" ("Kant's Antinomy," 29) – but he makes no attempt to remedy this deficiency in Kant's account.

[8] The Second Law of Mechanics also draws an important distinction between inert or lifeless matter (matter as such) and life (4:544), which one might be tempted to view as spelling out the meaning of "mechanical" in "mechanical laws."

The Antinomy of Teleological Judgment   157

for Thesis$_r$. Therefore, this first answer, which relies on the *Metaphysical Foundations* to justify Thesis$_r$, is clearly not satisfactory.

Another possible justification of Thesis$_r$ stems from the fact that teleological explanation presupposes mechanical explanation, despite being its rival. Because the parts of organisms not only are made possible by the organism as a whole, but also must contribute causally to the whole, teleological explanations cannot occur without also invoking mechanical explanations. For example, it is essential to the tree that its leaves contribute to its maintenance through mechanical processes, even if the leaves depend on the tree as a whole for their existence, functioning, and maintenance. Thus, when Kant says that we would have no cognition of nature without mechanical explanation, one might think that he is making this claim on the grounds that the only other kind of explanation available to us employs mechanical explanation too, so there is simply no way around it in our search for cognition. Such a justification would not address someone skeptical about our ability to provide any explanation at all, but Kant does not seem to be concerned with such an extreme view in this context. The fatal difficulty for this second justification, however, is that, given its very starting point (namely, teleological explanation), it precludes the possibility of a *purely* mechanical explanation of such phenomena, as Thesis$_r$ requires. That is, Thesis$_r$ states that the possibility of generation be judged in accordance with *merely* mechanical laws, not mechanical *and* teleological laws. As a result, this second answer is clearly inadequate as well.

A third, and perhaps most promising, answer draws on what reflective judgment is required for and what it is supposed to accomplish. In the first paragraph of §70, after distinguishing between general a priori and particular empirical laws, Kant notes:

> There can be such great diversity and dissimilarity among [the latter] that the power of judgment itself must serve as a principle even in order merely to investigate the appearances of nature in accordance with a law and spy one out, because it requires one for a guideline if it is to have any hope of an interconnected experiential cognition in accordance with a thoroughgoing lawfulness of nature or of its unity in accordance with empirical laws. (5:386)

That is, the unity of empirical laws is not given, but rather must be discovered, and reflecting judgment is required for that insofar as it must try to organize particular phenomena in such a way that they fall under particular laws that can, in turn, be unified within a larger theoretical framework of more general laws.

Even granting the necessity of the reflecting power of judgment for the discovery of the unity of empirical laws, however, the question still

158   Teleological Laws

remains as to what justifies Thesis$_r$, with its emphasis on specifically mechanical laws. Why think that mechanical laws are necessary to this end? Three bits of textual evidence hint at an answer to this question. First, Kant's initial description of this maxim is that the maxim "is provided to it [i.e., reflection] by the mere understanding a priori" (5:386). The idea here is that empirical phenomena and empirical laws will be constrained by a priori laws, and insofar as mechanical laws have an a priori foundation in the understanding (in the guise of the Second Analogy or the Laws of Mechanics), it makes sense to consider right away the constraints that they place on the discovery of particular empirical laws and any unity that they might possess at some later stage. Second, Kant begins §71 by arguing that one "can by no means prove the impossibility of the generation of organized products of nature through the mere mechanism of nature" (5:388). If one cannot prove that all generation of natural material products does not occur according to mechanical laws, one might be tempted to at least proceed on the assumption that it must always be possible to explain such generation according to mechanical laws. It would therefore make sense to start looking for an explanation along those lines.

Third, later in §71 Kant remarks that in reflection one "always remains open for any mechanical explanatory grounds, and never strays from the sensible world" (5:389). That is, while one might be tempted to appeal to highly theoretical concepts in attempting to explain the generation of natural phenomena, one must always be open to specifically mechanical explanation on the grounds that it keeps one firmly rooted in the sensible world, which must form the basis for any "interconnected experiential cognition." So not only should one look to build off the a priori constraints of the understanding's mechanical principles, which serve as a fixed point in the search for unity, but one should also try to keep as close to what is given in sensible experience in working up to a unified set of empirical laws, given that mechanical explanations stay close to the empirical evidence and should also always be possible, at least in principle. Though the textual evidence for this interpretation is both fairly scant and widely scattered so that one could certainly question whether it is ultimately convincing, it is still, I take it, the most attractive justification of Thesis$_r$ currently on offer.

7.2.4   The Second Challenge: The Proof of Antithesis$_r$

If this justification of Thesis$_r$ is adequate, what about Antithesis$_r$? Antithesis$_r$ states that the generation of some material objects cannot be judged as possible according to mere mechanical laws. In §§69–73 Kant does not

The Antinomy of Teleological Judgment

argue for this assertion beyond noting that "particular experiences" suggest such a "special principle" (5:386). Given the Analytic of the Teleological Power of Judgment, the reader can reasonably assume, however, that it is experiences of *organisms* that suggest *teleological* explanations. Later, as we saw above, Kant claims more explicitly that "it would be absurd for humans even ... to hope that there may yet arise a Newton who could make comprehensible even the generation of a blade of grass according to natural laws that no intention has ordered" (§75, 5:400), a claim that is reminiscent of very similar remarks he had made early in his pre-Critical period (e.g., 1:230). However, such assertions simply make one want to know all the more *why* the generation of blades of grass and other organisms cannot be judged according to mechanical laws. That is, why are organisms mechanically inexplicable for us?

McLaughlin has argued that an organism is not mechanically explicable because, as a natural end, "its parts (as far as their existence and their form are concerned) are possible only through their relation to the whole ... [and] its parts can be combined into a whole by being reciprocally the cause and effect of their form" (5:373).[9] That is, an organism has a different causal structure from what machines have, since its parts are possible only through the whole (the organism as a whole causes its organs, cells, etc.) and its parts form a whole due to their reciprocally causing each other (the cells and organs interact in ways that bring about the whole organism). More specifically, plants and animals have the powers of growth, reproduction, and self-maintenance. A machine or artifact, by contrast, is mechanically explicable because its parts have the properties and powers they do independently of any larger wholes that they might form. A clock may well have parts that interact with each other reciprocally, but a clock does not cause its parts and the parts do not cause each other, even if they are there for the sake of each other. In short, a clock does not grow, reproduce, or maintain its parts as an organism does. A further difference is that artifacts are not *natural* ends, given that they are caused by an external agent according to a conscious intention.

Hannah Ginsborg rejects this understanding of the mechanical inexplicability of organisms on the grounds that "there is no less of a need for teleology in understanding a machine such as a watch, than there is in understanding an organism."[10] That is, both watches and birds involve relations between their parts that are determined by the nature of the

---

[9] McLaughlin, *Kant's Critique of Teleology in Biological Explanation*, pp. 152–3.
[10] Hannah Ginsborg, "Two Kinds of Mechanical Inexplicability," *Journal of the History of Philosophy* 42 (2004): 33–65, p. 37.

160   Teleological Laws

whole (even if watches are not natural ends but rather artificial products). Granted, watches cannot reproduce or maintain themselves, but that does not detract from the fact that they are products of design and thus require teleological explanation just as much as birds do. Accordingly, Ginsborg argues that what makes an organism mechanically inexplicable is the fact that it cannot be explained in terms of "the mere forces of matter as such," or the fundamental properties of matter, whether it be matter in general or particular kinds of matter.[11] In the *Metaphysical Foundations*, for instance, Kant develops an account of attractive and repulsive forces inherent in matter that explains how bodies can fill a determinate region of space and communicate motion (e.g., in collisions according to the Laws of Mechanics). Insofar as an organism's reproduction, growth, and maintenance cannot be explained solely by such attractive and repulsive forces and the Laws of Mechanics, an organism is said to be mechanically inexplicable in Ginsborg's sense.

Two questions in this debate need to be distinguished. First: Is the antinomy concerned merely with the *origin* of organisms, or is it concerned primarily with the daily *functioning* of organisms? Second: Is an organism mechanically inexplicable because its parts are possible only through the causal efficacy of the whole, as McLaughlin maintains, or is it rather due to the special complexity inherent in an organism, one that is fundamentally different from the complexity that machines have, as Ginsborg holds?

Regarding the first question, it is somewhat surprising that no definitive answer is immediately provided by any of the contexts that are obviously relevant to Kant's discussions of organisms (even if certain statements, e.g., at 5:389–90, point in one direction). In fact, a careful reading of the statement of the antinomy shows that it is ambiguous on this very point, since Antithesis$_r$ refers to "products of material nature," which suggests that functioning is at issue, while Thesis$_r$ refers to the "generation of material things," which indicates that the origin of organisms is Kant's concern. Nor do Kant's various reflections on the debate between advocates of pre-formation and proponents of epigenesis decide the issue.[12] Given this impasse, one could appeal to the analogy between the origin of organisms and Kant's concern with the first state of the

---

[11] Hannah Ginsborg, "Kant on Understanding Organisms as Natural Purposes," in *Kant and the Sciences*, ed. Eric Watkins (New York: Oxford University Press, 2001), pp. 231–58, p. 244.

[12] See Mark Fischer, "Organisms and Teleology in Kant's Natural Philosophy," PhD dissertation, Emory University, 2007, for detailed discussion of Kant's position on this issue.

The Antinomy of Teleological Judgment   161

world in the first *Critique*'s First Antinomy. However, it is difficult to see that the origin of organisms is particularly crucial to the unity of laws, which is what reflective judgment is supposed to bring about. So insofar as the unity of empirical laws is the issue, it would *seem* to be the regular functioning of organisms that is the central topic of the Antinomy. However, this question is deserving of further research.

Regarding the second question, several striking passages seem relevant. In the first paragraph of §71, Kant emphasizes how the limitations of our cognitive faculties preclude us from comprehending how organisms are actually possible. Kant thus remarks about organisms: "we have no insight into their primary internal ground, and thus we cannot reach the internal and completely sufficient principle of the possibility of a nature (which lies in the supersensible) at all" (5:388). What this passage suggests is that we lack insight into what makes organisms possible, given that it lies in the supersensible and we have no insight into the supersensible.[13] Along similar lines, he considers seriously the possibility that what is specific to organisms requires a kind of causality that cannot lie either "in material nature or in its intelligible substratum" (5:388), and we cannot have a priori cognition of that kind of causality: "About this our reason, which is extremely limited with regard to the concept of causality if the latter is supposed to be specified a priori, can give us no information whatsoever" (5:389). Kant also says emphatically that he is claiming only that when we seek mechanical explanations, "**human reason** ... will never be able to discover the least ground of what constitutes what is specific in a natural end" (5:388). If we can grasp mechanical laws but cannot grasp what makes organisms possible, then it is natural to infer that mechanical laws cannot be used to explain the possibility of organisms so far as we can judge (even if mechanical laws could ultimately be used to explain the possibility of organisms in a way that we could not understand). Even if organisms turn out to be possible according to mechanical laws, or even if mechanical and final causation were ultimately grounded in a single principle, in its judgment our reason can neither reconcile these modes of explanation nor grasp their unifying principle, given that it would lie in "the inner ground of nature itself, which is unknown to us" (5:388). As a result of the limitations of our cognitive powers, we have no choice but to adopt a maxim that goes beyond mechanical laws if we are to have any chance of explaining, or even of starting to explain, organisms. These passages thus suggest that

---

[13] It is unfortunate that Kant does not directly address the question of how we can know that the possibility of an organism must lie in the supersensible.

162   Teleological Laws

Antithesis$_r$ is justified by our experiencing organisms as specific natural ends whose ground lies beyond the mechanical explanations that are available to us.

What thus emerges from identifying the antinomy of teleological judgment as constituted by Thesis$_r$ and Antithesis$_r$ is that they do contradict each other, as is required for an antinomy, and that lines of argument can be identified that would prove, or at least go some way toward providing argumentative support for, both Thesis$_r$ and Antithesis$_r$, which would satisfy another fundamental requirement for the presence of an antinomy. What is striking about the lines of argument we have found for Thesis$_r$ and Antithesis$_r$, tentative though they may be, is not only that they contribute to the unity of empirical laws but also that they do so in rather different ways. What recommends mechanical explanations in Thesis$_r$ is ultimately their proximity to the phenomena, since that must be one fixed point for reflecting judgment in its attempt to find unity among the laws of experience. What supports Antithesis$_r$, by contrast, is the fact – if it is one – that the possibility of organisms lies beyond experience in the supersensible and as such requires a mode of explanation different from that in terms of mechanical laws. In short, if Thesis$_r$ contributes to the unity of empirical laws by starting close to the phenomena, Antithesis$_r$ recognizes the necessity of allowing a role to what is distant from the immediate phenomena (in the supersensible).

7.3   The Resolution of the Antinomy of Teleological Judgment

The second main question that inevitably arises with respect to the Antinomy of Teleological Judgment concerns its resolution. Certain aspects of this resolution can be determined from the most basic features of the resolutions that Kant develops for the antinomies of pure theoretical and practical reason. Accordingly, Transcendental Realism is allegedly presupposed by the Thesis and the Antithesis, and Transcendental Idealism is required for the contradiction between the Thesis and Antithesis to be avoided and the resolution achieved. Since Kant seems to address these issues in a way that connects to the topic at hand in §§72–3, it is worth considering the content of these paragraphs and how they might contribute to the resolution before facing the resolution directly.

7.3.1   Four Alternative Accounts of Teleology (§§72–3)

In §72 Kant lays out four different kinds of objective systems that would attempt to explain purposiveness in some ultimate way. He first

The Antinomy of Teleological Judgment 163

distinguishes between an *idealism* and a *realism* of natural ends. The former asserts that, notwithstanding appearances to the contrary, all purposiveness in nature is *unintentional*, i.e., the result of causes that do not require conscious intentions, while the latter claims that some purposiveness is in fact *intentional*. He then focuses on two kinds of "idealist" positions. The purposiveness of nature can take the form, he asserts, of either a lifeless matter or a lifeless God.[14] (1) Epicurus and Democritus are proponents of the former view, (2) Spinoza of the latter. Kant thinks that the former view's reduction of final causation to a purely physical ground in the form of mechanical laws of motion is unworthy of serious consideration, though he does go on to refute it. The latter view, by contrast, which reduces final causation to the fatalism of a hyperphysical and supersensible ground of all of nature by saying that the world follows not from God's understanding or will but rather from the divine nature by a blind necessity, is more difficult to refute since the concept of the original being it employs is, he thinks, not even intelligible.

Kant continues his discussion by considering the "realist" positions, which likewise divide into physical and hyperphysical versions by tracing organisms back to either living matter or a living God. The former (3) asserts that nature is teleological, whether in the form of a plurality of individual living substances (as Aristotle seems to maintain in the *Metaphysica*) or a single world-soul (as one might try to understand Plato's view), and is called hylozoism. The latter (4) attributes purposiveness to the "original ground of the world-whole" (5:392), i.e., God, and is called theism. In a footnote, Kant claims that these four positions exhaust the possible options and suggests that one should give up all such objective assertions as to the ultimate explanation of purposes so as to "weigh our judgment critically, merely in relation to our cognitive faculty" (ibid.), which will result in non-dogmatic maxims for the use of our cognitive faculties.

In §73 Kant then argues that all four accounts just described are unsuccessful in their attempts to explain the purposiveness of nature. (1) Kant's objection to Epicurus' account is that by denying the difference between final and mechanistic causality and by asserting that everything, including what appears as a purpose in nature, is caused by blind chance, Epicurus cannot provide adequate accounts of two phenomena that stand in need of explanation. One is that our concepts of ends bear an analogy to generated products, or artifacts. The other is that generation actually occurs in accord with mechanical laws. The first

---

[14] Both positions invoke "lifeless" since, on the idealist position, purposiveness reduces to a "blind" mechanism of one kind or another.

164   Teleological Laws

phenomenon remains unexplained because ends, which on his account are produced by purely mechanical laws, are unlike objects that we produce according to our own intentions, and to say that they correspond due to blind chance explains nothing at all. Similarly, to say that blind chance brings it about that ends are generated according to the laws of motion is explanatorily vacuous, because what one wants to know is *how* the laws of motion produce such ends, and "blind chance" precludes insight on this point. In fact, Kant concludes by noting that given his reduction of natural events to the laws of motion Epicurus is not even in a position to explain the *illusion* of teleological judgments (that is, our being tempted to invoke final causes).

(2) Kant's analysis highlights several distinctive features of Spinoza's position. Instead of asserting that an original being endowed with understanding brings about living creatures according to certain intended ends, Spinoza holds that living beings subsist as necessary accidents within a necessary substance that is devoid of any understanding.[15] Spinoza's position has an immediate advantage over other accounts insofar as living organisms have a kind of unity by virtue of their subsisting in one and the same substance (rather than being distinct substances). However, Kant repeatedly emphasizes that this kind of ontological unity is distinct from the unity of ends or purposes, which is a unity of a very special kind. Specifically, on Spinoza's view living beings follow with blind necessity from a being that has no understanding, which is inconsistent with the possibility of either a unified purpose or any intentionality, both of which require contingency in the effect and intelligibility in the cause. As a result, Spinoza's position cannot account for what is specific to purposes.

(3) Kant's principal objection to hylozoism is based on its inability to explain the possibility of living matter a priori. Against the possibility of living matter, Kant repeats his objection from the *Metaphysical Foundations* (4:544) that the concept of living matter contains a contradiction in terms, since the concept of inertia, which is essential to matter as such, just means "lifelessness." Against the possibility of a living matter (whether in the form of individual substances or in the world-soul) his main point here is that there is no a priori and non-circular explanation of its basic concept. Experience might be able to establish the possibility of organisms by revealing their actuality, but the requisite kind of experience would be a posteriori, not a priori. One could derive the concept of an organism from the concept of living matter, but only if one has

---

[15] Insofar as Spinoza clearly maintains that thought is an attribute of the one infinite necessary substance, Kant's interpretation seems odd, if not uncharitable.

The Antinomy of Teleological Judgment 165

antecedent a priori grounds to accept the concept of living matter, and such grounds are precisely what was lacking for the concept of an organism in the first place. As a result, hylozoism cannot explain purposiveness, but rather presupposes it.[16]

(4) Kant concedes that theism has one advantage over the other three dogmatic explanations, namely, that by positing the divine understanding as the cause of the world, it at least *starts* with a notion that involves genuinely intentional causality. The problem it faces, however, is that its account of purposiveness is ultimately dogmatic, at least when determining judgment is involved. To establish that God is the cause of the purposiveness of organisms, one would have to prove that matter could not generate purposiveness by means of its mechanistic causality, but our cognitive abilities are too limited to rule out such a possibility. Instead, given our cognitive limitations, we have to judge the generation of organisms as caused by a supreme understanding, but such judgments occur only at the level of reflecting rather than determining judgment. Thus, a theistic account of purposiveness is not justified.

Now it would be natural to expect that these four accounts of the systematicity of nature would be relevant to the antinomy because they illustrate how important philosophers of the past make the assumption that generates the antinomial conflict, and that Kant's own position can avoid this conflict by rejecting that assumption. However, this natural expectation does not fit well with Kant's actual discussion. For one, Kant devotes all of §73 to refuting these accounts *on their own terms*, which is not at all required for the antinomy; he has already stated the propositions that form a contradiction and there is thus no need to argue their internal inconsistency. For another, Kant sometimes suggests that what leads these accounts astray is that they do not rest "satisfied with speculation within the boundaries of the mere cognition of nature" but rather attempt to connect the concept of final causes with the "highest point in the series of causes" (5:390), but what he repeatedly stresses about these accounts is their dogmatic intent. That is, their concern is with "objective principles of the possibility of things" (5:391) rather than with a properly critical analysis of our subjective faculties and the subjective maxims that we adopt. If, however, they are dogmatic in this sense, then they do not illustrate either Thesis$_r$ or Antithesis$_r$, do not make the assumption that leads to the antinomial conflict, and are not directly relevant to understanding Kant's resolution, however it is understood, given that it must be at the level of reflecting judgment and its maxims.

---

[16] Kant's argument against hylozoism seems to be either uncharitable or question-begging.

166   Teleological Laws

Unfortunately, not only are all four of these systems deemed inadequate, it is also difficult to see that they shed much light on the nature of Kant's own resolution to the antinomy. For as we saw above, no explicit reference is made to Transcendental Realism in Thesis$_r$ and Antithesis$_r$ or in the arguments one might formulate on their behalf, and Transcendental Idealism seems to be important in this context primarily insofar as it helps in the diagnosis of the failures of the dogmatic positions. How it is involved in resolving the contradiction and explaining the possibility and nature of organisms is not immediately obvious. These limitations suggest that the antinomy of teleological judgment has a special dynamic of its own.

7.3.2   The Notion of an Intuitive Understanding

So what is this special dynamic and how it is relevant to a philosophically satisfying resolution of the antinomy? In §§76–7 Kant devotes considerable attention to describing the discursive nature of our human understanding and how it contrasts with an intuitive understanding (whether or not such an understanding actually exists). Since our understanding uses concepts to grasp whatever particular objects happen to be given to us (through sensibility), there is a distinction for us between possibility and actuality as well as between constitutive and regulative principles. Since an intuitive understanding would grasp all features of all objects immediately, it would not, Kant claims, distinguish between possibility and actuality and it would also have no place for regulative principles. As a result of these remarks, several authors have claimed that Kant's discussion of these different kinds of understandings is crucial to his resolution of the antinomy.

For example, Eckart Förster, who has recently distinguished very carefully in Kant's texts between the notion of an intuitive understanding and that of an intellectual intuition,[17] argues that the notion of an intuitive understanding is central to Kant's resolution of the antinomy on the basis of two main points:

Because all perceptions are appearances that always arise individually in sensibility as passive (A99), the understanding must combine them according to mechanical perspectives in order to make cognition of them. That is the one point. Since we must at the same time judge some perceptions teleologically, we can combine them with the mechanism of sensibility by tracing the unity of both

---

[17] Eckart Förster, "Von der Eigentümlichkeit unseres Verstands in Ansehung der Urteilskraft (§§ 74–78)," in *Kooperativer Kommentar zu Kants Kritik der Urteilskraft*, ed. Otfried Höffe and Ina Goy (Berlin: Akademie Verlag, 2008), pp. 259–74, pp. 266–7.

The Antinomy of Teleological Judgment 167

back to the super-sensible substrate of nature. *We* can do that only with the help of concepts of ends, but since we cognize that the concept of an end is a peculiarity of a discursive understanding and not that of an intuitive understanding, we do not need to ascribe this concept of an end to the substrate itself. That is the other.[18]

So the basic idea underlying Förster's interpretation of the resolution is that because the concept of an end is peculiar to our discursive understanding, it need not be attributed to the substrate of nature.

However, two aspects of Förster's explanation of Kant's position are, it seems, unsatisfying. First, it is difficult to see, on Förster's account, how exactly it follows from the specifically discursive nature of our understanding that we must attempt to explain the world according to mechanical principles. Even if it is true that particulars are given to us and that we must then find general rules (or laws) to cover them, and even if it is true that there is an element of contingency involved when general rules (or laws) are selected to cover them, neither truth directly entails the necessity of *mechanical* explanation, which maintains the priority of the parts over the whole. For if one takes into account only the concept of a discursive understanding, such an understanding could, it seems, encounter, or be given, either a part or a whole. As a result, it is only if one assumes that the part is given and that the whole is not, that mechanical explanation becomes necessary for us. Yet nowhere has this claim been argued for. So it is not clear that the discursivity of our understanding is as closely connected to mechanism as Förster maintains.

Second, and more seriously for understanding Kant's resolution, Förster's idea of an end that is peculiar to our discursive understanding is not sufficient to resolve the contradiction asserted in Thesis$_r$ and Antithesis$_r$. The fact that an intuitive understanding might be able to understand the possibility of organisms does not entail that we can understand such a possibility, so Antithesis$_r$ remains in full force. At the same time, Thesis$_r$ is not threatened by what an intuitive understanding can do or by the fact that it operates differently from us.[19] As a result, nothing in this line of thought has shown that either Thesis$_r$ or Antithesis$_r$ is false (even if there could be a being for which neither would be true)

---

[18] Förster, "Von der Eigentümlichkeit unseres Verstands in Ansehung der Urteilskraft (§§ 74–78)," pp. 270–1.

[19] Alix Cohen, "Kant's Antinomy of Reflective Judgment: A Re-Evaluation," *Teorema* 23 (2004): 183–97, p. 193, similarly notes that the conflict between regulative principles for our discursive understanding is not immediately removed due to a reference to an intuitive understanding.

168 Teleological Laws

and therefore nothing has removed the contradiction between them.[20] While Kant's reflections on the differences between a discursive and an intuitive understanding and on their general philosophical importance are fascinating and one can immediately see why they would have such tremendous significance for later German Idealists, they are best seen as part of the larger context for Kant's resolution of the antinomy, rather than as articulating the resolution itself. Some further move is clearly still needed.

7.3.3 Subcontraries and the Assumption of Objective Inexplicability

Peter McLaughlin, by contrast, places much less explicit emphasis on the possible implications that an intuitive understanding might have for resolving the antinomy. Instead, his basic strategy is to use the specific resolution of the Antinomies in the first *Critique* as a model for understanding the resolution of the antinomy of teleological judgment. This strategy allows him to focus on (1) the formal resolution of the antinomy and on (2) whether we must in fact be able to explain everything, for the contradiction disappears, he maintains, once we give up that assumption. Regarding the first point, McLaughlin states: "The form in which this antinomy is resolved ... is the subcontrary form. It is shown that, the false presupposition having been exposed and rejected, both thesis and antithesis in their new forms *can* be true."[21] The First Antinomy in the first *Critique*, which asserts both that the world is finite and that it is infinite, is resolved by noting that Thesis and Antithesis contradict each other only on the assumption that the world must have a determinate magnitude. Once one rejects this assumption (which one can do by noting that the assumption holds only for things in themselves, not appearances), one can see that both are false (for the sensible world) insofar as the sensible world is indeterminately large. On the basis of the parallels between the first and third *Critiques*, McLaughlin's proposal

---

[20] Quarfood, *Transcendental Idealism and the Organism*, likewise accepts the idea that the notion of an intuitive understanding provides argumentative support for understanding the resolution in this way. For he argues that the elimination of time removes the most problematic aspect of the natural purpose, with its suggestion of final causality or reversed time-order (p. 189). However, even if one were to somehow remove temporality from a natural purpose, it is still not clear what implications that would have for *our* understanding. In particular, one should not immediately infer the regulative status of a principle simply because an intuitive understanding might not adopt that principle. Space and time are principles that an intuitive understanding would not have, yet space and time are not regulative principles. Quarfood concludes his treatment of the antinomy with a brief discussion of this problem, but refrains from endorsing any particular solution (pp. 207–8).

[21] McLaughlin, *Kant's Critique of Teleology in Biological Explanation*, p. 130.

The Antinomy of Teleological Judgment   169

thus holds that Thesis$_r$ and Antithesis$_r$ rest on a shared assumption and that, once one identifies and rejects that assumption, one will be able to avoid the contradiction between Thesis$_r$ and Antithesis$_r$, just as was the case in the First Antinomy.

McLaughlin then identifies the relevant assumption:

> Our understanding has, according to Kant, the peculiarity that it can only explain mechanistically, that it can genuinely understand only that which it can itself produce out of its parts. Due to this peculiarity, we *must* judge all natural things to be possible according to merely mechanical laws, because it is only such natural objects that we can explain at all. However, apparently due to the same peculiarity, we *cannot* explain some objects in this manner and have to introduce final (actually formal) causes. *We* must explain everything mechanistically, but nature need not always let itself be explained in this way. The incompatibility between the two maxims (R1, R2) [i.e., Thesis$_r$ and Antithesis$_r$] is based on the presupposition that the necessity and impossibility are objective. Our subjective inability to explain things otherwise than in a mechanistic manner and our incapacity to explain certain things mechanistically contradict one another only under the presupposition that we *must* be able to explain everything. If there is a difference between causality and reductionist mechanism, such that causality is constitutive of the objects of experience and mechanism is merely regulative since it is based on a subjective peculiarity of our understanding, then it is at least possible that there may be objects of experience that are not explainable for us.[22]

If not everything must be objectively explicable, then, McLaughlin claims, both Thesis$_r$ and Antithesis$_r$ can be true and the antinomy has been resolved.

However, despite its considerable attractions, this solution is unsatisfying on two main points. Now McLaughlin identifies as the crucial assumption the claim that everything must be objectively explicable. Yet it is difficult to see the relevance of specifically *objective* considerations to the actual antinomy. Thesis$_c$ and Antithesis$_c$ are objective principles, but, as we have seen above, they also do not represent the antinomy. Thesis$_r$ and Antithesis$_r$, by contrast, are not constitutive or objective principles, but are rather regulative and subjective (pertaining to how we must judge). It is the contradiction between subjective principles that must be resolved. What is novel about McLaughlin's position on this issue, however, is his claim that the antimony holds only if everything is explicable for us. For if one rejects that assumption, then Thesis$_r$ and Antithesis$_r$ can pertain to different domains, just as rejecting the identification of the sensible and intelligible worlds in the first *Critique*'s Third Antinomy allows one to hold that, e.g., determinism is true for the sensible world, while freedom is excluded for that class of objects,

---

[22] McLaughlin, *Kant's Critique of Teleology in Biological Explanation*, p. 162.

170   Teleological Laws

though not for the intelligible world. Accordingly, on McLaughlin's interpretation of the resolution, once one rejects the assumption that everything is explicable by us, Thesis$_r$ can be true of phenomena that are explicable by us, whereas Antithesis$_r$ can be true of phenomena that are not explicable by us.

The problem with this particular aspect of McLaughlin's interpretation is that although it does resolve the contradiction, it also generates unwelcome results. The main difficulty is that it does not provide any criterion that is independent of mechanical explicability for determining whether phenomena are explicable by us, and thus no criterion that would allow us to apply the regulative principles stated in Thesis$_r$ and Antithesis$_r$. That is, for any given phenomenon we would have no criterion that would determine whether it is explicable by us and thus no way of knowing whether we should judge the phenomenon as possible according to mechanical laws alone or not. Notice how very different such a resolution would be from how the first *Critique*'s Antinomy is resolved. For its distinction between the sensible and intelligible world provides us with an explicit criterion for distinguishing between the things of which the thesis and antithesis will be true or false. By contrast, the distinction between what can and cannot be explicable by us provides no criterion for applying the regulative principles that constitute the antinomy, leaving *us* unable to avoid a contradiction when confronted with a given phenomenon (even if there is, strictly speaking, no contradiction in the phenomenon).

McLaughlin's interpretation also faces some difficulty in accounting for the practical import of Kant's resolution. For Kant holds that we should try to explain any given phenomenon as far as we can according to mechanical laws. However, if the antinomy is resolved as McLaughlin proposes, it is not clear why this recommendation would apply. For if a phenomenon is not explicable by us, then McLaughlin's interpretation of Antithesis$_r$ would have it that we should judge that it is not possible according to mechanical laws. However, if we should judge that it is not possible according to mechanical laws, it is difficult to see why we should try to explain it as possible according to mechanical laws as far as we can (given that we do not think that such an explanation is even possible.) As a result, Kant would not be justified in making such a recommendation if McLaughlin's interpretation were correct.

7.3.4   Subordination

Ginsborg suggests yet a different resolution to the antinomy. Instead of denying that we are able to explain organisms, she argues that Kant must

The Antinomy of Teleological Judgment 171

show how Thesis$_r$ and Antithesis$_r$ "can be reconciled from the point of view of a discursive understanding applying these principles within the context of scientific enquiry, ... [a] step, which ... invokes the 'subordination' of mechanism to teleology."[23] Ginsborg's focus on the application of principles within scientific inquiry is important, but it also raises the question of how this subordination should be understood. Ginsborg spells this out by suggesting that when scientists attempt to explain the origin of organisms, they do so on the basis not of inanimate matter, as would be the case for, say, collisions of billiard balls, but rather of matter that is already organized in such a way that it is endowed with the kind of formative power that makes it possible for an organism to maintain itself and reproduce in ways that watches cannot.[24] Ginsborg develops her interpretation further as follows:

In effect, then, [Kant] completes the resolution of the antinomy by allowing two different, although related, senses of mechanical explanation. On the narrower sense, on which the mechanical explanation of a thing involves accounting for its existence in terms of the fundamental powers of inorganic matter, organisms are indeed ... inexplicable by us. But they can still be mechanically explained in a weaker sense which does not exclude teleology, namely in terms of the powers of organized matter.[25]

So Ginsborg's idea is that when we attempt to explain organisms, while mechanical laws are still invoked, they are not applied exclusively to inorganic matter. Ginsborg's interpretation has a clear advantage here in that it can find textual support in several sentences at 5:414 and 5:415 in §78, where Kant asserts the subordination of mechanical explanations to teleological explanations, as well as in several passages from §§80–1, where he provides examples of how we are to explain natural ends by considering what changes would occur to an organism if certain mechanical adjustments were made to it.

Though Ginsborg is right to note the importance of Kant's idea that mechanism is in some sense subordinate to teleology in Kant's resolution of the antinomy, her interpretation still faces two significant challenges. First, Ginsborg does not explain how the contradiction between Thesis$_r$ and Antithesis$_r$ is to be resolved. The mere fact that teleological explanations must involve mechanical laws may well

---

[23] Hannah Ginsborg, "Kant's Biological Teleology and Its Philosophical Significance," in *The Normativity in Nature: Essays on Kant's Critique of Judgement* (Oxford: Oxford University Press, 2015), pp. 316–31, p. 325.

[24] In a series of further articles, which are collected in *The Normativity of Nature*, Ginsborg has argued that a special kind of normativity is involved in such judgments.

[25] Ginsborg, "Kant's Biological Teleology and Its Philosophical Significance," 325.

172   Teleological Laws

constrain how the resolution is to be achieved, but it cannot represent the resolution itself insofar as it does not explain whether and how Thesis$_r$ and Antithesis$_r$ are, e.g., both false. While one might think that subordinating mechanical to teleological explanation would require a restriction in the scope of Thesis$_r$, in §80 Kant states quite clearly that Thesis$_r$ remains true: "The **authorization to seek** for a merely mechanical explanation of all natural products is in itself entirely unrestricted" (5:417), even though he then immediately notes that our ability to identify merely mechanical explanations is severely limited. In fact, Kant claims that this limitation even explains why mechanical explanation is subordinate to teleological principles. So it is clear that the notion of subordination that Ginsborg rightly draws our attention to is multifaceted, and its implications for the resolution of the antinomy are not immediately obvious.

Second, Ginsborg's interpretation does not take into account one feature that Kant seems to insist on as crucial to explaining his resolution of the antinomy. In §78, for example, he writes:

The two principles [of mechanism and teleology] cannot be united in one and the same thing in nature as fundamental principles for the explanation (deduction) of one from the other ... For one kind of explanation excludes the other, even on the supposition that objectively both grounds of the possibility rest on a single one, but one of which we take no account. The principle that is to make possible the unifiability of both in the judging of nature in accordance with them must be placed in what lies outside of both (hence outside of the possible empirical representation of nature), but which still contains the ground of both, i.e., in the supersensible, and each of these two kinds of explanation must be related to that. (5:411–12)

What is crucial here is not just that Kant invokes the supersensible, but the use to which he puts it. The unifiability of mechanical and teleological principles depends on the supersensible, since the supersensible is the ground of both. More specifically, in his explanation of the claim just quoted, Kant asserts that the principle that underlies both mechanism and teleology "justifies the maxims of natural research that jointly depend on it" (5:412). Kant thus seems to think not only that both Thesis$_r$ and Antithesis$_r$ depend on a supersensible principle but also that the way to see how these otherwise incompatible principles can be rendered compatible is by seeing that they both depend on such a principle.[26] Such claims obviously stand in need of considerable explanation and justification. However, rather than attempting to explain and justify them, Kant immediately goes on to assert that "we cannot form

---

[26] Section 7.2.2 suggests this point too.

The Antinomy of Teleological Judgment 173

the least affirmative determinate concept of this" and that therefore how these incompatible principles can be rendered compatible "can by no means be explained" (5:412–13). Instead, Kant suggests that we should pursue the laws of nature – whether mechanical or teleological – "without being troubled by the apparent conflict between the two principles for judging this product; for at least the possibility that both may be objectively unifiable in one principle (since they concern appearances that presuppose a supersensible ground) is secured" (5:413). These claims are deeply puzzling and raise many further questions. However, it is equally clear that Kant views them as playing a crucial role in the resolution of the antinomy. Unfortunately, neither Ginsborg's interpretation nor any one of the other views discussed above explains these claims or shows how they are to be incorporated into a single comprehensive resolution of the Antinomy of Teleological Judgment.[27]

7.4 Conclusion

We are now in a position to summarize the most significant results that emerge from considering our two basic questions concerning Kant's Antinomy of Teleological Judgment. The one major result is that after it became clear that the antinomy consisted in a genuine contradiction between two regulative principles (Thesis$_r$ and Antithesis$_r$), we were able to identify a significant problem concerning the requisite proofs of these principles, a problem with two sides: (1) Kant does not provide clear and explicit proofs of either Thesis$_r$ or Antithesis$_r$ and (2) no one has made adequate progress in articulating plausible lines of argument on his behalf (though there has been considerable productive debate about the meaning of his claim regarding the mechanical inexplicability of organisms). A second major result is that once the contradiction between Thesis$_r$ and Antithesis$_r$ was made precise in such a way that it could not be quickly dismissed as resulting from a simple confusion, finding a resolution to the antinomy from within the framework of Kant's Critical philosophy that would be based on direct textual evidence and be philosophically rigorous proved to be a challenge that remains.[28]

[27] Cohen, "Kant's Antinomy of Reflective Judgment," goes further in claiming (pp. 193–4) that the appeal to the supersensible shows that Kant *cannot* resolve the antinomy. Even though Kant's claims regarding the supersensible are undoubtedly difficult, I am not (yet) convinced that they necessarily reveal insoluble problems in Kant's view.

[28] For helpful discussion of some of the ideas contained in the first part of this chapter, I thank audience members (especially Eckart Förster, Hannah Ginsborg, and Ina Goy) at a conference in Tübingen in May 2007 on the third *Critique*. I am indebted to Karl Ameriks, Mark Fisher, Hannah Ginsborg, Peter McLaughlin, and Clinton Tolley for numerous conversations about the antinomy and earlier versions of this chapter.

8 Nature in General as a System of Ends

8.1 Introduction

Despite the many complexities, mysteries, and puzzles that one inevitably encounters reading the "Critique of the Teleological Power of Judgment," the basic structure of Kant's main line of argument would seem to be quite straightforward. What prompts Kant to write about teleological judgment in the first place is organisms, since organisms involve purposes, and purposiveness is a unifying theme of the *Critique of the Power of Judgment* as a whole (since judgment in general is purposive). Thus Kant begins his discussion of organisms by first providing analyses of what (material, intrinsic, natural) objective purposiveness is and of what an organism is, before asserting that organisms are natural purposes. In this way, his analyses reveal that organisms are different from inorganic matter, which can be explained according to the mechanical principles already laid out in, e.g., the *Metaphysical Foundations*. But since organisms are in some sense mechanically inexplicable, despite also involving matter, the existence of organisms presents a problem that can be expressed in the form of an antinomy concerning mechanical and teleological modes of explanation. Kant then solves the antinomy by invoking a supersensible ground that (for some reason) allows one to (somehow) privilege teleological over mechanistic explanation, though without thereby rejecting the possible applicability of the latter to organisms. Kant concludes his argument by explaining how this solution fits with his discussion of the physico-theological and moral arguments of the first and second *Critiques*, thus putting his solution to the antinomy into the larger context of his critical philosophy. In accordance with this three-fold structure of (1) conceptual analysis, (2) antinomial conflict and resolution, and (3) broader context-setting, Kant divides his treatment of organisms in the "Critique of the Teleological Power of Judgment" into (1) an "Analytic of the Teleological Power of Judgment," (2) a "Dialectic of the Teleological Power of Judgment," and (3) a "Methodology of the Teleological Power of Judgment." In this way,

174

Nature in General as a System of Ends 175

one has, it seems, an account of Kant's overall argument that corresponds to the load-bearing elements of this part of the third *Critique*.

Without denying any of these claims about the structure of the "Critique of the Teleological Power of Judgment," I want to assert that such an account omits a crucial element of Kant's main line of argument. For in a series of passages that have not received sufficient attention, Kant claims that once we start to reflect on organisms, we are necessarily led beyond this initial topic to think of nature in general.[1] That is, even if teleological judgment is prompted by our experience of (what we take to be) organisms, it does not then restrict itself to judgments about organisms, but rather necessarily goes further to make claims about all of nature, which will include at least some things that are not organisms. But this immediately raises two questions: (1) What exactly are Kant's claims about nature in general (as contrasted with his claims about organisms in particular)? (2) What are his arguments for these claims? I first argue that according to Kant, reflection on organisms necessarily leads to two further claims about nature in general. The first claim is that not just organisms, but in fact every specific thing *in* nature must also be judged teleologically, while the second is that nature as a whole is a system of purposes that itself has a purpose. I then argue that Kant's distinctive conception of reason as a faculty that searches for the unconditioned condition of all conditioned objects provides the key for understanding Kant's arguments for both of these assertions. Although the third *Critique* does depend in essential ways on the faculty of the power of judgment, the faculty of reason also plays an ineliminable role in its overall argument, since it motivates and justifies Kant's moving beyond organisms to what is his ultimate concern, namely, the final and unconditioned purpose of nature, which is the existence of human beings, not as natural organisms, but rather as free and rational noumenal agents.[2]

8.2 Two Claims

In the third paragraph of §67, whose title is "On the Principle of the Teleological Judging of Nature in General as a System of Ends," Kant argues:

---

[1] Paul Guyer, *Kant's System of Nature and Freedom* (Oxford: Oxford University Press, 2005), pp. 314–42, esp. p. 327, similarly argues that the step from organisms to nature as a whole is both intrinsically important and crucial to the structure of Kant's overall argument.

[2] Though scholars sometimes treat the third *Critique* as if it had to be about the faculty of judgment exclusively, the book can, I argue, involve reason as well. There is, to my mind, no genuine conflict between the faculty of judgment and reason, even if they have different ends and functions.

176   Teleological Laws

It is therefore only matter insofar as it is organized that necessarily carries with it the concept of itself as a natural end, since its specific form is at the same time a product of nature. However, this concept now necessarily leads to the idea of the whole of nature as a system in accordance with the rule of ends, to which idea all of the mechanism of nature in accordance with principles of reason must now be subordinate (at least in order to test natural appearance by this idea). The principle of reason is appropriate for it only subjectively, i.e., as the maxims that everything in the world is good for something, that nothing in it is in vain; and by means of the example that nature gives in its organic products, one is justified, indeed called upon [*berufen*] to expect nothing in nature and its laws but what is purposive in the whole. (5:378–9)

This passage contains two crucial moves. The first is Kant's assertion that organized matter is a natural purpose. This assertion, which is obviously central to Kant's entire argument, is clearly intended as a conclusion that is supposed to follow from his analyses of purposes and organisms in the previous sections (§§61–3 and §§64–6, respectively). The second, which Kant signals (with "now") as the novel claim that is his focus in this section, is that the notion of an organism "necessarily leads" to the idea of the entirety of nature. But how exactly should this second statement be understood?

Kant seems to have two different claims in mind here. First, he clearly asserts that one is not only justified, but even called on ("*berufen*") to expect that everything *in* nature has a natural purpose or end. Accordingly, not only organisms, the very concept of which entails the concept of a natural purpose, but also inorganic matter must be viewed in terms of the purposes it serves. The force of this claim is thus that the *scope* of teleological judgment is not limited to organisms, but rather extends *universally* to each and every thing throughout nature. This is the clear import of his remarks that "everything in the world is good for something" and "nothing in nature is in vain." I will call this claim the Claim of Universal Scope (CUS).[3]

Second, Kant seems to think not only that everything *in* nature has a purpose, but also that nature itself, or nature as a whole, must be a system of purposes. That is, there is a systematic connection between the different purposive things in nature. This point comes out not only in the title to §67, which makes mention of "nature in general as a system of

---

[3] Kant also states CUS in §66 of the third *Critique* (5:376). In the first passage in particular, Kant asserts not merely the limited claim that in our judgment "nothing in such a creature [an organism] is *in vain*" (5:376) (so that he is claiming only that everything in an organism has a purpose), but also "the general doctrine of nature that *nothing* happens *by chance*" (5:376), which I take to mean that we judge that nothing in the world at all is in vain, since otherwise there would be no contrast between the first and second claims.

Nature in General as a System of Ends 177

ends" (5:377), but also in his phrase "the idea of a whole of nature *as a system*" (5:370) as opposed to simply 'the whole of nature *as such.*' Accordingly, though CUS clearly applies to 'the whole of nature,' it does not obviously require thinking of all of nature 'as one system,' that is, in such a way that the various things in nature are related to each other in any systematic way. This second claim is also on display at the conclusion of the final paragraph of §67, when Kant clarifies that "the unity of the supersensible principle must then be considered as valid in the same way not merely for certain species of natural beings, but for the whole of nature as a system" (5:381).[4] However, Kant wants to go even further than simply claiming that the things in nature come together to form a system. For he also wants to claim both that nature itself is a system *of purposes* (i.e., the systematic connection of things in nature involves their being purposes) and that nature as a whole must itself have a purpose, just as all of the individual organisms within nature do.[5] Let me label this constellation of positions (that nature as a whole is a system of purposes and that nature as a whole has a purpose) the Claims about Nature as a Whole (CNW).

In the second paragraph of §67 (which immediately precedes the first quotation above and lays the foundation for it), Kant articulates the context for and the meaning of CNW more fully as follows:

> To judge a thing to be purposive on account of its internal form is entirely different from holding the existence of such a thing to be an end of nature. For the latter assertion we need not only the concept of a possible end, but also cognition of the final end (*scopus*) of nature, which requires the relation of nature to something supersensible, which far exceeds all of our teleological cognition of nature; for the end of the existence of nature itself must be sought beyond nature. (5:378)

In this passage, Kant begins by drawing a distinction between judging the natural purpose of a thing according to its *form* and determining the *existence* of a thing as a natural purpose. We judge that a thing has the form of a natural purpose when we judge that it is an organism (by displaying the special kind of causality that is definitive of organisms). But to judge the form of a thing as purposive is distinct from passing judgment on the purpose of the existence of that thing. I can judge that this object in front of me is a tree (because its parts and its whole stand in

---

[4] The centrality of Kant's point is revealed by the fact that he introduces the passage with: "In this section we have meant to say nothing except . . ." (5:380).

[5] Textual evidence for this claim can be found in §85 at, e.g., 5:437.

178   Teleological Laws

a certain reciprocal dependency relation that matter as such does not display) without judging why the tree exists (what ends it might satisfy), or indeed judging that it exists for any purpose at all.

In light of this distinction, Kant then clarifies that once we start thinking about the purpose of the existence of things in nature, we end up being committed to (i) a purpose for the existence of nature as a whole, (ii) the purpose of the existence of nature as a whole being a final purpose or end (*Endzweck*),[6] and (iii) this final end being something supersensible that lies outside of nature. The first claim amounts to one aspect of CNW as it was originally introduced – nature forms a system of purposes and nature as a whole has a purpose of its own. The second and third claims, by contrast, significantly extend his commitments about the purpose of nature as a whole and thus reveal the full meaning of CNW.

Moreover, Kant's expression of commitment to all three components of CNW is no fluke; in several passages from later on in the third *Critique* he expresses the same constellation of claims. Thus in §86 he asserts:

Now if we encounter purposive arrangements in the world, and ... subordinate the ends that are only conditioned to an unconditioned, supreme end, i.e., a final end, then one readily sees, first, that in that case what is at issue is not an end of nature (within it), insofar as it exists, but the end of its existence, with all its arrangements, hence the ultimate *end of creation*, and in this, further, what is actually at issue is the supreme condition under which alone a final end (i.e., of the determining ground of a highest understanding for the production of the beings of the world) can obtain. (5:443)

And in §88, he reiterates:

But we certainly do find ends in the world, and physical teleology presents them in such measure that ... we will ultimately have reason to assume as the principle for research into nature that there is nothing in nature at all without an end; yet we try in vain to find the final end of nature in nature itself. (5:454)

As a result, Kant understands CNW to involve a robust commitment not only to nature as a system of purposes and to a purpose of nature as a whole, but also to a final purpose that lies outside of nature in the supersensible.[7]

---

[6] For the sake of brevity, I am abstracting from the distinction between "ultimate end" (*letzter Zweck*) and "final end" (*Endzweck*), helpfully clarified by Guyer (*Kant's System of Nature and Freedom*, p. 318).

[7] Note that Kant's commitment here is not to full-fledged cognition, but rather to a weaker kind of assent (though one that has reasons to support it).

Nature in General as a System of Ends 179

8.3 Kant's Arguments

If Kant thus maintains that reflection on individual organisms "necessarily leads" (5:379) to asserting CUS and CNW, how is one led beyond organisms to these claims, and what arguments does he develop in support of them? Why not be a biologist who is committed to understanding (the functioning of) organisms and leave it at that? Kant's most explicit statement in regard to CUS is found in §66:

For this concept [of a natural end] leads reason into an order of things entirely different from that of a mere mechanism of nature, which will no longer satisfy us here. An idea has to ground the possibility of the product of nature. However, since this is an absolute unity of the representation, while the matter is a multitude of things, which by itself can provide no determinate unity of composition, if that unity of the idea is even to serve as the determining ground *a priori* of a natural law of the causality of such a form of the composite, then the end of nature must extend to *everything* that lies in its product. For once we have related such an effect in the *whole* to a supersensible determining ground beyond the blind mechanism of nature, we must also judge it entirely in accordance with this principle; and there is no ground for assuming that the form of such a thing is only partially dependent on the latter, for in such a case, in which two heterogeneous principles are jumbled together, no secure rule for judging would remain at all. (5:377)

Kant is making two main points here. First, the discovery of even a single natural purpose (in the form of an organism) leads the faculty of reason, Kant says, and not the faculty of judgment, as one might expect, to "an order of things that is completely different" (5:377) from the mechanistic order laid out in, e.g., the *Metaphysical Foundations*.[8] For in a natural purpose, everything is both cause and effect of itself (5:370) such that the whole depends on its parts at the same time that the parts depend on the whole, a distinctive causal ordering that is evident, Kant thinks, in the maintenance and growth of an organism as well as in the preservation of the species through reproduction. It is because of this special kind of reciprocal dependence that Kant speaks in this passage of a unity that matter, which essentially involves a plurality (but not a principle that necessarily unifies the plurality), does not have. Given the analyses of the previous §§62–5, this point is not fundamentally new, even if it does stress the importance of the distinctive kind of order and unity found in organisms.

---

[8] Again, though there is no conflict between reason and the faculty of judgment, in this case the distinctive features of reason make it more appropriate for Kant to refer to it explicitly.

180   Teleological Laws

Second, and more importantly, Kant suggests that if we posit a super-sensible ground outside of nature as responsible for the distinctive order and purpose found in an organism, then we are committed to viewing everything in that organism as ordered in that same kind of way. However, if the appeal to a supersensible ground requires the application of a single criterion in order to explain a given object (including its constituent parts and structure), then one can reconstruct an argument for CUS based on CNW by noting that CNW requires that the object we hope to explain is simply the world in its entirety. Specifically, once one has claimed that nature as a whole forms a system of purposes and posited a supersensible ground to account for the final purpose of nature as a whole (as CNW maintains), it follows that one must consider all specific things *in* nature with respect to what purpose they have, because we consider them to be essential members of the system of purposes of nature that is brought about by this supersensible ground. But investigating whether each and every thing has a purpose is simply tantamount to CUS. So it is plausible to think that CUS follows straightforwardly from CNW.[9]

However, Kant does suggest a line of thought in support of CUS that runs independently of CNW, at least to a certain extent. At the end of the quotation, he notes that if one attempted to explain the form of a thing as depending in part on its relation to the supersensible principle invoked in CNW and in part on something else, then we would have two heterogeneous principles that worked independently of each other, which would entail that we would have "no secure rule" (5:377) for judging what makes such a form possible. That is, such a scenario would require that one judge some features of an object in nature according to mechanistic principles and other features according to teleological principles, which would be confusing since one would have no criterion to determine which principle should be used to explain any given feature. At the same time, it is not clear that Kant intends for it to be an argument that carries much independent weight. For it is not obvious (at least not without

---

[9] I should note that Kant does not explicitly formulate this argument. His explicit argument is only that the appeal to a supersensible ground requires the application of a single criterion to an organism. I am proposing that this argument be extended to the world as a whole, however, because it seems to be the most promising way to justify CUS. I do not rule out the possibility that there are other ways of justifying CUS. (Perhaps one might argue that CUS follows simply from nature having an end, and then nature forming a system of purposes follows from CUS plus some other assumptions.) What the textual justification for such arguments might be cannot easily be anticipated. The interpretation presented above is at least based on the text, even if it requires extending the argument's scope so as to encompass the world in its entirety (which, given CNW, Kant is committed to).

Nature in General as a System of Ends 181

more explicit argument than Kant provides here) why it is necessary that we must have only one criterion for judging the different features of things. There are all sorts of cases in which we use multiple criteria in a given explanatory context, even if there is a hierarchy among them. Granted, it is useful to have a single criterion for all cases, and also convenient, but its necessity is not particularly perspicuous. Fortunately, CUS follows from CNW, so this result is not damaging to Kant's position.

In the very next paragraph, Kant clarifies that the conclusion of his argument is still consistent with the possibility that some of the things in nature might not themselves have purposes, but rather are explicable according to purely mechanical laws. For example, CUS does not entail that everything in nature is itself an organism, which is important given that water, for example, clearly is not an organism. Nor does it even necessarily imply that everything in nature must serve as a purpose for something else. Water serves as a purpose for the existence of other organisms in nature insofar as it is necessary for the sustenance of plants and animals, but it is not metaphysically impossible that things serving no purpose might exist, such as, e.g., small bits of matter in a distant galaxy that have no effect on us or on any other rational living being.[10] Neither the fact that a whole has a purpose (or is viewed as having a purpose) nor the fact that there is a system of purposes within nature as a whole immediately entails that absolutely everything within nature must actually have a purpose (or must be viewed as having a purpose). In short, the system of natural purposes need not be completely coextensive with all of the objects in nature. Instead, the demand is that one *consider* whether all things in nature have either intrinsic or extrinsic purposes. CUS is, in short, no more than a regulative principle, and its truth depends, as we have seen, on the truth of CNW, just as Kant claims.

So what is Kant's argument for CNW? The passage that comes closest to containing an explicit argument for CNW can be found in the latter half of the second paragraph of §67 (the first half of which was quoted earlier). After claiming that the purpose of the existence of nature must be sought beyond nature, Kant provides the following by way of justification:

The internal form of a mere blade of grass can demonstrate its merely possible origin in accordance with the rule of ends in a way that is sufficient for our human

---

[10] I understand regulative principles in this case in such a way that what they presuppose is not that the relevant feature that is governed by the content of the principle is metaphysically possible, but rather that it might be metaphysically possible (or is metaphysically possible for all we know).

182   Teleological Laws

faculty of judging. But if one leaves this aside and looks only to the use that other natural beings make of it, then one abandons the contemplation of its internal organization and looks only at its external purposive relations, where the grass is necessary to the livestock, just as the latter is necessary to the human being as the means for his existence; yet one does not see why it is necessary that human beings exist (a question which, if one thinks about the New Hollanders or the Fuegians, might not be so easy to answer); thus one does not arrive at any categorical end, but all of this purposive relation rests on a condition that is always to be found further on, and which, as unconditioned, (the existence of a thing as a final end) lies entirely outside of the physical-teleological way of considering the world. But then such a thing is also not a natural end; for it (or its entire species) is not to be regarded as a natural product. (5:378)

Kant's argument contains racist views that are highly objectionable. He also seems to argue that once one distinguishes between the inner form of natural purposes in organisms and the purpose of the existence of things and then looks beyond the former, one will see that it is not possible to explain the purpose of the existence of things by way of external purposive relations within nature.[11] Even if the existence of grass is necessary for the existence of cattle and the existence of cattle is in turn necessary for the existence of human beings, it is not necessary that human beings exist. Indeed, there are, Kant maintains, no necessarily existing things within nature. So if one searches for the purpose of the existence of things, external purposive relations within nature cannot suffice. Instead, the only thing that could possibly suffice to explain the purpose of the existence of things is, Kant wants to argue, an unconditioned final end that lies outside of nature. But Kant's argument raises two questions: (1) What is it that moves one to seek a sufficient explanation of the purpose of the *existence* of things? (2) Why must a sufficient explanation take recourse specifically to an unconditioned final end that lies *outside* of nature?[12]

I want to suggest that the answer to both of these questions derives from Kant's distinctive conception of reason. For current purposes, Kant's conception of reason can be summarized in three claims.[13] First, reason is a faculty that searches for the conditions for whatever is

---

[11] By distinguishing between these two cases Kant is in effect operating with two different instances of purpose, one pertaining to the properties of a thing, the other concerning the existence of the thing. While one might think that Kant is thus illegitimately sliding from the one notion to the other, one might think that both are instances of conditioning relations and thus both are equally of interest to reason.

[12] That is, in effect, the second question asks: Why is CNW true?

[13] Both Guyer (*Kant's System of Nature and Freedom*) and Angela Breitenbach, *Die Analogie von Vernunft und Natur. Eine Umweltphilosophie nach Kant* (Berlin: Walter de Gruyter, 2009), suggest that reason is important in drawing this inference due to its desire for unification. I am arguing that one can take this point further by showing that it is not just

conditioned that is given. For example, in syllogistic logic (as Kant understands it), reason searches for the conditions for a conditioned judgment, since if successful, it can then formulate a syllogism, with the premises serving as the conditions for the conclusion, which is 'conditioned' by its premises. However, reason is not restricted to judgment and the realm of logic, but rather applies to any object of experience; for any conditioned object that is given to us, reason necessarily searches for the conditions that would explain it, such as when reason searches for the cause of some change of state that we experience. Reason is thus the faculty that is interested in identifying the conditions for anything that is conditioned.

Second, reason searches not simply for conditions but also for the *totality* of conditions and thus the *unconditioned*. There is obviously an analytic connection between anything that is conditioned and its conditions, because to characterize something as conditioned entails conditions on that thing. However, reason's interest in the unconditioned, which alone offers it a satisfactory resting place (since if it obtained the object of its inquiry, it would have nothing else to pursue), goes beyond this analytic connection and can be satisfied only by seeking the totality of conditions. For the totality of conditions cannot be a totality if it does not contain *all* conditions, but if it contains *all* conditions, then it must be unconditioned, because if this totality were itself conditioned, it would not have included the condition that conditions it and would thus not in fact be the totality of conditions. As a result, if reason could find all of the conditions for something conditioned, it would necessarily have found the unconditioned as well. Moreover, because reason seeks the totality of conditions for what is conditioned by starting with something conditioned and moving to its conditions, which, because they are themselves conditioned, leads reason to yet further conditions, etc. until it reaches the unconditioned, the unconditioned also provides a principle of organization, Kant thinks, for all the conditions that fall under it. In this way, it leads to a systematic interconnection of conditioned elements under a single unconditioned principle. That is, the unconditioned serves as the principle for the system of condition–conditioned relations that reason discovers in its search for the totality of conditions.

---

any unity that reason wants to produce, but one that would culminate in an idea of something unconditioned that serves as the condition for all conditioned things. For more discussion of Kant's conception of reason, see Eric Watkins, "Kant on Real Conditions," in *Proceedings of the 12. International Kant Congress Nature and Freedom*, ed. Violetta Waibel and Margit Ruffing (Berlin: Walter de Gruyter, 2019), pp. 1133–40.

184   Teleological Laws

Third, Kant holds that the unconditioned object that alone could provide reason with a satisfying resting place can never be given to us through the senses and thus can never be an object that we could cognize in nature.[14] Since the objects of traditional metaphysics that interest us most, such as God, freedom, and the soul, are characterized as unconditioned, it follows that we cannot have immediate cognition of them through the senses.[15] At the same time, since reason does not, on that account, lose its interest in the unconditioned, our ideas of this kind of object function as regulative principles that guide our understanding's judgments such that we strive to come ever closer to approximating these ideals. So, even though reason does not find satisfaction in cognition of the unconditioned, it still functions as a regulative principle that unifies its subject matter in a distinctive and systematic way. In this way, it finds as much satisfaction as is possible for a faculty that is limited by the fact that objects must be given to it through sensible intuition.

This account of Kant's conception of reason puts us in a position to understand his argument for CNW. First, as we saw above, Kant identifies reason as the faculty that leads us to move beyond the purely mechanistic order of inert matter to the distinctive order of organisms. Specifically, the experience of organisms reveals a special kind of conditioning relationship, where both the whole and its parts reciprocally condition each other according to some unified principle. It is precisely because a distinctive kind of conditioning relationship is involved in organisms that reason is the faculty that moves us beyond mechanisms to this new order. Moreover, it does so in several ways. On the one hand, reason, with its desire for conditions, is interested in the *internal form* of organisms, since this form involves a distinctive unity with complex conditioning relations. Yet reason also discovers that organisms, like all other objects in nature, can be conditioned by external circumstances. For example, plants require sunlight, water, and nutrients from the soil in order to grow, maintain, and reproduce themselves.[16] In this way reason is able to discover vibrant ecosystems as well as understand how they might be endangered. In short, the internal form of organisms involves

---

[14] There are passages to this effect scattered throughout Kant's corpus. There are not, however, clearly stated arguments that would justify this claim.

[15] This claim coincides perfectly with transcendental idealism's claim that we cannot have cognition of things in themselves, such as God, freedom, and the soul. However, Kant's reasons in this case, whatever they are, turn out to be quite different.

[16] For a detailed discussion of this issue, see Ina Goy, "On Judging Nature as a System of Ends. Exegetical Problems of §67 of the *Critique of the Power of Judgment*," in *Akten des XI. Internationalen Kant-Kongresses, Pisa 2010*, ed. Claudio LaRocca, Stefano Bacin, Alfredo Ferrarin, and Margit Ruffing, vol. 5 (Berlin: Walter de Gruyter, 2013), pp. 65–76.

Nature in General as a System of Ends

185

external conditions that reason must seek out.[17] On the other hand, and more importantly for present purposes, reason is also compelled to search for the purpose and thus the condition of the *existence* of organisms. In this case, it is an *external* or relative purposiveness that is pivotal. When reason seeks the purpose for the existence of one thing (organism A) and finds that it cannot lie in that thing, it seeks its purpose in another thing in nature (e.g., organism B). Thus, plants exist for animals, which exist in turn for humans, etc. The purpose of the existence of things, since it contains a conditioning relation, is of fundamental interest to reason as well.[18] So, just as Kant suggests in several places, it is reason that leads us to consider the special status of organisms, both in their internal form and with respect to purposive relations that condition their existence.

Second, CNW specifically asserts further that nature as a whole must itself have a purpose and that it must, moreover, be a final and unconditioned purpose. Why this demand and why in this specific form? If reason's ultimate interest is with the unconditioned, it is clear that though reason begins by seeking the purpose, or condition, for the existence of one finite thing in another, it continues to seek ever further conditions such that it ultimately ends up inquiring into the purpose for the existence of nature as a whole.[19] And it is clear that the purpose of the existence of nature as a whole must be a final purpose, one not conditioned by anything else; i.e., it must be unconditioned. Put more informally, the purpose of nature as a whole cannot be something that exists for the sake of something else, but is rather something that exists for its own sake. Kant's repeated references to a "final end" (5:378), a "condition that is always to be found further on, and which, as unconditioned, . . . lies entirely outside of the physical-teleological way of considering the world" (5:378), are clear expressions of the structure of reason's interest in finding the unconditioned.[20] Thus, Kant's understanding of reason reveals why it claims that nature as a whole must have a purpose that is both a final and an unconditioned purpose.

Moreover, taking these two points together, we can see why nature as a whole must also be regarded as a system of purposes. As the first point

---

[17] Indeed, because organisms involve both internal and external conditions, reason's search for conditions provides a direct justification of CUS.

[18] In a later passage, Kant adds that in this way, one can discover "many laws of nature which, given the limitation of our insights into the inner mechanisms of nature, would otherwise remain hidden from us" (5:398).

[19] There are significant similarities between this account of why nature as a whole involves the notion of an unconditioned purpose and Kant's explanation of the ideas of reason in "On the Transcendental Ideas" in the first *Critique* (A321/B377).

[20] Another relevant passage can be found at 5:436: "*Physicotheology* is the attempt of reason to infer from the *ends* of nature (which can be cognized only empirically) to the supreme cause of nature and its properties."

186   Teleological Laws

shows, reason seeks the conditioning relations between the purposes of things that exist in nature, but that alone would not require a unifying principle that would organize these purposes into a single system. (Perhaps some ecosystems are completely distinct from others or perhaps things are more like an aggregate than a system.) As the second point shows, however, reason, in seeking the totality of conditions for something conditioned, seeks something unconditioned that subordinates to itself everything that it conditions. The final, unconditioned purpose it seeks subordinates (or conditions) the purposes of the things that exist in nature in such a way that they form a system in Kant's specific sense of the term.[21] That is, it is only because of the unconditioned purpose of nature that nature as a whole must also form a system of purposes and not a mere aggregate.

Third, not only is the final end of nature unconditioned, for Kant, but it also lies beyond the limits of our cognition, in the supersensible. Why? (In particular, why is the supersensible introduced?) Given that we cannot experience anything unconditioned and given that the final purpose of nature is unconditioned, it follows immediately that we cannot have experience of the final purpose of nature. Indeed, Kant explicitly asserts that nature as a whole is not given to us *as organized* (5:398). At the same time, because reason does not lose interest in the unconditioned simply because it cannot cognize it, it posits the unconditioned as something that lies beyond what we can experience, that is, beyond the sensible world, and thus in the supersensible. As a result, it functions not as an object in nature that we could cognize as such, but rather as a regulative ideal that we use to organize what we do experience into a systematic whole. In this way, an appreciation of Kant's conception of reason allows one to understand what his justification is for both CNW and CUS.

8.4   Conclusion

One might naturally start reading the "Critique of the Teleological Power of Judgment" with the expectation that Kant will (simply) try to explain the distinctive status of living organisms. As philosophers of biology will attest, providing such an explanation is no mean feat, and if Kant has accomplished such a significant task, we should be glad. However, what

---

[21] Though Kant's position here may (or may not) be plausible, he would need an additional argument to show that everything in nature must be related as a single system of purposes. For, at least prima facie, one could imagine several causal chains that were all subordinate to a single unconditioned condition, but that were nonetheless distinct from each other. For example, perhaps there could be a plurality of ecosystems that are each conditioned by some further purpose, yet completely separate from each other.

Nature in General as a System of Ends 187

we have come to see is that reason, on Kant's distinctive understanding of that faculty, leads us to expectations that have an even grander scope and even more fundamental ambitions. For reason, as the faculty that searches for any and all conditions until it finds the unconditioned, has legitimate interests not only in the inner form of organisms, but also in the external conditions on these organisms and in the purpose for the existence of objects in nature. However, given its essential interest in the unconditioned, reason does not stop there. It also seeks systematic connections within nature as well as a final unconditional purpose for nature as a whole that must itself lie outside of nature. It is at this point that Kant's grandest ambition becomes apparent.[22] For this question is simply the question of why the world (along with everything in it) exists at all. And in line with the fundamental results of his moral philosophy, his answer is that a human being, or any being that has the supersensible ability to act freely and thus morally, can be both unconditioned and yet still necessary in itself, that is, man considered not as an organism within nature, but rather as a noumenon (5:435).[23] For a free, rational, and spontaneous being is the only kind of entity of which one cannot ask why it exists, given that it is the kind of entity that could be "a final end to which the whole of nature must be subordinated" (5:436).[24] Identifying human beings as the final end of creation has implications, in turn, for the kind of systematic relations that obtain within the members of the system of ends in nature, such as for the kinds of laws that obtain, because they must, as Kant argues in the second *Critique*, make possible the highest good that rational agents presuppose is possible in acting morally.[25] In this way, we see how Kant unifies major elements of his entire critical project, while addressing one of the most basic questions that we can raise about our existence.[26]

---

[22] For an excellent discussion of Kant's intentions toward the end of the third *Critique* (and in the third *Critique* as a whole), see Karl Ameriks, "The End of the *Critiques*: Kant's Moral 'Creationism,'" in *Rethinking Kant*, ed. Pablo Muchnik (Newcastle: Cambridge Scholars Publishing, 2009), pp. 165–90, esp. pp. 165–7.

[23] It is at this point that reason, which had been theoretical in investigating the conditioning relations that obtain between organisms, becomes practical as well.

[24] For a more extensive account of Kant's views on this point, see Paul Guyer, "Freedom, Happiness, and Nature: Kant's Moral Teleology," in *Kant's Philosophy of Biology*, ed. Ina Goy and Eric Watkins (Berlin: Walter de Gruyter, 2014), pp. 221–37.

[25] For discussion of this issue, see Eric Watkins, "The Antinomy of Practical Reason: Reason, the Unconditioned, and the Highest Good," in *Kant's Critique of Practical Reason: A Critical Guide*, ed. Andrews Reath and Jens Timmerman (New York: Cambridge University Press, 2010), pp. 145–67.

[26] I thank Karl Ameriks, Hannah Ginsborg, Ina Goy, Paul Guyer, Peter McLaughlin, James Messina, Günter Zöller and all of the participants at the "International Symposium: Kant's Theory of Biology" held in Tübingen in December 2010, for helpful discussion of an earlier version of this chapter.

Part IV

Laws as Regulative Principles

As we have seen in several of the previous chapters, it is distinctive of Kant's position that he views both certain a priori laws of nature (such as the Second and Third Analogies of Experience) and a number of mechanical laws (such as the Three Laws of Mechanics) as what he calls constitutive principles, since the former make experience in general possible, while the latter make experience of objects of outer sense, or matter, possible. However, Kant also accepts a number of laws that he calls regulative rather than constitutive. For example, he views several a priori laws in his theoretical philosophy that were traditionally at home in rational cosmology, namely, those of no fate, no chance, no leap, and continuity, as regulative principles, that is, as broadly explanatory principles that constrain what our experience of the world could be like, yet without constituting our experience. Though these laws do not prescribe how the world must be, they do determine how we have to view the world. Their necessity thus attaches to how we must explain the world (rather than how the world is). Chapter 9 is devoted to describing the content and historical context for these principles as well as their unique status in Kant's Critical philosophy.

Chapter 10 is devoted to the principles of homogeneity, specificity, and continuity, which Kant calls "logical laws" and discusses in both his logic lectures and the Appendix to the Transcendental Dialectic. Like the principles of rational cosmology, these principles are regulative principles that specify that for any object that falls under a concept, one should *seek* higher (more general) concepts, lower (more specific) concepts, as well as concepts that would lie in between any two concepts. The chapter also argues that Kant's justification not only of these principles' status as regulative principles, but also of their content is based in his distinctive conception of reason, which fits well with his general view that laws are based in our spontaneous faculty of reason.

9 Kant on Rational Cosmology

9.1 Introduction

Kant's views on what one might call rational cosmology[1] have not received a great deal of attention, for a variety of reasons.[2] One likely reason is that Kant does not seem to place any special emphasis on rational cosmology in his Critical publications, given that he neither uses it there as a standard technical term nor designates it in any consistent fashion as one of the main branches of metaphysics.[3] Further, one might think that Kant's attitude toward rational cosmology is similar to his attitude toward rational psychology and rational theology insofar as he considers these disciplines to be primarily dogmatic and illegitimate. The main reason in virtue of which rational psychology's and rational theology's arguments must be fallacious and their claims to synthetic a priori cognition illegitimate would seem to apply to rational cosmology as well. And insofar as the Antinomies are supposed to reveal the contradictions into which reason is inevitably drawn when it attempts to determine the fundamental features of the world as a totality, it would be natural to think that reason is entirely dialectical in rational cosmology

---

[1] I use the term "rational cosmology" to indicate a cosmology that "borrows its principles not from experience, but rather from pure reason" (28:195) or a "cosmology of pure reason" (29:956). Kant's concern with what one might naturally call "empirical cosmology" is well established by, e.g., his *Universal Natural History and Theory of the Heavens, or Essay on the Constitution and Mechanical Origin of the Entire Universe, Treated in Accordance with Newtonian Principles* (1755).

[2] Exceptions to this claim are Karl Ameriks, "The Critique of Metaphysics: Kant and Traditional Ontology," in *The Cambridge Companion to Kant*, ed. Paul Guyer (Cambridge: Cambridge University Press, 1992), pp. 249–79, and Eric Watkins, "Kant's Theory of Physical Influx," *Archiv für Geschichte der Philosophie* 77 (1995): 285–324.

[3] Within the Wolffian tradition, it is traditionally one of the four branches of (theoretical) metaphysics, which also includes ontology, psychology, and rational (i.e., natural) theology. When Kant lectures on metaphysics using Baumgarten's *Metaphysica*, he follows this division and divides metaphysics into psychology, rational (or natural) theology, rational cosmology, and at times either ontology or rational physics (29:754–5).

192   Laws as Regulative Principles

too, and thus incapable of delivering positive conclusions for Kant's own natural philosophy. Finally, Kant's acceptance of a broadly Newtonian dynamical and mechanical physics (e.g., in the *Metaphysical Foundations*) leads many to focus on his relation to Newton, implicitly assuming that his adherence to fundamentally Newtonian principles would preclude the possibility that a Wolffian-sounding rational cosmology could have a significant positive influence on Kant.

In this chapter I argue that Kant's views on rational cosmology play a surprisingly important role in his overall philosophical system. To this end, I first briefly explain the fundamental principles of rational cosmology as it was understood by Baumgarten. I then explore how Kant develops four principles of rational cosmology that stem either directly or indirectly from Baumgarten. I conclude by considering how Kant's views on rational cosmology fit into his Critical philosophy as developed in the first *Critique*. The thesis I defend in this final section is that Kant's four cosmological principles are closely related to his Principles of Pure Understanding, though they also go significantly beyond these Principles. Thus, Kant's views on rational cosmology form a crucial and independent part of his theoretical philosophy. This result implies that the Critical turn does not consist in a wholesale rejection of ontological issues in favor of broadly epistemological ones.

9.2   Rational Cosmology in Baumgarten

Alexander Baumgarten's *Metaphysica*, which Kant used as a textbook for several decades, divides metaphysics into four branches: ontology, rational cosmology, psychology, and theology. Each section begins with a definition of the relevant object (being in general, the world, the soul, and God) and then derives a variety of principles from more fundamental, ultimately self-evident principles, such as the principles of contradiction and sufficient reason.[4] Baumgarten's discussion of cosmology takes place in three main chapters. The first chapter introduces the notion of the world, with sections explaining both positive and negative concepts of the world. The second chapter considers the parts of the world, treating both the simples out of which the world is composed and the composites they thereby form. The third chapter discusses the perfection of the world, with sections on the idea of the perfection of the world and on the means necessary for its perfection. Throughout these chapters,

---

[4] Kant seems to endorse this general conception of the principles of rational cosmology in the Metaphysics Mrongovius when he remarks: "Little is presented of the intelligible world (*mundo intelligibili*) since we can cognize little more of it through the understanding than what follows from the definition [of the world]" (29:850).

Kant on Rational Cosmology

Baumgarten discusses a wide range of important issues. For example, his treatment of the perfection of the world considers the three theories of causality widely disputed in the seventeenth and eighteenth centuries – pre-established harmony, occasionalism, and physical influx – as well as the nature and possibility of miracles. In various other passages he discusses egoism, materialism, idealism, atomism, and corpuscularianism. He also attempts to prove that there can be no change in the world without motion (§415), and, though he does not mention Newton, he argues for the law of the equality of action and reaction (§412) after first proving that action cannot occur without reaction (§410).[5]

Rather than focusing on these topics (which deserve discussions of their own), let us turn to the chapter on the concept of the world where Baumgarten introduces the following set of cosmological principles, which govern all events in the world:

> §382. Fate is the necessity of events in the world. Fate from the absolute necessity of the world is Spinozistic and is not a being, §361, 105, to be assumed either in this or in any other world, §354, 58.
>
> §383. An event in the world of which the sufficient reason is unknown is chance. Pure chance, for which there is no sufficient reason, is impossible, §22, and is to be assumed neither in this nor in any other world, §354, 58 ...
>
> §386. An event without a proximate sufficient reason is an absolute leap. An event without an ordinary proximate sufficient reason is a relative leap.
>
> §387. What exists without any proximate sufficient reason, §27, exists through pure chance, §22, 383, such an absolute leap is impossible, §386, 284, and is to be assumed in neither this nor any other world, §354, 58. (17:107–8)

Accordingly, Baumgarten presents three cosmological principles that can be referred to in abbreviated form as the principles of no fate (*non datur fatum*), no chance (*non datur casus*), and no leap (*non datur saltus*). This last principle is sometimes also referred to as the law of continuity (*lex continui*).[6] To these three principles, Kant will add a fourth principle, closely related to the law of continuity, namely, the principle of no gap (*non datur hiatus/abyssus*).

---

[5] For a fuller discussion of which of Newton's laws of motion were discussed and provided with non-empirical justifications, see Chapters 4–6 in this book.

[6] One finds the law of continuity stated explicitly by, e.g., Georg Bernhard Bilfinger in *Dilucidationes philosophicae de Deo, anima humana, mundo, et generalibus rerum affectionibus*, [Tübingen], reprinted in Abt. 3, Bd. 18 of Christian Wolff, *Gesammelte Werke* (Hildesheim: G. Olms Verlag, [1725] 1982), pp. 168–74.

194   Laws as Regulative Principles

9.3   Kant on the Four Cosmological Principles

What is remarkable about the cosmological principles Baumgarten states and what stands in need of explanation is the fact that Kant explicitly *accepts* all four principles in his Critical period (though Kant's acceptance of them may differ significantly from Baumgarten's). After the Third Postulate of Empirical Thought (and following the Refutation of Idealism), Kant states:

Hence the proposition "Nothing happens through blind chance" (*in mundo non datur casus*) is an *a priori* law of nature; likewise, [the proposition] "No necessity in nature is blind, but is rather conditioned, consequently comprehensible necessity" (*non datur fatum*). Both are laws of the sort through which the play of alterations is subjected [*unterworfen*] to a **nature of things** (as appearances), or, what is the same thing, to the unity of the understanding, in which alone they can belong to one experience, as the synthetic unity of appearances. Both of these belong to the dynamical principles. The first is properly a consequence of the principle of causality (under the analogies of experience). The second belongs to the principle of modality, which adds to the causal determination the concept of necessity, which, however, stands under a rule of understanding. The principle of continuity forbade any leap in the series of appearances (alterations) (*in mundo non datur saltus*), but also any gap or cleft between two appearances in the sum of all empirical intuitions in space (*non datur hiatus*). (A228–9/B280–1)

Now Kant's explanation of these principles in the first *Critique* is quite brief, presumably because he assumes that his readers are sufficiently familiar with these principles. We, however, must look to other sources to be able to determine the meaning of this passage, i.e., to explain how Kant can accept what could appear to be dogmatic principles in his Critical period.

The best (albeit still imperfect) sources for Kant's views on traditional metaphysical topics are the various transcripts from his metaphysics lectures, since, instead of focusing on an independent and autonomous project, as the first *Critique* does, they react more or less directly to specific claims advanced by either Baumgarten or others in the Wolffian tradition. Accordingly, we now turn to the relevant cosmology lecture transcripts to consider Kant's discussion of each of these principles, starting with fate and chance.

9.3.1   Fate and Chance

Kant's discussion of the principle of no fate is, in one important sense, uniform throughout his metaphysics lectures, for he consistently rejects

Kant on Rational Cosmology

fate.[7] More significant, however, is Kant's discussion of the different kinds of fate and his reasons for rejecting each. For he distinguishes (with some textual basis in Baumgarten) between absolute fate and conditioned fate (28:663). Absolute fate, which he sometimes also calls blind destiny, occurs when the necessity of the relevant event(s) is absolute, while conditional fate involves merely conditioned necessity. The idea underlying this distinction is not Leibniz's distinction between God's antecedent and consequent will, but rather the idea that conditioned necessity is a necessity that depends on a ground, cause, or law of some sort, whereas an absolute necessity is a necessity that has no ground, cause, or law that necessitates the event.[8] Given this distinction, Kant's basis for rejecting absolute fate is expressed most clearly in a passage in the Metaphysics Mrongovius lectures (1782–3):

Of that, that something should be without any grounds and causes, and yet be necessary, we have not the slightest concept. For we find nothing at all contradictory in this, that something would also not have happened. To want to explain something by destiny is nonsensical, for calling upon destiny just means that I cannot explain something. (29:926)[9]

In this passage, Kant seems to be raising two separate objections to absolute fate or destiny. The first objection is that the necessity of absolute fate lacks justification or grounding. Something is necessary if its denial involves a contradiction. But denying something that is allegedly the result of absolute fate does not involve a contradiction because, as Hume famously points out, the denial of any particular event (i.e., a matter of fact) can never involve a contradiction. Further, since absolute fate precludes any ground, cause, or law, no ground, cause, or law can be used to generate a contradiction. But if no contradiction can be generated, then the necessity involved in absolute fate cannot be justified. The second objection is that absolute fate, even if it were somehow justified, would violate valid principles of explanation. In an earlier passage (from the Metaphysics Herder lectures (1762–4)) Kant explains that nature and freedom alone "are the two explanatory grounds of our understanding" (28:200) and that explanations that do not appeal to these two grounds "serve only as a cushion for ignorance, and deprive

---

[7] See 28:199 ("All phenomena in the world do not exist by fate"), 29:925 and 28:663 ("There is no fate in the world"), and, very briefly, at 29:1006.

[8] See Leibniz's Letters to Arnauld in Gottfried Wilhelm Leibniz, *Philosophical Essays*, ed. and trans. Roger Ariew and Daniel Garber (Indianapolis: Hackett Publishing, 1989), pp. 69–70.

[9] Kant sometimes thinks that absolute necessity pertains to "the highest cause" (28:200), i.e., God.

196   Laws as Regulative Principles

the understanding of all use" (28:200). Similarly, in a passage from the Metaphysics Mrongovius lecture transcripts: "Destinies are deviations from maxims ... Destinies conflict with the interest of reason. For if I accept them, then I must renounce the use of reason" (29:925–6). Accordingly, we must appeal either to nature (in the form of the laws of nature) or to freedom (in the form of practical reason) to provide satisfactory explanations.[10]

Kant's endorsement of explanatory appeals to freedom is limited by significant constraints.[11] The main constraint is that no physical event can be explained by means of freedom, a point Kant makes explicitly in transcripts from the Metaphysics Mrongovius lectures: "When we do something, insofar as it proceeds from physical causes, we must explain it from the laws of nature and not from spontaneity, otherwise we would come to intelligible grounds which belong to the noumenal world; and that would be passing over into another genus, which takes place only in moral relations" (29:926). At the same time, as Kant's Third Antinomy shows, explanations based solely on the laws of nature are necessarily incomplete. Interestingly enough, Kant makes this point as early as the L1 lecture transcripts (from the mid-1770s): "The necessity of nature cannot be the explanatory ground of everything; the first ground of origination must happen through freedom, because nothing but freedom can furnish a ground of origination" (28:200).

The fundamental point of Kant's discussion of fate in the transcripts from his metaphysics lectures is that one cannot accept something as necessary unless one can identify a ground that our understanding can comprehend. As it turns out, the only grounds our understanding can comprehend are derived from nature or freedom, and grounds of freedom can be invoked only under certain, quite limited conditions. Thus, the only kind of necessity that could be fully endorsed would be one based on the laws of nature. Since absolute fate or destiny asserts a necessity that appeals neither to such laws nor to freedom, Kant rejects fate as unintelligible.

This account, based on Kant's lecture transcripts, is consistent with Kant's brief rejection of fate in the first *Critique*, which similarly invokes the laws of nature. After making the preliminary point that necessity applies not to the existence of things (or substances) but rather to their states, Kant notes:

---

[10] The same arguments apply if absolute necessity (and thus absolute fate) stems from God, for Kant repeatedly stresses that it is inappropriate to appeal to God instead of to physical causes in explaining any event.

[11] Kant explicitly restricts the role of freedom in his Critical period.

Kant on Rational Cosmology

Thus it is not the existence of things (substances) but of their state of which alone we can cognize the necessity, and moreover only from other states, which are given in perception, in accordance with empirical laws of causality. From this it follows that the criterion of necessity lies solely in the law of possible experience that everything that happens is determined *a priori* through its cause in appearance. Hence we cognize the necessity only of **effects** in nature, the causes of which are given to us, and the mark of necessity in existence does not reach beyond the field of possible experience ... Necessity therefore concerns only the relations of appearances in accordance with the dynamical law of causality, and the possibility grounded upon it of inferring *a priori* from some given existence (a cause) to another existence (the effect). Everything that happens is hypothetically necessary. (A227–8/B279–80)

In short, since (1) any necessity we could cognize applies only to states and (2) the laws of nature dictate necessity only for the relation between states, the only necessity we can cognize is hypothetical; that is, we can know that state B is necessary only if both state A and a law of nature asserting 'if A, then B' are given. Further, this necessity must be internal to nature; i.e., state A must be one that we can cognize in nature. But if the sense of necessity at issue is hypothetical and internal to nature, there can be no absolute fate or destiny, which necessarily appeals beyond nature.

Kant's discussion of chance parallels his treatment of fate in many ways, although (or precisely because) the position to be excluded in this case is the direct opposite of fate.[12] For the merely conditional necessity established by the arguments that exclude fate is still a necessity based on the laws of nature. Accordingly, it rules out events that have no necessity or cause whatsoever, that is, chance.

Kant's fullest explanation of his rejection of chance is developed in the L1 transcripts to his metaphysics lectures. He explains blind chance or accident as follows:

Blind accident [*Blindes Ungefähr*] is an event that is contingent, and indeed, that the contingency takes place in every regard. But something can be contingent in one regard and necessary in another regard; only that which is contingent in *every* regard is a blind accident [*blindes Ungefähr*] ... If I assume a blind accident [*blinden Zufall*], something contingent absolutely and in every regard, then it is an exception to all laws and all grounds. (28:199–200)

The idea Kant is expressing here is that if something were truly to occur by chance (in the strict sense of the word), it would be absolutely

---

[12] In the L1 lecture transcripts, Kant treats fate and chance jointly, because they are both blind (i.e., blind necessity and blind accident), and it is precisely their blindness that makes them "contrary to reason" (28:199).

198   Laws as Regulative Principles

contingent. But since "every ground determines its consequence necessarily" (28:41), such an occurrence would lack entirely a ground or cause. Given this, it is clear that chance cannot occur.

9.3.2   Gaps

Kant does not explicitly refer to the principle of no gap in his published work until his Critical period, and, in line with this fact, it does not appear in the transcripts we have of his metaphysics lectures until the Metaphysics Mrongovius (1782–3). At this point Kant also explicitly orders the four cosmological principles according to the headings of his table of judgments/categories. The principle of no leap is related to quality, no gap to quantity, no chance to relation, and no fate to modality.[13] Kant's assignment of each of these principles to a categorial heading provides a plausible explanation for the addition of the law of no gap. Only if there are four cosmological principles can one be assigned to each heading, and it would be natural (at least for Kant) to think that the world would have quantitative, qualitative, relational (e.g., causal), and modal features and thus that the world must be determinable in some fundamental way with respect to each feature. Kant provides a partial explanation of his particular assignments in two cases. He suggests that the principle of no chance falls under the heading of relation since, as we saw in the previous section, chance is excluded by causal considerations which are expressed in the relational categories of causality and community. One might think that the strong parallels between fate and chance would imply that fate too would fall under the heading of relation. As we have seen, however, Kant suggests that fate belongs to modality insofar as it adds "to the causal determination the concept of necessity" (A228/B281). Unfortunately, Kant does not clarify the precise relations between the notion of necessity involved in the category of modality and the notion of necessity involved in the category of causality.

What Kant means by a gap is empty space or empty time, and he distinguishes between empty space and time within the world from empty space and time without, since his arguments are sometimes different for each. In the Metaphysics Mrongovius lectures his main argument against empty space and time outside the world is based on the familiar point that we cannot cognize such a space or time insofar as they lie outside any possible experience. Further, since the sensible world has no determinate boundaries and cognition of such boundaries would be

---

[13] Kant suggests such a correspondence in the first *Critique* (at A229/B282). We return to this passage later.

Kant on Rational Cosmology

required to know that any empty space or time is outside the world, we could never cognize space or time as *extra mundanum*.

His argument against empty space and time within the world is fourfold. First, like empty space and time outside the world, they cannot be an object of experience; we could have, in principle, no intuition of them.[14] Second, Kant presents an argument against them based on an analysis of change. The claim is that they would be inconsistent with change. "For if a body merely moved in an empty space, then nothing would be altered, neither in itself nor outside it. There would thus have happened no alteration at all" (29:922). In short, the motion of a body in an empty space or time (where motion is understood as change of place) would, *per impossibile*, not involve any change, since the body that is changing its state with respect to empty space or time is changing its state with respect to nothing, that is, is not in fact changing its state. Third, if two (presumably spatiotemporal) objects in the world were separated by empty space or time such that they were separated causally, then, given Kant's definition of the world, these things would not belong to the same world, which is contrary to the initial assumption (as well as to Kant's Critical claim that there is only one space and time).[15] Kant's final argument is that a gap would entail a leap,[16] but since, as we shall see below, leaps are not possible, neither are gaps. It is to leaps that we now turn.

9.3.3 Leaps and the Law of Continuity

Kant's views on the law of continuity are by far the most complex and most interesting. Kant defines leaps and continua by noting that a leap "is an immediate sequence of two states wholly unconnected with each other, without passing through the states that are between them" (29:863), whereas a quantity is continuous if "one cannot determine in and for itself how many parts are in it. Continuity is thus the absolute indeterminability of the parts in the whole" (28:200). Continuity has this feature in virtue of the fact that for any continuous quantity there are always further points or moments between any two points or moments; two points or moments are never immediately next to each other if they are points or moments of a continuous magnitude.

---

[14] Kant's argument for this claim is to be found in the first *Critique*'s Anticipations of Perception. See Chapter 3 in this book.

[15] I consider Kant's account of the world in transcripts from his metaphysics lectures in more detail later.

[16] See 29:922–3.

200   Laws as Regulative Principles

As early as the Herder lectures (1762–4) Kant distinguished between logical, mathematical, and physical versions of this law.[17] Kant understands logical continuity to mean that whatever applies to something having a certain magnitude will also apply to it if it has any other degree of that magnitude (28:41). One of Kant's examples is that of a body in motion. If a body is in motion, whatever quantity (other than motion) one attributes to it (e.g., extension) will also be applicable to it at rest (i.e., if it has a vanishingly small degree of motion) (28:662). Kant seems to accept such a version of the law of continuity, though without giving any explicit argument for it.

Kant understands the physical law of continuity to apply to kinds or species of things and to entail that "no kind or species is so closely related to another that another intermediate kind or intermediate species might not be able to occur between them" (29:921). One version of this law that was commonly held at the time states that all beings are ordered continuously according to their degree of perfection.[18] If God is to create the best possible world, then he must create as much being as possible with the greatest amount of diversity. If God cannot create two beings with the same degree of perfection, then creating the best possible world implies creating one being for every possible degree of perfection, that is, an infinity of beings, each with a different degree of perfection.[19] In this way, there would be a continuum of beings from the very least to the very greatest (excepting God, who lies outside the series). Kant does not think that any such version of the law of continuity can be proved (29:921–2). In fact, in the Dohna lectures (1792–3) Kant argues against it on the grounds that "it is a mere chimera, for if we are talking about things, then there is no necessary ground of connection for it at all" (28:662). Similarly, in the L1 lectures Kant states: "If creatures exist, there must still be a space between one and the other creature, in which there is no infinite degree of intermediate creatures; thus the physical law of continuity is only *comparative*" (28:205).

It is what Kant calls the mathematical law of continuity, however, that is of greatest interest, not only because it "is the first law of nature, whose necessity can be comprehended *a priori*" (28:203) but also because it applies to a wide variety of important topics: (1) both extensive and

---

[17] Kant makes such a distinction throughout his metaphysics lectures (up through *Metaphysics Dohna* in 1792–3).

[18] Leibniz would seem to hold such a version. In the Herder lectures Kant seems to understand the physical law differently, namely, as pertaining to how beings attempt to perfect themselves (cf. 28:42).

[19] The Principle of the Identity of Indiscernibles might be taken to exclude the possibility expressed in the antecedent.

Kant on Rational Cosmology

intensive magnitudes, (2) composition, and (3) alteration or change. Consider first intensive and extensive magnitudes. Kant applies the law of continuity to extensive and intensive magnitudes by noting that between zero and any particular quantum there are infinitely many intermediate degrees. This law clearly holds for extensive magnitudes such as space and time, since space and time are obviously continuous quanta, but it also holds for intensive magnitudes such as the real in space and time insofar as it is a quantum.[20] As Kant notes in the Metaphysics Mrongovius lectures: "For internally the real is the sensations, externally that which corresponds to them. But sensation has a degree and an infinite multitude of degrees" (29:862). Kant illustrates this point with the example of bodies. "Each body has extensive magnitude insofar as it is in space and in time, and also intensive magnitude or a degree of reality. No bodies are so closely related to one another that the difference between them could not be still smaller" (29:863). Kant's point here is that in the mere comparison of any quantities (whether extensive or intensive magnitudes) any differences must be related as continuous magnitudes.

Kant also applies the law of continuity to composition in the Metaphysics Mrongovius lectures as follows: "With respect to quanta, the simple is zero. From that to the quantum are infinitely many parts. A thing thus consists not of finite degrees, also not of finite parts, for that would be an infinite given, but rather the regression in division is infinite" (29:862–3). In other words, the law of continuity implies that the world is not composed of simples, a view that directly contradicts the monadologist's position.[21] The monadologist's position is that since the (spatiotemporal) world is a composite, it must ultimately consist of (either finitely or infinitely many) simple parts. Kant objects that the world cannot consist of simple parts given an appropriate understanding of continuity. For spatial parts cannot be simple (on account of the infinite divisibility of space), and spatial simples, i.e., points, cannot constitute a spatially extended world, since such a world has a quantum

---

[20] One limitation of Kant's argument regarding extensive magnitudes is that it is difficult to see that *every* extensive magnitude must be continuous. For being an extensive magnitude implies merely that the properties of the whole are determined by the properties of its parts. Thus, the definition of an extensive magnitude does not, by itself, entail that its parts could not be finite and discrete. However, Kant's ultimate concern with extensive magnitudes reaches no further than spatiotemporal magnitude. Insofar as this case is clear, he sees no need to pursue the issue further.

[21] Kant's justification of simples is found not in the Metaphysics Herder, but rather in the Metaphysics L1.

202   Laws as Regulative Principles

that cannot be attained through the addition of (even infinitely many) points,[22] given that the magnitude of a simple point is zero.[23]

In the L1 lectures Kant qualifies his claim that there are no simples in appearances by noting: "There is indeed something simple, that is, a point in space and a moment in time; but those are not parts of space and of time; for otherwise one could think of them before space and time. But now I think a moment in time and a point in space; thus, they are determinations and not parts" (28:204). In other words, there may be simples in the world, but they are not *parts* of the world; that is, they do not *compose* the world. Rather, they are mere determinations, limits, or boundaries of what is not simple (28:201).[24] He then continues his line of reasoning in the L1 lectures as follows:

> But are substances nonetheless simple? Of course! But when I see bodies, then I see no substances, but rather appearances. I also cannot at all perceive the substances, for no being, other than the creator alone, can perceive the substances of another thing ... Although all experiences happen through the senses; thus, we can still anticipate appearances through the understanding, and comprehend *a priori* the conditions of objects. (28:204)

In this passage Kant seems to be claiming that bodies qua appearances do not consist of substances; rather, substances exist only in the noumenal world.[25] However, Kant will change his position on this point in his Critical period. For he comes to argue that the concept of substance, which is thought through the understanding, must apply to objects given through the senses. But since objects of the senses cannot be simple, Kant must revise his conception of substance by giving up the Leibnizian requirement that being must have true unity, that is, simplicity.

---

[22] Kant's thoughts on this issue are obviously more complicated than this isolated passage can reveal. For example, see his pre-Critical *Physical Monadology* (1756) and his Critical *Metaphysical Foundations of Natural Science* (1786). For discussion, see Eric Watkins, "On the Necessity and Nature of Simples: Leibniz, Wolff, Baumgarten, and the Pre-Critical Kant," *Oxford Studies in Early Modern Philosophy* 3 (2006): 261–314.

[23] Kant also expresses the argument as follows: "no appearance can consist in the simple, because from the simple to matter there would be a sudden transition to something which is distinguished from it generically (*in genere*)" (29:863). The idea is that there is a qualitative difference between zero and other quantities, because adding zero to itself will never produce a finite (non-zero) quantity. Kant makes the latter connection more explicit in the following passage: "The world cannot consist of monads, for with respect to quanta the simple is a null. But the transition from null to a quantum is a leap. I can put together as many simples as I want, but they will never become a quantum" (29:921).

[24] At 28:202–3 Kant presents an extended argument for the claim that any appearance cannot consist of simple parts based on the fact that all appearances are in time, which is a continuous magnitude.

[25] If this is right, Kant's position in the L1 lectures is not identical to that of either his Inaugural Dissertation or his first *Critique*, both of which posit phenomenal substances.

Kant on Rational Cosmology

Another significant application of the law of continuity is to alteration or change.[26] This law states simply that all change is continuous; that is, if an object changes from one state to another, it must successively pass through all of the continuous states that lie between these two states. Kant's position on the continuity of change in the first *Critique* might seem to be ambiguous. On the one hand, he seems to accept this law in the Second Analogy when he concludes: "That is, now, the law of the continuity of all alteration, the ground of which is this: that neither time nor appearance in time consists of smallest parts, and that nevertheless in its alteration the state of a thing passes through all these parts, as elements, to its second state" (A209/B254). Similarly, in the Anticipations of Perception Kant notes: "Now if all appearances, considered extensively as well as intensively, are continuous magnitudes, then the proposition that all alteration (transition of a thing from one state into another) is also continuous could be proved here easily and with mathematical self-evidence [*Evidenz*]" (A171/B213). On the other hand, there is also textual evidence that seems to contradict this view. For the passage just quoted from the Anticipations of Perception continues:

... if the causality of an alteration in general, did not lie entirely beyond the boundaries of a transcendental philosophy and presuppose empirical principles. For the understanding gives us no inkling *a priori* that a cause is possible which alters the state of things, i.e., determines them to the opposite of a certain given state, not merely because it simply does not give us insight into the possibility of this (for this insight is lacking to us in many *a priori* cognitions) but rather because alterability concerns only certain determinations of appearances, about which experience alone can teach us, while their cause is to be found in the unalterable. But since we have before us here nothing that we can use except the pure fundamental concepts of all possible experience, in which there must be nothing at all empirical, we cannot anticipate general natural science, which is built upon certain fundamental experiences, without injuring the unity of the system. (A171–2/B213)[27]

In this passage Kant is expressing reservations about the law of continuity, apparently based on the idea that "experience alone" can provide us with cognition of the continuity or discontinuity of the changes that appearances undergo.

Fortunately, Kant's metaphysics lectures clarify his position on precisely this point. First, the metaphysics lectures confirm that Kant accepts the law of the continuity of change. For Kant provides an explicit

---

[26] For extensive discussion of this particular version of the law of continuity, see Tim Jankowiak, "Kant on the Continuity of Alteration" (unpublished manuscript).

[27] Kant then immediately adds: "Nevertheless, we are not lacking proofs of the great influence that our principle has in anticipating perceptions" (A172/B213).

204   Laws as Regulative Principles

justification of the law of the continuity of change in a wide range of lectures over many decades. Consider, for example, the following passage from the Ll lecture transcripts:

Every state[28] has two limits (*terminos*): from which (*a quo*) and to which (*ad quem*). Each of these states is in a particular distinct moment. With each transition the thing is in two moments distinct from one another. The moment in which the thing is in the one state is distinct from the moment in which the thing arrives in the other state. But between two moments there is a time, just as between two points a space. Thus the transition happens in time; for in the moments in which it moves from A to B there is a time in which it is neither in A nor in B. But in this time it is in the mutation, in the transition. Thus a thing never goes immediately from one state into the other, but rather through all intermediate states, and thereby the alteration of the state of a thing is possible. The differences of the states all have a magnitude, and in this magnitude is continuity. (28:201)[29]

The main idea here is that due to the continuity of time there will always be a period of time between the two states that represent the starting and ending points of a change, and it is during this period of time that the transition through all of the intermediate states that lie continuously between the starting and ending points must occur.

Now one might object that this argument begs the question by simply assuming that the intermediate states must all be gone through.[30] Why is it not possible that an object change its state from, say, A to D without going through B and C?[31] While Kant does not explicitly formulate this objection, he makes two points that provide resources for a response. First, he seems to advance the following line of argument. In virtue of the infinite divisibility of time one can identify intermediary moments that lie between the moments in which the object is in states A and D. Now, the object must be in some state during these moments. The intuitively natural option is that the object is in states B and C during the intermediary moments. This option seems even more natural (perhaps

---

[28] I suggest that Kant intends "change" rather than "state."

[29] Three brief remarks are in order here. First, the argument is obviously based in important ways on time. Kant recognizes this fact in several passages (e.g., 28:202). Second, Kant presents a very similar argument a few lines later at 28:202–3. The notable difference is that in this later passage Kant seems to emphasize that this argument will work for all objects because all objects must be given in time through the form of inner sense. Third, Kant suggests a similar argument at 29:863–4 and in the Second Analogy at A208/B253–4.

[30] One might object to the very positing of intermediate states. However, given Kant's argument above (namely, that the mere comparison of magnitudes, whether extensive or intensive, necessarily reveals continuity), it is clear that there must be infinitely many possible intermediate states.

[31] Using letters to represent states is misleading insofar as letters are discrete in ways that states are not supposed to be.

Kant on Rational Cosmology

natural enough to seem compelling) if one considers how this possibility would apply to the case of motion, which is Kant's primary instance of change.[32] If a body is said to move along a line segment from point A to point D, it is very natural to assume that it does so by passing through points B and C (which lie between points A and D). If it did not pass through points B and C, then it must simply have passed out of existence when it 'left' point A and then popped back into existence when it 'arrived' at point D. Obviously, bodies do not (in fact) move in such a fashion.[33] Therefore, they must pass through all intermediate points when they change from one state to another. It is, I confess, difficult to maintain that this series of natural moves by Kant amounts to a non-question-begging argument.

Second, Kant appeals to a claim that is based on an analysis of the concept of a leap. In the Dohna lectures, after introducing the law of continuity, Kant notes that a "leap is the immediate connection of a conditioned (of a consequence) with a distant ground without an intermediate ground [*Grund ohne Zwischengrund*] – [which is] a contradiction" (28:662). The idea is that it is simply a contradiction to claim that A conditions D without A being connected to D either immediately or mediately (that is, through intermediate grounds). Now A cannot ground D immediately because A is, by definition, a distant ground.

---

[32] Kant considers such a case at 28:201: "If something could transfer from one location to another without running through all intermediate locations, then this would be a change of place through a leap. But no thing goes immediately from one location to another except through all intermediate locations; it must go through the infinitely many parts of space."

[33] Kant sometimes calls such a transition a leap, but if one takes the metaphor seriously, even leaping implies that there is a continuous line in space from the takeoff spot to the landing spot. The picture underlying the idea of a leap is something like the following. A body simply moves from state A to state D in one discrete change. At one moment of time it is in state A and at the next moment of time it is in state D, having leapt from A to D without going through B and C. However, the continuous nature of time (and perhaps space) shows that such a picture is in fact incoherent. The problem is that given the continuous nature of time no two moments of time are immediately next to each other and thus one cannot say that it is in state A at one moment and then at D in the very next moment. Given that it cannot be in state A and state D at the same moment of time (change presupposes contradictory predicates), they must be in these states at different moments of time. Given that they are different moments of time, there are moments between the moments in which the body leaves A and enters D and in these moments they must be in some kind of state, namely, the intermediary ones. Kant still has not given any compelling reason to think that they must be in the intermediary states other than the fact that bodies do in fact seem to move that way. Another problem with the argument lies in its status. For in the case of a body it is ambiguous whether the fact that bodies do not move by leaps is supposed to be supported empirically or non-empirically. If the support is empirical, then Kant can hardly claim (as he does) that the law of continuity can be proved a priori. If the support is supposed to be non-empirical, then even after the above analysis, it is difficult to see what the connection is supposed to be.

206   Laws as Regulative Principles

But A cannot ground D through intermediates such as B and C, since intermediate grounds are excluded. Yet if A cannot ground D either immediately or mediately, then it cannot ground D at all, which contradicts the claim that A (qua distant ground) is connected with D (qua conditioned). Kant might hope to invoke this analytic claim by arguing that since there are infinitely many degrees between any two states (say, A and D), any ground that explains why the object in question comes to be in state D from state A must also be able to explain the transition from state A to state D, that is, must be able to explain how the object "moved" from state A to state D through all of the intermediate states. If one were to accept a leap, one would be accepting a ground explaining why the object comes to be in state D from state A that did not also explain how the object "moved" through all of the intermediate states. Since such a ground is impossible, all change must be continuous. Again, though Kant does seem to endorse this line of consideration, it is not obviously compelling.[34]

Kant applies the law of the continuity of change to a variety of particular instances. With respect to physics, for example, Kant argues that the law applies to both speed and direction.[35] It also applies to the construction of geometrical figures, where Kant refers to Kästner's discussion of the issue, and to optics, where Kant cites Newton's account of refraction as an instance of the law. Kant even suggests that it holds true of our conscious states (which are an example of an intensive magnitude): "If there are obscure representations in my soul, then it must seek to make the representations ever clearer until they finally obtain an adequate degree of clarity" (29:864).

All this evidence from Kant's metaphysics lectures suggests that he accepts the law of the continuity of change and even presents arguments in its favor (even if we might have serious reservations about their plausibility). But how is Kant's acceptance of this law to be reconciled with his statement (quoted above) that only experience could determine the truth of this law? In the Dohna lectures, Kant explains that "we always make leaps, for we cannot possibly cognize the infinite

---

[34] Though Kant does seem to suggest such an argument, it has a serious defect. Even if one grants that there can be no leaps in the order of grounds, it does not immediately follow that there could not be leaps in the order of states. And since grounds are required for states (rather than vice versa), it is far from clear that denying leaps in the former requires the denial of leaps in the latter.

[35] It applies to speed as follows: "If a body is brought from rest into motion, then it goes through all of the smallest degrees of speed up to the highest degree of speed with which it has power, and if it is again brought to rest: then this happens through smaller degrees of speed" (28:41–2). (See 28:203 for a very similar passage.) Kant applies it to direction at 29:921 and 28:203.

Kant on Rational Cosmology

intermediate states" (28:662). This remark suggests that the point behind the reservations Kant expresses in the first *Critique* is that we do not immediately perceive all the intermediate states that an object goes through in changing from one state to another. The law of continuity expresses an ontological, not an epistemological claim: There is a continuous series of intermediate states that lie between the initial and terminal states of a changing object. This claim in no way implies that we actually cognize all the intermediate states. The only way to cognize these states is by consulting what is given to us in experience; it is not possible to infer any determinate information about these states solely from the initial and terminal states. In this way Kant can assert the law of the continuity of change as an ontological principle without threatening his epistemological doctrine that cognition requires that objects be both given and thought.

9.4   Rational Cosmology and the Critical Kant

To summarize briefly Kant's discussions of the principles of no fate, no chance, no gap, and no leap: It is now clear that Kant not only accepts these four principles as a priori laws of rational cosmology, but also presents arguments for them and applies them in a wide variety of contexts. The issue that must still be addressed, however, is how these principles (along with the arguments Kant provides for them) relate to his position in the first *Critique* and what their status is.

One might initially have been tempted to think that any principles forming part of rational cosmology are for that reason simply dogmatic remainders from Kant's pre-Critical period that he would (or at least should) reject in his Critical period.[36] More specifically, one might have thought that these four cosmological principles are applicable only to the noumenal world and as such cannot be cognized according to the conditions laid down in the first *Critique*. However, in light of our discussion above, such an attitude is untenable. For not only are these principles endorsed throughout the Critical period (e.g., in the Mrongovius and Dohna lectures as well as in the first *Critique*), but they also do not appear to hold for the world of things in themselves, since things in themselves are not spatiotemporal and at least the principle of continuity has senses that require temporality.

---

[36] For example, in line with the so-called patchwork theory, one might read the passage in the Postulates of Empirical Thought in which Kant endorses these principles as an older passage that he should have omitted.

208   Laws as Regulative Principles

Further, in the K3 lectures (from 1794–5) Kant explicitly states (with uncharacteristic clarity) that they hold for the *phenomenal* world:

The world is thus a substantial whole that is not part of another ... Now if one thinks the world as noumenon, then it is nothing further than an absolute whole of substances; but one is also not in the position *a priori* to determine further what it might have as properties or determinations. But if one thinks the world as phenomenon, therefore the things in space and time as their real relations, in which they must stand opposed to each other, then the following four principles can be established, under which the determinations of the world must be thought: [in the world there is no (1) abyss, (2) leap, (3) chance (blind accident), fate (blind necessity) *in mundo non datur* (1) *abyssus*, (2) *saltus*, (3) *casus* (...), *fatum* (...)]. (29:1006)

This brief passage is highly suggestive for Kant's understanding of rational cosmology and for how the four cosmological principles fit into rational cosmology as a whole. Kant initially defines the world in such a manner that its most general features will hold for any world whatsoever (that is, for both the phenomenal and noumenal worlds). For example, the world is "a substantial whole that is not part of another."[37] He also distinguishes between the matter and the form of the world in such a way that the matter is substance and the form mutual interaction. (In this way, the form of the world binds the matter together in such a way that we can speak of a single world with a plurality of elements in it.) After noting the principal traits that can be attributed to any world whatsoever (that is, merely in virtue of being a world), he then distinguishes between the noumenal and phenomenal worlds, specifying what further features each will have. Accordingly, although he expresses some skepticism in this passage about the possibility of determining any further features of the noumenal world, other passages make it clear that a bit more can be said: e.g., that its substances must be finite in number and simple in nature.[38] Similarly, Kant understands the phenomenal world to consist of substances that are infinitely divisible and thus not simple in nature. Given this general understanding of the structure of rational cosmology, this passage clearly indicates that the four cosmological principles are to be understood as principles that pertain specifically to the phenomenal world.

One might still object, however, that the four cosmological principles are, if not dogmatic remainders from his pre-Critical period that would

---

[37] See, e.g., 29:849 and 28:657.
[38] See, e.g., 29:856 for the finitude of the intelligible world and 29:859 for the simplicity of the substances of the intelligible world.

Kant on Rational Cosmology

properly hold only of the noumenal world, then at best merely analytic principles that do not add any significant content to what the first *Critique* establishes. Yet it is difficult to view these principles as analytic, given that the arguments that Kant presents in support of them are not based simply on analyses of the relevant concepts. As we have seen above, the principle of continuity, for example, depends on the nature of time in addition to the concept of continuity.

But that simply makes more pressing the question concerning the status of these principles. They are, Kant says, a priori laws, and are neither dogmatic nor analytic. So they must be synthetic a priori principles. At the same time, they are not identical to the Principles of Pure Understanding. To see this, it is helpful to recall how Kant introduces these four principles. In the context of explaining the notion of necessity involved in the Third Postulate of Empirical Thought, he first notes that this necessity is not logical (relating to concepts), but material (relating to the existence of the states of things). He then notes that one can cognize this kind of necessity only in accordance with the laws of experience, where the laws of causality receive special mention. It is at this point, as we saw above, that he introduces the first two laws of rational cosmology (no chance and no fate), describes them both as dynamical principles, explicitly refers to the principle of no chance as "a consequence of the principle of causality under the analogies of experience," and suggests that the principle of no fate "belongs to the principles of modality" (A228/B281). After introducing the other two principles (no gap and no leap), he provides the following clarification:

> We could easily represent the order of these four propositions (*in mundo non datur hiatus, non datur saltus, non datur casus, non datur fatum*) in accordance with the order of the categories, just like all principles of transcendental origin, and show each its position, but the already practiced reader will do this for himself or easily discover the clue to it. However, they are all united simply in this, that they do not permit anything in the empirical synthesis that could violate or infringe the understanding and the continuous connection of all appearances, i.e., the unity of its concepts. For it is in this alone that the unity of experience, in which all perceptions must have their place, is possible. (A229/B282)

In this dense passage, Kant makes his most explicit remarks about the status of the four principles of rational cosmology. He clearly wants to connect the four principles to the four headings of the table of categories (or perhaps to their corresponding Principles of Pure Understanding), but he does not state explicitly what the connection is (suggesting, wrongly, that practiced readers will have no trouble discovering the connection on their own). The principle of no chance does seem to follow immediately from the Second Analogy, since both claim that an

210 Laws as Regulative Principles

event cannot have no cause. However, the three other principles do not follow in similar fashion from their corresponding Principle of Pure Understanding, so the principle of no chance would seem to be an exception in this regard. Instead, what the passage just quoted seems to suggest is that the four principles of rational cosmology must be distinct from the Principles of Pure Understanding. For when Kant explains what unites the four principles (in the face of their obvious differences), he notes that they cannot violate the understanding and its syntheses that make experience possible. This suggests that the understanding and its syntheses are one thing and that the principles of rational cosmology are another, since the latter cannot violate or conflict with the former, a concern that could arise only if they were distinct.

What's more, the principles of rational cosmology and the Principles of Pure Understanding are clearly distinct in terms of their content. The former, which stress that there can *be* no chance, no fate, no leaps, and no gaps in the phenomenal world, are broadly ontological in character, while the latter, which highlight the conditions on the possibility of our *experience*, stress the conditions of our cognition, which involve broadly epistemological (or semantic) features. While epistemological and ontological principles could come into conflict, it is also not necessary. At the same time, the logical possibility of conflict between these two kinds of principles does make it important to specify, as we have just seen, that such a conflict does not in fact take place.

But if the principles of rational cosmology are synthetic a priori principles that are not epistemological in their basic orientation, but instead concern the ontology of the phenomenal world, what is their status? Why should we accept such ontological claims, if they do not make experience possible by constituting the objects of experience the way that, say, the categories do? They are best understood, I believe, not as constitutive principles, but rather as regulative principles that serve to satisfy the explanatory demands of reason. For example, the Second Analogy states that every event must have a cause, but it does not itself specify what kinds of causes could be explanatory for us. The principle of no fate adds that we cannot accept blind necessity as a cause, since it would not explain anything for us. Similarly, Kant objects to the idea that we would accept God as the proximate cause of a natural event. Even if God were somehow the cause of spatiotemporal events, invoking God as the cause of whatever particular features they have does not give rise to a useful explanation.

As we saw above, Kant remarks that only nature and freedom can be explanatory grounds for us, and this claim is grounded in the nature

Kant on Rational Cosmology

of our reason.[39] The principles of rational cosmology are, I suggest, specifications of the idea that only nature and the objects in it can be explanatory for us in theoretical contexts (just as only freedom and its requirements, such as the highest good, can be explanatory for us in practical contexts). That is, reason has certain explanatory needs that the understanding tries to satisfy. But since not any arbitrary application of the categories will satisfy reason's needs, the principles of rational cosmology specify how the understanding's categories need to be applied to the world so that it can provide explanations that can contribute to satisfying reason's needs. They regulate the use of our understanding so as to satisfy reason. These principles can thus be synthetic and a priori, because they are informative and precede experience, but they do not constitute objects of experience. Instead they are necessary guides for our attempts at explaining the world. This is the ultimate justification for the laws of rational cosmology.[40]

---

[39] For more discussion of this claim, see the Conclusion of this book.

[40] I thank audience members at the conference "Kant and the Sciences" held at Virginia Tech, March 6–8, 1998, for their valuable comments. In particular, I thank Karl Ameriks, Michael Friedman, and Paul Guyer for their comments on an earlier version of this chapter.

10 Kant on *Infima Species*

10.1 Introduction

Kant repeatedly claims that there can be no lowest species (A655/B683, 24:911, 9:97). In the *Jäsche Logik* he goes much further by claiming first that there also cannot be a next species and then that both of these claims follow from a principle that he calls the law of continuity.[1] On the face of it, these claims are puzzling. It is far from clear how either one of these claims can be justified at all, much less from the principle of continuity, and it is also unclear how these claims have their proper place and justification in *logic*, given that they seem to be objective principles about the world. For the fact, if it is one, that there can be no lowest species – no species that does not contain yet further species subordinated to it – would seem to be a fact about the world to be discovered by science, not true simply as a matter of logic. The same goes for the fact, if it is one, that there must always be intermediary species in between a genus and its species. I argue that these puzzles can be resolved by close consideration of passages scattered throughout Kant's logic lectures and, especially, of his discussion in the Appendix to the Transcendental Dialectic's section "On the Regulative Use of the Ideas of Pure Reason." For in the course of this discussion, we can see that while the positions in question do not receive a purely logical justification, they do follow straightforwardly from Kant's distinctive conception of reason as the faculty that searches for the totality of conditions of what is conditioned and thus for the unconditioned. These considerations also reveal that Kant's reasons for emphasizing the limits to our cognition include not only his famous claim that we can cognize not things in themselves, but only appearances, which are given to us through our sensibility's merely subjective spatiotemporal forms of intuition, but also his view that our discursive

---

[1] "As a consequence of the law of continuity, however, there can be neither a *lowest* nor a *next* species" (9:97). Kant repeats this claim at *Refl. 2893* (16:564) and *Refl. 4211* (17:458).

Kant on *Infima Species* 213

understanding and the finite range of the concepts it can form are more limited than what reason and the unlimited scope of its ambitious search for the unconditioned call for.

10.2 Lowest and Next Species in the Logic Lectures

Kant's claims about lowest and next species typically take place within the context of his broader account of concepts as representations that refer mediately to possibly many objects. He notes, following standard logics at the time, that concepts contain other concepts both in and under themselves. So the concept "living thing" contains the concepts of "substance" and "living" *in* it and the concepts "plant" and "animal" *under* it. The concept "animal," which contains "living thing" in it, in turn contains further concepts under itself (such as those of mammal, amphibian, arthropod, etc.). In light of the hierarchical structure that is generated by such conceptual containment relations Kant introduces several terminological distinctions: "concepts are called higher insofar as they have other concepts under themselves, which are called lower concepts in relation to them" (9:96). The higher a concept is in this structure, (1) the more concepts fall under it, (2) the greater is its domain (i.e., the more objects it refers to), (3) and the fewer concepts are contained in it. Similarly, the lower a concept is, (1) the fewer concepts fall under it, (2) the smaller is its domain, (3) and the more that are contained in it. Further, for two concepts that are related via a direct containment relation, Kant follows common scientific practice in calling the higher concept the genus and the lower concept the species. Thus Kant's claim that there is no lowest species is simply the claim that every species is also a genus, containing further species under it. This much seems clear and relatively unproblematic.

However, matters are immediately complicated by a fundamental asymmetry in Kant's account of concepts. While he denies that there is a lowest concept, he affirms the existence of a highest concept, which he explicitly refers to as a *conceptus summus* (9:97) and identifies in different passages as the concept of something (24:911), a thing (24:755), or a possible thing (24:259). One can obtain a higher, less determinate concept by removing content (i.e., a determination) from a given concept via a process of logical abstraction. Similarly, one can obtain a lower, more determinate concept by adding content to a given concept via a process of logical determination (9:99). Now Kant argues that a highest concept must exist, because at some point "nothing further may be abstracted from it as such without the whole concept disappearing" (9:97). As a result, although logical abstraction and logical determination are

214   Laws as Regulative Principles

symmetrical operations, which differ solely in whether they add or subtract determinations, it turns out that the availability of the determinations that are to be added or subtracted provides asymmetrical constraints. Content can, Kant thinks, always be added such that there is no end to the process of logical determination. However, there are certain representations, e.g., the categories, that have no *empirical* content and very little *non-empirical* content that could be removed by way of logical abstraction before they disappear entirely, which places an absolute limit on the process of logical abstraction.

So, why think that there is an infinite amount of content that can be added in the process of logical determination such that one can never specify concepts with enough content to ensure direct reference to unique individuals? And how can that be a matter decided by logic? Kant claims: "as soon as I have a concept that I apply to *individua*, it would still be possible for even smaller differences to take place among the *individua*, although I make no further distinction" (24:911). But one wants to know exactly what Kant's principled reason is for asserting these "even smaller differences." In particular, a Leibnizian might say that if one has included in the content of a concept all of the properties that an individual has, then (1) no more content can be added, (2) one has obtained a complete concept, and (3) one has thus found the lowest concept. Kant rejects this kind of view, but on what grounds?

Kant's denial that there could be a *next* species requires both a clarification of its precise meaning and an appreciation of the account of division that underlies it. One issue involves the relation *between species*, specifically whether there must be a finite number of discrete natural kinds with qualitative distinctions between them, or whether there must be an infinite number of kinds between the species that fall under a genus. How many different kinds of beetles should we be prepared to accept? (350,000, which is the current estimate, or infinitely many?) The formal conceptual structure underlying this issue is whether the number of species (A, B, C, etc.) into which a genus can be divided must be finite or infinite.

A second issue involves the relation between a *genus* and *its species*, specifically whether there must always be a further kind between any genus and its species. Must there be some further kind between "bear" and "grizzly bear" such as "brown bear" (but then also a further kind between "bear" and "brown bear" as well as between "brown bear" and "grizzly bear") or is it possible that "brown bear" is as "close" to "bear" as one could ever get? The formal conceptual structure underlying this issue is whether the division of a genus A into B, C, D, etc. must allow for the introduction of a distinct new species E in between that

Kant on *Infima Species* 215

of A and B such that A would contain E under itself and E would then contain B under itself.

Kant's "no next species" claim takes a stand on this second issue. It entails that it must always be possible to introduce further species immediately under any genus. However, to understand Kant's position on both of these issues, several basic features of his account of different kinds of divisions must be brought to light. The *division* of a concept (in its most generic sense) requires only (1) that there be opposition between a concept's member concepts, and (2) that its member concepts fill up the entire sphere of the concept.[2] Thus, the division of bears into black, brown, polar, etc., is acceptable as long as one has identified all of the different kinds of bears. *Codivision* occurs when a single concept is divided into *only two* members in some respect or relation.[3] For example, all humans are either learned or unlearned with respect to cognition and either virtuous or non-virtuous (i.e., vicious) with respect to character. *Subdivision* occurs when one divides the members of a concept that has already been divided. Thus, learned humans can be learned in matters of reason or in matters of experience. Those learned in matters of reason are either philosophers or mathematicians, etc.

Given Kant's denial of a lowest concept, he is obviously committed to subdivision going to infinity. However, he also explicitly asserts:

Codivision also proceeds to infinity. E.g., I can divide the triangle, with respect to its *latera*, into equilateral and non-equilateral, with respect to its angles, into right-angled and oblique-angled. More cannot be set forth here. But with respect to the things of nature, uncountably many codivisions can be given. (24:927)

That is, for any given concept (and thus for any genus), there are infinitely many codivisions and thus infinitely many species that could be next. Just as subdivision is associated with the no lowest species claim, codivision is associated with the no next species claim. Though this clarifies the primary meaning of Kant's claims in the *Jäsche Logik* about lowest and next species, we still have no justification for either one, nor an explanation of how they are both to follow from the principle of continuity.

But how does Kant treat the division of a genus into more than two species? He calls division into more than two members polytomy (9:147) and claims that it is "a subdivision in every case" (24:928) because every

---

[2] Kant provides a more complete account of the specific rules for division in the *Jäsche Logik* (9:146) and in *Logik Dohna* (24:761–2).
[3] If a concept is divided into A and ~A, Kant calls it *logical* division.

216   Laws as Regulative Principles

immediate division is really a dichotomy that is brought about by the word "not." As a result, every polytomy can be reduced to a subdivision. He illustrates the reasoning behind his claim with an example from mathematics: "triangles are either equilateral or not equilateral. Equilateral triangles are either *aequicrura* or *scalena*. When mathematicians divide triangles into *aequilatera*, *aequicrura*, and *scalena*, they have consequently brought the subdivision under the immediate division and divided falsely" (24:928). So, instead of dividing triangles into three different kinds, mathematicians should divide them first into equilateral and non-equilateral and then non-equilateral into *aequicrura* (two equal sides) and *scalena* (non-equal sides), which is just subdivision. Similarly, the division of bears into discrete species is a simply case of polytomy and thus, if properly handled, an instance of subdivision. But if subdivision goes to infinity, then the number of species that fall under any genus also goes to infinity, since the latter is nothing other than the former. As a result, this issue, when suitably clarified, turns out not to introduce any significant extra complications.

10.3   Appendix to the Dialectic

Kant's most detailed discussion of these topics occurs in the first *Critique*'s Appendix to the Dialectic, where he introduces three logical principles, which he also refers to on occasion as laws, namely that of "*homogeneity, specification,* and *continuity*" (A658/B686). The law of homogeneity, or genera, is similar to the principle of parsimony that admonishes one not to multiply entities needlessly. As Kant understands it, it states that "all manifoldness of individual things does not exclude the identity of the *species*; that the various species must be treated only as different determinations of a few *genera*, but these [latter] of still higher *families*, etc." (A651/B679). In short, particularity does not preclude universality. Individuals can be referred to by a series of increasingly higher, or more universal, concepts, up to the highest concept of all.

The law of specification, "which demands manifoldness and variety in things despite their agreement under the same genus" (A654/B682), proceeds in the other direction, from universality to particularity, stating that "every *genus* requires different *species*, and these [require] *subspecies* ... and reason demands in its entire extension that no species be viewed as in itself the lowest" (A655/B683). This is the doctrine of no lowest species. In this way, Kant sets up two principles that are based on "interests that conflict with each other: on the one hand, an interest in the *domain* (the universality) in regard to genera, on the other, an interest in *content* (the determinacy) in respect to the manifoldness of species,

Kant on *Infima Species*   217

because in the first case the understanding thinks much *under* its concepts, but in the second it thinks all the more *in them*" (A654/B682).

The law of continuity of species, which corresponds to the "no next species" claim, is then added as a third principle such that one does not have only the extremes of universality and particularity, but also the richest possible connection linking the two. Thus instead of having only the highest genus, "something" (or "possible thing"), and then an infinite (or at least indefinitely large) number of very determinate species, the law of continuity is designed to fill in all of the intermediary species/genera that could lie between these extremes such that we have a single interconnected conceptual framework. Thus in between the most abstract concept of "something" and the various particular species of plants or animals identified in science, which, though not of course the lowest, are still very rich in empirical content, lie a potentially infinite number of further concepts of genera, family, order, class, phylum, kingdom, domain, life, etc.

There is, however, an important difference between the scholastics' principles, which are straightforwardly metaphysical, and these three principles, which Kant characterizes as "logical."[4] For Kant characterizes these laws as *regulative* principles and contrasts them with constitutive laws (A647/B675). Regulative principles do not dictate what objects must be like, as strictly metaphysical principles would, but rather direct the understanding's activities in judgment. Thus, the "logical" principle of homogeneity claims not that there must *be* a single fundamental power or law of nature that underlies all of the particular empirical powers or laws of nature in the world, but rather only that our understanding must *seek* to unify our experience of particular powers under a fundamental power or law of nature. There is no metaphysical guarantee that it will succeed, but our understanding is directed by such principles to try.

At the same time, Kant distances himself from the view that these principles are therefore merely principles of "economy" (A650/B678) or are to be recommended "merely as methodological devices [*bloss als Handgriffe der Methode*]" (A661/B689). Indeed, he argues that each of these logical principles presupposes a *transcendental* one. Regarding the principle of homogeneity, for example, he notes:

one cannot even see how a logical principle of rational unity of rules could take place unless a transcendental principle were presupposed ... For by what authority can reason in its logical use demand to treat the manifoldness of the powers that nature gives to our cognition as merely a concealed unity ... if reason

---

[4] For a detailed discussion of the status of the laws of logic, see Clinton Tolley, "Kant and the Nature of Logical Laws," *Philosophical Topics* 34 (2006): 371–407.

218   Laws as Regulative Principles

were free to admit that it is just as possible that all powers were different in kind and that its derivation of them from a systematic unity did not conform to nature? For then reason would proceed precisely contrary to its definition by setting as its goal an idea that completely contradicts the arrangement of nature. (A650–1/B678–9)

Kant makes analogous points about the second and third laws at A656/B684 and A657/B685.[5]

Though these three "logical" laws are not straightforwardly metaphysical principles since their most immediate task is simply to regulate our judgments, they are also not *merely* methodological because they also make a non-trivial metaphysical presupposition about the world, namely, that what these principles instruct us to do is not inconsistent with the way we take the world to be. More specifically, if we are to have cognition of the world through the application of more and less general concepts, we must assume that the world *could* be such as to allow for the application of these concepts (even in the face of the metaphysical possibility that the world does not oblige, which cannot be ruled out). Kant is explicit about the epistemological (or transcendental) warrant for this assumption. "For the law of reason to seek it [unity in the law of homogeneity] is necessary, because we would have no reason without it, and without that, no coherent use of the understanding, and, lacking that, no sufficient mark of empirical truth, and therefore in regard to the latter we must presuppose the systematic unity of nature simply as objectively valid and necessary" (A651/B679). The assumption is thus not only necessary, but also has a metaphysical component that is expressed by its *objective* validity. Yet it is not objective in the same sense that empirical judgments about the world are since in that case it would be a constitutive rather than a regulative principle. Instead, Kant remarks: "none the less, they [these principles], as synthetic propositions *a priori*, have objective, but indeterminate validity" (A663/B691). That is, they are *objective* (i.e., are ontological principles that concern how the world is – whether there are higher and lower species in the world) and therefore not mere principles of economy, yet *without determining* the world (i.e., without adding a determination to an object in a judgment that would amount to cognition), and they do so by *directing* us to add determinations whenever we have reason to accept that the

---

[5] Later it will be important that Kant also notes explicitly that the second law "cannot be borrowed from experience" (A657/B685) and the third must also "depend on pure transcendental and not empirical grounds. For in the latter case it would come after the systems; but it really first produced what is systematic in the cognition of nature" (A660/B688).

Kant on *Infima Species* 219

determinations whose possibility we have assumed for epistemic reasons are indeed actual. Thus, like the principles of rational cosmology discussed earlier in Chapter 9, these "logical" laws are regulative principles that are nonetheless broadly ontological in character.

If these logical laws, together with their transcendental correlates, thus capture more precisely the content and status of Kant's claims in the *Jäsche Logik* about lowest and next concepts, then the crucial question is this: Can Kant's remarks in the Appendix also clarify their justification? The key claim Kant repeatedly makes in the Appendix is that these logical laws are principles of *reason* (which goes some way toward explaining why he calls them *logical*). This is relevant in two respects. First, Kant's account of the distinctive kind of activity that our faculty of reason undertakes is capable of explaining the regulative status these principles have.

Second, and more importantly, Kant's distinctive conception of reason makes it possible to justify the content and not simply the status of these principles. Kant sometimes defines reason as the faculty that searches for the unconditioned by seeking out the totality of conditions for whatever conditioned objects it encounters. That is, reason considers the understanding's judgment as to whether the object of its judgment is conditioned or unconditioned. If it is conditioned (as all appearances are, according to Kant), reason directs the understanding to make a judgment about whatever conditions the conditioned object. (Indeed, it is because Kant understands causality as a kind of conditioning relation, with the cause serving as the condition of the effect, that our reason demands that we seek the *cause* of an event rather than its *effect*.) If whatever conditions a conditioned object is itself conditioned, reason once again directs the understanding to identify its conditions until it finds something that is not itself conditioned, that is, until it finds the unconditioned. Several objects that have been of perennial interest in metaphysics, namely, God, freedom, the immortality of the soul, and the world as a totality, are, for Kant, unconditioned objects and are also, for that reason, ideas of reason. Indeed, part of the power and point of Kant's Critical project derives from his view that reason cannot have cognition of precisely those objects that it would view as a satisfactory resting place for its explanations, which the objects of traditional metaphysics happen to be.

But how does Kant's characterization of reason as the faculty that searches for the unconditioned justify the specific content of the claims to no lowest and no next species (which make no explicit mention of conditions, much less the unconditioned)? The crucial idea here is that Kant views the containment relation that obtains between concepts of

220 Laws as Regulative Principles

differing levels of generality as a kind of conditioning relation, one which reason, given its nature, must seek out. To see this point, it is important to understand that many different relations qualify as conditioning relations for Kant. Causal relations are one obvious instance, given that a cause is quite naturally said to be a condition of its effect, but Kant also characterizes part–whole and spatiotemporal relations as conditioning relations. Unfortunately, Kant never provides an explicit definition of what a condition is, and, what's more, he talks of conditions in the context of relations between objects, cognitions, and concepts. This suggests that the core notion of a condition is abstract and allows for different kinds of conditioning relations between different kinds of items such that one can speak of at least real, logical, and conceptual conditions.[6] Against this background, it is plausible to hold that Kant thinks that containment relations involve conditioning relations. That is, the idea is that if one concept contains another in itself, then the content of the one conditions that of the other.[7] E.g., if we apply the concept "bachelor," then we can infer that a bachelor must be not only unmarried and male, which is immediately entailed by the explicit definition of the concept, but also a mammal, animate, a substance, etc. This is based on the facts that (1) the concepts that represent these features are contained in the concept "bachelor" (according to a standard conceptual hierarchy) and (2) concept containment is a kind of conditioning relation.

Now if it is granted that containment relations are conditioning relations, then the claims to no lowest and no next species follow relatively straightforwardly. Consider first the no lowest species claim. If reason seeks further conditions in its search of the unconditioned and if containment relations are conditioning relations in the sense just explained, then reason must search for increasingly specific concepts, since these concepts would contain the conditions for the higher concepts. But since the unconditioned can never be given through the senses and no empirical concept can be formed that would refer to the unconditioned (as such), reason will always be forced to search for more specific concepts; that is, there will be no lowest empirical concept, just as Kant claims. The line of argument in support of the no next species claim runs analogously to the extent that it too is based on the idea that containment relations are

---

[6] Kant does frequently speak of real and logical grounds, and he clearly thinks of the grounding relation as a conditioning relation. The relations Kant maintains between real, logical, and epistemic grounds are too complex to address in the context of this chapter. For a preliminary account, see Eric Watkins, "Kant on Real Conditions," in *Proceedings of the 12. International Kant Congress Nature and Freedom*, ed. Violetta Waibel and Margit Ruffing (Berlin: De Gruyter, 2019), pp. 1133–40.

[7] See 9:148, 5:197, and 16:623 for the clearest textual evidence on this point.

Kant on *Infima Species*

a kind of conditioning relation. However, the point of difference is that the conditions reason searches for need not be more specific concepts. These conditions can instead lie in between two concepts of different levels of generality. In other words, because concepts have different degrees of generality and because concepts of different degrees of generality can, through the containment relations they can enter into, have conditions of different degrees of generality, reason's search for conditions requires that one be open to infinitely many concepts in between any two concepts; that is, reason requires the no next species claim.

These two lines of argument also allow one to see how the shape of the hierarchical structure of concepts (with a top, a bottom, and a middle that connects the two) allows Kant to posit three different principles, each with content that moves us in a different direction, corresponding to where the conditions for it could be located, despite the fact that reason ultimately has a single interest (in cognizing the totality of conditions in a systematic whole). If the question that was posed for the claim that there could be no lowest species was why we must always be open to the possibility that more content, more determinations, be added, the answer is not simply that we could always experience something new, but also that in pursuing the conditions that are responsible for some phenomenon, we must be open to the possibility that they are more specific. But for the same reason, we can also see that we must be open to the possibility that they are less specific, that is, that we might need to accept intermediary concepts and thus conditions. That is, we can now see not only that both the claims to no lowest species and to no next species follow from reason's search for conditions, but also that both of these principles are supposed to follow from a single source, which is a claim Kant made, but did not explicitly argue for in the *Jäsche Logik*.

Indeed, we can even appreciate Kant's reason for ascribing a certain kind of priority to the no next species claim in the *Jäsche Logik*. (1) Technically, if there is no lowest species, then every species except for the highest one will be in between two others, and for every new species that is introduced there will be both a higher and a lower species, which just means that the new species will in fact be the "next" one (albeit only provisionally). (2) Kant provides the following explanation in the Appendix: "The last one [i.e., the principle of continuity] arises by unifying the first two, according as one has completed the systematic connection in the idea by ascending to higher genera, as well as descending to lower species; for then all manifolds are related to one another, because they are all collectively descended from a single highest genus through all degrees of related determinations" (A658/B686). The principle of continuity ensures that we seek a single conceptual hierarchy

222   Laws as Regulative Principles

capable of capturing the broadest class of specific phenomena whose various higher and lower species form a continuum such that no possible condition, and thus no possible species we might encounter, is excluded. The principle of continuity is thus indispensable for the unity of our conceptual hierarchy of species as well as for its completeness, which neither of the other two principles can guarantee on their own.

10.4   Conclusion

The considerations noted above regarding Kant's claims that there can be neither a lowest nor a next species, reveal that he thinks of them as expressing a certain kind of "logical law." On the one hand, these laws are regulative principles of reason that direct the understanding to seek cognition of certain kinds of features of objects (both general and specific). On the other hand, they express a special kind of ontological principle that concerns how we take the world to be (namely, as at least potentially having the features that our understanding is attempting to cognize), despite the fact that the world may not in fact oblige, which prevents these principles from being ontological in a straightforward or unqualified way. Indeed, for this reason, these ontological claims cannot guarantee cognition, even though they are required by reason for the perfection of our cognition. In several respects, these principles are like the laws of rational cosmology and represent a special kind of law that Kant accepts and makes use of within his systematic philosophy.

In light of this interpretation of Kant's justification for claiming that we cannot find any lowest or next species, it would be natural to think that these restrictions are due to the limits of our sensibility, which Kant famously stresses throughout his Critical period. Only a determinate number of objects can come before our senses at any given time and, in fact, over the course of time as well. Just as we cannot experience either the outer edge in space or the first moment in time due to principled limitations in what sensible intuitions we could have, so too one might think that our senses are too limited to experience a lowest species, especially if that were to require an infinite amount of empirical data (sensible manifold). However, reflection on Kant's justification for the no lowest and no next species claims reveals that Kant's most explicit argument emphasizes that these claims presuppose principled limits to our discursive understanding as well. Our understanding is discursive in the sense that (1) objects must be given to it, (2) our understanding must use general rules that capture abstract similarities between objects rather than grasping them in isolation, but also (3) it is capable of capturing only a finite number of concepts or species at any particular time, and this in

Kant on *Infima Species* 223

the face of reason's demand that the understanding find a potentially infinite number of conditions. So what Kant objects to about Leibniz's doctrine of complete concepts is not simply that our sensible intuitions are never sufficient for cognition, but rather that our understanding is too limited to represent *complete* concepts, since complete concepts would contain an infinity of concepts in itself. From Kant's perspective, the Leibnizian is right to note that reason demands complete concepts, but wrong to think that our understanding is actually able to form such concepts. Hence, in addition to the limitations of our sensibility and of the empirical intuitions that derive from it, there is a further unbridgeable gap between what reason demands (the unconditioned) and what our understanding can deliver (a finite set of conditioned conditions).

Part V

The Moral Law

In many of the preceding chapters, our focus has been on the different roles that the notion of law plays in different parts of Kant's theoretical philosophy. Yet Kant makes important use of the notion of law in his practical philosophy as well, since he emphasizes that our various moral obligations depend on the moral law and its applicability to us. The fact that Kant uses the notion of law in this way is neither an accident nor a mere linguistic fact. For he conceives of morality and of the moral law in terms of many of the same core features of the notion of a law that are prevalent throughout his discussions of laws of nature. Chapter 11 contributes to the argument for such a conception by pointing out the deep parallels between laws of nature and the moral law that come to light by considering whether Kant's account in the *Prolegomena* of how we prescribe laws to nature might have led to his distinctive doctrine of autonomy in the *Groundwork of the Metaphysics of Morals*. For the crucial idea underlying autonomy, namely, that the moral law is necessary for us because we legislate it to ourselves, is one that Kant emphasizes in a particularly clear and distinctive way in the *Prolegomena* by arguing that, "even though it sounds strange at first," we must prescribe laws to nature.

The main goal of Chapter 12 is to show that it would be a mistake to think that Kant is simply replacing God with human beings when he asserts that human reason (rather than God) prescribes laws either to nature (resulting in laws of nature) or to itself (issuing in the necessity of the moral law's applicability to us). Though Kant does place increased importance on the human order as compared with many of his early modern predecessors, who had often given pride of place to the divine order (albeit in starkly different ways), it is important to Kant's position that God not fall out of the picture altogether, since he insists on a notion of God (as an active rational agent) that is consistent with the moral law, and he also thinks that reason requires that we assent to God's existence. To illustrate the pervasiveness of God throughout Kant's philosophy, this chapter argues that Kant constructs a multifaceted argument for God's existence that makes a crucial start in the first *Critique* (by establishing that all possibility requires an idea of the existence of an *ens realissimum*, which involves only transcendental and not moral predicates), continues in the second *Critique* (by showing the necessity of moral attributes to account for the possibility of the highest good), and concludes in the third *Critique* (by showing how it is that God must be responsible for at least those empirical laws that are required for mechanism to be subordinate to teleology and for virtue possibly to be an indirect systematic cause of happiness). By attending to Kant's complex reasons for asserting the necessity of God, one can see how it is that the notion of law that is so central to Kant's philosophy is consistent with a new conception of the relationship between the natural, moral, human, and divine orders, one that reestablishes their priority relations rather than simply eliminating the divine order.

11 Autonomy and the Legislation of Laws in the *Prolegomena*

11.1 Introduction

In the *Prolegomena to Any Future Metaphysics*, Kant never uses the word "autonomy" or, for that matter, any of its cognates. Further, its subject matter, theoretical cognition, and its primary goal, that of ascertaining whether metaphysics can be a science, differ significantly, at least at first glance, from those of the *Groundwork of the Metaphysics of Morals*, which concerns morality and establishing its supreme principle. These differences could easily lead one to infer that the development of Kant's moral philosophy runs on a track that is generally separate from that of his theoretical philosophy and thus that the *Prolegomena* is not especially relevant to the emergence of the notion of autonomy in the *Groundwork*. However, matters are not as obvious as they might initially seem and such inferences may turn out to be mistaken. For Kant is writing the *Prolegomena* in 1782 and 1783, just as he is thinking about how to compose the metaphysics of morals that he had long been interested in and that finds preliminary expression in the *Groundwork*. More importantly, the *Prolegomena* builds into its basic argument the view that the understanding legislates, or prescribes, laws to nature, a view that parallels the *Groundwork*'s claim that practical reason legislates the moral law. As a result, one cannot dismiss out of hand the possibility that Kant developed (or at least expressed) his doctrine of autonomy in the *Groundwork* on the basis of the parallels that he discovered while composing the *Prolegomena*'s account of how the understanding prescribes laws to nature.

In this chapter, I consider whether the *Prolegomena* could play a significant role in explaining the emergence of Kant's doctrine of autonomy in the *Groundwork* and, if so, what its role might be. I do so, in the next section, by presenting textual evidence from the *Prolegomena* establishing that and how, for Kant, the understanding prescribes laws to nature, and, in the section that follows, by drawing attention to points of similarity and contrast between the ways in which reason, construed broadly so as

228   The Moral Law

to include the understanding, prescribes laws in theoretical and practical contexts according to Kant.[1] What this investigation shows is that despite important points of difference between the cases of theoretical legislation of the laws of nature and autonomy in moral philosophy, their extensive parallels make a strong, even if not definitive case in favor of the *Prolegomena* forming an important part of the explanation of the emergence of autonomy in the *Groundwork*.[2] In any event, the comparison proves instructive insofar as it reveals deep structural parallels between Kant's theoretical and practical philosophy regarding his conception of laws.

11.2   Legislation and Laws of Nature in Kant's Theoretical Philosophy

11.2.1   Kant's Project in the Prolegomena

To understand Kant's view that reason, construed broadly, prescribes laws to nature, along with the argument he advances in its favor, it is useful to recall his basic project in the *Prolegomena*. The official topic of the *Prolegomena* is whether metaphysics is possible as a science, but its main focus is not on whether metaphysical claims are *systematically organized* in such a way that they would qualify as *science*, but rather on whether they can amount to *synthetic a priori cognition*. For this reason, he considers in detail the conditions under which synthetic a priori cognition in general is possible.

Now, unlike the *Critique of Pure Reason*, the *Prolegomena* follows an analytic method by first presupposing that we have actual instances of synthetic a priori cognition and then analyzing the various specific conditions that make those instances possible. Thus in its first two parts, Kant considers mathematics and the pure principles of physics so as to determine what conditions are satisfied by the synthetic a priori cognitions they contain. After identifying the relevant conditions, he then turns, in the third part of the *Prolegomena*, to determining whether the claims of traditional metaphysics satisfy these conditions and therefore qualify as synthetic a priori cognition. The conclusion Kant reaches is

---

[1] Though Kant asserts that the *understanding* legislates the laws of nature rather than *reason*, he often takes reason broadly so as to include not only speculative reason (whose objects cannot be given in sensibility), but also reason as it is applied to objects that are given in sensibility, which he then typically refers to as the understanding.

[2] I refer to the legislation of the laws of nature as "theoretical legislation" rather than theoretical autonomy because, prior to 1790, Kant does not use the term "autonomy" in theoretical contexts. In the third *Critique*, he does start to use the term in such contexts and contrasts it with heautonomy.

that the claims of traditional metaphysics do not satisfy these conditions and therefore that metaphysics (in the dogmatic sense) cannot be a science, though he also holds that this conclusion is definitively established only on the basis of the more detailed and differently structured argument found in the *Critique of Pure Reason*.[3]

In the *Prolegomena*'s First Part (§§6–13) Kant's central question is: How is pure mathematics possible? In discussing this question, he starts with the idea that mathematical cognition is both synthetic and a priori, and then considers the conditions that must be satisfied if mathematical cognition is to have these features.[4] Since the truths of geometry – arguably the clearest case of synthetic a priori cognition – are based on constructing geometrical objects in our a priori intuition of space, it is plausible for Kant to argue that mathematical cognition in general is based on a priori sensible intuitions of space and time and thus that the synthetic a priori cognitions found in mathematics are possible on the basis of a priori sensible intuition. However, since intuitions are defined as representations that relate immediately to singular objects, it is not obvious how there could be such a thing as an a priori intuition, i.e., a representation that refers immediately to an object without that object being given in empirical intuition. Kant responds by claiming that our intuitions of space and time can be a priori only if they concern what he calls forms of sensibility, which are subjective principles (or capacities) through which objects are given to us and that thus pertain not to things in themselves, but rather to appearances, i.e., objects given through the senses. He concludes that the a priori intuitions of space and time cannot relate to things in themselves, but rather only to appearances, and the spatiotemporal forms of sensibility through which objects must be given serve as conditions on the possibility of synthetic a priori cognition in mathematics.

In the *Prolegomena*'s Second Part (§§14–39), Kant's central question is: How is pure natural science possible? Analogous to his argument concerning mathematics in the First Part, he assumes that we do have a science, namely, pure natural science, that contains synthetic a priori cognition (as well as, ultimately, a transcendental metaphysical science that explains this possibility). Though he does not provide a detailed or exhaustive account of the principles of this science in the *Prolegomena*,

---

[3] Kant's conclusion here is consistent with his claim that metaphysics is not only possible, but even actual, if considered as a natural predisposition of reason (4:365).

[4] Though Kant rightly puts the question in terms of "pure" mathematics insofar as he wants to emphasize that it is not an empirical science, I will not repeat the qualification in my discussion.

230   The Moral Law

he does provide two examples: that substance remains throughout all change and that everything that happens is determined by a cause according to constant laws (i.e., that every event is causally determined according to a universal law). He then argues that these synthetic a priori propositions of pure natural science are possible only if the objects referred to by these principles (e.g., substance and causes and effects) are thought through pure concepts of the understanding, i.e., categories, since only the categories can underwrite the kind of objectivity and necessity that is expressed in the basic principles of pure natural science. So, just as the forms of sensible intuition make mathematics possible, so too the forms of discursive thought, or categories, make pure natural science possible.

Further, just as mathematical cognition does not pertain to things in themselves, so too pure natural science delivers cognition only of appearances, not of things in themselves. Because the categories do not immediately relate to objects and cognition requires a relation to an object, the categories do not deliver cognition of things in themselves (because they require a relation to intuition, which, in our case, is sensory). As a result, for the categories to make cognition possible, the objects that are thought through the understanding's categories must also be given through the forms of sensibility. So while it is true that the categories are forms of thought that make pure natural science possible, the forms of sensibility, which make mathematics possible, are also required for the cognition contained in pure natural science.[5]

In the *Prolegomena*'s Third Part (§§40–60), Kant returns to his main question of whether metaphysics is possible. Insofar as the synthetic a priori claims of metaphysics are based solely on reason, construed narrowly, and not on sensibility, it is appropriate that Kant focuses on reason's distinctive representations and on the proper and improper uses that reason might make of them. To this end, he provides a brief account of reason's ideas, which he defines as concepts whose objects cannot be given in intuition, and describes in highly abbreviated form some of the fallacious arguments to which reason can succumb. But what is crucial about Kant's ultimate answer to the main question concerning (traditional) metaphysics is his view that because reason is dealing with ideas, which have no relation to objects that could be given in sensibility, it cannot give rise to cognition, since, as noted above, cognition requires a

---

[5] Kant also holds that cognition in mathematics requires the understanding's forms of thought. Mathematics and natural science are thus symmetrical in that each one requires both forms of sensibility and forms of thought.

Autonomy and the Legislation of Laws in the *Prolegomena*   231

relation to objects.[6] By contrast, mathematics, as we have seen, has a relation to objects insofar as it is based on the forms of sensibility through which objects are immediately given, and the a priori principles of natural science have a relation to objects insofar as the categories used in these principles are the forms of thought through which the objects that are given through sensibility must be understood. Since the claims of metaphysics lack any relation to an object, they cannot be cognition and therefore cannot attain the status of science (in the strict sense), despite the positive uses to which reason's ideas might be put (in the guise of principles that would regulate our theoretical inquiry).[7]

11.2.2 *Legislation in the* Prolegomena

What is of interest about the *Prolegomena* for current purposes, however, is not Kant's specific reasons for denying traditional metaphysical claims the status of synthetic a priori cognition, but rather his account of the laws of nature and the role that the understanding's forms of thought play in that account. This issue arises in the context of Kant's question, in the Second Part, about how pure natural science is possible, where he takes that question to benefit from clarification of how the 'nature' that is the subject matter of pure natural science is to be understood. He starts with the following definition of nature: "*Nature* is the *existence* of things, insofar as that existence is determined according to universal laws" (4:294), where it is noteworthy that he asserts that the very definition of nature involves universal laws. He immediately clarifies this definition by distinguishing between nature in the material and formal senses. Nature taken in the material sense is simply "the sum total of all objects of experience" (4:295). The formal aspect of nature, by contrast, is "the conformity to law of all objects of experience, and, insofar as this conformity is cognized a priori, the *necessary* conformity to law of those

---

[6] The phrases "relation to an object" and "cognition" are technical terms. Since an idea can *represent* and possibly even refer to its object, the notion of "relating to an object" must be construed more narrowly. As for cognition, Kant invokes both broader and narrower senses such that an idea seems to qualify as cognition in the broad sense of a conscious objective representation (specified at A320/B377), but not in the narrow sense of a conscious representation of the existence and general features of an object (A92/B125). For discussion of Kant's conception(s) of cognition, see Eric Watkins and Marcus Willaschek, "Kant's Account of Cognition," *Journal of the History of Philosophy* 55 (2017): 83–112, and "Kant on Cognition and Knowledge," *Synthese* (2017): https://link.springer.com/article/10.1007%2Fs11229-017-1624-4.

[7] Kant's use of the term "metaphysics" is ambiguous. Sometimes, he has traditional metaphysics in mind. However, in other cases he views the principles that make experience (or synthetic a priori cognition) possible as metaphysical.

232 The Moral Law

objects" (4:296). That is, the material aspect of nature is the set of objects we can cognize (i.e., all appearances), while the formal aspect of nature signifies that these objects necessarily conform to law, are necessarily lawful, or are necessarily governed by universal laws.

In light of this distinction, Kant then divides the question about how pure natural science is possible into two more specific questions, concerning the material and formal senses of nature:

1. "How is nature possible in general in the material sense, namely according to intuition, as the sum total of appearances?"
2. "How is nature possible in the *formal* sense, as the sum total of the rules to which all appearances must be subject if they are to be thought as connected in one experience?" (4:318)[8]

His answer to the first question is admirably succinct: "by means of the constitution of our sensibility" (ibid.), and he refers back to his explanation of the possibility of mathematics in the First Part of the *Prolegomena*. Insofar as the objects of experience are appearances, i.e., objects given in sensibility, the sum total of such objects must be given through the forms of sensibility that are also involved in mathematics. His answer to the crucial second question is similarly succinct, at least initially: "it is possible only by means of the constitution of our understanding" (ibid.). Kant's answer is supposed to be intelligible, even in this rather terse form, on the basis of the evident parallels between the forms of understanding and the forms of sensibility. Just as sensibility is the faculty through which the objects of experience are given, the understanding is the faculty through which these objects are thought. As a result, while the former is responsible for the material aspect of nature, the latter is responsible for its formal aspect. And given that cognition requires that any object of cognition must be both given and thought, both sensibility and the understanding are necessary for the cognition of nature.

However, Kant recognizes the need to clarify and add detail to his answer to the second question in particular. Indeed, it is in the course of what follows that Kant provides his most extensive account in the *Prolegomena* of what is responsible for the laws of nature (or, to be more precise, for the necessary conformity to law of the objects constituting nature):

Even the main proposition that has been elaborated throughout this entire part, that universal laws of nature can be cognized *a priori*, already leads by itself to the

---

[8] Kant also poses the question about the formal aspect of nature as follows: "How is it possible in general to cognize a priori the necessary conformity to law *of things* as objects of experience?" (4:296).

Autonomy and the Legislation of Laws in the *Prolegomena*

proposition: that the highest legislation for nature must lie in ourselves, i.e., in our understanding, and that we must not seek the universal laws of nature from nature by means of experience, but, conversely, must seek nature, as regards its universal conformity to law, solely in the conditions of the possibility of experience that lie in our sensibility and understanding; for how would it otherwise be possible to become acquainted with these laws *a priori*, since they are surely not rules of analytic cognition, but are genuine synthetic amplifications of cognition? Such agreement, and indeed necessary agreement, between the principles of possible experience and the laws of the possibility of nature, can come about only from one of two causes: either these laws are taken from nature by means of experience, or, conversely, nature is derived from the laws of the possibility of experience in general and is fully identical with the mere universal lawfulness of experience. The first one contradicts itself, for the universal laws of nature can and must be cognized *a priori* (i.e., independently of all experience) and set at the foundation of all empirical use of the understanding; so only the second remains. We must, however, distinguish empirical laws of nature, which always presuppose particular perceptions, from the pure or universal laws of nature, which, without having particular perceptions underlying them, contain merely the conditions for the necessary unification of such perceptions in one experience; with respect to the latter laws, nature and *possible* experience are one and the same, and since in possible experience the lawfulness rests on the necessary connection of appearances in one experience (without which we would not be able to cognize any object of the sensible world at all), and so on the original laws of the understanding, then, even though it sounds strange at first, it is nonetheless certain, if I say with respect to the universal laws of nature: *the understanding does not draw its* (a priori) *laws from nature, but prescribes them to it.* (4:319–20)

Kant's explanation here is complex, consisting of a multistep argument that leads from the premise that universal laws of nature can be cognized a priori, which is itself, according to Kant, a presupposition of the existence of pure natural science, to the conclusion that it is the understanding that prescribes those laws to nature.

Abstracting from various details, the argument proceeds as follows. The first step asserts that if there are universal laws of nature that can be cognized a priori, then the principles of possible experience (such as that we must employ the categories as forms of thought to have experience) must agree with the laws of the possibility of nature (that is, with its necessary conformity to law, or the necessary lawfulness of nature). However, there are, Kant claims, only two ways in which one could attempt to explain this necessary agreement.[9] Either the principles of the possibility of experience are derived from the laws of nature or the

---

[9] On occasion Kant does acknowledge a third option, namely, that there might be a common cause of both.

234   The Moral Law

laws of nature are derived from the principles of the possibility of experience. The former option can be ruled out because if it obtained, the principles of the possibility of experience would be cognized empirically rather than a priori.[10] Therefore only the second possibility remains.

The second step of the argument then asserts that the principles of possible experience that make the lawfulness of nature possible depend on the activity of our understanding and its laws. For to have "one experience," i.e., empirical cognition of a single world, the disparate representations of objects provided by sensibility in empirical intuition must be combined or connected in a specific way (so that we cognize a single set of causally interacting objects), but only the understanding is in a position to combine or connect these representations in this way, and it can do so only according to its own laws. In fact, the activity of the understanding in connecting appearances into one experience has a normative dimension that is essential both to its effect, namely, the lawfulness of the laws of nature, and to the way in which its effect depends on it. For if one abstracts from the kind of object on which the understanding operates (namely, sensible objects), the activities it engages in rely on the very same functions as those that reason depends on in its purely logical use and which are naturally thought of as having a normative dimension.[11] As a result, it is appropriate to say, just as Kant does in the conclusion of his argument, that the understanding *prescribes* laws to nature. For the notion of prescription, or legislation, includes the notion of (1) a normatively justified act that establishes (2) a law, and (3) the idea that a law has authority over or governs a subject matter, and all of these features are present in the dependence of the laws of nature on the understanding and its activities.

Though the long passage quoted above is the clearest instance in the *Prolegomena* of Kant's view that the understanding prescribes laws to nature, aspects of the view are also expressed in both editions of the Transcendental Deduction of the *Critique of Pure Reason*. In the first edition, Kant argues as follows:

The understanding is thus not merely a faculty for making rules through the comparison of the appearances; it is itself the legislation for nature, i.e., without understanding there would not be any nature at all … Thus as exaggerated and contradictory as it may sound to say that the understanding is itself the source of

---

[10] Kripke has famously resisted this line of argument, insisting that we can know necessity empirically.

[11] For discussion of the normativity and constitutivity of the laws of logic for thought, see Clinton Tolley, "Kant on the Nature of Logical Laws," *Philosophical Topics* 34 (2006): 371–407.

Autonomy and the Legislation of Laws in the *Prolegomena*   235

the laws of nature, and thus of the formal unity of nature, such an assertion is nevertheless correct and appropriate to the object, namely experience. (A126–7)

Though Kant uses the term "legislation" rather than "prescription," they share the same core features mentioned above – on its own authority the understanding establishes laws that would not obtain without its activity.

In the second edition of the first *Critique*, and with the benefit of further reflection, Kant repeats several features of the position described above, albeit with important clarifications:

> Categories are concepts that prescribe laws *a priori* to appearances, thus to nature as the sum total of all appearances (*natura materialiter spectata*), and, since they are not derived from nature and do not follow it as their pattern (for otherwise they would be merely empirical), the question now arises how it is to be conceived that nature must follow them, i.e., how they can determine *a priori* the combination of the manifold of nature without deriving from the latter. Here is the solution to this riddle.
> Now it is not at all stranger how the laws of appearances in nature must agree with the understanding and its a priori form, that is, with its faculty of **combining** the manifold in general, than how the appearances themselves must agree with the sensible form of intuition a priori. For laws exist just as little in the appearances, but rather exist only relative to the subject in which the appearances inhere, insofar as it has understanding, as appearances do not exist in themselves, but only relative to the same being insofar as it has senses. The lawfulness of things in themselves would necessarily pertain to them even without an understanding that cognizes them. But appearances are merely representations of things that exist uncognized with respect to what they may be in themselves. As mere representations, however, they do not stand under any law of connection other than the law that the understanding prescribes … [A]ll appearances of nature, as far as their combination is concerned, stand under the categories, on which nature (considered merely as nature in general) depends, as the original ground of its necessary lawfulness (as *natura formaliter spectata*). (B163–4)

In this passage, Kant rehearses his position that the a priori laws of nature necessarily involve the categories and the understanding's activities that combine appearances into experience. However, he provides further clarification of two points. First, he makes it explicit that it is because appearances are mere representations that the only laws that could obtain for them would have to be prescribed by the understanding. That is, because appearances do not exist independently of the subject in which they inhere, laws cannot govern them unless the subject that has them is responsible for prescribing laws to them. Things in themselves, by contrast, could be subject to laws that do not depend on any understanding (but rather only on the natures of the things in themselves), due to their subject-independent ontological status.

236   The Moral Law

Second, Kant notes that there are similarities and differences in the ways in which appearances depend on the forms of sensibility and the forms of the understanding. On the one hand, Kant argues that one should not find it any stranger to say that the understanding is responsible for the agreement between the laws of appearances and its own laws than it is to say that sensibility is responsible for the agreement of appearances with the forms of sensibility. For in both cases, one of the mind's basic faculties has a form that makes appearances/experience possible. On the other hand, given the centrality of these similarities, it is natural to wonder why Kant does not extend the analogy further to say that sensibility prescribes laws to nature just as the understanding does.[12] For if the forms of sensibility are just as necessary to the appearances that constitute nature as the forms of thought are, then it could seem that one should say that sensibility prescribes laws to nature, just as the forms of thought do.

However, this passage from the second edition of the first *Critique* indicates why Kant does not (and cannot) extend the analogy in this way. Kant holds that sensibility and the understanding are different in kind due to the relative passivity of the former and the spontaneous activity of the latter.[13] Specifically, whereas sensibility represents what is "given" to us (e.g., from without, by being "affected"), the understanding not only *compares* representations, but also is responsible for the spontaneous act of *combining* appearances according to its own rules, or laws, in thought or judgment. In fact, Kant describes the understanding in precisely these terms: "Now we can characterize it [i.e., the understanding] as the **faculty of rules.** This designation is more fruitful, and comes closer to its essence ... Rules, so far as they are objective (and thus necessarily pertain to the cognition of objects), are called laws" (A127).[14] In light of the distinction Kant draws between the two faculties and his characterization of the understanding, sensibility's lack of spontaneity explains why it cannot be said to prescribe laws to nature. For even if sensibility is responsible for both the sensory content and the spatiotemporal location of the appearances that constitute nature (in its material

---

[12] Kant does seem on occasion to be attracted to the idea that there are laws of sensibility in the *Inaugural Dissertation* (see, e.g., 2:401 and 2:404), but it is striking that these formulations drop out by the time of the first *Critique*.

[13] For further discussion of the distinction between sensibility and understanding, see Eric Watkins, "The Foundations of Transcendental Idealism: The Origin of Kant's Distinction between Sensibility and Understanding," in *Kant's Critique of Pure Reason: A Critical Guide*, ed. James O'Shea (Cambridge: Cambridge University Press, 2017), pp. 9–27.

[14] I do not take a stand on whether rules are themselves laws or whether the ability to justify a claim about a rule requires appealing to a law.

Autonomy and the Legislation of Laws in the *Prolegomena*   237

sense), it depends on affection from without, does not combine the appearances into objects with general properties, and has no authority of its own with which it could justify any one connection of appearances over any other. The understanding, by contrast, is an active faculty that on its own authority *combines* what is given *under concepts*, which are rules that depend on specific functions of unity and which, since they are objective, are explicitly identified with laws of nature (in the formal sense). For this reason it is appropriate to say that the understanding prescribes or legislates laws to nature and that sensibility does not.

In sum, in the *Prolegomena* Kant articulates and defends a view according to which reason, in the guise of the understanding, prescribes laws to nature in a robust sense. Insofar as we have a priori cognition in the pure part of natural science, the only possible account of the necessary agreement of the lawfulness of nature and the principles of possible experience must involve our understanding actively *prescribing* or *legislating* laws to nature (so that they are properly called "laws of nature"). Otherwise the a priori character of our cognition of the lawfulness of the laws of nature would be inexplicable. What's more, we have seen that Kant's view about the understanding prescribing laws to nature a priori is not a peripheral doctrine, but rather central to his project in the *Prolegomena*, for one can make sense of his account of how the synthetic a priori cognitions that constitute pure nature science are possible only by appealing to the forms of thought that the understanding prescribes to nature in such a way that it can be an object of experience for us as opposed to a mere play of representations.[15]

11.3   Points of Comparison and Contrast

Kant understands autonomy in his moral philosophy in terms of the legislation of reason, where such legislation includes reason's legislation of the moral law both (1) *by itself*, independently of anything else,[16] and (2) *for itself*, as applying to itself, or as having itself as its object (and also serving for us as a kind of end). More specifically, reason is understood as an *impartial* and *spontaneous* faculty that serves as the *legislator* of the moral law while also being *subject* to the moral law. Moreover, this

---

[15] For a fuller description of Kant's conception of the laws of nature, see Chapter 1 in this book.

[16] See, for example, Karl Ameriks, "'Pure Reason of Itself Alone Suffices to Determine the Will,'" in *Interpreting Kant's Critiques* (New York: Oxford University Press, 2003), pp. 249–62, though his discussion focuses on the *Critique of Practical Reason*. For discussion of the *Groundwork*, see Karl Ameriks, "Kant's Groundwork III Argument Reconsidered," also in *Interpreting Kant's Critiques*, pp. 226–48.

238   The Moral Law

legislation is responsible for (3) the formulation of the law and its content, (4) the motivation necessary to be able to comply with the law, and (5) its binding force.[17] Though it was not uncommon (for earlier rationalist moral philosophers) to hold that reason can be responsible for the moral law's formulation, content, and motivation, what is most distinctive about Kant's view is that on his account the binding force of the moral law holds in virtue of reason's autonomy. That is, it is because reason legislates the law to itself that the law is binding for it, which contrasts with, e.g., divine command theory, according to which the moral law is binding simply because God commands it.

Though one can raise important questions about various details of Kant's account of autonomy within his moral philosophy, the issue that is relevant at present concerns the most basic points of comparison and contrast between the legislation of reason in theoretical and practical contexts. To that end, it is appropriate to examine the legislation of the laws of nature with respect to each of the five main points described above that characterize autonomy in Kant's moral philosophy.

(1) Despite the terminological differences noted above between reason and the understanding, Kant is clearly committed to the idea that in both practical and theoretical contexts, reason is responsible for legislating the law, and it does so by itself, independently of anything else and on its own authority.[18] On the practical side, reason is said to "give itself" the moral law.[19] Though Kant does note that the moral law can be viewed as a divine command (with God as the legislator of the moral law), he also makes it clear (by way of his criticism of traditional versions of divine-command theory) that this way of considering the moral law is justified only insofar as God, too, is (practically) rational; it is the rationality shared by God and human beings that legislates the moral law.[20] Further, reason's legislation is entirely impartial in the sense that the moral

---

[17] Karl Ameriks has pointed out an ambiguity in the word "binding," which can mean simply "applies to," but can also mean "obligating."

[18] The act of legislation involves, for Kant, the will, since he identifies practical reason with the will.

[19] In several passages (e.g., 27:282–3, 29:633–4), Kant denies that there is an *author* of the moral law, so to claim that reason legislates the moral law is not to claim that it is the author of the moral law. Kant seems to think that only contingent, or "arbitrary," laws can have an author (19:247), despite one (parenthetical) remark in the Groundwork (at 4:431). For further discussion, see Patrick Kain, "Self-Legislation in Kant's Moral Philosophy," *Archiv für Geschichte der Philosophie* 86 (2004): 257–306, and Stefano Bacin, "Legge e obbligatorietà: la struttura dell'idea di autolegislazione morale," *Studi kantiani* 26 (2013): 55–70.

[20] See Patrick Kain, "Interpreting Kant's Theory of Divine Commands," *Kantian Review* 9 (2005): 128–49.

Autonomy and the Legislation of Laws in the *Prolegomena* 239

law is the same for human beings and God, even though God does not encounter the moral law in imperatival form, as human beings do. It is also independent insofar as reason does not require anything beyond itself (e.g., inclinations) to legislate the moral law (as is clear from the divine case, since God has no inclinations, even if there is in his case a special kind of "satisfaction").[21]

In theoretical contexts, as we have seen above, it is crucial to Kant's position and argument in the *Prolegomena* (and both editions of the first *Critique*) that it is the understanding that prescribes, or legislates, laws to nature. There is, he argues, no other way to account for the a priori status of the cognition of the laws of nature contained in the pure part of natural science. As we saw in the first edition Transcendental Deduction, Kant explicitly calls the understanding "the source of the laws of nature" (A126–7). Further, it is clear from this argument that the understanding legislates the laws of nature independently of anything else and impartially, since the laws of nature are *objective* rules that do not vary from subject to subject. Indeed, Kant makes it clear that in legislating the laws of nature, the understanding is an active and even spontaneous faculty. This first point of similarity between practical and theoretical legislation is especially important insofar as it serves as a presupposition for several other aspects of Kant's position.[22]

(2) The most significant difference between theoretical legislation and practical autonomy concerns what the law governs in each case. In the case of practical legislation, the moral law applies to *any rational agent* who legislates the moral law and who has the capacity to choose how (or whether) to act, which thus gives rise to a reflexive structure, whereas in theoretical legislation, the laws are laws of nature and thus apply to any and all *appearances* that are given to us through sensibility (so that the legislator is not also being legislated to, at least not in a strict sense). These appearances need not be rational or possess any faculty of choice. The object of the law thus represents an important point of difference between theoretical legislation and autonomy in morality. Kant puts this difference as follows in the Introduction to the *Critique of the Power of Judgment*: "morally practical precepts, which are grounded entirely on the concept of freedom to the complete exclusion of the determining

---

[21] For discussion of how the subject of self-legislation is to be understood, see Karl Ameriks, "Vindicating Autonomy," in *Kant on Moral Autonomy*, ed. Oliver Sensen (Cambridge: Cambridge University Press, 2013), pp. 53–70.

[22] For a broader discussion of reason and its legislative functions in both theoretical and practical philosophy, see Onora O'Neill, *Constructions of Reason* (Cambridge: Cambridge University Press, 1989), esp. chapters 1–3.

240   The Moral Law

grounds of the will from nature, constitute an entirely special kind of precept: which are also, like the rules that nature obeys, simply called laws, but which do not, like the latter, rest on sensible conditions, but on a supersensible principle" (5:173). But note that this difference derives not from the core notion of legislation that is at issue, but rather from the different contexts of theory and action in which legislation plays a central role.[23] As a result, this difference is to be expected and does not nullify the deep similarities between these two kinds of legislation.

(3) Despite the clear difference in the objects to which the law applies in each case, it is striking that there are significant similarities in the content of the law in each case and that reason is responsible for both the formulation and the content of the law. Specifically, the moral law and the laws of nature are both *formal* and *universal* in scope. That is, in both cases the law has a form that remains the same even as the specific (empirical) content (or matter) changes, and that form is best described by way of its necessity and universality. The formality and universality of the moral law finds its most obvious and most explicit expression in the Formula of Universal Law, which stresses the necessity of universalizing one's maxims (4:436) and which Kant explains by way of an explicit appeal to laws of nature (4:421 and 4:437). And it is clear that reason is responsible for precisely these features. On the theoretical side, despite differences in the empirical content of the various empirical laws of nature, they all imply (or take the form of) exceptionless generalizations. For example, the causal principle asserted in the Second Analogy invokes universality in a two-fold manner by asserting that *every* event is determined according to *universal* laws. And reason (in the guise of the understanding) is responsible for the lawfulness and thus the universality of the laws. The *Prolegomena* brings out this point nicely by drawing the distinction between the material and formal aspects of nature and emphasizing that the understanding is responsible for the formal aspect of nature, which is explicitly identified with necessary conformity to universal law. Thus, the way that Kant formulates the content of both the moral law and laws of nature reveals several significant points of similarity.

(4) Comparing reason's role in the generation of moral motivation to what occurs in cases of the legislation of laws of nature calls for some speculation. While Kant provides an explanation of how one can be motivated to act morally, an explanation that involves an a priori feeling of respect for the moral law, there is no strictly analogous question in the

---

[23] I return to this issue in the Conclusion to this book.

Autonomy and the Legislation of Laws in the *Prolegomena* 241

case of theoretical legislation insofar as motivation is a distinctively practical issue with no exact theoretical counterpart.[24] However, even acknowledging this difference, one can see that a somewhat looser, but still interesting analogy could obtain, even if Kant does not explicitly draw attention to it. For if one thinks not about the representational content of motivational states per se, but about how a motive is required to explain how one could be led to *act* in a particular way – where the motive (which Kant often calls a "*Triebfeder*") serves as a kind of efficient cause (as opposed to how one could be *justified* in acting a certain way) – then one might similarly think that one ought to be able to explain how one could be led to *assent* to a certain proposition (regardless of whether one would be justified in assenting to it). And just as reason produces the feeling of respect, which is required to serve as an efficient cause of a moral action, so too one might suppose that reason could produce a cognitive state that leads one to assent to a priori laws obtaining in nature.[25] Granted, Kant does not explicitly endorse such a point of similarity, but one might nonetheless see room for a structural parallel there, in spite of the difference in kind between motivational states and whatever states lead one to assent to the laws of nature.

(5) Central to Kant's doctrine of autonomy is the idea that the moral law is binding, or obligatory, for us precisely because reason legislates the moral law to itself.[26] To see what parallels obtain between autonomy and theoretical legislation in this regard, it is crucial to distinguish between the scope of the law's applicability and the kind of necessity that it has. On the one hand, the moral law applies to, and is binding for, all rational agents, and it does so because all rational agents can legislate it to themselves. As a result, the moral law applies both to God and to finite rational agents, such as ourselves. This point can be put in more familiar terms by saying that the law is not merely hypothetically necessary, depending on the desires one has, but rather is categorically necessary, binding for all rational agents.

On the other hand, as we saw in Chapter 1, the kind of necessity that the moral law expresses can vary between different kinds of rational agents. The moral law is necessary for us in the sense that we ought to

---

[24] A different way of seeing the disanalogy between the cases is to note that, unlike the moral case, in the case of nature the objects that are subject to the laws are (in many cases) not sentient beings that would even have motivational states.

[25] In the Canon of the first *Critique*, Kant acknowledges that a subjective ground of assent is necessary (but also that it is not sufficient) for knowledge. See Andrew Chignell, "Kant's Concepts of Justification," *Nous* 41 (2007): 33–63, for discussion.

[26] See the more detailed discussion of this issue in Chapter 1 of this book.

242   The Moral Law

act in accordance with it (it binds us or is obligatory for us), even if we can also act contrary to the moral law (in virtue of our susceptibility to act on sensible inclinations that run contrary to its demands). That is, we are obligated by the moral law without it being the case that we inevitably act as it demands. In this respect, there is an important difference between the kind of necessity that the moral law takes on in the divine and human cases. For the moral law does not take the form of an imperative for God, since God could not have acted otherwise, whereas finite rational agents experience the moral law as an imperative because of the possibility of acting contrary to it. That is, we are obligated by the moral law without it being the case that we necessarily act as it demands. Kant makes this distinction clear as follows:

Now the laws of freedom are either

1. **purely necessary**, or **leges objective mere necessariae**. These are found only in God. or
2. **necessitating**, **necessitantes**. These are found in man, and are objectively necessary, but subjectively contingent. Man, that is, has an urge to trespass against these laws, even when he knows them, and thus the legality and morality of his actions are merely contingent. (27:481)

That is, the very notion of a law involves necessity, but it takes on different forms in different cases. In the case of God, the law determines what God will necessarily do, whereas in the case of human beings, the necessity of the law is characterized as necessitation rather than determination or as necessitat*ing* rather than determin*ing*. In short, in all cases reason legislates the moral law, which is an objectively necessary principle. The necessity of the law then either *determines* purely rational beings to act in accordance with the law or it *obligates* rational beings that are not purely rational in such a way that they ought to act in accordance with the law. The law thus prescribes necessity to different kinds of beings in different ways without the law itself being different.

Now one might think that theoretical legislation must be fundamentally different from practical autonomy with respect to the question of whether reason can be responsible for the binding force of the laws of nature. After all, the laws of nature do not entail that the objects found in nature *ought to* behave as the laws dictate, and such objects could not disobey these laws.[27] For inanimate objects do not possess either reason or a power of choice and therefore cannot in any strict sense be said to

---

[27] Hannah Ginsborg, *The Normativity of Nature: Essays on Kant's Critique of Judgement* (Oxford: Oxford University Press, 2015), argues that there is a kind of primitive normativity in nature itself.

obey or disobey the laws of nature. Since the laws of nature are not imperatives, it is clear that theoretical legislation does not involve obligation.[28]

However, a case can be made that theoretical legislation does still involve a kind of necessity that is at least similar to the first notion described above. For insofar as a law involves the necessity of an action and the necessity of an action can be said to bind whatever is acting under that necessity, then a law of nature also involves the binding of whatever it is that acts, even if it is not capable of choosing to act otherwise. It is in this sense that one can say that inanimate objects can be said to act *according to* the laws of nature or that the laws of nature *govern* or *determine* the behavior of inanimate objects.[29] Billiard balls hit, collide, and act in sundry ways. It turns out that, unlike finite rational agents, they are determined to act in such ways by the laws of nature so that they have no choice; they are bound or governed by the laws of nature even more strictly than we are by the moral law. But in both cases, there is a genuine sense in which the law concerns "the *necessity* of what is and what happens or the necessity of what ought to happen" (4:463).

If it is appropriate to speak of the laws of nature as necessary in this sense, then, in light of Kant's claim that reason (in the guise of the understanding) prescribes laws to nature, it is clear that it is ultimately reason that is responsible for the necessity of the laws of nature.[30] In fact, Kant clearly endorses this point insofar as he maintains that appearances would not have the kind of order or necessity that is characteristic of the laws of nature if they were not combined according to the understanding's own laws. It is thus the legislation of reason that is responsible for the necessity that the laws of nature bring to nature. As a result, there is a fundamental similarity concerning the necessity of the law for practical autonomy and theoretical legislation.

---

[28] Kain develops an argument for the claim that Kant's notion of practical legislation is not (what has come to be called) constructivist, or even anti-realist, in "Self-Legislation in Kant's Moral Philosophy." The current account agrees with Kain's interpretation in not viewing the act of legislation as something that particular empirical subjects might (or might not) do. Instead, the law carries necessity with it on the basis of reason's legislative authority. See also Karl Ameriks, *Interpreting Kant's Critiques* (Oxford: Oxford University Press, 2003), chapter 11. For the most thorough constructivist interpretation of Kant's position, see Andrews Reath, "Legislating the Moral Law," *Nous* 28 (1994): 435–64.

[29] For detailed discussion of Kant's account of causality, according to which it makes sense to say that (even inanimate) substances act according to laws (and their natures and powers), see Eric Watkins, *Kant and the Metaphysics of Causality* (New York: Cambridge University Press, 2005), especially chapter 4.

[30] Though Kant's account is complex, what is necessary can depend not only on reason, but also on the natures of things.

244   The Moral Law

This account of the necessity of the law then straightforwardly entails what might otherwise seem to be a surprising result. It might have been tempting to think that the binding force of the moral law derives from the reflexive structure of autonomy. That is, reason is not only what legislates the law, but it also legislates the law *to itself*. And one might have thought, much as Rousseau seems to have for political contexts, that the law is genuinely binding for us only because we are binding ourselves in legislating the law. How can we reasonably object to a law that we ourselves have enacted? Put differently, for any externally imposed law the possibility of illegitimate coercion (and exploitation) seems unavoidable. But a self-imposed law cannot be coercive insofar as coercion requires an *external* agent imposing his or her will on us from without and there is no external agent in the case of a *self*-imposed law. We seem to be bound in such a case precisely because *we* have bound *ourselves*. Yet, without denying the presence and importance of the reflexive component of autonomy, the account of necessity and obligation described above suggests that the moral law has binding force in virtue of the necessity of the law where that necessity derives from reason's legislation.[31] If we are rational beings and enact a law, that law has a necessity that binds all rational agents in virtue of the *rationality* of both the legislator and the law and not in virtue of it being their *own* law.[32]

In sum, what emerges from comparing the most fundamental points of Kant's doctrine of autonomy in the moral realm and Kant's view of theoretical legislation presented earlier is that we find points of similarity and points of contrast. The basic points of similarity are that in both cases reason legislates a law that is formal and universal, and this law is necessary for its object as a result of reason's legislation. The most prominent differences are that the object of the law is significantly different in each case – rational agents as opposed to nature as a whole – and that Kant does not explore the possibility of a theoretical analog to the issue of moral motivation, even if one could investigate such an option independently. But these differences arise not from some

---

[31] Kain ("Self-Legislation in Kant's Moral Philosophy," p. 301) suggests that the reflexivity of legislation is an expression of the immediacy and unconditional nature of our being bound by the law we self-legislate. Stefano Bacin ("Legge e obbligatorietà: la struttura dell'idea di autolegislazione morale") similarly argues that the reflexive expressions indicate not a genuine reflexiveness, but rather the inner nature of the legislation.

[32] This consequence might be viewed by some as a welcome result, since one line of thought (developed by Anscombe) maintains – in a way that can seem hostile to Kant's position – that one cannot obligate oneself, since one can simply release oneself from the obligation whenever one so desires. Since the necessity of the moral law does not depend on any contingent feature of ourselves, it is unclear how one could release oneself from an obligation at will.

Autonomy and the Legislation of Laws in the *Prolegomena*   245

fundamental difference in legislation per se, but rather from the particular contexts – theoretical and practical – in which a core notion of legislation by reason is invoked. In short, autonomy in the practical realm and theoretical legislation in nature share deep and important parallels.

11.4   Conclusion

At this point, the following question naturally arises: Do the substantive philosophical parallels between practical autonomy and theoretical legislation that Kant envisions justify the historical claim that he was led by the development of the account of theoretical legislation in the first edition of the first *Critique* and the *Prolegomena* to develop his account of practical autonomy in the *Groundwork*? There is, it seems, no explicit textual evidence in the *Groundwork* that would provide a definitive answer. Nor does Kant make any autobiographical remarks in other works that would settle the question. As a result, there is no conclusive textual evidence that would resolve the issue. Instead, we must consider more indirect evidence, e.g., by looking to how and when he develops and adopts doctrines that are relevant to his account of autonomy and then evaluating the possible connections between them.[33]

In light of the fact that Kant's doctrine of theoretical legislation is not developed prior to 1781, is explicitly endorsed in 1781, and then forms a crucial element of the most basic argumentative structure of the *Prolegomena* in 1783, it is certainly tempting to think that this doctrine plays a significant role in the development of his doctrine of practical autonomy, which first makes an appearance in the *Groundwork* in 1785. This is especially tempting because Kant's doctrine of theoretical legislation is so strikingly original in maintaining that the laws of nature are not an independent feature of the world, but rather derive from our spontaneous faculties. It is plausible to maintain that thinking of legislation in this way in the theoretical sphere opens up the possibility that it would obtain, with suitable modification, in the practical sphere as well. So without claiming that Kant's acceptance of theoretical legislation is the *only* consideration that led him to see the advantages of adopting his account of practical autonomy, we do have some reason to think that Kant comes to hold certain aspects of his views in morality by way of the distinctive views that he comes to adopt in his theoretical philosophy.[34]

---

[33] For extensive discussion of precisely this issue, see *The Emergence of Autonomy*, ed. Stefano Bacin and Oliver Sensen (Cambridge: Cambridge University Press, 2018).

[34] Indeed, as we saw in Chapter 1 of this book, Kant is drawing on the natural law tradition in conceiving of his univocal notion of law.

246   The Moral Law

Whatever the historical influences may be, however, the comparison of theoretical legislation and practical autonomy is instructive in several respects. For one, the comparison makes clear that if we are to take laws seriously as laws, then it is fitting to have an account that can explain their special normative status. Reason is the legislator of both the moral law and the lawfulness of the laws of nature, and reason is a spontaneous faculty that is endowed with legislative authority; thus it is plausible to view reason as a crucial faculty in Kant's account of law in general.[35] For another, the comparison reveals an important aspect of the unity of reason, as Kant understands it. Though Kant has a more robust conception of reason that distinguishes his view fundamentally from his predecessors' (by focusing on what he calls "the unconditioned"), this comparison shows that reason is also concerned with laws, whether they be theoretical or practical, and with their formulation, content, and necessity. This aspect of Kant's account of reason is especially important in the current context because it suggests that his explanation of the necessity of the moral law in particular is not ad hoc. That is, if reason legislates laws as objective principles that involve necessity, then there is at least some reason to accept that practical autonomy can explain rather than simply presuppose the necessity, or bindingness of the moral law. In this way, it provides valuable insight into the core of Kant's position in both his theoretical and practical philosophy.[36]

---

[35] See the discussion in Chapter 1 for further argument.

[36] For comments on an earlier version of this chapter I thank Karl Ameriks, Stefano Bacin, Pierre Keller, Pauline Kleingeld, Heiner Klemme, Georg Mohr, Andy Reath, Oliver Sensen, Susan Shell, Jens Timmermann, and Marcus Willaschek.

12 Kant on the Natural, Moral, Human, and Divine Orders

12.1 Introduction

What many find appealing about Kant's philosophy today is that his rejection of traditional metaphysics allows one to jettison an idea that is prominent both among many early modern thinkers and in the various narratives offered to account for their views, namely, that a perfect and transcendent God is ultimately responsible for the order found in nature and among human beings within it. That is, on this view, his critical stance on metaphysics leads him to dispense with the view that God is the ultimate legislator, or law-giver, both of the moral law and of the laws of nature, and to advance the revolutionary idea that human beings alone are essentially responsible for creating order within the natural and moral world. Thus, not only does our conception of the world become increasingly secularized throughout the modern period, as Taylor, Israel, and Dreyfus and Kelly have argued recently, but it also appears to be anthropomorphized, or made dependent on the constructive activities of human beings, as Rawls and Schneewind have suggested.[1] In short, what many value in Kant's thought today is that his rejection of metaphysics in favor of a distinctively human epistemology and practical philosophy allows him, in effect, to replace God with human beings within his philosophy, thereby contributing to the fulfillment of the Enlightenment's agenda of progress wrought solely by human effort.

This view of the role of Kant's position within modern philosophy and its contemporary significance is based on genuine and important features

---

[1] See Charles Taylor, *A Secular Age* (Cambridge, MA: Harvard University Press, 2007); Jonathan Israel, *The Enlightenment Contested* (New York: Oxford University Press, 2006); Hubert Dreyfus and Sean Dorrance Kelly, *All Things Shining: Reading the Western Classics to Find Meaning in a Secular Age* (New York: Free Press, 2011); John Rawls, "Kantian Constructivism in Moral Theory," *The Journal of Philosophy* 77 (1980): 515–72; and Jerome Schneewind, *The Invention of Autonomy: A History of Modern Moral Philosophy* (New York: Cambridge University Press, 1997).

248   The Moral Law

of his philosophy. For as we have seen in several earlier chapters in this book, Kant clearly asserts that reason, broadly construed, has a strong prescriptive role with respect to both nature and morality. As Kant argues in the *Critique of Pure Reason*, reason (in the guise of the understanding) prescribes lawfulness to nature a priori such that we are responsible for the regularities in nature, and in the *Groundwork of the Metaphysics of Morals*, the moral law is based on autonomy, which is a specific kind of self-legislation of reason. Thus the laws of nature and morality are both based in the first instance on us and not simply on God alone.

I argue, however, that Kant's actual position is both more nuanced and more interesting than this standard narrative has it, and I do so by considering one central issue from each of Kant's three *Critiques*. First, while Kant does clearly deny in the first *Critique* that we can have theoretical cognition of God's existence, he nonetheless also argues that, even in its purely theoretical use, reason requires that we form an idea of an ontologically most real being, and that we assent to the existence of such a being so as to be able to explain the possibility of the empirical objects that we can cognize. This point – that reason requires us to accept an ontologically most real being that grounds possibility – not only provides a more comprehensive metaphysical account of the world, but also turns out to open up more plausible interpretive options for other claims and arguments that Kant makes throughout his corpus.

Second, Kant argues in the second *Critique* that practical reason requires belief in God's existence, since God is needed to bring about the proper proportion of happiness to virtue that is required for the highest good, the possibility of which we necessarily presuppose in acting morally. What's more, Kant repeatedly asserts that we can recognize our moral obligations as divine commands, even as he rejects certain (more voluntarist) versions of divine command theory.[2] Thus, even in the face of his emphasis on human autonomy in the moral realm, Kant does not view the acceptance of God's existence as optional, much less as prohibited. Now Kant's moral argument for the necessity of postulating God's existence has been widely criticized and I do not intend to defend it against all objections, but I do want to suggest that if one takes the specific context in which it arises into consideration, one can see how to defend it against two particularly important objections. Kant's argument can appear in a better light if one (1) assumes what Kant takes himself

---

[2] See Patrick Kain, "Interpreting Kant's Theory of Divine Commands," *Kantian Review* 9 (2005): 128–49.

to have already established in the first *Critique*, namely, that we are required to assent to the existence of an ontologically most real being that grounds all possibility, and (2) views his task in the second *Critique* as demonstrating the necessity of such a being's specifically *moral* attributes. It also represents a further instance of the kind of argument that Kant deploys in systematic ways throughout his philosophy.

Third, in the *Critique of the Power of Judgment*, Kant argues that the contradiction expressed in the Antinomy of Teleological Judgment regarding the mechanical inexplicability of organisms can be resolved only if (1) mechanistic laws are subordinated to teleological laws and (2) appeal is made to a supersensible ground. What has remained mysterious about Kant's views here is, specifically, how these claims actually allow one to avoid the contradiction between the thesis and antithesis that form the antinomy as well as, in general, what implications they have for understanding the ensuing system of nature, with its mechanistic and teleological laws. If, however, we identify the supersensible ground with the most real being endowed with perfect moral qualities, i.e., with the being Kant had established in the first and second *Critiques*, then we can dispel at least some of the puzzles that currently obscure our understanding of his resolution of the antinomy. We can resolve the contradiction between the thesis and antithesis because what appears possible for a merely discursive understanding such as our own can be different from what is possible for the divine intellect. Moreover, given what Kant is committed to in the second *Critique*, his position can best be understood as asserting that God (i.e., the supersensible principle) uses the metaphysically necessary mechanistic laws to further the teleological aims of rational agents that are ends in themselves by proportioning the natural goodness aimed at in teleology to the moral goodness that rational agents have managed to achieve.

I present some considerations in support of these three sets of interpretive claims in the following three sections. Taken together, however, they reveal a broader and more satisfying interpretation of Kant's views on the relations that obtain between the natural, moral, human, and divine orders. Specifically, instead of simply making dogmatic metaphysical claims about God, in several contexts Kant begins with undeniable features of our experience of the natural and moral orders and argues that they are possible only if supported by highly specific features of a divine order at the same time that he still allows for the human order to play an important, albeit restricted role with respect to the laws that are definitive of the natural and moral orders. This mode of argumentation can thus avoid the weaknesses that some early modern philosophers faced and allow his position to appear attractive in contemporary contexts as well.

250   The Moral Law

12.2   The Ground of Possibility

Much attention has been devoted to Kant's rejection, in the first *Critique*, of traditional metaphysics in general, and of the three traditional theistic proofs in particular.[3] This is especially true of his famous criticism of the ontological argument, which relies on the insight that existence cannot be understood exactly as other properties (or "real predicates") can.[4] Relatively little consideration has been given, by contrast, to Kant's positive assertions about God within his theoretical philosophy.[5] To redress the comparative neglect of this issue, I argue for two central claims about his position before noting three crucial qualifications. In this way, we can come to a more accurate picture of Kant's actual position and see more clearly what his contribution to modern philosophy is, yet without having to sacrifice what could make his position appear appealing today.

The first and most basic claim is that Kant does think that we can form a meaningful idea of God and that we do so by extending our categories beyond what can be given to us in sensible intuition. It is true that Kant does sometimes say that when we free the categories from their sensible conditions, such representations are without sense and meaning (*"ohne Sinn und Bedeutung"*), which has in turn led some to think that for Kant the very idea of God must be literally meaningless and akin to a mere feeling.[6] However, reflection on the terms Kant uses and on the nature of his project in the first *Critique* clearly shows that we must be able to form some kind of meaningful idea of God. Kant's point in saying that the categories are without "sense and meaning" when freed from their sensible conditions is typically that the conditions for theoretical *cognition* cannot be satisfied, not that these ideas are literally meaningless. For "sense" and "meaning" are technical terms with the former denoting, at least sometimes, a (sensible) grasp of the sort of thing that is intended by a given concept, or of what it would be like for us to encounter it (A241/B300), while the latter (which is sometimes translated as "significance") indicates something akin to demonstrable reference. Thus to say that our idea of God is without sense and meaning is to say that we do not know

---

[3] For recent discussion, see, e.g., Michelle Grier, *Kant's Doctrine of Transcendental Illusion* (New York: Cambridge University Press, 2001).

[4] See, for example, Alvin Plantinga, "Kant's Objection to the Ontological Argument," *The Journal of Philosophy* 63 (1966): 537–46, which generated a significant literature in response.

[5] However, there are important exceptions, such as Allen Wood, *Kant's Rational Theology* (Ithaca: Cornell University Press, 1978), and Andrew Chignell, "Belief in Kant," *The Philosophical Review* 116 (2007): 323–60.

[6] See Peter Strawson's "Principle of Significance," in *The Bounds of Sense: An Essay on Kant's Critique of Pure Reason* (London: Methuen, 1966).

Kant on the Natural, Moral, Human, and Divine Orders 251

what it would be like for us to experience an object that corresponds to that idea and that we cannot demonstrate that and how our idea refers to such an object, not that we have no idea at all of what we mean when we use the term. Indeed, if such an idea were truly meaningless, Kant's objection to the three traditional theistic proofs would be simply that we cannot even conceive of their subject matter, an objection that would beg the question against his opponents in a rather crude and uninteresting way. Instead, the detailed objections that he actually formulates against these arguments in the Ideal of Pure Reason presuppose that we have at least a rudimentary understanding of what we are talking about when we employ our idea of God.

The second claim is that although Kant rejects the three traditional arguments for God's existence, he affirms a (suitably) revised version of his own pre-Critical theistic proof. Though there is no need, for current purposes, to reconstruct this pre-Critical argument in detail, it is useful to recall its general structure.[7] The basic idea is that the principle of determining ground ought to apply not only to what is actual, but also to what is possible. Slightly more specifically, Kant notes that to speak of any possibility, not only must what is to be possible satisfy the logical ground of possibility, namely, the principle of contradiction (by not contradicting itself), but a certain material or content must also be given that is subject to the principle of contradiction; i.e., there must be a material condition of possibility. Kant then argues that whatever is the ground, or reason, of the material contained in any possibility cannot itself be merely possible – a vicious regress would loom down that road – but must instead be actual. He concludes by inferring that this actual ground of the content of any possibility must be a necessary, unique, simple, immutable, eternal mind that contains the most fundamental realities, and hence be God. In short, God is required to ground not only the existence of all contingent things, but also the very possibility of these things.

In the first *Critique* Kant sees the need to recast this argument in several respects and also to note the status of its conclusion and limitations. He sometimes reframes the argument in terms provided by his Critical characterization of reason as the faculty that searches for the totality of conditions, and thus the unconditioned, that conditions whatever conditioned items are given and stand in need of explanation.[8]

---

[7] See Robert M. Adams, "God, Possibility, and Kant," *Faith and Philosophy* 4 (2000): 425–40, and Andrew Chignell, "Kant, Modality, and the Most Real Being," *Archiv für Geschichte der Philosophie* 91 (2009): 157–92.

[8] See especially A577/B605ff.

252   The Moral Law

Described in these terms, the argument asserts that (1) the possibilities of things are given as conditioned – possibilities are not brute facts, accepted as inexplicable primitives; (2) reason seeks a ground, or condition, of these conditioned possibilities – it is analytically true that the existence of something conditioned entails the existence of a condition or set of conditions that condition it; and (3) reason is satisfied only with the totality of conditions of these conditioned items, which is necessarily unconditioned, and, in this case, must be the *ens realissimum* whose necessary existence explains all possibility.

Kant's statement of the argument in the first *Critique* also involves further complications. For example, in Section Two of the Ideal of Pure Reason he introduces not only the principle of determinability, which is a version of the principle of excluded middle, but also the principle of thoroughgoing determination, which involves the "whole of possibility as the sum total of all predicates of things in general" (A572/B600). He also holds that we must think of certain properties as realities and others as negations thereof, and that limited instances of real properties are in some way grounded in, or conditioned by, the full realities.[9] And he then moves, on a less than straightforward path, from this position to the ideal of an *ens realissimum*. Further, in Section Three of the Ideal of Pure Reason he suggests that since this argument alone might not be fully persuasive, one is naturally tempted to try to supplement it with a version of the cosmological argument, though he criticizes the effectiveness of this supplementation. Fortunately, however, sorting out these details is not necessary for understanding the basic structure of the argument, according to which reason requires that we think of an *ens realissimum* as the condition, or ground, of all possibility, and it is important to note that the acceptance of this thought of an *ens realissimum* does significant philosophical work for Kant, since it puts him in a position to extend the scope of the principle of determining ground so that it applies not only to actual things, but also to possible things.[10]

---

[9] It requires that we "represent every thing as deriving its own possibility from the share that it has in the whole of possibility" (A572/B600).

[10] There is significant disagreement about the nature and intended conclusion of Kant's argument. While I do not have space to discuss the issue in the detail it deserves, I do want to point to an ambiguity that could significantly affect how one understands and evaluates the argument. When Kant talks about possibility, he often does so in terms of predicates. (For example, the principle of determinability is phrased in this way.) This word choice suggests that Kant is interested in the semantic content of predicates that we might attribute to objects. However, Kant also talks about possibility in terms of the determinations of things, which can be understood as pertaining to the properties of things. (The principle of thoroughgoing determination is phrased in this way.) If one focuses on Kant's talk of predicates and reads his interest in the Ideal of Pure Reason as

Kant on the Natural, Moral, Human, and Divine Orders 253

Now for three crucial qualifications. First, what the argument establishes is nothing more than "God thought of in a transcendental sense" (A580/B608), which falls well short of the traditional Judeo-Christian conception of God, since this latter concept involves an essential moral dimension. That is, if all we need is some being that is capable of serving as the ground for all possibility, it is not necessary to attribute any specifically *moral* qualities to such a being, nothing about such a being's will or goodness.[11] In the Appendix contained in the Methodology of the Teleological Power of Judgment, Kant similarly notes that "the objective reality of the idea of God as the moral author of the world cannot of course be established by means of physical ends *alone*" (5:456, cf. also 5:473 and 5:480), despite the fact that the so-called physico-theological argument does warrant acceptance of "an intelligent world cause" (5:437).[12] In fact, elsewhere, Kant is explicit that God does not ground possibilities by willing them, and here he explicitly notes that the argument goes awry if the supremely real being is "**personified**" (A583/B611).[13] As a result, the predicates ascribed to "God" cannot go beyond what can be represented by means of the unschematized categories. Thus, what Kant's argument here purports to establish is the existence only of an *ens realissimum* that grounds all possibilities, not a God endowed with moral properties.

Second, Kant notes that even if one takes the ground of possibility to be understood in such minimal terms, reason "would already be overstepping its bounds" by "demanding that this reality should be given objectively" (A580/B608).[14] In other words, for us to have theoretical

---

exclusively semantic, one is likely to think that Kant could never draw any ontological conclusion and that his analysis of the argument is objecting to drawing precisely that kind of conclusion. However, if one thinks that Kant holds that predicates and properties go hand in hand (despite being distinct), then one might think that Kant is willing to accept that there must be some (actual) ground for the reality of the real properties that our predicates refer to, even as Kant rejects inferences to ontological commitments (or properties) that are unwarranted by the metaphysical considerations with which he starts.

[11] In his lectures on the philosophical doctrine of religion, Kant makes it clear that both will and understanding cannot be represented solely through non-empirical transcendental predicates. Insofar as goodness depends on a notion of will, the same holds for it.

[12] I thank Caroline Bowman for discussion of the role of teleological arguments in the context of the moral argument in the third *Critique*.

[13] In *The Only Possible Argument*, Kant says: "Accordingly, if I assert that God contains the ultimate ground even of the internal possibility of things, everyone will easily understand that this can only be a non-moral dependency, for the will makes nothing possible" (2:100). See also Eric Watkins, "The Early Kant's (Anti-)Newtonianism," *Studies in History and Philosophy of Science* 44 (2012): 429–37.

[14] Surprisingly little attention has been devoted to what it means, according to Kant, for something to be given objectively. It might mean, for us at least, that it must be given through intuition or through the senses. For an analysis of what givenness means in

254   The Moral Law

cognition of an object, that object would have to be given to us through the senses, which is not possible in the case of God (or even an *ens realissimum*).[15] Reason can demand that we assent to the object's existence in thought, but it cannot demand that the object be given to us through the senses (especially since reason and sensibility are distinct faculties). Insofar as one expects any theistic proof to establish God's existence by way of objective evidence (that is, evidence that derives in some way from the presence or existence of the object as opposed to reason's demands and its search for conditions), one will, he argues, be disappointed by the proof. The argument thus suffers from what he refers to as an "objective insufficiency" (A589/B617). This critical point, which is limited to *objective* considerations, is thus perfectly consistent with the critical thrust of the Transcendental Dialectic as a whole.

Third, Kant proposes that we accept such a being as a regulative principle of reason, not as a constitutive principle of objects (which would wrongly "hypostatize" this being).[16] That is, given that such a being cannot be given to us through the senses and thus cannot be cognized as an object, it must be accepted solely on *subjective* grounds. But since these grounds are based on an *essential* feature of our subject, namely, our rationality, it is not a contingent principle that we might dispense with. Nor does it depend on anything that we might or might not do. As a result, though the principle is subjective in one sense – it depends on one of our faculties rather than on a being distinct from us – it is not contingent for us and thus qualifies as what we would now think of as objective in a robust sense. In short, it is a regulative principle that directs us to think such a being as grounding the possibilities of things, and though we cannot have objective theoretical cognition of it (and of how we might encounter it), we must nonetheless assent to its existence.[17]

If we take these three qualifications into account, we can see that Kant's purely theoretical case for the existence of an *ens realissimum* does not in fact entail a full-scale rejection of metaphysics (in favor of,

---

Kant, see Eric Watkins and Marcus Willaschek, "Kant's Account of Cognition," *Journal of the History of Philosophy* 55 (2017): 83–112.

[15] See Eric Watkins, "Kant on the Hiddenness of God," *Kantian Review* 14 (2009): 81–122.

[16] Though Kant is referring to the being that is posited on the basis of cosmological considerations rather than reasons pertaining to the grounding of possibility, he is quite explicit about the ideal of pure reason being a regulative principle of reason at A619/B647.

[17] Andrew Chignell has articulated the kind of theoretical assent, or belief, that Kant has in mind here in "Belief in Kant" and "Kant's Concepts of Justification," *Nous* 41 (2007): 33–63.

e.g., purely epistemic conditions), even if certain kinds of specific metaphysical claims are to be rejected *insofar* as they are taken to amount to objective theoretical cognition in his technical sense of the term. Instead, what Kant advances, at least by his philosophical practice in this instance, is that certain metaphysical claims are presupposed as conditions on the possibility of cognition of empirical objects in the natural world. That is, given that the natural order must be understood in terms of what is and what is not possible and given that we take all possibility to be grounded in an *ens realissimum*, we must take the natural order to be grounded in what can be reasonably characterized as a metaphysical (quasi-)divine order (even if certain features traditionally associated with a divinity cannot be established on the basis of these considerations). In short, we see in the first *Critique* that the natural order is ultimately grounded in a metaphysically prior quasi-divine order that grounds the possibility of all things in nature.

However, note that Kant's understanding of this grounding relation is interestingly different from that of his predecessors in ways that allow his position to avoid some of the weaknesses of their positions and thus to remain relevant to a contemporary audience. For Kant does not argue *from* features of God (e.g., God's immutability or will) *to* attributes of the natural order (as Descartes, Malebranche, and Leibniz did), but rather *from* features of the natural order *to* the rationally necessary conditions that are associated with the divine order.[18] That is, since he starts with what could be an object for us in the natural world and moves to its presuppositions, he is not starting with dogmatic and thus inherently controversial metaphysical assertions. At the same time, even as he insists on the necessity of the human order to the natural order by emphasizing how human reason inserts lawfulness into nature a priori (thereby defining the natural order), he is not forced into the extreme position of denying that metaphysics has any role at all to play in explaining the fundamental features of the natural order of our world (as, e.g., Hume does). Instead, as we have seen, he asserts that it is a distinctive feature of human reason in particular that requires that we assent to the divine order being a (metaphysical) presupposition of the natural order. Granted, experience cannot confirm that the divine order exists as reason claims it is, but if we are to make genuine sense of the world in the way in which our reason demands and if our claims are to survive the tribunal of reason, which is the ultimate authority for any claim we might make, positing such an order is fundamental to the comprehensibility of our

---

[18] This claim does not exclude the possibility that the divine order provides some constraints on the natural order.

256   The Moral Law

experience of the world just as it is essential to the kind of cognitive beings that we are.

12.3   Kant's Moral Argument

If Kant's theoretical philosophy is understood in this way, it brings with it important implications for his practical philosophy and the moral order that it envisions. This can be seen most clearly with respect to Kant's so-called moral argument for the existence of God, which asserts that we must postulate God's existence if the moral law is not to be illusory for us. Specifically, Kant asserts not only that we should act morally, but also that to do so rationally, we must assume the possibility of the ultimate end or object of our action, namely, the highest good. However, since the highest good, with its distinctive combination of virtue and happiness, does not lie fully in our control, we must assume that God exists as a guarantor of the possibility of the highest good.

Kant's moral argument can be reconstructed, roughly and in its barest essentials, as follows.[19]

(1) If the moral law is not false, then the highest good must be possible as an object of pure practical reason.
(2) The highest good can be possible as an object of pure practical reason only if there is a necessary connection between virtue and happiness.
(3) There can be a necessary connection between virtue and happiness only if either happiness necessarily causes virtue or virtue is necessarily the cause of happiness.[20]
(4) Happiness does not necessarily cause virtue.
(5) If virtue necessarily causes happiness, it must do so either directly or indirectly, by way of a being that has the knowledge, power, and moral character to do so, i.e., by God.
(6) Virtue does not cause happiness directly.
(7) The moral law is not false.
(8) Therefore, God, understood as a being that has the knowledge, power, and moral character to cause happiness to be proportionate to virtue, must exist.

---

[19] For a more detailed discussion of Kant's practical argument, see Allen Wood, *Kant's Moral Religion* (Ithaca: Cornell University Press, 1978), and Eric Watkins, "The Antinomy of Practical Reason: Reason, the Unconditioned, and the Highest Good," in *Kant's Critique of Practical Reason: A Critical Guide*, ed. Andrews Reath and Jens Timmerman (New York: Cambridge University Press, 2010), pp. 145–67.

[20] Kant argues that the necessary connection cannot in this case be analytic, but rather must be synthetic.

Kant on the Natural, Moral, Human, and Divine Orders   257

Needless to say, the moral argument has numerous controversial features. In presupposing that reason must not only legislate the moral law but also have the highest good as its necessary object, Kant is basing his view on a more robust conception of reason than the kind of purely formal conception of instrumental rationality that is typically assumed in contemporary discussions of the justification of principles of normative ethics. He also makes substantive assumptions about the relations between happiness and virtue, since he takes happiness (or flourishing) to be distinct from virtue, in opposition to a broadly Aristotelian account, and he holds, unlike the Stoics, that virtue does not necessarily cause happiness.

However, insofar as Kant at least explicitly adduces reasons in support of these assumptions, one might think that his moral argument is more vulnerable to two objections that he seems not to address. First, one might think that the argument, if successful, establishes only the possibility and not the actuality of God. For if what must be explained is the possibility of the highest good, it can seem that the mere possibility of God suffices. That is, if it is possible that God exists, then it is also possible that the highest good exists. Now if one wanted to establish the *actuality* of the highest good, then perhaps the *actuality* of God would be required, but given the starting point of the moral argument – we must take the highest good to be possible – it can seem as if only the weaker conclusion follows.

Second, even if one granted that the moral argument establishes the existence rather than the mere possibility of a being that makes the highest good possible, one might still object to identifying that being with (the Judeo-Christian) God. Specifically, even if one were warranted in inferring the moral perfection of a being that could guarantee the possibility of the highest good (since attributing goodness to such a being is based on its being responsible for the best possible moral state of affairs), it is not clear that one could establish all of the attributes that would be necessary to identifying that being with the Judeo-Christian God, insofar as such a being is thought to possesses all perfections. Take, for instance, omniscience and omnipotence. To proportion virtue and happiness, such a being would presumably need to know the moral character of every rational agent, but not the state of everything else in the world, so omniscience is not obviously required to bring about the highest good. Similarly, such a being would not have to create anything in the world *ex nihilo*, much less everything. Instead, all that such an argument would establish is the necessity of a moral architect who arranges states of happiness in the world according to a certain design. As a result, even if the moral argument were successful in establishing

258   The Moral Law

the existence of an actual cause of the proportion of happiness to virtue that is required for the highest good, it could still seem to fall short of establishing its intended conclusion.

However, a proper appreciation of Kant's position in the first *Critique* relieves some of the pressure placed on Kant's moral argument by these objections. Specifically, if Kant has already established the necessity of an *ens realissimum*, which is understood in terms of transcendental predicates as the ground of all possibility, then he has resources with which to address both of these objections. First, Kant would clearly reject the attempt to explain the possibility of the highest good in terms of the mere possibility of God, as the first objection would have it, for when it comes to ultimate explanations, Kant firmly maintains the priority of actuality over possibility, as he makes clear in the *New Elucidation* and *The Only Possible Argument*, where possibility presupposes actuality.[21] More importantly, however, insofar as Kant has already provided an account of the logical possibility of everything and thus of that of the highest good as well, what is at issue in the moral argument clearly must be something more robust than logical possibility. What might that be? Kant claims that when we act, we are necessarily interested in the realization of the end or object of our actions.[22] The interest we take in that object presupposes not simply that it be *logically* possible, but rather that so far as we know, it is actually attainable or *genuinely possible* in these circumstances.[23] As a result, when reason demands that we act according to the moral law and we assume that the highest good must be possible as the ultimate end of our moral actions, then reason requires the existence of something that makes this end genuinely attainable, given that we do not have complete control over whether the ends of our actions are realized. The mere possibility of God would not make the highest good genuinely attainable for us. Only the actuality of God could accomplish that task.

Second, the fact that the moral argument, if successful, establishes only the moral attributes of whatever grounds the real possibility of the

---

[21] This priority comes out most clearly in the *New Elucidation*, where he grounds all possibility in the necessary existence of God, for whom there is no ground. That is, for Kant, while the principle of determining ground accounts for all possibility, God's existence is itself inexplicable. See Eric Watkins, "Breaking with Rationalism: Kant, Crusius, and the Priority of Existence," in *Leibniz and Kant*, ed. Brandon Look (Oxford: Oxford University Press, 2019).

[22] I note, as an aside, that this is an assumption Kant makes about human agency in particular, which is not obviously true for agency in general.

[23] Robert M. Adams makes a closely related point in "Moral Faith," *The Journal of Philosophy* 92 (1995): 75–95.

Kant on the Natural, Moral, Human, and Divine Orders   259

highest good need not be viewed as problematic if the moral argument is neither intended nor needed to prove any non-moral predicate of God.[24] If we supplement the moral argument with the conclusion of Kant's argument from the first *Critique*, a more robust case for God's existence emerges. Specifically, if the argument from the first *Critique* that accounts for possibility establishes the existence of a simple, eternal, necessary mind containing the most fundamental non-moral properties, such as omnipotence and omniscience, then the moral argument from the second *Critique* is really needed only to establish the moral predicates of goodness and justice so that the predicates typically associated with God by philosophers in the Judeo-Christian tradition will have been established.[25]

It is striking that Kant explicitly divides up his treatment of God and the divine attributes in precisely this way in the Pölitz transcripts from his lectures on the philosophical doctrine of religion from 1783–4 (or 1785–6). After distinguishing rational and empirical theology – which corresponds roughly to our distinction between natural and revealed religion – Kant divides rational theology into transcendental, natural, and moral theology. Transcendental theology proceeds independently of all experience, merely from pure understanding and reason; natural theology compares God with our own natures as physical beings; whereas moral theology considers what can be inferred about God as the highest moral good. In line with this classification, he distinguishes between what he calls transcendental, physical, and moral perfections, which correspond to our conceptions of God as cause, author, and ruler of the world. The entire structure of his lectures is then built on this classificatory framework. He starts with transcendental theology, arguing that it establishes considerably less than is sometimes thought, but still more than nothing, namely, a deistic conception of God, proceeds then to natural theology, which establishes theism (a living God), and finally moves on

---

[24] In the third *Critique*, Kant does explicitly claim that "moral teleology" establishes omniscience, omnipotence, and omnipresence (5:481). He does not, however, present an extended argument that justifies these properties.

[25] There is a missing step here. In addition to an argument showing that there must be a moral guarantor of the possibility of the highest good, one needs an argument showing that it must be the same as the being that grounds possibility. While it would be more economical, metaphysically speaking, to make such an identification, such a rationale is not impeccable. However, Kant is attentive to this kind of issue in the third *Critique* (at 4:456 and 4:480). While he recognizes a range of possibilities, he also expresses a (rational) preference for a unified account in terms of a single being.

260   The Moral Law

to moral theology, which is devoted to the moral attributes of God. Specifically, Kant says:

> In transcendental theology I think of God as having no limitation ... But do I become acquainted with God at all in this way? – Hence the deist's concept of God is wholly idle and useless and makes no impression on me if I assume it alone. But if transcendental theology is used as a propaedeutic or introduction to the two other kinds of theology, it is of great and wholly excellent utility. (28:1001–2)

Even if it faces significant challenges on a number of fronts, Kant's strategy of establishing belief in God's existence by means of such a multistep procedure has obvious advantages over attempts that hope to establish such a conclusion on the basis of a single thought.

If we step back from the details of Kant's moral argument, however, what is striking is that, despite its fundamental practical orientation, its basic structure parallels that of the theoretical argument in the first *Critique* described in the previous section. For in the second *Critique*, too, the moral order, as represented by the moral law and the highest good, is, for Kant, grounded in a metaphysically prior divine order insofar as (the actuality of) God (or his moral attributes) must be invoked to explain the possibility of the highest good. Moreover, it is crucial to note, again, that Kant's understanding of the grounding relation is unlike that of his predecessors in ways that seem advantageous to his position from a contemporary perspective. For Kant does not argue, as Malebranche and Leibniz do, *to* the moral order (the moral law and its object, the highest good) *from* features of God (such as his justice and will), which would have to assume metaphysical claims that would be highly controversial and correspondingly unattractive in a contemporary context.

Instead, Kant argues *from* specific indisputable features of the moral world (such as the lack of a conceptual connection between virtue and happiness in the natural world) *to* the necessity of (moral properties of) a God who is responsible for proportioning happiness to virtue. In fact, the parallel even extends to the way in which the human order is attributed an indispensable, albeit limited role in his broader account. For Kant insists on the necessity of (human) reason in accounting for specific aspects of the moral order, namely, that the moral law and its binding force for us as sensible beings cannot be explained without appealing to autonomy. At the same time, he does not fall into the extreme (quasi-Humean) position of suggesting that the moral law and its binding force might depend on activities that human beings might or might not be inclined to perform or feelings that occur in us as a purely contingent

Kant on the Natural, Moral, Human, and Divine Orders   261

matter, if they occur at all. Instead, he emphasizes that it is the essential features of human rationality that are required for the moral law.[26] Moreover, insofar as he recognizes that ensuring the possibility of the highest good is not among the powers of human beings, he sees that there are aspects of the moral order that cannot depend on the human order, and that must depend on God instead. Thus, just as in the theoretical case, the moral argument shows that the moral order depends on a metaphysically prior divine order, even as it involves the human order in a crucial way, and it does so in ways that avoid the pitfalls that some kinds of more extreme metaphysical claims are prone to, rendering it attractive in that respect in current discussions as well.

12.4   Mechanical and Teleological Laws

The third issue concerns Kant's interpretation of the relationship between mechanical and teleological laws. There is a fascinating history to this topic, both in early modern thinkers and in Kant's own pre-Critical works, especially *The Only Possible Argument*, but for current purposes we can focus exclusively on his treatment of this issue in the third *Critique*, which represents his most considered and sophisticated view on the topic. A straightforward approach to the text naturally gives rise to three significant puzzles, which can be resolved, I submit, by taking recourse to features of the interpretation developed in the previous two sections.

In the second half of the third *Critique*, Kant turns his attention from aesthetics to organisms, and after providing an analysis of objective purposiveness, which shows that we must regard organisms as natural ends, he argues that an antinomy of judgment arises from our experience of organisms, which display a distinctive kind of causality that seems to defy mechanical explanation. Though Kant presents (somewhat confusingly) two sets of contradictory principles, one constitutive and the other regulative, a genuine antinomy arises only for the regulative pair.[27] According to the regulative thesis, all generation of material things must be judged as possible according to mechanical laws alone, whereas according to the regulative antithesis, some material things cannot be judged as possible according to merely mechanical laws (since judging

---

[26] For an explanation of the sense in which Kant's claims are subjective and objective, see Karl Ameriks, "On Two Non-Realist Interpretations of Kant's Ethics," in *Interpreting Kant's Critiques* (Oxford: Oxford University Press, 2003), chapter 11.

[27] See Chapter 7 in this book.

262   The Moral Law

them requires an entirely different law of causality, namely, that of final causes and teleological laws). In short, the contradiction arises when we experience organisms because although we are supposed to explain everything through mechanical principles alone, organisms, given their unique causal structure, defy mechanical explanation and call for explanation in terms of teleological laws instead.

It is important to note that these principles, despite their regulative status, are truly contradictory. For example, they are not simply recommending that one look for either mechanical or teleological laws to explain things in nature. For there is no contradiction in explanatory multitasking by being open to a range of explanations of any given phenomenon. Instead, these judgments are genuinely contradictory insofar as the one asserts that mechanical laws all by themselves can be used to judge the possibility of the generation of natural things, while the other claims that mechanical laws alone cannot be used to make such judgments. Whatever makes the generation of natural things possible in our judgment, it must involve either mechanical laws alone or laws other than mechanical ones as well. Accordingly, if one sought explanations that involved both mechanical and teleological laws at the same time, one would be performing activities that contradicted the thesis insofar as one would be looking for explanations that were not restricted to mechanical laws alone. So it is clear that the thesis and antithesis are in fact contradictory on strictly philosophical grounds.

At first glance, Kant's solution to the antinomy raises three significant puzzles. Kant begins by noting that the thesis concerning the necessity of mechanistic explanation is one that derives from the discursive nature of our understanding. For beings such as ourselves, who obtain cognition by applying concepts to objects given through the senses, the parts necessarily precede the whole. As a result, we cannot have cognition of organisms as such, since the reciprocal causal connection between the parts and the whole involved in organisms affords a priority to the whole that is incompatible with our discursive understanding (except in practical contexts). Thus, the first puzzle is: Does this consideration not entail the outright falsity of the antithesis (since our understanding simply cannot attribute a priority to the whole in the way in which organisms seem to require)?

Kant then suggests that the antinomy can be resolved if one appeals to a supersensible ground that somehow underlies both mechanistic and teleological laws, though he concedes that we cannot have objective cognition of such a supersensible ground. This gives rise to the second puzzle: How can positing something unknown and, in fact, unknowable help to avoid a contradiction between the thesis and antithesis?

Kant on the Natural, Moral, Human, and Divine Orders 263

Kant seems to conclude his resolution by saying that the supersensible ground allows one to subordinate mechanistic explanations to teleological explanations, which generates the third puzzle: Why should positing a supersensible entity lead one to prioritize teleology over mechanism rather than vice versa (or to denying any priority at all)? It is not especially surprising that the initial excitement that accompanied Kant's interest in organisms in the third *Critique* has never been matched by a deep and lasting satisfaction with the position that he ends up adopting.

If, however, we keep in mind what Kant takes himself to have established in the first and second *Critiques* concerning possibility and the highest good, a more optimistic perspective on Kant's resolution of the antinomy emerges. For if we recall that reason requires that we think of God as the ground of possibility and note that the thesis and antithesis are about the possibility of things (both inanimate and animate), what otherwise seems extremely puzzling can be rendered more intelligible. First, if we recognize that God is the ground of possibility, then it is highly relevant to point out that our discursive understanding provides but one limited kind of cognition, since that allows our grasp of possibility to be similarly limited. That is, just as the resolution of the Antinomy of Pure Reason in the first *Critique* turns on distinguishing between things in themselves (apart from how they would be given to beings with distinctive forms of sensibility) and appearances, so too the resolution to the antinomy of teleological judgment requires a distinction between possibility in itself (apart from how it would be accounted for by beings with our distinctive forms of explanation) and possibility for us (with the limited explanatory resources that attach to the principles of our reflecting judgment). As a result, we can allow that we can cognize the possibilities of things only in terms of mechanical laws (which is what the thesis claims), while still acknowledging that God can ground possibilities (of organisms) that we cannot cognize in this way, even if we (have to) pass judgment on them on the basis of our distinctive experience of them (which is what the antithesis asserts). By accepting this distinction, we can maintain both the thesis and the antithesis (suitably modified), yet without embracing any contradiction, which points toward a solution of the first puzzle.[28]

---

[28] This solution is, in certain respects, similar to Peter McLaughlin's. See Peter McLaughlin, *Kant's Critique of Teleology in Biological Explanation: Antinomy and Teleology* (Lewiston: Edwin Mellen Press, 1990).

264   The Moral Law

Second, as we have seen above in the third section, the fact that we cannot have cognition of the supersensible ground of the possibility of things does not entail that we have no conception of what the supersensible being is or of what it can do. Moreover, even if we do not *know* or *cognize* that the supersensible being grounds possibilities and causes happiness to be proportionate to virtue, we can be entitled to believe (or assent to) these claims. This distinction creates space for us to hold that God could similarly reconcile mechanical and teleological laws, even if we cannot attain theoretical cognition of God. By appealing to the distinction between cognition and weaker forms of assent (such as belief), we can see how one might go about solving the second puzzle, at least in its main outlines.

Third, progress can even be made on the most difficult question of why and how mechanical laws should be subordinate to teleological laws (rather than vice versa). Since we know a priori that the mechanical laws are necessary, it is clear that God has no choice about whether they obtain. Now if God is supposed to proportion happiness to virtue, then it is clear that he must use (or at least cannot violate) these mechanical laws to promote whatever contingent laws will support the proportioning of happiness to virtue. Since our happiness depends, at least in part, on the state of our body, which is an organism, those laws clearly must include an empirical teleological dimension. That is, for our rational activity not to be pointless, God must make use of mechanical laws in determining how empirical teleological laws can further the happiness of rational agents, which are ends in themselves. By considering the means by which God will make the highest good attainable through our action, we can see why and in what sense mechanical laws are subordinate to teleological laws rather than the reverse, which points toward a solution of the third and final puzzle.

If this preliminary outline of an interpretation is correct, it suggests that on Kant's overall account, God can be highly relevant to at least some of the laws of nature after all. While the mechanical laws are grounded in the legislation of the human understanding, the teleological laws, which are in some sense contingent, derive from God's will. In fact, transcripts from Kant's lectures on metaphysics contain clear assertions to this effect. In the Pölitz lectures, he says: "if we ask who has established the laws of nature so firmly and limited its operations, then we will come to God as the supreme cause of the entirety of ... nature" (28:997). Moreover, Kant thinks that this is compatible with his view that we prescribe laws to nature. For in the Metaphysics Mrongovius transcripts, Kant says that "the understanding does not prescribe all laws of nature ... but rather only those that belong to the possibility of

Kant on the Natural, Moral, Human, and Divine Orders 265

experience" (29:993), at which point he then refers to principles that are readily identifiable as versions of the Analogies of Experience.[29] This claim explicitly leaves room for a wide range of *empirical* laws, such as teleological laws, that could derive from God's will.

What this brief look at the third *Critique* reveals is that Kant's ultimate account of the relation between mechanics and teleology retains certain elements of the traditional early modern view of laws of nature, though it introduces an important moral motivation at its foundation. For he adheres to the idea that God can be legitimately viewed as responsible for at least some (aspects of some) of the laws of nature. But his support for this position, lest it appear dogmatic in a clearly objectionable sense, depends on the thought that the only way that God can be morally perfect in the way that is required by our moral demand that the highest good be genuinely possible for us is if God uses the laws of mechanics that are necessary to underwrite those teleological laws that allow for a proportionate ordering of virtue and happiness. In this way, we can see how the third *Critique* contributes to and indirectly confirms the relations between the natural, moral, human, and divine orders that were established by the first two *Critiques*.

12.5   Conclusion

If I am correct about these three specific claims in each of the previous three sections, not only do they help to solve some long-standing interpretive puzzles and thereby provide a more satisfying philosophical interpretation of systematically central texts in Kant's corpus, but they also fundamentally alter what our view of his contribution to modern thought is and, as a result, what we might find worth exploring further about it today. It is still true on this interpretation that Kant's analysis of our epistemic faculties brings about a Critical philosophical revolution; one need not deny the existence of a "critical turn." However, it is clearly false to say that for Kant, God drops out of the philosophical picture entirely and is simply replaced by human beings. While there is, according to Kant, a genuine sense in which human beings are responsible for order in the natural and moral world in a way that had not been the case according to earlier thinkers, he retains three foundational roles for God: God is required (1) to ground all possibility, (2) to proportion happiness to virtue, and (3) to subordinate mechanical laws to teleological laws so that happiness can be proportionate to virtue. God does not disappear

---

[29] See Eric Watkins, *Kant and the Metaphysics of Causality*, especially chapter 3, for discussion of the Analogies of Experience.

266   The Moral Law

from the picture, even if his existence is not obvious in the way that empirical objects are and is thus "hidden."

More generally, we see that Kant has no interest in abandoning metaphysics altogether, even though he does genuinely want to reject certain kinds of dogmatic claims. Whatever one thinks of the particular metaphysical claims that Kant proposes, his suggestion about the *kind* of argument that could justify such metaphysical claims is interesting and important, even today. For he emphatically rejects the idea that such claims could be decided either by means of straightforward empirical inquiry or by simply dogmatically assuming them. Instead, he views them as deep-seated rational presuppositions of (1) the empirical questions that we pursue in our everyday lives and scientific practice, which, taken by themselves, are not fully intelligible, and (2) the moral demands we face as we encounter other rational agents in a wide range of situations of potential and actual conflict. In this way, Kant can be seen as suggesting not only that the world, with all of its empirical content, is essentially rational in its basic form, but also that the rational order of the world is neither arbitrarily imposed for purely heuristic or pragmatic reasons nor dogmatically asserted on allegedly objective grounds, but rather taken to be a subjectively necessary presupposition of activities that are both rational and essential to us. If we thus abstract from all of the controversial details of Kant's full-blown position, what can seem quite attractive is his attempt to identify principles that are neither objective (but dogmatic) nor subjective (but therefore thoroughly contingent), but rather subjectively necessary insofar as they are required for the most essential features of ourselves as rational human beings. This is not to say that identifying such principles is a straightforward task, but rather only that it could be valuable in many respects.

Finally, Kant's philosophy provides an important model for how one might think about order today. If we live in a fully secular and naturalized world dominated by science and technology, one might be tempted to think either that there is ultimately no order to the world at all (in which case Humeans are right that laws of nature – if any happen to exist – are nothing more than convenient summaries of empirical facts) or that human beings are responsible for the only order that we might find in the world (which might sound Kantian, if one accepted a certain story about Kant). Either way, it comes as no surprise when the world looks dappled.[30] These are clearly possible options, which many are convinced of today, since they can seem to be the picture that emerges if one latches

---

[30] For a powerful description of such a view, see Nancy Cartwright, *The Dappled World: A Study of the Boundaries of Science* (Cambridge: Cambridge University Press, 1999).

onto the specific practices we are in fact engaged in and is pessimistic about our ability to address broader, more systematic questions. However, Kant's position illustrates how one might pursue another option. Perhaps one can, without falling back into dogmatic metaphysics, distinguish between different kinds of order and consider whether it might be necessary for us (with our rationality) to presuppose dependency relations among them and, if so, to look for some kind of unconditioned or absolute ground that would provide guidance in our practices and a kind of ideal resting place for our explanatory endeavors. Kant's own specific suggestion, as I understand it, is that reason requires that both the natural and moral orders presuppose an ultimate metaphysical and, in fact, divine order without which neither scientific practice nor moral agency makes sense. Such a position, despite its assertion of order and dependency relations, is by no means reductionistic, and it also allows for the kind of messiness on display in our actual practices that motivates empiricist options, yet without requiring them. The details of the position that Kant himself adopts may or may not be defensible in the end, but the kind of project that he undertakes could point us in a direction worth exploring further.[31]

---

[31] I thank the participants and audience members at the conference held at UCSD in March of 2011 and Andrew Chignell for helpful discussion of an earlier version of this chapter.

Conclusion

C.1 Introduction

Suppose that the interpretation of Kant's account of laws described in the preceding chapters is (more or less) correct (at least in its barest essentials). Suppose, that is, that Kant is in fact committed to a univocal concept of law that underlies the different kinds of laws discussed above, one that includes as distinctive elements (1) necessity and (2) a legislative authority. With respect to the first element, both the moral law and the a priori laws of nature are clearly necessary, since the validity of the moral law is in no way contingent (even if it is contingent whether human beings act in accordance with it) and a priori laws of nature are necessary, in the sense that they are conditions both of the very possibility of experience and of nature (in its formal sense). Now empirical laws might seem to be contingent in light of their empirical content, but insofar as they are laws, they too must have an element of necessity according to Kant. For even if it were contingent whether this or that empirical feature of an object causes a certain effect, it is necessary that there be *some* feature that causes that effect. However, Kant's view is stronger than this, for in the third *Critique* he attempts to show how a system of laws can reveal the necessity of even empirical laws (even if that necessity is conditional and cannot be confirmed).[1] For example, I take it that for Kant it is necessary that human beings are mortal and that this necessity follows from the (purported) necessity of all animals being mortal and all humans being animals. And the regulative principles Kant adopts are more like Categorical than Hypothetical Imperatives insofar as their normative force is unconditioned and thus necessary rather than contingent. As a result, every law, whether practical or theoretical, empirical or a priori, constitutive or regulative, contains an element of necessity.

---

[1] See, e.g., Paul Guyer *Kant's System of Nature and Freedom* (Oxford: Oxford University Press, 2005).

Conclusion 269

With respect to the second element, Kant requires that a law be properly established by a spontaneous act because he accepts the basic insight behind the motto "No law without a lawmaker."[2] More specifically, as is particularly clear in the case of political (or positive) laws, a law can be valid only if a proper authority has prescribed it to a particular domain through an appropriate legislative act. Analogously, in the case of the moral law, Kant holds that reason spontaneously "gives" the moral law in such a way that it applies to all rational beings. In the case of a priori laws of nature, Kant similarly holds that the understanding "prescribes" laws to nature, specifically, to appearances in such a way that one can say that the laws of nature govern appearances (or, alternately, that appearances are subject ("*unterworfen*") to law, i.e. A228/B281, cf. A552/B580). In all cases, a spontaneous faculty engages in an activity that makes a law necessary for some domain that is marked out by a distinguishing feature, whether it be rational beings (the moral law), possible experience (a priori laws), or some subset of appearances (mechanical or chemical laws). Thus, in all of these cases, Kant is committed to a univocal notion of law that includes both an element of necessity and a spontaneous act that gives rise to that necessity.

So where does that leave us? On the one hand, one might welcome such a result insofar as it sheds light on a range of otherwise puzzling passages, reveals a unity to Kant's thought that is not immediately apparent, and articulates a conception of law that nicely unifies seemingly disparate strands within modern philosophy. These three accomplishments are not easy to come by.

On the other hand, it naturally gives rise to a fundamental and potentially critical question about Kant's position. If Kant accepts a univocal concept of law, one that is present in the different kinds of laws throughout his philosophy, what accounts for their diversity? As we have seen above, for Kant laws can be theoretical or practical, empirical or a priori, constitutive or regulative, mechanistic or teleological. How could the kinds of laws to which he is committed be so different from each other if they are all instances of one and the same concept? Having established their unity, their diversity can now seem to be in danger.

In this concluding chapter, I address this question by drawing on specific discussions in the above chapters so as to offer an account of what gives rise to the differences between the different kinds of laws. I argue that their most substantive differences can be explained, at least in part, (1) by differences in the kinds of necessity, faculty, and act that

---

[2] See John Locke, *Essays on the Laws of Nature*, ed. Wolfgang von Leyden (Oxford: Clarendon Press, 1954), p. 173.

270   Conclusion

are involved in laws and (2) by the nature of reason (taking into account Kant's view of reason's objects, needs, interests, and essential ends). This latter explanation has the additional merit of indicating how the different kinds of laws that Kant employs contribute to satisfying the aims of his Critical project as a whole.

C.2   Different Kinds of Necessity, Faculty, and Acts

Some of the differences between the different kinds of laws Kant discusses arise from (1) the different kinds of *necessity* involved, (2) the different kinds of *faculties* that are responsible for the law and its necessity, and (3) the different kinds of spontaneous *acts* that the faculties in question engage in with respect to the law. In this section I consider these three sources of difference in turn.

C.2.1   Necessity

The notion of necessity involved in all the different kinds of *laws of nature* is that of *determination*.[3] One natural way to illustrate the notion of determination within Kant's system would be with a case of *causal* determination in which, say, two billiard balls collide. When one body communicates its motion to another in impact according to the Laws of Mechanics, the one body *causally determines* an acceleration in the other body just as the second body causally determines a corresponding deceleration in the first. It does so by acting according to its nature (as an extended and impenetrable object endowed with a certain mass), by means of the exercise of its distinctive causal powers (e.g., its repulsive force), and in such a way that its action is necessarily equal and opposite to the reaction of the other body according to the Third Law of Mechanics.[4] In this example, the body that serves as a cause determines, or makes necessary, the effect, but it does so according to the law of the equality of action and reaction, where it is this law that expresses the necessity of the actions that cause the precise changes of motion in the two bodies in such a way that the acceleration and deceleration are equal and necessarily so.

---

[3] For a useful disambiguation of Kant's many senses of determination, see Karl Ameriks, "On the Many Senses of 'Self-Determination,'" in *Freedom and Spontaneity in Kant*, ed. Kate Moran (Cambridge: Cambridge University Press, 2018), pp. 171–94.

[4] For a more detailed description of this kind of case, see Eric Watkins, *Kant and the Metaphysics of Causality* (New York: Cambridge University Press, 2005).

Conclusion 271

The notion of necessity involved in the case of the moral law is more complicated. For here it is crucial to distinguish, as Kant explicitly does, between the kinds of necessity that obtain in the human and divine cases. In the divine case, the moral law determines what God will do (if God acts at all). Given that the moral law is completely objective for God, God could not have done otherwise (as far as morality is concerned) even though God acts freely. As a result, the notion of necessity that is involved in the moral law in the divine case is the same as that involved in laws of nature (even if the "mechanics" of divine action are opaque and radically different in certain respects). By contrast, for finite (and imperfect) rational beings such as human beings the notion of necessity involved in the moral law is different, since the moral law is expressed in the form of a Categorical Imperative and imperatives do not determine actions (in the mode of an efficient cause). That is, it is *possible* for us to act contrary to the moral law, even if we *ought* not to. The necessity that is involved in the moral law for human beings is thus not one of determination, but rather one of obligation. Accordingly, when the moral law takes the form of a Categorical Imperative, the necessity of the law is obligation, which Kant also calls necessitation.[5]

The various regulative principles to which Kant is committed in his theoretical philosophy have a status similar to that of the Categorical Imperative in his practical philosophy insofar as both involve an obligation to act (broadly construed) rather than determination. However, these regulative principles are different insofar as they prescribe a "theoretical" (rather than a moral) action or aim at theoretical cognition rather than practical cognition. That is, they do not determine either the world or our thought, but rather represent rational constraints on what we should do as we attempt to obtain (a certain kind of) theoretical cognition.

C.2.2 Faculties

Laws can also be differentiated by means of the faculty that is responsible for the act that enacts the law. According to Kant, *reason* is the faculty that is responsible for the lawfulness of the moral law. This is fitting insofar as Kant characterizes reason as an active and spontaneous faculty of principles, and the moral law, simply qua law, requires an active spontaneous faculty.[6] However, reason's involvement in the moral law is even more extensive, according to Kant. For reason, as the highest

---

[5] See, e.g., 29:611, a passage I discuss in some detail in Chapter 1.
[6] See Chapter 11 in this book for more detailed discussion.

272   Conclusion

faculty, answers only to itself and thus has the authority to legislate the moral law. Further, reason is responsible for both the content of the moral law and its bindingness. As Kant understands it, the content of the moral law is universal, in the sense of admitting of no exceptions either across time or over different agents; reason is the same for all and at all times. Reason is also responsible for the bindingness of the moral law, because, on Kant's distinctive view, a person is subject to the moral law only because reason acts autonomously, i.e., gives itself the law. In other words, Kant's doctrine of autonomy is possible only on the basis of his account of reason, since he understands autonomy not as in any way contingent or as dependent on particular empirical acts, but rather as relying on our basic capacity to reason for ourselves.[7] The moral law is thus related to the faculty of reason in several notable respects.

Kant is equally clear that it is the faculty of the *understanding* that is responsible for the a priori laws of nature.[8] As he notes in the Introduction to the *Critique of the Power of Judgment*: "Legislation through concepts of nature takes place through the understanding and is theoretical. Legislation through the concept of freedom takes place through reason, and is merely practical" (5:174). The understanding is in a position to prescribe a priori laws to nature because, like reason, it is an active and spontaneous faculty, though it is unlike reason insofar as its concepts must be applied to objects given in sensible intuition. That is, the understanding, unlike reason, is restricted in its scope to appearances. Further, as the faculty of a priori rules, the understanding can also account for the lawfulness of the laws of nature, i.e., for their strict universality and necessity (albeit a necessity that has to do with things that do not themselves necessarily exist, thus necessities for a contingent realm of existence). For the rules that the understanding operates in accordance with in forming judgments can give rise to the rules that are characterized as laws of nature (A126). The understanding is able to prescribe laws to the sensible world in part because it is superior to sensibility (given its activity and relative independence and the latter's passivity and relative dependence) and in part because, according to Kant's so-called Copernican Revolution, the understanding makes sensible objects conform to it by putting its forms into the object, rather than the other way around.[9]

---

[7] See, e.g., Karl Ameriks, *Kant and the Fate of Autonomy* (New York: Cambridge University Press, 2000) and *Interpreting Kant's Critiques* (Oxford: Oxford University Press, 2003).

[8] Kant employs both broader and narrower conceptions of reason. Reason in the broad sense encompasses both the understanding and reason in the narrow sense.

[9] There is, however, an interesting similarity between this and the previous case. In the case of both the moral law and a priori laws of nature, an active faculty gives rise to an a priori form that is prior to an empirical matter, which is subordinate to it, whether the matter is contingent desires in the one case or sensations (sensible intuition) in the other.

Conclusion 273

Empirical laws of nature can be accounted for, at least in part, in a way that is analogous to the explanation just given for a priori laws. For empirical laws of nature are the result of the combination of the lawfulness of the a priori laws prescribed by the understanding with an empirical content that has its source in our sensibility and in the empirical objects represented through sensibility. Granted, special issues arise for the complexities pertaining to how sensible content is generated, but even so, on Kant's view, the understanding has a certain kind of priority over whatever sensible content is given to it. Now, as noted above, it may be the case that the empirical content of an empirical law can also be shown to be necessary by being entailed by higher-level laws that are discovered through the reflective power of judgment and by the natures of the relevant empirical objects, but that is not essential to their status as laws of nature. Thus empirical laws of nature are based on the faculty of the understanding, just as the a priori laws of nature are, even if they also depend on empirical content deriving from sensibility and the reflective use of judgment, and the nature of the objects that affect sensibility.

The laws of homogeneity, specificity, and continuity, by contrast, have a somewhat more complicated origin, though one that is still fully consistent with Kant's general conception of law.[10] On the one hand, considerable evidence suggests that Kant thinks that these laws derive from reason. He explicitly states that by means of these principles "reason prepares the field for the understanding" (A657/B685). That is, they all direct the understanding to employ a certain concept for the sake of a particular explanatory role (of revealing similarities or differences among objects at various levels of generality and specificity). Also, the laws of homogeneity and specificity seem to have a connection with reason insofar as they aim at totalities that are bound by limits (highest and lowest concepts). Finally, Kant claims that the "continuity of forms is a mere idea for which a corresponding object can by no means be displayed in experience" (A661/B689). That Kant invokes an idea, in his technical sense, shows that reason must be involved.

On the other hand, it is tempting to think that reflective judgment is involved in these laws insofar as they start with a given particular object and then attempt to find different kinds of concepts that cover the particular in question, a process that the faculty of judgment would be responsible for in its reflective use. The differences that are apparent here in determining whether reason or reflective judgment is involved in these laws may be due either to Kant's changing his mind or simply to his supplementing his view from the first to the third *Critique*. Whatever the

---

[10] For further discussion, see Chapter 10 in this book.

274 Conclusion

nature of the changes to his position is, however, the employment of reflective judgment does not *preclude* the involvement of reason. As we shall see in more detail shortly, the faculties of reason and judgment can complement each other in the case of these laws.

As for the laws of no fate, no chance, no gap, and no leap, two options seem immediately tempting.[11] If we note that these laws are discussed not in the Transcendental Dialectic, which focuses on reason, but rather at the end of the Transcendental Analytic right after the Postulates of Empirical Thought, it would be natural to attribute these laws to the understanding. What is unclear about this interpretive option, however, is how these laws are related to the Analogies of Experience (as the most important instances of the Principles of Pure Understanding discussed in the Analytic). They do not seem to follow directly from the Analogies, because their content goes well beyond the claim that, say, every event is caused according to a law. If, by contrast, we take our cue from the fact that Kant discusses these laws in the rational cosmology section of his metaphysics lectures, it would be most natural to assume that they are laws prescribed by reason, though then one wonders why Kant chooses to discuss them in the Transcendental Analytic rather than later in the first *Critique*.

The best position to take here, I suggest, is to note that while these laws do have their ultimate basis in reason and are thus distinct from the Analogies of Experience, they are explanatory principles that presuppose the Analogies of Experience in order to do their explanatory work. For example, if the Second Analogy states that every event is caused according to a law, the principle of no fate goes beyond that by stating what kinds of causal laws can and, more importantly, cannot be involved, since some laws would be entirely lacking in explanatory value for us. Specifically, it states that the kind of causal conditioning that is required by the Second Analogy cannot be absolutely necessary, but must rather be only hypothetically necessary (since it presupposes that we have experience in Kant's specific sense of cognition of a single spatiotemporal world). Similarly, regarding the case of fate, Kant notes: "To want to explain something by destiny is nonsensical, for calling upon destiny just means that I cannot explain something" (29:926). Confirmation for viewing the cosmological laws as arising from reason can be found shortly thereafter: "Destinies conflict with the interest of reason. For if I accept them, then I must renounce the use of reason" (29:926). If this is correct, the

---

[11] For further discussion, see Chapter 9 in this book.

Conclusion   275

cosmological laws are ultimately grounded in reason, which, as an active
and spontaneous faculty, is able to underwrite them.

In short, some laws (the moral law) derive from reason alone, while
others (the a priori laws of nature) are prescribed by the understanding
alone, and yet others arise from some combination of reason, the understanding, and reflective judgment (empirical laws of nature, the laws of
no fate, no chance, and no leap as well as the laws of homogeneity,
specificity, and continuity of forms).[12]

C.2.3   Differences in Acts

The different kinds of laws that Kant accepts can also be differentiated
by the different kinds of acts that are involved. Specifically, in various
passages Kant claims that moral and juridical laws arise on the basis of
reason engaging in acts of *legislation* (*Gesetzgebung*) (5:27, 6:28); laws
of nature result from the understanding *prescribing* (*vorschreibt*) laws
to nature (4:320); while reason *commands* (*gebiete*) or *makes demands*
(*verlangt*) with the regulative principles of homogeneity, specificity, and
continuity (A655/B683).[13] To account for these different kinds of acts,
I briefly describe how Kant understands the conditions under which
they occur.

Juridical laws are the clearest illustration of the act by means of which
a law is enacted. Rousseau, who greatly influenced Kant, held that
(political) laws must be enacted by means of an open legislative process
that gives rise to a general will through public deliberation and that
requires full participation by those who would be subject to the law.
Kant's own political philosophy differs from Rousseau's on many points,
but he agrees on the importance of a public declaration when it comes to
asserting, e.g., that I have a right to an external object as my private
property, a declaration that generates an obligation for all other citizens
to respect that right, just as I am in turn obligated to respect the property
rights established by others' similar declarations.[14] Kant and Rousseau
also agree that political laws must be established by citizens endowed
with reason, which makes them legislators of the laws to which they are
themselves subject. Since the term 'law' derives from and is most at

---

[12] In fact, empirical and teleological laws derive, in part, from sensibility and God,
respectively.

[13] See also, e.g., 4:469, where Kant speaks of the "demands of reason."

[14] For a recent account of property rights in Kant, see Arthur Ripstein, *Force and Freedom:
Kant's Legal and Political Philosophy* (Cambridge, MA: Harvard University Press, 2009).

276   Conclusion

home in political contexts, it is natural to require the public act of a legislator to underwrite an (in this case, legal) obligation.

The case of the moral law is trickier than that of juridical laws, despite the fact that in both cases reason is the relevant faculty and the necessity at issue is one of obligation rather than determination.[15] Part of what makes the moral case more difficult is that some ambiguity surrounds the exact meaning of the notion of legislation when Kant says that reason "legislates" the moral law. What he most often says, literally, is that reason "gives" the moral law. For example, in the second section of the *Groundwork*, where he is trying to be as clear and explicit as possible on this point, he asserts, in the Gregor translation: "the will is not merely subject to the law but subject to it in such a way that it must be viewed as also giving the law to itself and just because of this first subject to the law" (4:431).[16] The crucial German phrase here is "*selbstgesetzgebend*," rendered "giving the law to itself."[17] Unfortunately, the meaning of the term "giving" or "*gebend*" is not particularly clear, though when used in the context of law, it is not obviously wrong to translate it as "legislation" (though "lawgiving" is more literal). But note that Kant does not always stick to the term "giving." In one passage he defines autonomy as "a property of the will by which it is a law to itself" (4:440, cf. also 4:447). Thus, in this case, practical reason (or, what is the same for Kant, the will) does not *give* itself the law, but rather *is* the law, that is, is somehow identical with it. But if the law just *is* reason, how could it require an act?

Further, in the case of the moral law reason's "legislation" need not involve a public declaration. For one, the moral law obligates regardless

---

[15] Reath offers an interesting interpretation of the legislation of the moral law: "the parallels are rich enough to warrant Kant's talk of legislating the moral law. The proposal is that we regard the Formula of Universal Law as the 'constitution' of the rational will. It is the fundamental law that sets out the procedure that agents (citizen-legislators) must follow in order to enact substantive principles as law, just as a political constitution sets out the procedure that a sovereign body must follow in order to create law. Substantive moral requirements are the results of the proper application of this procedure, and receive their authority from this fact. When agents guide their deliberations and subsequent actions by the Categorical Imperative, they enact their maxims as law (enact law through their wills)"; Andrews Reath, *Agency and Autonomy in Kant's Moral Theory* (New York: Oxford University Press, 2006), p. 109.

[16] "Der Wille wird also nicht lediglich dem Gesetze unterworfen sondern so unterworfen, daß er auch als selbstgesetzgebend und eben um deswillen allererst dem Gesetze ... unterworfen angesehen werden muß."

[17] For careful analysis of this phrase, see Karl Ameriks, "Kant's Ambivalent Cosmopolitanism," in *Kant und die Philosophie in weltbürgerlicher Absicht*, ed. Claudio La Rocca, Stefano Bacin, Alfredo Ferrarin, and Margit Ruffing, vol. 1 (Berlin: Walter de Gruyter, 2013), pp. 55–72.

Conclusion 277

of whether anyone ever explicitly says so.[18] For another, even if the moral law is stated publicly (or commanded by God), what one is obliged to do could not be different after the public statement from what it was before. For both the content and necessity of the moral law do not depend on anyone acting at a particular moment in time and do not require a public act of endorsement, as juridical laws do. Instead, the moral law is always binding, regardless of what one says or does at any moment in time. But if this is the case, the notion of act involved in reason's legislation of the moral law cannot be any ordinary empirical act, which would be in some sense optional in any given case.

Similar issues arise for the case of the understanding and laws of nature. Though Kant states (in both the *Prolegomena* and the first *Critique*) that the understanding prescribes laws to nature, he does not mean to say that particular empirical subjects must prescribe laws to nature before particular empirical laws obtain for the world of appearances.[19] These acts of prescription are not datable historical events, in the absence of which the spatiotemporal world would be an indeterminate and lawless chaos. Instead, the laws of nature obtain, regardless of what particular act one particular person's understanding performs. But without empirical subjects engaged in particular acts at particular moments in time, it is natural to wonder what it means for the understanding to be *prescribing* laws to nature, just as the question arises for reason's *legislation* of the moral law.[20]

What these considerations suggest is that the acts that are supposed to give rise to the different kinds of laws are a matter not of *empirical* but rather of *transcendental* psychology. While one might follow Strawson in rejecting transcendental psychology as hopelessly confused and unnecessary, this would create serious obstacles to understanding Kant's actual position. For the transcendental aspect of transcendental psychology can be quite useful for understanding the normative dimension of Kant's philosophy. As a result, to understand Kant's position on laws it is useful to attend to the normative dimension of the acts that are instantiated under particular empirical circumstances, and to note that the normativity does not derive from the empirical circumstances, but rather from

---

[18] In the *Metaphysics of Morals*, Kant distinguishes between internal and external legislation as forming part of the contrast between juridical and moral laws, and explicitly notes that some external laws do not require "actual external lawgiving" (i.e., positive law) (6:224).
[19] Such acts can be required for actual cognition.
[20] The regulative laws of homogeneity, specificity, and continuity and the four cosmological laws are easier to accommodate on this particular point, since they involve explanatory principles that are specific to finite rational cognizers.

278   Conclusion

the normative principles that guide the activities that take place in a particular empirical situation. Thus, instead of thinking of the relevant act as an efficient cause of the law, it is better understood as what one might think of as a formal cause or constituent principle of law.[21]

If we pursue this line of thought, we can see that reason and the understanding are both spontaneous faculties performing "acts" that are responsible for unifying a plurality of one kind into a unity of another. The understanding unifies the sensible manifold given in intuition under concepts in judgments that can be true or false, while reason, at least in its logical use, unifies a plurality of cognitions into syllogisms. But what is crucial here is that these faculties are guided in their unifying acts by what Kant refers to as "functions" (A68/B93), which we might think of as normative rules.[22] The understanding is guided by the functions that find expression in the table of judgments and the table of categories, while reason is guided, in its purely logical use, by what we would call logically valid inference rules (whose structure is given by the relational forms of judgment). Thus, the acts are crucial insofar as they are responsible for, or are at least indicative of, a distinctive kind of normativity in our judgments about the world and in the world too insofar as it either depends on these judgments or corresponds to them. This is consistent with the idea that laws of nature are said to govern the world and the moral law is a normative standard for rational behavior. Thus the normativity that these faculties involve in their acts is a crucial feature of the laws that Kant is trying to explain. Unless one rests content with brute necessities, one will need a story about what the ground of necessity is in a world that can seem to be populated entirely by purely natural entities, as well as how and why they are necessary for beings like us, that is, how we can and must recognize their necessity.[23] Kant's account involves acts that will happen under various empirical circumstances, but what is crucial about the acts is not so much that they unify something *at a particular moment in time* as that the unity they bring about embodies certain *functions* that allow them to support normative principles that can underwrite necessity of various sorts.[24]

---

[21] See Karl Ameriks, *Interpreting Kant's Critiques* (Oxford: Oxford University Press, 2003), esp. chapter 10 ("'Pure Reason of Itself Alone Suffices to Determine the Will'").

[22] For discussion of how functions are relevant within Kant's epistemology, see Eric Watkins, "Kant and the Myth of the Given," *Inquiry* 51 (2008): 512–31.

[23] For one account of this kind of issue in Kant, see Hannah Ginsborg, *The Normativity of Nature: Essays on Kant's Critique of Judgement* (Oxford: Oxford University Press, 2015).

[24] Much more would need to be said about Kant's theory of normativity. For recent discussion, see Konstantin Pollok, *Kant's Theory of Normativity* (New York: Cambridge University Press, 2017).

Conclusion 279

Though this account of acts and their constitutive functions captures a distinctive and important part of Kant's views on laws, it still leaves unexplained certain features of laws and of the different kinds of laws that he envisions. For example, though reason is responsible for the legislation of moral and juridical laws as well as for the demands of the principles of rational cosmology and those of homogeneity, specificity, and continuity, reason has only one set of unifying functions on which it can rely. But how can one set of functions account for the different kinds of laws that reason is responsible for? It cannot be a difference in faculty, since reason is involved in all of these acts. Nor can we appeal to a different set of functions, given the unity of reason on which Kant insists.[25] The notion of necessity is different in some of these cases, but only in some, and that is a *result* of the different kinds of acts, not the *source* of their differences. To make progress on this question, we must briefly consider some distinctive features of Kant's account of reason.

C.3 Reason's Objects, Interests, and Ends and the Project of the *Critique of Pure Reason*

Kant repeatedly notes that reason has two distinct objects, nature and freedom. For example, in the Doctrine of Method's Architectonic of Pure Reason, he writes: "The legislation of human reason (philosophy) has two objects, nature and freedom, and thus contains the natural law [*Naturgesetz*] as well as the moral law, initially in two separate systems but ultimately in a single philosophical system" (A840/B868).[26] What this passage makes clear is that the difference between reason's legislation of juridical laws and the moral law, on the one hand, and its activities in theoretical philosophy, on the other, derives from a difference in its object, since in the former case its object is freedom (whether internal or external), and what ought to be, while in the latter its object is nature (whether material or thinking), and what is or will be.[27] Unfortunately, Kant does not specify whether all rational beings have these two objects,

---

[25] See, e.g., 5:89 and 4:392 for explicit statements (and endorsements) of the unity of reason.

[26] See also the Introduction to the *Critique of the Power of Judgment*, e.g., 5:171, 5:174, and 5:195.

[27] In the Introduction to the *Critique of the Power of Judgment*, Kant introduces distinctions between a "field," a "territory," and a "domain," so as to differentiate those objects with respect to which concepts are related, those objects with respect to which cognition is possible, and those objects with respect to which the concepts are legislative. Given this distinction, he then makes the same point as follows: "Our cognitive faculty as a whole has two domains: that of the concepts of nature and that of the concept of freedom" (5:174).

280   Conclusion

or only human beings. Nor does he ever try to deduce these two objects from any more ultimate object that could somehow unite them (although he does think that they must be united in a single philosophical system). But the crucial point for present purposes is that since at least human reason does have these different objects, it is natural that its laws (and legislation) with respect to those objects will be different as well.[28]

At the same time, this difference in reason's objects cannot account for all of the differences between the different kinds of laws in Kant. Instead, this difference (between what is and will be and what ought to be) explains only the basic distinction between practical and theoretical laws. As a result, one must appeal to something other than reason's object to account for the further differences we find between the different kinds of laws.

One significant factor here lies in the fact that Kant takes reason to have needs, interests, and essential ends.[29] Consider first Kant's view on the needs of reason (which contrast with the needs of inclination). In one of his more ambitious moments Kant claims that reason seeks to achieve "insight into the unity of the whole pure rational faculty (theoretical as well as practical) and to derive everything from one principle" (5:91). This ambition is based, he thinks, on "the undeniable need of human reason, which finds complete satisfaction only in a complete systematic unity of its cognitions" (ibid.). That is, reason has a "need" to derive all cognitions, whether theoretical or practical, from a single principle and it can satisfy this need only by developing a complete systematic unity of cognition. In short, reason has a need for systematic unity.

Now 'interest' is a technical term for Kant, which indicates a need of which a rational being is also aware. That is, if I am rational and aware of a need, then I have an interest in satisfying that need. Kant employs this notion in different contexts. For example, he invokes it when he claims that "all interest of my reason (the speculative as well as the practical) is united" (A800/B828) in the three questions about what I can know, what I should do, and what I may hope. Thus, we not only have a need for a complete systematic unity of cognition, but are also interested in precisely that complete systematic unity of cognition that would allow us to answer these basic questions.

At the same time, Kant uses this notion of an interest in more specific contexts. For example, he notes that the principles of homogeneity and specificity express "two interests that conflict with each other"

---

[28] This difference is also responsible for Kant's division of metaphysics into a metaphysics of freedom and a metaphysics of nature.
[29] See Pauline Kleingeld, "The Conative Character of Reason in Kant's Philosophy," *Journal of the History of Philosophy* 36 (1998): 77–97, for discussion of the conative character of reason.

Conclusion 281

(A654/B682), since the one pushes toward ever more generality in our concepts while the other pushes toward ever greater specificity. However, he goes on to resolve this apparent conflict by noting that "reason in fact has only a single unified interest and the conflict between its maxims is only a variation and reciprocal limitation of the methods satisfying this interest" (A666/B694). Though Kant does not clarify what the "single unified interest" is, I take it that one must have both increasingly general and ever more specific concepts to have the kind of concepts that are necessary to achieve the kind of *complete* systematic unity of cognition that could satisfy reason's need. For without a broad range of concepts, including both the more general and the more specific, we might not be able to cognize certain features of the world, which would render impossible the completeness of our cognition.

But the crucial point about these needs and interests for our purposes is their relation to the essential *ends* of reason.[30] For a need of reason (and therefore every interest as well) presupposes an end of reason. For only if my end is not already satisfied do I have a need. In fact, the nature of the need can be determined by both the nature of the end and the resources that would be needed to attain it.

The fundamental question then is what the essential end of reason is. Kant asserts that "reason demands to cognize the unconditioned, and with it the totality of all conditions, for otherwise, it does not cease to question, just as if nothing had been answered yet" (20:326).[31] That is, reason's essential end is to cognize not only the conditions for whatever conditioned items are given, but also the totality of these conditions, and therefore the unconditioned, since cognition of the unconditioned alone represents a resting place where all of its needs and interests have been satisfied. In theoretical philosophy reason pursues its essential end by attempting to achieve theoretical cognition of God, the world as a totality, and our soul, since these objects of traditional metaphysics are unconditioned. In practical philosophy, reason pursues its essential end by cognizing either the moral law, as a synthetic a priori principle that binds categorically and thus unconditionally, or the highest good, which contains virtue, an unconditioned good, and, proportionate to it, happiness, which is good only on the condition that one's actions are virtuous enough to make one worthy of happiness.[32] By conceiving of the essential

---

[30] For discussion of the ends of reason, see Richard Velkley, *Freedom and the End of Reason: On the Moral Foundation of Kant's Critical Philosophy* (Chicago: University of Chicago Press, 1989).

[31] See also 20:287.

[32] For discussion of the role of the unconditioned in Kant's practical philosophy, see Eric Watkins, "The Unconditioned Goodness of the Good Will," in *Kant on Persons and Agency*, ed. Eric Watkins (Cambridge: Cambridge University Press, 2018), pp. 11–28.

282   Conclusion

ends of reason in terms of what is unconditioned and then understanding the unconditioned along both theoretical and practical dimensions, Kant conceives of reason as committed to the possibility of a complete systematic unity of cognition. This conception of the essential end of reason allows for the unity of reason, despite obvious differences between its objects (nature and freedom).

The *Critique of Pure Reason* and the *Critique of Practical Reason* then undertake full-scale investigations of the nature and limits of our cognitive capacities so as to determine whether we are in fact in a position to attain the kind of complete systematic cognition that could be adequate to reason's essential ends. As it turns out, detailed analysis of our theoretical faculties of sensibility, understanding, and reason (in the narrow sense) reveals the limitations that prevent us from having theoretical cognition of the unconditioned objects of traditional metaphysics so that reason's end cannot be attained on purely theoretical grounds. Fortunately, however, a similarly detailed analysis of our practical capacities of desiring and willing and our awareness of the fact of moral obligation reveals that we *can* have practical cognition of the moral law, along with the (unconditioned) freedom that is a prerequisite of it, and of the possibility of the highest good, along with its presuppositions of God's existence and the immortality of the soul. As a result, the "self-cognition" (Axi) that reason acquires through its investigation of our cognitive capacities establishes that its own ends can ultimately be fully satisfied on practical grounds, or at least can provide adequate responses to the most significant threats that have been raised against it.

But note that the various kinds of laws to which Kant is committed play crucial roles within his larger project of attaining complete systematic theoretical and practical cognition of the unconditioned. For example, the a priori laws of nature, since they constitute the possibility of experience, provide necessary conditions on any systematic theoretical cognition of nature, since they make out the lawfulness of the laws that constitute nature taken in its formal sense. Since these laws concern nature only in its formal sense and reason is interested in systematically complete cognition, nature in its material sense must also be included. Empirical laws of nature, along with those principles that make possible the discovery and justification of such laws, are therefore also required for this kind of systematic and complete cognition of nature. Specifically, the laws of homogeneity, specification, and continuity are required because the *completeness* of the systematic unity of cognition could not be achieved if our cognition did not involve the richest possible conceptual resources, and these laws direct the understanding to develop and deploy the fullest possible range of concepts. The laws of rational

Conclusion 283

cosmology – no gap, no leap, no chance, and no fate – contribute to the systematic cognition of nature insofar as they give expression to the explanatory demands that reason requires for the systematic unity of cognition to be as rich as possible so that it can approximate completeness. That is, the point of a system of cognitions is not simply to relate all cognitions to each other in an arbitrary way, but rather to relate them to each other in such a way that both the whole and its various parts become intelligible in virtue of their interrelations. Since each kind of theoretical law makes an indispensable contribution to the complete systematic unity of cognition of nature, legislation is necessary for the theoretical cognition we are able to achieve, even if we end up only approximating cognition of what is unconditioned rather than actually attaining it.

The moral law plays an even more fundamental role in our systematic cognition. Toward the end of the third *Critique*, Kant clarifies that the final end of all creation can be nothing other than human beings considered as noumenal moral beings (5:435). But on Kant's analysis, we cannot be moral beings unless we legislate the moral law to ourselves. Thus our legislation and action in accordance with it are essential to the end of all creation. Further, the moral law (along with, in a different way, the highest good) involves the unconditioned in an essential way. For as we have seen earlier, morality takes the form of imperatives whose normative force for us is unconditioned, a status that can be explained only if we legislate the law to ourselves (freely and rationally). Thus by cognizing the moral law and the highest good that necessarily accompanies it, we are able to have practical cognition of the unconditioned, which can thus satisfy reason's ultimate end. In this way we can see that the moral law lies at the foundation of Kant's Critical system. Kant makes this connection between the moral law and the end of reason explicit in the Canon of Pure Reason: "Pure practical laws, whose end is given by reason completely a priori, and which do not command under empirical conditions but absolutely, would be products of pure reason. Of this sort, however, are the moral laws; thus these alone belong to the practical use of reason and permit a canon" (A800/B828).[33]

---

[33] I thank Clinton Tolley and the audience at the Leverhulme conference held in Edinburgh in June 2015 for helpful discussion of and comments on an earlier version of this chapter. Special thanks go to Michela Massimi and Angela Breitenbach for organizing the project on Kant and the laws of nature of which this conference was one central part.

Bibliography

Adams, Robert M., "Moral Faith," *The Journal of Philosophy* 92 (1995): 75–95.
  "God, Possibility, and Kant," *Faith and Philosophy* 4 (2000): 425–40.
Allison, Henry, "Kant's Antinomy of Teleological Judgment," *Southern Journal of Philosophy* 30 (Supplement) (1991): 25–42.
  Kant's Transcendental Idealism: An Interpretation and Defense (New Haven: Yale University Press, 2004).
Ameriks, Karl, *Kant's Theory of Mind* (Oxford: Oxford University Press, 1982).
  "The Critique of Metaphysics: Kant and Traditional Ontology," in *The Cambridge Companion to Kant*, ed. Paul Guyer (Cambridge: Cambridge University Press, 1992), pp. 249–79.
  Kant and the Fate of Autonomy (New York: Cambridge University Press, 2000).
  Interpreting Kant's Critiques (Oxford: Oxford University Press, 2003).
  "The End of the Critiques: Kant's Moral 'Creationism,'" in *Rethinking Kant*, ed. Pablo Muchnik (Newcastle: Cambridge Scholars Publishing, 2009), pp. 165–90.
  "Kant's Ambivalent Cosmopolitanism," in *Kant und die Philosophie in weltbürgerlicher Absicht*, ed. Claudio La Rocca, Stefano Bacin, Alfredo Ferrarin, and Margit Ruffing, vol. 1 (Berlin: Walter de Gruyter, 2013), pp. 55–72.
  "Vindicating Autonomy," in *Kant on Moral Autonomy*, ed. Oliver Sensen (Cambridge: Cambridge University Press, 2013), pp. 53–70.
  "On the Many Senses of 'Self-Determination,'" in *Freedom and Spontaneity in Kant*, ed. Kate Moran (Cambridge: Cambridge University Press, 2018), pp. 171–94.
Armstrong, David, *What Is a Law of Nature?* (Cambridge: Cambridge University Press, 1983).
Bacin, Stefano, "Legge e obbligatorietà: la struttura dell'idea di autolegislazione morale," *Studi kantiani* 26 (2013): 55–70.
Bacin, Stefano, and Sensen, Oliver (eds.), *The Emergence of Autonomy* (Cambridge: Cambridge University Press, 2018).
Baumeister, Friedrich, *Institutiones Metaphysicae*, [Wittenberg], reprinted in Abt. 3, Bd. 25 of Christian Wolff, *Gesammelte Werke* (Hildesheim: G. Olms Verlag, [1738] 1988).
Beck, Lewis White, *Selected Essays on Kant*, ed. Hoke Robinson (Rochester: University of Rochester Press, 2006).
Beebee, Helen, "The Nongoverning Conception of Laws of Nature," *Philosophy and Phenomenological Research* 61 (2000): 571–94.

Bibliography

Beeson, David, *Maupertuis: An Intellectual Biography* (Oxford: Oxford University Press, 1992).

Bilfinger, Georg Bernhard, *Dilucidationes philosophicae de Deo, anima humana, mundo, et generalibus rerum affectionibus*, [Tübingen], reprinted in Abt. 3, Bd. 18 of Christian Wolff, *Gesammelte Werke* (Hildesheim: G. Olms Verlag, [1725] 1982).

Breitenbach, Angela, *Die Analogie von Vernunft und Natur. Eine Umweltphilosophie nach Kant* (Berlin: Walter de Gruyter, 2009).

Brittan, Gordan, *Kant's Theory of Science* (Princeton: Princeton University Press, 1978).

Brook, Andrew, *Kant and the Mind* (Cambridge: Cambridge University Press, 1994).

Buchdahl, Gerd, *Metaphysics and the Philosophy of Science* (Oxford: Blackwell, 1969).

"Gravity and Intelligibility: From Newton to Kant," in *The Methodological Heritage of Newton*, ed. Robert Butts and John Davis (Toronto: University of Toronto Press, 1970), pp. 74–102.

Butts, Robert, "The Methodological Structure of Kant's Metaphysics of Science," in *Kant's Philosophy of Physical Science*, ed. Robert Butts (Reidel: Dordrecht, 1986), pp. 163–99.

Calinger, Ronald S., "Frederick the Great and the Berlin Academy of Sciences (1740–1766)," *Annals of Science* 24 (1968): 239–49.

"The Newtonian-Wolffian Confrontation in the St. Petersburg Academy of Sciences," *Cahiers d'histoire mondiale* 11 (1968): 417–35.

"The Newtonian-Wolffian Controversy (1741–1759)," *Journal of the History of Ideas* 30 (1969): 319–30.

Carnap, Rudolph, "Empiricism, Semantics, and Ontology," *Revue Internationale de Philosophie* 11 (1950): 20–43.

Carrier, Martin, "Kant's Relational Theory of Absolute Space," *Kant-Studien* 83 (1992): 399–416.

Cartwright, Nancy, *How the Laws of Physics Lie* (Oxford: Oxford University Press, 1983).

Nature's Capacities and Its Measurement (Oxford: Oxford University Press, 1989).

The Dappled World: A Study of the Boundaries of Science (Cambridge: Cambridge University Press, 1999).

Cassirer, Ernst, *Kants Leben und Lehre* (Berlin: B. Cassirer, 1921).

Das Erkenntnisproblem in der Philosophie und Wissenschaft der neueren Zeit (Berlin: B. Cassirer, 1922).

Chignell, Andrew, "Belief in Kant," *The Philosophical Review* 116 (2007): 323–60.

"Kant's Concepts of Justification," *Nous* 41 (2007): 33–63.

"Kant, Modality, and the Most Real Being," *Archiv für Geschichte der Philosophie* 91 (2009): 157–92.

Clark, William, "German Physics Textbooks in the Goethezeit, Parts 1 and 2," *History of Science* 35 (1997): 219–39 and 295–363.

Cohen, Alix, "Kant's Antinomy of Reflective Judgment: A Re-Evaluation," *Teorema* 23 (2004): 183–97.

286 Bibliography

Cramer, Konrad, *Nicht-reine synthetische Urteile a priori. Ein Problem der Transzendentalphilosophie Immanuel Kants* (Heidelberg: Carl Winter Verlag, 1985).

Crusius, Christian, *August, Entwurf der nothwendigen Vernunft-Wahrheiten* (Leipzig: Gleditsch, 1745).

Dahlstrom, Daniel O., "Kant's Metaphysics of Nature," in *Nature and Scientific Method*, ed. Daniel O. Dahlstrom (Washington: Catholic University Press of America, 1991) pp. 271–90.

Dreyfus, Hubert, and Kelly, Sean Dorrance, *All Things Shining: Reading the Western Classics to Find Meaning in a Secular Age* (New York: Free Press, 2011).

Erxleben, Johann Christian Polykarp, *Anfangsgründe der Naturlehre* (Göttingen, 1772 [1st edition], 1787 [4th edition]).

Ewing, Alfred C., *Kant's Treatment of Causality* (London: Kegan Paul, 1923).

Fischer, Mark, "Organisms and Teleology in Kant's Natural Philosophy," PhD dissertation, Emory University, 2007.

Förster, Eckart, "Is There 'a Gap' in Kant's Critical System?," *Journal for the History of Philosophy* 25 (1987): 533–55.

"How Are Transcendental Arguments Possible?," in *Reading Kant*, ed. Eva Schaper and Wilhelm Vossenkuhl (Cambridge: Blackwell, 1989), pp. 3–20.

"Von der Eigentümlichkeit unseres Verstands in Ansehung der Urteilskraft (§§ 74–78)," in *Kooperativer Kommentar zu Kants Kritik der Urteilskraft*, ed. Otfried Höffe and Ina Goy (Berlin: Akademie Verlag, 2008), pp. 259–74.

Friedman, Michael, "Causal Laws and the Foundations of Natural Science," in *The Cambridge Companion to Kant*, ed. Paul Guyer (New York: Cambridge University Press, 1992), pp. 161–99.

Kant and the Exact Sciences (Cambridge, MA: Harvard University Press, 1992).

Kant's Construction of Nature: A Reading of the Metaphysical Foundations of Natural Science (Cambridge: Cambridge University Press, 2013).

Ginsborg, Hannah, "Kant on Understanding Organisms as Natural Purposes," in *Kant and the Sciences*, ed. Eric Watkins (New York: Oxford University Press, 2001), pp. 231–58.

"Two Kinds of Mechanical Inexplicability," *Journal of the History of Philosophy* 42 (2004): 33–65.

"Kant's Biological Teleology and Its Philosophical Significance," in *The Normativity in Nature: Essays on Kant's Critique of Judgement* (Oxford: Oxford University Press, 2015), pp. 316–31.

The Normativity of Nature: Essays on Kant's Critique of Judgement (Oxford: Oxford University Press, 2015).

Goy, Ina, "On Judging Nature as a System of Ends. Exegetical Problems of §67 of the Critique of the Power of Judgment," in *Akten des XI. Internationalen Kant-Kongresses, Pisa 2010*, ed. Claudio LaRocca, Stefano Bacin, Alfredo Ferrarin, and Margit Ruffing, vol. 5 (Berlin: Walter de Gruyter, 2013), pp. 65–76.

Grier, Michelle, *Kant's Doctrine of Transcendental Illusion* (New York: Cambridge University Press, 2001).

Guyer, Paul, *Kant and the Claims of Knowledge* (New York: Cambridge University Press, 1987).

Bibliography

Kant's System of Nature and Freedom (Oxford: Oxford University Press, 2005).
"Freedom, Happiness, and Nature: Kant's Moral Teleology," in *Kant's Philosophy of Biology*, ed. Ina Goy and Eric Watkins (Berlin: Walter de Gruyter, 2014), pp. 221–37.

Haakonssen, Knud, *Natural Law and Moral Philosophy: From Grotius to the Scottish Enlightenment* (Cambridge: Cambridge University Press, 1996).
"German Natural Law," in *Cambridge History of Eighteenth-Century Political Thought*, ed. Mark Goldie and Robert Wokler (Cambridge: Cambridge University Press, 2006), pp. 249–90.

Hankins, Thomas, "Eighteenth Century Attempts to Resolve the Vis-Viva Controversy," *Isis* 56 (1965): 281–97.
"The Influence of Malebranche on the Science of Mechanics during the 18th Century," *Journal of the History of Ideas* 28 (1967): 193–210.
"The Reception of Newton's Second Law of Motion in the 18th Century," *Archives internationales d'histoire des sciences* 20 (1967): 43–65.
"The Concept of Hard Bodies in the History of Physics," *History of Science* 9 (1970): 119–28.
Jean d'Alembert: Science and the Enlightenment (New York: Oxford University Press, 1970).

Harnack, Adolf, *Geschichte der Königlich-Preussischen Akademie der Wissenschaften zu Berlin* (Berlin: Reichsdruckerei, 1900).

Harrison, Peter, "Voluntarism and Early Modern Science," *History of Science* 40 (2002): 63–89.

Hartung, Gerald, *Die Naturrechtsdebatte: Geschichte der Obligatio vom 17. bis 20. Jarhhundert* (Freiburg: Verlag Karl Alber, 1998).

Henry, John, "Metaphysics and the Origins of Modern Science: Descartes and the Importance of Laws of Nature," *Early Science and Medicine* 9 (2004): 73–114.

Hochstrasser, Tim, *Natural Law Theories in the Early Enlightenment* (Cambridge: Cambridge University Press, 2000).

Hoppe, Hansgeorg, *Kants Theorie der Physik. Eine Untersuchung über das Opus postumum von Kant* (Frankfurt: Klostermann, 1969).

Hunter, Ian, *Rival Enlightenments: Civil and Metaphysical Philosophy in Early Modern Germany* (Cambridge: Cambridge University Press, 2001).

Iltis, Carolyn M., "D'Alembert and the Vis Viva Controversy," *Studies in the History and Philosophy of Science* 1 (1970): 135–44.
"Leibniz and the Vis Viva Controversy," *Isis* 62 (1971): 21–35.
"The Leibnizean-Newtonian Debates: Natural Philosophy and Social Psychology," *British Journal for the History of Science* 6 (1972): 341–77.
"The Decline of Cartesian Mechanics: The Leibnizian-Cartesian Debates," *Isis* 64 (1973): 356–73.

Iltis, Carolyn, "Madame du Chatelet's Metaphysics and Mechanics," *Studies in the History and Philosophy of Science* 8 (1977): 29–48.

Irwin, Terence, *The Development of Ethics*, vol. 2 (New York: Oxford University Press, 2008).

Israel, Jonathan, *The Enlightenment Contested* (New York: Oxford University Press, 2006).

288   Bibliography

Jankowiak, Tim, "Kant on the Continuity of Alteration" (unpublished manuscript).

Kain, Patrick, "Self-Legislation in Kant's Moral Philosophy," *Archiv für Geschichte der Philosophie* 86 (2004): 257–306.

"Interpreting Kant's Theory of Divine Commands," *Kantian Review* 9 (2005): 128–49.

Kant, Immanuel, *Critique of Pure Reason*, trans. W. Pluhar (Indianapolis: Hackett, 1987).

Vorlesung zur Moralphilosophie, ed. Werner Stark (Berlin: Walter de Gruyter, 2004).

Kitcher, Philip, "Kant's Philosophy of Science," in *Contemporary Perspectives on the History of Philosophy*, ed. Peter A. French, Theodore E. Uehling, Jr., and Howard K. Wettstein, vol. 8 (Minneapolis: University of Minnesota Press, 1983), pp. 387–408.

Kleinert, Andreas, "Mathematik und anorganische Naturwissenschaften," in *Wissenschaften im Zeitalter der Aufklärung*, ed. Rudolf Vierhaus (Göttingen: Vandenhoek and Ruprecht, 1985), pp. 218–48.

Kleingeld, Pauline, "The Conative Character of Reason in Kant's Philosophy," *Journal of the History of Philosophy* 36 (1998): 77–97.

Laudan, Larry, "The Vis Viva Controversy: A Post-Mortem," *Isis* 59 (1968): 131–43.

Leibniz, Gottfried Wilhelm, *Philosophical Essays*, ed. and trans. Roger Ariew and Daniel Garber (Indianapolis: Hackett Publishing, 1989).

Lind, Gunter, *Physik im Lehrbuch 1700–1850* (Springer: Berlin, 1992).

Locke, John, *An Essay Concerning Human Understanding* (Oxford: Oxford University Press, 1689).

Essays on the Laws of Nature, ed. Wolfgang von Leyden (Oxford: Clarendon Press, 1954).

Longuenesse, Béatrice, *Kant and the Capacity to Judge* (Princeton: Princeton University Press, 1998).

Maupertuis, Pierre Louis Moreau de, *Recherche des loix du mouvement* (Berlin, 1746).

Examen philosophique de la preuve de l'Existence de Dieu employee dans l'Essai de Cosmologie (Berlin, 1758).

Discours sur les différentes Figures des Astres, Paris, [1732], reprinted in Pierre Louis Moreau de Maupertuis, *Oeuvres* (Lyon, 1768).

McLaughlin, Peter, *Kant's Critique of Teleology in Biological Explanation: Antinomy and Teleology* (Lewiston: Edwin Mellen Press, 1990).

McMullin, Ernan, *Newton on Matter and Activity* (Notre Dame: University of Notre Dame Press, 1978).

Milton, John R., "The Origin and Development of the Concept of the Laws of Nature," *Archives Européennes de Sociologie* 22 (1981): 173–95.

Musschenbroek, Pieter van, *Grundlehren der Naturwissenschaft, nach der zweiten lateinischen Ausgabe*, trans. Johann Christoph Gottsched (Leipzig, 1747).

Newton, Isaac, *Mathematical Principles of Natural Philosophy and His System of the World*, trans. Andrew Mott, revised by Florian Cajori (Berkeley: University of California Press, [1729] 1934).

Oakley, Francis, "Christian Theology and the Newtonian Science: The Rise of the Concept of the Laws of Nature," *Church History* 30 (1961): 433–57.

Bibliography

O'Neill, Onora, *Constructions of Reason* (Cambridge: Cambridge University Press, 1989).

Palter, Robert, "Kant's Formulation of the Laws of Motion," *Synthese* 24 (1972): 96–116.

Papineau, David, "The Vis Viva Controversy," *Studies in History and Philosophy of Science* 8 (1977): 111–42.

Pierson, Stuart, "Two Mathematics, Two Gods: Newton and the Second Law," *Perspectives on Science* 2 (1994): 231–53.

Plaass, Peter, *Kants Theorie der Naturwissenschaft. Eine Untersuchung zur Vorrede von Kants "Metaphysischen Anfangsgründen der Naturwissenschaft"* (Göttingen: Vandenhoek & Ruprecht, 1965).

Plantinga, Alvin, "Kant's Objection to the Ontological Argument," *The Journal of Philosophy* 63 (1966): 537–46.

Pollok, Konstantin, *Kant's Theory of Normativity* (New York: Cambridge University Press, 2017).

Pulte, Helmut, *Das Prinzip der kleinsten Wirkung und die Kraftkonzeption der rationalen Mechanik* (Stuttgart: Franz Steiner Verlag, 1989).

Quarfood, Marcel, *Transcendental Idealism and the Organism* (Stockholm: Almquiest and Wiksell, 2004).

Rawls, John, "Kantian Constructivism in Moral Theory," *The Journal of Philosophy* 77 (1980): 515–72.

Reath, Andrews, "Legislating the Moral Law," *Nous* 28 (1994): 435–64.

  Agency and Autonomy in Kant's Moral Theory (New York: Oxford University Press, 2006).

Reusch, Johann Peter, *Systema metaphysicum antiquiorum atque recentiorum item propria dogmata et hypotheses exhibens*, [Jena], reprinted in Abt. 3, Bd. 27 of Christian Wolff, *Gesammelte Werke* (Hildesheim: G. Olms Verlag, [1735] 1990).

Ripstein, Arthur, *Force and Freedom: Kant's Legal and Political Philosophy* (Cambridge, MA: Harvard University Press, 2009).

Ruby, Jane E., "The Origins of Scientific 'Law,'" *Journal of the History of Ideas* 47 (1986): 341–59.

Schneewind, Jerome, "Kant and Natural Law Ethics," *Ethics* 104 (1993): 53–74.

  The Invention of Autonomy: A History of Modern Moral Philosophy (New York: Cambridge University Press, 1997).

Schönfeld, Martin, *The Philosophy of the Young Kant: The Pre-Critical Project* (New York: Oxford University Press, 2000).

s'Gravesande, Willem Jacob van, *Mathematical Elements of Natural Philosophy Confirmed by Experiments or an Introduction to Sir Isaac Newton's Philosophy*, 2nd edition, trans. John Theophilus Desaguliers (London, 1721).

Smith, Norman Kemp, *A Commentary to Kant's Critique of Pure Reason* (New York: Humanities Press, 1962).

Stan, Marius, "Kant's Early Theory of Motion," *The Leibniz Review* 19 (2009): 29–60.

  "Rebellious Wolffian: Kant's Philosophy of Mechanics in 1758," in *Rethinking Kant*, ed. Oliver Thorndike, Vol. 3 (Cambridge: Cambridge Scholars Press, 2011), pp. 158–79.

290   Bibliography

"Newton and Wolff: The Leibnizian Reaction to the Principia, 1716–1763," *The Southern Journal of Philosophy* 50 (2012): 459–81.

"Kant's Third Law of Mechanics: The Long Shadow of Leibniz," *Studies in History and Philosophy of Science* 44 (2013): 493–504.

"Kant and the Object of Determinate Experience," *Philosopher's Imprint* 15 (2015): 1–19.

"Euler, Newton, and Foundations for Mechanics," in *The Oxford Handbook of Newton*, ed. Chris Smeenk and Eric Schliesser (New York: Oxford University Press, 2017), pp. 1–22.

"Newton's Concepts of Force among the Leibnizians," in *Reading Newton in Early Modern Europe*, ed. Mordechai Feingold and Elizabethanne Boran (Leiden: Brill, 2017), pp. 244–89.

"Emilie du Chatelet's Metaphysics of Substance," *The Journal of the History of Philosophy* 56 (2018): 477–96.

"Rationalist Foundations and the Science of Force," in *The Oxford Handbook of 18th Century German Philosophy*, ed. Brandon Look and Frederick Beiser (New York: Oxford University Press, forthcoming).

Steinle, Friedrich, "The Amalgamation of a Concept – Laws of Nature in the New Sciences," in *Laws of Nature: Essays on the Philosophical, Scientific and Historical Dimensions*, ed. Friedel Weinert (Berlin: de Gruyter, 1995), pp. 316–68.

Strawson, Peter, *The Bounds of Sense: An Essay on Kant's Critique of Pure Reason* (London: Methuen, 1966).

Suarez, Francisco, *On Laws and God the Lawgiver*, 8 vols., ed. and trans. L. Perena et al. (Madrid: Consejo Superior de Investigaciones Cientificas, 1971–81).

Sutherland, Daniel, "The Point of Kant's Axioms of Intuition," *Pacific Philosophical Quarterly* 86 (2005): 135–59.

Taylor, Charles, *A Secular Age* (Cambridge, MA: Harvard University Press, 2007).

Terrall, Mary, "Maupertuis and Eighteenth-Century Scientific Culture," PhD thesis, UCLA, 1987.

Thümmig, Ludwig Philipp, *Institutiones philosophiae Wolfianae*, [Frankfurt], reprinted in Abt. 3, Bd. 19 of Christian Wolff, *Gesammelte Werke*, (Hildesheim: G. Olms Verlag, [1725–6] 1982).

Tolley, Clinton, "Kant and the Nature of Logical Laws," *Philosophical Topics* 34 (2006): 371–407.

Tooley, Michael, "The Nature of Laws," *Canadian Journal of Philosophy* 7 (1977): 667–98.

Tuck, Richard, *The Rights of War and Peace: Political Thought and the International Order from Grotius to Kant* (Oxford: Oxford University Press, 1999).

Velkley, Richard, *Freedom and the End of Reason: On the Moral Foundation of Kant's Critical Philosophy* (Chicago: University of Chicago Press, 1989).

Walker, Ralph C., "The Status of Kant's Theory of Matter," in *Kant's Theory of Knowledge*, ed. Lewis White Beck (Dordrecht: Reidel, 1974), pp. 151–6.

Washburn, Michael, "Did Kant Have a Theory of Self-Knowledge?," *Archiv für Geschichte der Philosophie* 58 (1976): 40–56.

Bibliography

Watkins, Eric, "The Development of Physical Influx in Early Eighteenth-Century Germany: Gottsched, Knutzen, and Crusius," *Review of Metaphysics* 49 (1995): 295–339.

"Kant's Theory of Physical Influx," *Archiv für Geschichte der Philosophie* 77 (1995): 285–324.

Kant and the Metaphysics of Causality (New York: Cambridge University Press, 2005).

"On the Necessity and Nature of Simples: Leibniz, Wolff, Baumgarten, and the Pre-Critical Kant," *Oxford Studies in Early Modern Philosophy* 3 (2006): 261–314.

"Kant and the Myth of the Given," *Inquiry* 51 (2008): 512–31.

Kant's Critique of Pure Reason: Background Source Materials (New York: Cambridge University Press, 2009).

"Kant on the Hiddenness of God," *Kantian Review* 14 (2009): 81–122.

"The Antinomy of Practical Reason: Reason, the Unconditioned, and the Highest Good," in *Kant's Critique of Practical Reason: A Critical Guide*, ed. Andrews Reath and Jens Timmerman (New York: Cambridge University Press, 2010), pp. 145–67.

"Making Sense of Mutual Interaction: Simultaneity and the Equality of Action and Reaction," in *Kant and the Concept of Community*, ed. Charlton Payne and Lucas Thorpe (Rochester: Rochester University Press, 2011), pp. 41–62.

"The Early Kant's (Anti-)Newtonianism," *Studies in History and Philosophy of Science* 44 (2012): 429–37.

(ed.), *The Divine Order, the Human Order, and the Order of Nature: Historical Perspectives* (New York: Oxford University Press, 2013).

"The Foundations of Transcendental Idealism: The Origin of Kant's Distinction between Sensibility and Understanding," in *Kant's Critique of Pure Reason: A Critical Guide*, ed. James O'Shea (Cambridge: Cambridge University Press, 2017), pp. 9–27.

"The Unconditioned Goodness of the Good Will," in *Kant on Persons and Agency*, ed. Eric Watkins (Cambridge: Cambridge University Press, 2018), pp. 11–28.

"Breaking with Rationalism: Kant, Crusius, and the Priority of Existence," in *Leibniz and Kant*, ed. Brandon Look (Oxford: Oxford University Press, 2019).

"Kant on Real Conditions," in *Proceedings of the 12. International Kant Congress Nature and Freedom*, ed. Violetta Waibel and Margit Ruffing (Berlin: Walter de Gruyter, 2019), pp. 1133–40.

Watkins, Eric, and Willaschek, Marcus, "Kant's Account of Cognition," *Journal of the History of Philosophy* 55 (2017): 83–112.

"Kant on Cognition and Knowledge," *Synthese* (2017): https://doi.org/10.1007/s11229-017-1624-4.

Wolff, Christian, *Allerhand nützliche Versuche dadurch zu genauer Erkantnis der Natur und Kunst der Weg gebahnet wird* (Halle, 1721).

Cosmologia Generalis, [Frankfurt], reprint of the 2nd edition in Abt. 2, Bd. 4 of Christian Wolff, *Gesammelte Werke* (Hildesheim: G. Olms Verlag, 1964).

292   Bibliography

Vernünfftige Gedancken von Gott, der Welt und der Seele des Menschen, auch allen Dingen überhaupt, [Halle], reprint of the 11th edition in Abt. 1, Bd. 2 of Christian Wolff, *Gesammelte Werke* (Hildesheim: G. Olms Verlag, [1719] 1983).

Wood, Allen, *Kant's Moral Religion* (Ithaca: Cornell University Press, 1978).

Kant's Rational Theology (Ithaca: Cornell University Press, 1978).

Zilsel, Edward, "The Genesis of the Concept of Physical Law," *Philosophical Review* 51 (1942): 245–79.

Index

a posteriori 24, 36–7, 56, 164
acceleration 22–3, 28, 34, 67–8, 84–6,
 90–1, 105, 121–2, 131, 142–4, 270
action and reaction 23, 35, 66, 83–6, 90–1,
 96–100, 113, 115, 119, 133–8, 144–5,
 193, 270
action at a distance 84n42, 139–42
Allison, Henry 60n10, 152n3, 155, 156n7
Ameriks, Karl 187n22, 191n2, 237n16,
 238n17, 239n21, 243n28, 261n26,
 270n3, 272n7, 276n17
Analogy of Experience
 First 58–61, 74
 Second 11, 33, 44, 61–5, 74, 86, 132,
 151, 155
 Third 57, 61, 65–8, 75–6, 83n40, 86n46
Analytic of Principles 51
Analytic of the Teleological Power of
 Judgment 159, 174
Anticipations of Perception 52, 54–6, 73,
 75, 199n14, 203
Antinomy of Teleological Judgment 5, 147,
 149–73, 249, 263
applied mathematics 107–9
Aquinas, Thomas 17–18
Aristotle 17, 19, 163
Armstrong, David 16, 31
*Attempt to Introduce the Concept of
 Negative Magnitudes into Philosophy*
 112n69
autonomy 7, 26, 225–6, 237–48, 260, 272,
 276
Axioms of Intuition 52–4, 73–4, 75n15, 78

Bacin, Stefano 244n31
Bacon, Francis 93
Baumeister, Friedrich 99n33
Baumgarten, Alexander Gottlieb 82n37,
 101, 125n13, 191n3, 192–5
Beeson, David 103n45
Bernoulli, Daniel 101
Bernoulli, Johann 101

Bilfinger, Georg Bernhard 97–9, 100n34,
 101, 193n6
biology 186
Brittan, Gordan 77n21
Buchdahl, Gerd 140–1
Buffon, Georges Louis Leclerc 101

Carnap, Rudolf 30, 41–6
Cartesian 94, 102, 104
Cartwright, Nancy 32
category(ies)
 of causality 16, 33, 57, 62, 65, 198
 of modality 198
 of quality 16, 52, 54–5
 of quantity 16, 53
causal determination 22–3, 270
causality 11, 16, 23n29, 34–5, 40, 64–8, 76,
 84n41, 151, 154, 161, 163, 165,
 168n20, 169, 193, 203, 209, 243n29,
 261–2
change of state 15, 64, 66, 113, 131n23,
 132–8, 144–5, 183
chemistry 109
Chignell, Andrew 241n25, 250n5, 254n17
Clarke, Samuel 94n10
cognition
 analytic 233
 complete systematic unity of 8, 280–3
 empirical 4, 40, 45, 78
 mathematical 229–30
 practical 271, 282–3
 synthetic a priori 11, 36–7, 44, 52, 116,
 191, 228–31, 237
 systematic 282–3
 theoretical 7, 227, 248, 250, 253–5, 264,
 271, 281–3
concept(s)
 empirical 70–3, 75–6, 144, 220
 pure 51, 230
*Concerning the Ultimate Ground of the
 Differentiation of Directions in Space*
 102n39

293

294 Index

condition(s)
  empirical 283
  necessary 32, 52, 78n21, 86–7, 96, 255, 282
construction
  in intuition 86, 116, 141
  of objective space 80–1
contingent 2, 12, 16, 25, 31, 39, 43–5, 58, 77, 81, 87n48, 136–7, 150, 197–8, 242, 244n32, 251, 254, 260, 264, 266, 272
Continued Observations on the Earthquakes that have been Experienced for some Time 138n33
Critique of Practical Reason 7, 174, 187, 226, 237n16, 248–9, 259, 263, 265, 282
Critique of Pure Reason 3–4, 7, 11, 21, 32–4, 49–51, 61, 69–73, 75–9, 83n40, 85n43, 87–8, 121, 125, 132–3, 142, 155, 161, 168–70, 174, 185n19, 192, 194, 196, 198n13, 199n14, 202n25, 203, 207–9, 216, 226, 228–9, 234–6, 239, 241n25, 245, 248–52, 255, 258–60, 263, 265, 274, 277, 282
Critique of the Power of Judgment 5, 7, 14, 24n32, 133, 147, 156, 168, 174–5, 176n3, 178, 226, 228n2, 239, 249, 253n12, 259n24, 261, 263, 265, 268, 272–3, 279n26, 283
Crusius, Christian August 18, 51, 82n37, 99–100, 135

d'Holbach, Paul Henri Thiry 101
de Spinoza, Baruch 163–4
Democritus 163
Descartes, René 4, 7, 12, 19–22, 92, 96, 102, 119–20, 126n14, 134, 255
Dretske, Fred 31
Dreyfus, Hubert 247
dynamics 55, 73–5, 94, 118n1, 126, 139, 142

Einstein, Albert 37
empiricism 32, 45, 51
Epicurus 163–4
epistemic 3, 9, 30, 44, 64, 79, 147, 219, 220n6, 255, 265
epistemology 133, 247, 278n22
Erxleben, Johann Christian Polycarp 107, 109n59, 112–13
Euler, Leonhard 101–2, 104–7, 113–14

faculty(ies)
  cognitive 3, 46, 79, 161, 163
  of imagination 62
  of judgment 175n2, 179, 274

of reason 175, 179, 189, 219, 272, 274, 282
of sensibility 62, 282
subjective 43, 165
of understanding 62, 282
Fontenelle, Bernard le Bovier de 101
force(s)
  of attraction 92, 105, 139, 141–2
  centripetal 106
  dynamical 94
  impressed 90, 96n20, 104, 106, 118, 131, 134n28, 144
  Newtonian conception of 106
Formey, Pierre Samuel 101
Förster, Eckart 166–7
freedom 1, 8, 14, 22, 25, 27–9, 169, 184, 195–6, 210–11, 219, 239, 242, 272, 279, 282
Friedman, Michael 41, 45, 77n21, 89, 91n5, 93n9, 124n12, 132n24

Galilei, Galileo 12, 19, 105
general metaphysics 70–1n5, 122, 132
geometry
  Euclidean 36–8, 40
  non-Euclidean 9, 41
Ginsborg, Hannah 159–62, 170–3
God 7, 13, 22, 25, 27, 103, 119–20, 135, 138, 163, 165, 184, 192, 195–6, 200, 210, 219, 225–6, 238–9, 241–2, 247–51, 253–61, 263–5, 271, 275n12, 277, 281–2
Gottsched, Johann Christoph 101, 111–12, 135
gravity(ation) 4, 20, 34n7, 58, 66–7, 93, 101, 104, 107, 109, 111–13
Guyer, Paul 54n3, 63–4, 175n1, 178n6, 182n13, 187n24, 268n1

Helvétius, Claude Adrien 101
highest good 187, 210, 226, 248, 256–61, 263–5, 281–3
History and Natural Description of the most Noteworthy Occurrences of the Earthquake that Struck a large Part of the Earth at the End of the Year 1755 138n33
Hoppe, Hansgeorg 70–1n5
Hume, David 11, 13, 16, 31, 34n5, 43, 45, 51, 64–5, 67–8, 195, 255
Huygens, Christiaan 20
hylozoism 163–5

imagination 52–3, 62–3, 65
impenetrability 104, 106, 112–13, 127n17, 141–2

Index

Imperative(s)
Categorical 19, 268, 271, 276n15
Hypothetical 268
Inaugural Dissertation 102n39, 202n25, 236n12
Inquiry Concerning the Distinctness of the Principles of Natural Theology and Morality 141
intuition(s)
a priori 53–4, 116, 142n41, 229
empirical 54, 223, 229, 234
Israel, Jonathan 247

Jäsche Logik 212, 215, 219, 221

Kain, Patrick 243n28, 244n31
Karsten, Wenceslaw Johann Gustav 107–9
Kästner, Abraham Gotthelf 206
Kelly, Sean Dorrance 247
Kepler, Johannes 92, 96, 100n34, 112, 114, 137
Kitcher, Philip 72n10
Knutzen, Martin 51, 127, 135

Lambert, Johann Heinrich 101
law(s)
causal 6, 11, 33, 62, 64, 274
of continuity 56, 94n11, 99, 100n34, 106, 193, 199–207, 212, 217
dynamical 85n44, 91n5, 93n8, 197
empirical 3, 7, 11, 24, 35–6, 150, 157–8, 161, 226, 240, 265, 273, 275, 277, 282
of homogeneity 216, 218, 273, 275, 282
of inertia 31, 91, 95, 97–100, 106, 110, 112, 114, 116, 120n6, 131–3, 136–7
of mechanics 2, 4–5, 8, 21–3, 28, 34–5, 37, 49–50, 66n23, 76–7, 83–4, 85n44, 86–7, 89–92, 115–17, 130–8, 142–5, 150–1, 154–64, 169–73, 189, 261–6, 270
moral 1–3, 6–9, 13–14, 19, 21–2, 25–7, 225–6, 256–8, 260–1, 268–9, 271–2, 272n9, 275–9, 281–3
of motion 20n22, 89–117, 142–5
a priori 5–6, 8, 11, 23–4, 32, 35n9, 150, 158, 189, 207, 209, 235, 241, 268, 275, 282
teleological 147–8, 249, 261–6, 275n12
transcendental 3, 9, 30–47
of universal gravitation 4, 21, 93, 101, 107, 109, 111–12, 114
lawfulness 18, 23–4, 26–7, 39, 157, 233–5, 237, 240, 246, 248, 255, 271–3, 282

lawmaker 3, 269
legality 25, 242
legislation 6–8, 14–16, 22–3, 26–7, 227–8, 231–46, 248, 264, 272, 275–80, 283
Leibniz, Gottfried Wilhelm 18, 20, 21n26, 51, 83, 93–5, 97–100, 102n43, 104n48, 106, 112, 115, 119, 127, 132, 134–5, 140, 195, 200n18, 222, 255, 260
Lichtenberg, Georg Christoph 112
Locke, John 51, 59, 93
logical abstraction 213–14
Logik Dohna 215n2

magnitude(s)
determinate 53, 141, 168
extensive 53–5, 73–5, 125–6, 129, 200–1
intensive 54–6, 125–6, 200–1, 206
Malebranche, Nicolas 7, 21n26, 255, 260
mass 23, 34, 39, 58, 61, 67, 72n10, 84n42, 91n5, 92, 104, 106, 121–2, 130, 270
matter
empirical concept of 77
quantity of 56, 73, 90, 115–16, 119–26, 129–31, 145
Maupertuis, Pierre-Louis 101–7, 114, 116
maxim(s) 26–7, 150–1, 153, 156, 158, 161, 163, 165, 172, 196, 240, 276n15, 281
McLaughlin, Peter 155, 159–60, 168–70
mechanical 5, 8, 82n33, 85n44, 120n6, 124n12, 149–50, 153, 156–62, 166–7, 170–3, 249
Meier, Georg Friedrich 101, 125n13
Metaphysical Foundations of Natural Science 4, 11, 15–16, 21, 34–5, 49–50, 52n2, 55, 61, 69–81, 83n40, 86–90, 115, 121, 137, 139–43, 156–7, 160, 164, 174, 179, 192, 202n22
Metaphysics Dohna 200n17, 207
Metaphysics Mrongovius 192n4, 195–6, 198, 201, 207, 264
monad(s) 95n18, 124–30, 201–2, 202n23
moral obligation(s) 6, 12, 18–19, 225, 248, 282
morality 6–7, 13, 18–19, 25–6, 225, 227, 239, 242, 245, 248, 271, 283
motion(s)
apparent 80, 93n9
objective 80
relative 84–5, 145
mutual interaction 51, 56–7, 65–7, 75n14, 76–7, 145, 208

nature(s)
cognitive 36, 40–1, 43–4, 46–7
epistemic 3, 30

296   Index

necessity 1–3, 6, 8–9, 11–12, 14–16, 22–9, 31–4, 36, 38–40, 43, 44n17, 63, 65, 67, 70, 97, 134, 139, 141, 145, 157, 162–4, 167, 169, 181, 193–8, 200, 208–10, 225–6, 230, 234n10, 240–4, 246, 248–9, 255, 257–8, 260, 268–72, 276–9
New Elucidation of the First Principles of Metaphysical Cognition 258
Newton, Isaac 4–5, 12, 20–1, 31, 39–40, 50, 57–8, 67, 80n27, 89–93, 95–117, 120, 131–4, 137–9, 142–5, 192–3, 206
normative 3, 234, 246, 257, 268, 277–9, 283
noumenal 175, 196, 202, 207–9, 283

object(s)
  conditioned 175, 183, 219
  empirical 3, 30, 36, 248, 255, 266, 273
  of experience 6, 32, 37, 40–5, 54, 70, 78, 183, 199, 210–11, 231–2, 237
  unconditioned 184, 219, 282
On the Causes of Earthquakes 138n33
ontology 19, 34, 40–1, 70–1n5, 94–7, 99–100, 103, 106–7, 114–16, 134, 138–9, 141, 191n3, 192, 210
Opus postumum 4, 49, 69, 71

Phenomenology 73, 80
philosophy
  practical 1, 9, 13, 17, 68, 225, 228, 239n22, 246–7, 256, 271, 281
  theoretical 1, 9, 11, 28, 68, 98n26, 189, 192, 225, 227–8, 239n22, 245, 250, 256, 271, 279, 281
Phoronomy 73–4, 75n15, 121, 143
Physical Monadology 124–5, 128n19, 141, 202n22
physics 19, 30, 34, 37, 39–41, 49, 52, 61n11, 66, 72n8, 78n21, 100–1, 107–17, 131, 135–6, 140, 145, 156, 191n3, 192, 206, 228
Plaass, Peter 70–1n5, 77n18
Plato 163
Ploucquet, Gottfried 101
Poincaré, Henri 41
possibility
  logical 210, 258
  real 258
Postulates of Empirical Thought 52, 73, 207n36, 274
pre-Critical 102n39, 115n75, 118n1, 125n13, 135, 141–2, 159, 202n22, 207–8, 251, 261

principle(s)
  constitutive 11, 42, 44–5, 150–5, 189, 210, 254
  of continuity 189, 194, 207–9, 212, 215, 221–2, 275, 279
  dynamical 194, 209
  explanatory 5, 189, 274, 277n20
  of homogeneity 6, 189, 216–18, 273, 275, 279–80, 282
  mathematical 92, 114
  a priori 41–3, 49, 52–4, 70, 209–10, 231, 281
  regulative 6, 8, 26n36, 149, 151–5, 166, 167n19, 170, 173, 181n10, 184, 189, 210, 217–19, 222, 254, 268, 271
  of specificity 189, 275, 279–80
  teleological 5, 8, 172, 180
Principles of Pure Understanding 50–2, 52n2, 69, 71–2, 78n22, 192, 209–10, 274
Prolegomena to Any Future Metaphysics That Will Be Able to Come Forward as Science 7, 21, 23–4, 25n34, 38, 142, 225, 227–46, 277
psychology
  cognitive 62
  rational 95, 191
  transcendental 277
purpose(s)
  natural 168n20, 174, 176–7, 179, 181–2
  system of 5, 148, 175, 177–8, 180–1, 185–6
  unconditioned 175, 185–6

quantity of substance 61, 122
Quarfood, Marcel 152n2, 168n20
Quine, Willard Van Orman 42–5

rational cosmology 6, 95, 101, 108, 189, 191, 211, 219, 222, 274, 279, 283
Rawls, John 247
reason
  ideas of 185n19, 219
  practical 26, 162, 196, 227, 238n18, 248, 256, 276
Reath, Andrews 276n15
Reflexion 71n5, 212n1
Refutation of Idealism 6, 52, 194
Reichenbach, Hans 41
Reusch, Johann Peter 97–9, 106

Schneewind, Jerome 247
space
  absolute 81n32, 85, 93n8, 106, 112
  relative 85
Stan, Marius 82n34, 84n42, 86n47, 93n8, 118n1, 134n28

Index

297

state of motion or rest 132, 136
Strawson, Peter 63, 277
Suarez, Francisco 17–18, 22
Sulzer, Johann Georg 101
syllogism(s) 183, 278
synthesis 52–5, 62, 209

Taylor, Charles 247
teleology 7, 162–6, 170–2, 178, 226, 249,
    259n24, 263, 265
Tetens, Johannes Nikolaus 51
*The Only Possible Argument in Support of a
    Demonstration of the Existence of God*
    102n39, 258, 261
theology
    moral 259–60
    natural 259
    rational 95, 191, 259
    transcendental 259–60
theory(ies)
    divine command 7, 238, 248
    natural law 17–18
    political 3
    relativity 9, 37, 39, 87
    scientific 3, 30
*Thoughts on the True Estimation of Living
    Forces* 3, 49, 120
Thümmig, Ludwig Philipp 97–9, 115
Tooley, Michael 16, 31
Transcendental Aesthetic 32, 54, 58, 85n43
Transcendental Analytic 33, 71, 274
Transcendental Deduction 15–16, 51, 54,
    78n23, 234, 239

Transcendental Dialectic 6, 189, 212, 254,
    274
Transcendental Idealism 47, 58, 68, 162,
    166, 184n15
Transcendental Realism 162, 166

unity
    of apperception 52–3
    of nature 218, 235
    of reason 246, 279, 282
*Universal Natural History and Theory of the
    Heavens, or Essay on the Constitution and
    Mechanical Origin of the Entire Universe,
    treated in accordance with Newtonian
    Principles* 3, 61, 142, 191n1

van Musschenbroek, Pieter 107,
    110–13
van s'Gravesande, Willem Jacob 107,
    109–13
velocity 74, 85, 90, 98, 110, 143–4
Voltaire 101–2, 110n64
von Wolff, Christian Freiherr 51, 92–101,
    93n8, 102n41, 103, 106–8, 111, 116,
    127, 133–5

Walker, Ralph 79, 81
world
    intelligible 169–70, 192n4,
        208n38
    noumenal 207–9
    sensible 70, 158, 186, 198, 233, 272
    spatio-temporal 4, 79, 274, 277

Printed in the United States
By Bookmasters